Library of
Davidson College

Criminal Justice
Organization and Management

Criminal Justice Organization and Management

Thomas F. Adams
   Dean, Applied Arts and Sciences
   Santa Ana College

Gerald Buck and Don Hallstrom
   Orange County, California Probation Department

Goodyear Publishing Company
Pacific Palisades, California

Copyright © 1974 by Goodyear Publishing Company, Inc.
Pacific Palisades, California

All rights reserved. No part of this book
may be reproduced in any form or by any means
without permission in writing from the publisher.

Current printing (last digit):
10 9 8 7 6 5 4 3 2 1

ISBN: 0-87620-181-8

Library of Congress Catalog Card Number: 73-83390

Y-1818-7

Printed in the United States of America

NORINA .... This one is for you. TFA

Our contribution to this book was made possible through the encouragement and patience of our wives Barbara and Charlotte.   GSB and DEH

Contents

PREFACE xi

1 THE CRIMINAL JUSTICE SYSTEM 1
    Through the System 2
    The Systems Approach 5
    The Criminal Justice System 9

2 ORGANIZATION PRINCIPLES AND PRACTICES 15
    Specify Goals and Objectives 16
    Develop an Organizational Plan 17
    Organize According to the Plan 18
    Prescribe Relationships 21
    Minimize Dual Accountability 24
    Limit the Scope of Supervision 27
    Integrate and Coordinate the Functional Units 34
    Staff the Organization for Maximum Effectiveness 36
    Develop Methods for Control 36

3 STRUCTURING THE ORGANIZATION 42
    Division of Work 42
    Specialization 48
    Authority Relationships 53
    Assistance for the Chief Executive 54
    Staff Authority 56

Line Authority 56
Coordination and Control 56
Appropriate Attention 57
Organizational Design and Relationships 59

4 ADMINISTRATIVE COMMUNICATIONS 67
Authority-Responsibility Hierarchy 68
Barriers to Communication 70
Overcoming the Barriers 72
Mass Communication 74
Policies 75
Manuals of Rules and Regulations 75
Committees 77
Meetings 78
Staff Communications 80
Inspections 81
Appeal Channels 83
Informal Organization 84

5 PERSONNEL MANAGEMENT 87
Task Analysis 87
Recruitment and Selection 94
Personnel Evaluation 101
Promotional Procedure 114
Guidelines for Personnel Management 116

6 SUPERVISION 123
Leadership 124
Motivation 129
Measurement Devices 133
Development of People 133
Direction 134
Authority 135
Coordination 136
Discipline 138

7 TRAINING AND EDUCATION FOR CRIMINAL JUSTICE 142
Training and Education 145
Curriculum Development 147

Training or Education Revisited 152
The College and University Role in Criminal Justice
   Education 154
College-affiliated Seminars and Specialized Training
   Courses 188
In-service Training 190
Training the Police Officer 195

8 RESEARCH AND PLANNING FOR EFFECTIVENESS 207
Planning, Defined 208
A Need for Planning 208
The Planning Process 209
Value of Planning as a Management Tool 218

9 FISCAL MANAGEMENT 221
Budget, Defined 223
Budget as a Planning Tool 223
Getting Everyone into the Act 224
Types of Budgets and Budgeting 226
PPBS (Planning Program Budgeting System) 230
The Budget Process 232
Purchasing 237
Inventory Control 238

10 THE POLICE ORGANIZATION 242
Principles of Management 242
Organizing the Department 246
Police Records System 274
Statistics for Efficiency and Effectiveness 278

11 COURT ADMINISTRATION 286
Records and Reporting 289
The Crime Commission Report and the Courts 291

12 PROBATION AND PAROLE ADMINISTRATION 299
Definitions of Probation and Parole 299
Historical Development of Probation and Parole 300
Legal Framework—Functional Authority 301
Trends toward Noninstitutional Corrections 302
The Goals and Objectives of Probation and Parole 304

Organizational Structure 314
Probation Organization 317
Probation Functions 318
Parole Organization 326
Contemporary Corrections and Management in the Future 332
Evaluation and Research 341

13 ADMINISTRATION OF CORRECTIONAL INSTITUTIONS 346
Early Development 348
Purpose of Correctional Institutions 350
Institutional Organization and Management 356
Administrative Organizational Structure 360
Personnel Management 367
Physical Plant—Facility Functions 369
Correctional Costs and Location of Juvenile and Adult Offenders 371
Diagnosis and Classification 372
Record and Statistical Controls 375
Community-based Corrections 376
Research and Evaluation 379

14 PUBLIC RELATIONS 386
Community Relations 389
Public Relations 393
Press Media Relations 396

BIBLIOGRAPHY 401

INDEX 405

Preface

Organization and management of the many agencies of the three basic components of the Criminal Justice System—*Police, Court,* and *Corrections*—involve principles and practices common to all, yet are distinctively different in the manner they might be utilized for each. In this text it is our desire to bring to the total system the most essential information necessary to the effective management of an agency involved in the administration of justice in modern American society.

Criminal justice involves a vast network of interrelated, people-oriented service agencies with the common purpose of administering the affairs of the American people in accordance with the responsibilities and constraints of the laws imposed to assure the constitutionally guaranteed "due process" rights of the accused and equity for all.

Criminal Justice Organization and Management is designed to bring to the Criminal Justice System certain principles and philosophies concerning agency administration which have proved effective in business, industry, and many agencies of government, including those of the Criminal Justice System. The book is not intended for use by any single segment of the system, but has been written and compiled as a fundamental text for any or all of the many agencies of law enforcement, corrections, or courts.

For a more authoritative presentation of the materials on each of the criminal justice components, the knowledge and expertise of currently employed practitioners in the fields of courts and corrections were called upon to augment the work of the principal author. The real strength of the material in this text is that the authors have relied heavily upon the knowledge and successful experience of many highly knowledgeable and respected writers and practitioners in the various fields represented between these covers.

Thanks should be directed to many individuals who must remain nameless because they are so numerous, but the authors have a special thank you for an outstanding editor: Jack Pritchard.

1 The Criminal Justice System

The administration of criminal justice in the United States involves many thousands of individuals functioning within their own distinctive organizations and specialized work patterns, sometimes working toward common goals but more often toward the accomplishment of their individual objectives. The so-called system of criminal justice more appropriately resembles a conglomerate of nonrelated operations that work within separate spheres with an apparent disregard for the many other spheres within this system. Yet, there does emerge some semblance of continuity and cohesiveness which somehow brings about the accomplishment of the objectives of the overall administration of justice.

The Criminal Justice System consists of three identifiable components, each operating within its own sphere of influence and communications. These three components can be categorized generally as *Police, Court,* and *Corrections*—or in systems terminology, the input, process, and output components. The generic term *Police* includes all law enforcement and investigative agencies directly or indirectly involved in the process of identifying and apprehending individuals who are suspected of disobeying some law or administrative regulation, and in arresting or by some other means causing those individuals to be brought before some tribunal to answer to the allegations of such violations. The *Court* component includes all judicial and quasi-judicial bodies that operate as criminal courts or administrative bodies having the authority to determine the facts and take appropriate action in the form of punishment or some other form of sanctions prescribed by law. This second component involves the judicial body as well as legal representatives for both the defense and the prosecution and "processes" each case as individually and constitutionally as possible under the procedural rules and attendant circumstances for each case.

Once the case has been processed, or adjudicated according to the adjective laws governing their operations, the individual is either out of the system, or he is remanded to the *Corrections*, or output component of the system. The purpose and function of this component is to enforce such sanctions as may be provided according to law in the form of punishment, imprisonment, supervision, or combinations of sanctions prescribed for getting the individual out of the system and redirecting him into lifestyles or behavior patterns that are intended to prevent him from reentering the system.

THROUGH THE SYSTEM

As an example of the manner in which an individual may be processed through the various components of the Criminal Justice System, consider the narcotics smuggler who is eventually arrested by the local police and charged with a felony.

The initial phases of the investigation may involve officers and investigators from many agencies. If the smuggler is an alien, the Federal Bureau of Immigration and Naturalization investigates the legality of his entrance and presence in the United States; customs officers are concerned with the smuggled merchandise; the Bureau of Narcotics and Dangerous Drugs investigates the international narcotics trafficking as well as the operational aspects of the smuggling ring; the many local law enforcement agencies and the various state narcotics bureaus in whose jurisdictions the trafficking activities occur are concerned with the overall operation but specifically with those criminal law violations they are charged with enforcing. Working alone and in teams consisting of representatives of the several agencies, the officers—each working his respective case on the same suspect—close in on the suspect and effect his arrest. They make the decision to arrest the suspect on a state charge of illegal possession for sale and to place a hold on him for several federal charges.

Following the arrest, the officers from the several agencies present their cases to the prosecuting attornies representing the different involved jurisdictions. The prosecutors, in turn, may meet and discuss their ideas on how to proceed. Reaching a consensus, the prosecutors decide that they will hold their respective cases in abeyance while the county district attorney in whose jurisdiction the arrest was made will proceed with the prosecution of three counts of illegal possession of narcotics for sale. The other jurisdictions may or may not file their charges at some later date, possibly upon the suspect's release from jail or prison in the event he is subsequently found guilty.

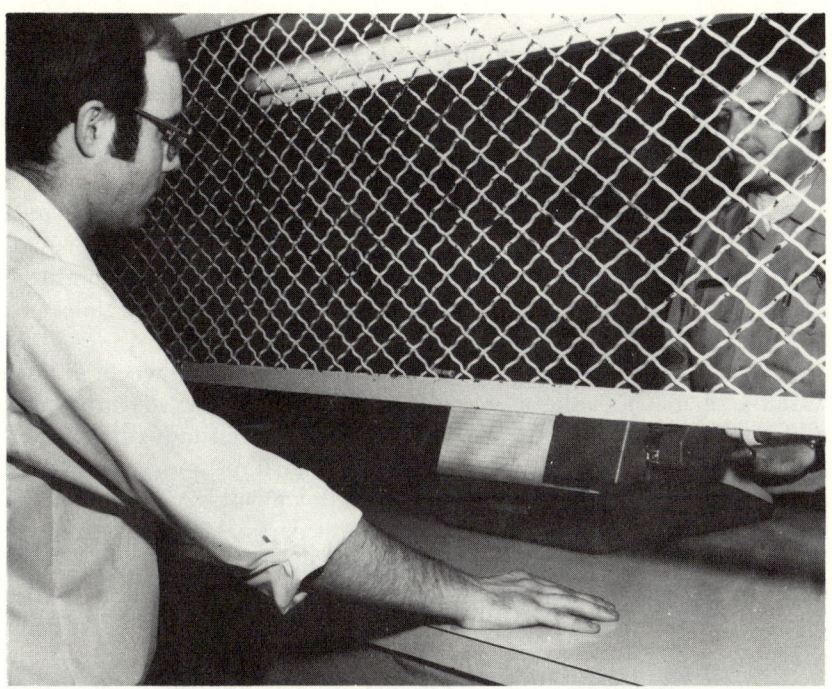
Introduction to the criminal justice system is sometimes by way of the booking desk . . .
Courtesy: Sheriff's Department, Riverside County, California

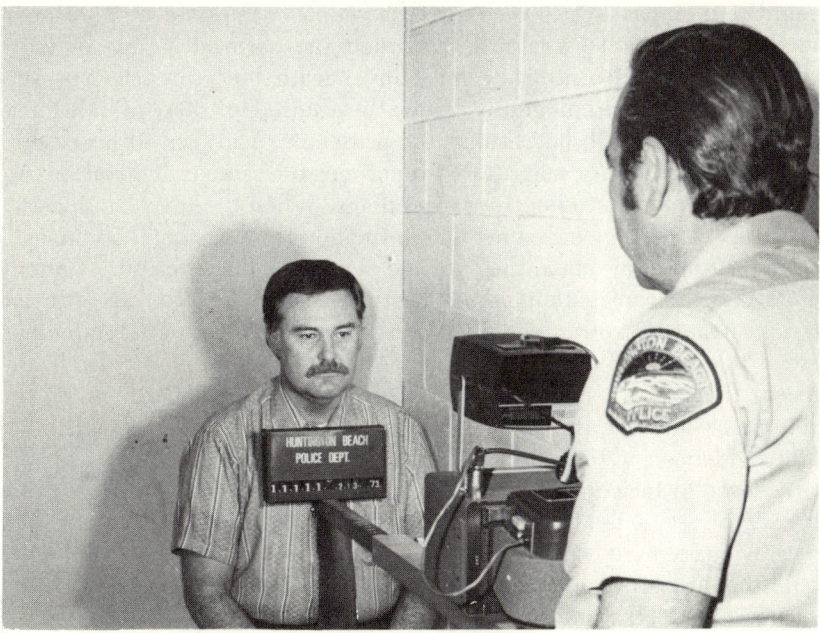
. . . and the "mugging" process.
Courtesy: Police Department, Huntington Beach, California

The suspect, in the meantime, has been arrested and booked, and has posted bail or was released on his own recognizance with his promise to appear in court as his bail. He has gone through the first component of the system, the input. The next phase will be in the process, or *Court* component. Constantly bearing in mind the fact that the suspect is "innocent until proven guilty" as provided by the Constitution, the operants in the *Court* component are charged with the sacred responsibility of providing for the accused a fair trial and assuring him that judgment will be made as a result of evidence presentation and that a finding of guilt must be based upon criteria established by law.

The *Court* component involves the bailiff of the court, who is either a constable, marshal, or sheriff (in a felony case probably the sheriff), whose responsibility involves security in the courtroom and custody of the defendant if he is incarcerated during the trial. Although imprisonment is in itself (according to many experts) punishment, the defendant is still innocent and must be afforded consideration as an innocent person—this practice is an extremely difficult and delicate one. The other principals in this process are the judge, the prosecutor, and the defense attorney. Each is charged with a separate role but with a common purpose—to assure the accused of a fair trial.

The prosecutor is charged with the burden of proving the defendant guilty of the offense "beyond all reasonable doubt" and coordinating his prosecution with the prosecutors from the other juridictions so as not to prejudice their cases. He represents the people of the state while respecting the constitutional guaranties afforded the accused as one of those people. The defense attorney must investigate the circumstances surrounding the case and diligently defend the accused to assure him that if he is found guilty, it will be because the prosecutor had proved his case.

The judge and/or magistrate (sometimes the same individual serving a dual role) referees the entire proceedings. When the investigating officers believe that they have enough information through their own investigation or from informants, they see the magistrate and present testimony supporting their allegations; the magistrate issues a search warrant or an arrest warrant, or both, depending on the circumstances of the individual case at that stage of the investigation. After the arrest and/or search, the officers then return to the magistrate and report their findings. At the preliminary hearing, the magistrate determines the legality and reliability of the evidence and testimony and makes a determination whether to hold the accused to answer to the charges brought against him. The magistrate, who is not serving as a judge at this time, may rule that evidence seized or an arrest made as a direct response to his warrant may not be sufficient to "bind the suspect over" for trial.

The role of the judge in this process is to referee the case to assure the defendent a fair trial according to laws and court-ruled precedent. He passes on the legality and constitutionality of all issues brought before him, and he instructs the jury on legal issues of the trial. If there is a jury, the jury determines what is fact and truth, and subsequently determines guilt. In the absence of a jury, the judge decides on both issues of law and truth, and he makes the determination of guilt. If guilt beyond reasonable doubt cannot be proved by the prosecution, the judge must order the trial ended and the case dismissed or the defendant not guilty, depending on the point in the process where he makes that determination.

Another officer of the court enters the process phase of the system. The probation officer, who serves a dual role in the administration of justice in both the *Court* and *Corrections* components, is delegated the responsibility of conducting a presentencing investigation into the offense from a socio-psychological point of view and into the personal life of the defendant for the purpose of aiding the judge in his determination of the most appropriate manner to prescribe punishment or some variation of correctional treatment. In some jurisdictions, the probation report may actually be brought into the process and used as one of the factors in the bartering process when the defendant and his attorney study the recommendations of the probation officer and decide to plead guilty on condition that a certain type of punishment will be prescribed.

Once the defendant has been found guilty, if such is the case, he is then introduced to the third phase of the Criminal Justice System: *Corrections*. He may be sentenced to a local jail, where his punishment is to serve in the custody of the local police department or the county sheriff. Following a term in jail, the prisoner may be remanded to the probation department or he may be assigned directly to probation without a jail sentence. Still a third alternative in this system approach is that he may be remanded to the custody of the state department of corrections to serve a sentence under their jurisdiction in any one of a wide variety of institutions or residential centers. The *Corrections* component consists of three distinctive parts: probation, local or state or federal institutions, and parole. Federal probation and parole are both supervised by federal probation officers.

THE SYSTEMS APPROACH

When studying the entire process, it becomes apparent that the administration of justice is most effective when it is approached with a "systems" point of view. Justice is a process, and the various components of the system—although each is organized for the accomplishment of certain goals and objectives—are similarly operating as systems through which services are rendered and individuals are processed in accordance with certain laws and procedures. If each organization is viewed as a structure with the development and maintenance of that structure as an institution, or an entity in itself with no purpose other than its own perpetuation, then conceptualizing the organization as a system would be incongruous.

Paul Whisenand said of the systems approach to the police organization:

> The first reason (toward a systems point of view) . . . is found in the increased complexity and frequency of change in our society. This is evident in both our social relations and technological innovations. Further, such complexity and change is equally prevalent within the organization itself. The second reason is seen in the limitations of the . . . organizational themism . . . that both the classical and neo-classical theories viewed an organization as a *closed* structure. Such nearsightedness produces an inability to recognize that the organization is continually dependent upon its environment for the inflow of materials and human energy. Consequently, we often find supervisors coping with organizational problems as if they were independent of changes in the environment. Thinking of an organization as a closed structure, moreover, results in a failure to develop a feedback capability for obtaining adequate information about changes in environmental forces and goal accomplishment. Hence, today we find societal change, complexity, and inappropriate organizational theories generating an urgent need for an open-system approach to organization.[1]

There seems to be no difficulty in overcoming the concept of "organization" as a rigid pyramidal-type structure once the beholder divests himself of the idea that a criminal justice organization must retain its status quo in a bureaucratic context and begins to think of the system and its components as dynamic, changing, fluid, and continuously interacting organisms within its various parts. If the improvement is little more than in attitude toward the organization as a dynamic and "moving" entity, as opposed to a nonchanging Gibraltar, we are on the right track. We should avoid the tendency to build a structure of lifeless building blocks that are unbending, unchanging, bureaucratic, and totally unpalatable to the modern administrator.

There are five distinct benefits to the police organization when the systems approach is applied to it, according to Whisenand: "(1) A vehicle for permeating organizational boundaries of a police structure, (2) a way to deal with complexity, (3) a new perspective on organization, (4) a conceptual underpinning for an empirical tool (system and design), and (5) a potential fund of scientifically pragmatic information."[2]

The rigid administrator, sometimes referred to as the "traditionalist," often has a tendency to adhere to certain fundamentals or principles of administration with such slavish devotion that he becomes a victim of the "within" structure of the organization. By that I mean that the higher he is in rank and the more he becomes devoted to the "book," the greater the chance he will lose sight of the true objectives—to provide protective and beneficial services to the community, to process as many defendants through fair trials as practicable, and to redirect the behavior patterns of parolees—and grow devoted to the internal operation of the organization, considering that perpetuation of the institution will be more important. It is not unusual to encounter the administrator who could "sure accomplish some of the work that I have to get done" if only he could shut down the organization once in a while just to catch up with the administrative "busy work" so zealously generated by some executives.

The benefits suggested by Whisenand provide a strong argument for taking the chance and risking the criticism of the traditionalists. A table of organization that carefully depicts hierarchical relationships, authority–responsibility flow, communications channels, and lines of supervision and command is essential to all organizations, and one that utilizes the systems approach is no exception. However, there are exceptions and circumstances that cause an individual to use personal judgment and "violate" the organizational mandate that a certain procedure be followed. To the systems-oriented individual, if such an occasion were repeated too often, there would be an indicated need to study the existing regulations with a view to changing them—if necessary—toward the changing needs of the environment. The traditionalist, on the other hand, might find it much easier and "wiser" to put the violator back into line and enforce the regulations as they stand because, "we have always done it that way." This is not intended to imply that traditions are bad and should be destroyed, nor that change just for the sake of change is good, but that organizations must change to meet the changing demands of a changing society. The Criminal Justice System cannot change on whim or caprice, because lives and ideals are directly related to laws and legal procedures. Certain practices within the system can change when the need is based upon sound exploration and reasoned decisions. Systems analysis provides the data for more valid decisions.

There are several characteristics of an "open system" described by Katz and Kahn.[3] Every one of these characteristics may be identified as "natural" to the individual criminal justice organization or to several of those organizations functioning in a cooperative fashion to serve their individual and collective needs. Consider the *Corrections* component, and a penal institution in particular:

> 1. Input. The prison input involves prisoners who are assigned for punishment or rehabilitation; this is one type of input. Another type of input is in the form of expert and professional services for the instruction and spiritual

guidance of the inmates, and various other personnel services provided by counselors, psychologists, and custodial personnel.

2. Processing. The system of the prison organization processes the input, by maintaining custody—which is the punishment of the inmate—and by employing all of the ongoing counseling and other programs to rehabilitate and redirect the inmates.

3. Output. The product returned to the environment by this system consists of the men and women who are released on parole to enter another system: parole. The output, hopefully, includes many individuals who have actually "changed" during the process of imprisonment and rehabilitative efforts and who never return to the institution. Even those who do eventually return may have benefitted from the process temporarily.

4. Cyclic character. The correctional institution as a system does have an obvious cyclic characteristic in that individuals are introduced into the system, go through the "corrective" process, and then go on to the output category. There is a continuous flow of new people into the system for more of the same type of corrective treatment, and at the same time the recidivists return for another turn at the process.

5. Arresting of disorganization. Routinization of the institution's daily operations tends to become somewhat standard, and for the time the inmates are in custody their lives are more regulated and less disorganized. The system tends to organize and level out human lives and activities within it.

6. Information is a separate form of energy that flows throughout the organization. In the correctional institution, there are several varieties of information going through the input, process, output, and feedback stages. The organization itself and the management generate information and attempt to stimulate its free flow, including the feedback that is vital to the healthy state of an organization. At the same time there is a concurrent and sometimes interrelated flow of information regarding the progress and activities of the inmates. Informal communications, the "grapevine," and informal organizations are very significant in personnel management and inmate control, and feedback in this area is vital to the security and smooth

operation of the institution. Information from outside, such as reports on the progress or failures of former inmates, and studies to determine ways and means to improve continuing programs within the institution, is another valuable source of feedback.

7. The steady state. Within the system, the steady state is not necessarily a nonchanging procedure or a maintenance of the status quo. There is a steady flow of feedback and a study of existing procedures, a comparison of the input and output, and a continuous process of adjustments to make the system a viable and effective operation.

8. Specialization. Open systems involve specialization. The correctional institution as a system is no exception. There are specialists in all phases of custodial and professional services throughout the institution. The skills and bodies of knowledge that must be mastered span such a wide spectrum that it would be impossible to expect everyone to master them all.

9. Equifinality. Open systems can reach the same final state from differing initial conditions and by a variety of paths. Individuals who are assigned to an institution come from a variety of backgrounds and are convicted of as wide a variety of criminal offenses. The objective of the institutional process is to return all of those individuals to their respective private lives in a "rehabilitated" state.

Study of these characteristics in relationship to a police department, a prosecuting attorney's office, or a municipal court operation would yield similar results. It seems apparent that an organization could be organized and managed with a "systems" point of view and the result would be a smoothly functioning criminal justice organization—operating consistently in accordance with laws and court procedures as well as management principles. The consistency would be in the form of responsiveness to the current needs and demands of society, and to changing trends in criminal and asocial behavior. The organization would be viewed in a more appropriate perspective as a vehicle designed to move toward accomplishment of its goals, in contrast to a structure that is an end in itself.

THE CRIMINAL JUSTICE SYSTEM

A cursory review of the various components of the Criminal Justice System shows a conglomeration of agencies that, although sometimes referred to as a "nonsystem,"[4] somehow manage to accomplish a great deal of common objectives in a cooperative manner. The individual who finds himself going through the system—a criminal violator, for example—may find that he is moved from one component to another as if he were in some sort of system. It is true that there are many negative factors working against the smooth coordination of the many organizations within the system, but it is important that this study be made from a positive point of view.

Police

Although sometimes referred to as levels of government, the various agencies in all components of the system can be studied from the standpoint of jurisdiction and scope of responsibility. Federal agencies that are charged with investigation and law enforcement have very limited powers, each agency having a specific set of limitations on its jurisdiction, although geographically broader in scope—on a national or international basis—than a local police agency. State agencies are similarly structured and more highly specialized—with statewide scope but narrow legal jurisdiction, such as traffic enforcement or alcoholic beverage control. The local law enforcement agencies, such as the municipal police or county sheriff, are the most general agencies, usually charged with the broad legal jurisdiction within their geographical limits.

Law enforcement and investigative agencies of the federal government are involved in matters of interstate and international commerce and diplomatic relationships, protection of the president, integrity of the national currency and legal tender, taxation and revenue, and specific matters prescribed by the legislature. "The national government has no specifically delegated police power—power to regulate the interests of health, safety, morals, convenience, and welfare of the people—such as the Supreme Court has recognized as existing in the states under the individual powers of the Tenth Amendment."[5]

Law enforcement agencies of the Treasury Department include the Secret Service, which is responsible for the protection of the president and the nation's currency; the Intelligence Unit of the Internal Revenue Service, which is involved in income tax and related investigative matters; and the Division of Alcohol, Tobacco, and Firearms (ATF), which is charged with investigative and enforcement matters involving tax-related violations concerning alcohol, tobacco, and the National Firearms Act. The ATF also investigates bombs and bombings with principal emphasis on federal buildings and offices. Under the administration of the Attorney General, the Justice Department has several law enforcement divisions, including the Federal Bureau of Investigation (FBI), the Bureau of Narcotics and Dangerous Drugs, and the Immigration and Naturalization Service. Many other units are responsible for the enforcement functions required by law attendant to the jurisdiction of such agencies as the Federal Aviation

Authority of the Department of Transportation, the Civil Service Commission, Federal Communications Commission, Federal Trade Commission, and the Interstate Commerce Commission.

The states have primary police powers, which are those powers vested in a government to make and enforce laws in the areas of health, welfare, safety, and morals. Most criminal, health, and licensing laws are a part of the powers of the states. In spite of a growing number of new federal laws governing these same areas, the primary control over the police power zones is still retained by the states.[6] Each state has its own network of law enforcement and administrative bodies that are directly concerned with the problems of the public health, safety, welfare, morals, and general prosperity. On the state jurisdictional level, agencies of the state governments are concerned with statewide problems in the areas of motor vehicle and operator licensing, traffic regulation and accident prevention on the state's highway system, and other such matters.

Each state has its own distinctive assortment of agencies, depending on needs and traditions. In California, the law enforcement and administrative control bodies include the following departments and offices: Alcohol Beverage Control, Consumer Affairs, Fire Marshal, Fish and Game, Forestry, Highway Patrol, Horse Racing Board, Industrial Relations, Mental Hygiene, Military, Motor Vehicles, Narcotics and Drug Abuse, Parks and Recreation, Social Welfare, and the several State Police organizations located at the state colleges and universities and the state facilities. The attorney general and the Department of Justice are responsible for coordination of statewide statistics, special investigations and advisory services as well as assortment of related services in coordination and training within the various components of the Criminal Justice System. A 1966 provision of the California Constitution delegates to the attorney general the authority to supervise sheriffs, local police, and district attorneys.[7]

At the local level the system is explained by Gourley: "There is . . . no such thing in the United States as a police system nor even a set of police systems within any reasonable accurate sense of the term. Our so-called systems are more collections of police units having some similarity of authority, organization or jurisdiction but they lack any systematic relationship to each other."[8] The U.S. Bureau of the Budget in 1966 reported that there were 50 federal agencies, 200 state agencies, and 39,750 local agencies directly involved in law enforcement in the United States.[9]

Court

The court system in the United States is similarly organized, or disorganized; so many of the jurisdictions involved at the various strata of government operate within their own sphere of authority and responsibility. The local courts, existing in numbers corresponding to law enforcement agencies throughout the system, have primary jurisdiction over criminal cases of misdemeanor and felony categories that constitute violations of municipal, county, or state laws. An appeals procedure according to a series of adjective laws provides for certain cases to be appealed through the state court system to the highest court of appeal—the United States Supreme Court.

The national court system consists of the U.S. Supreme Court, the appellate courts, and the courts of first instance. Jurisdiction of the Supreme Court includes appeals in matters of constitutionality and controversies involving certain public officials and those in which a state is a party. The eleven circuit, or federal, courts of appeal have principal jurisdiction over appeals from the district courts. Also at the appeals in the national judicial system are the Court of Systems and Patent Appeals, and the Court of Military Appeals. At the trial level there are 93 district courts, the Court of Claims, the Customs Court, and courts martial.

State court systems have similar levels of jurisdiction, ranging from justice courts to municipal courts, superior courts and the courts of appeal, including the appellate courts and the state supreme courts. The state supreme court hears appeals from decisions of the appellate courts and considers matters of constitutionality. In states having the death penalty, the Supreme Court automatically reviews all appeals from capital convictions. The courts of appeal hear appeals from the county or superior courts throughout the state.

Superior or county courts number one per county in most jurisdictions, with up to more than 100 divisions in a county such as Los Angeles, California. The municipal, or city, or justice courts are distributed throughout each state and serve the needs of the Criminal Justice System depending on the size of the judicial district and the volume of cases processed.

Corrections

The Corrections component of the Criminal Justice System serves a population described by the corrections task force: "The jails, workhouses, penitentiaries, and reformatories of the nation admit, control, and release an estimated 3 million individuals each year. On an average day, approximately 1.3 million people . . . are under correctional authority in the United States, roughly one-third of whom being in institutions and the balance on parole or probation."[10]

Federal institutions in the correctional system include a network of facilities at 38 locations throughout the nation.[11] That number includes six penitentiaries, a medical center, a behavioral research center, intermediate and short-term adult institutions; centers for young adults, youths, and juveniles; and community treatment centers. The Federal Bureau of Prisons is also planning the development of eight metropolitan federal correctional centers to replace traditional jails, most of which are obsolete and overcrowded.[12]

Throughout the 50 states there are approximately 432 correctional institution systems, including over 1,200 separate facilities for adults and juveniles.[13] As of March 1970, there were 4,037 locally administered jails (city and county).[14]

Probation and parole systems in the United States, many operating as combination organizations, including the federal probation system, totalled 1,647 in 1966.[15]

SUMMARY

A study of the many agencies of the three basic components or subsystems of the Criminal Justice System yields the finding that hundreds of thousands of individuals functioning for these agencies in their respective occupations and professional positions throughout the United States are taking part in a systems-like process that affects directly the lives of millions of people each year, and ultimately the lives of every resident and guest of the nation. Although not a system according to the purist, it seems most logical that administrators and supervisors should look upon their organizations and their operations as systems involved in the process of accomplishing a series of specific service-oriented objectives. The organization-structure approach may tend to lead those practitioners in the system to leave the dead-end trail leading to the organization as an end in itself.

Throughout this text reference will be made to the "system" of law enforcement (police), the courts, or corrections, or the Criminal Justice System. The intention of this approach is to carry out the concept of systems orientation with a view to organizing and managing the agencies as viable, dynamic, and fluid entities designed to continually move toward the goals of the administration of justice.

Notes

1. Paul M. Whisenand, *Police Supervision Theory and Practice* (Englewood Cliffs, N.J.: Prentice-Hall, © 1971), p. 112. Reprinted by permission of the publisher.
2. Ibid., pp. 112–13.
3. Daniel Katz and Robert L. Kahn, *The Social Psychology of Organizations* (New York: John Wiley & Sons), pp. 19–26.

4. Thomas F. Adams, *Law Enforcement* (Englewood Cliffs, N.J.: Prentice-Hall, 1973), p. 69.
5. Jewell Cass Phillips, Henry J. Abraham, and Cortez A. M. Ewing, *Essentials of National Government*, 3rd ed. (New York: Van Nostrand Reinhold, 1971), p. 343.
6. Jay A. Sigler and Robert S. Getz, *Contemporary American Government: Problems and Prospects* (New York: Van Nostrand Reinhold, 1971), p. 165.
7. Article 5, Section 13, Constitution of the State of California.
8. G. Douglas Gourley, *Effective Municipal Police Organization* (Beverly Hills, Calif.: Benziger, Bruce & Glencoe, 1970), pp. 21–22.
9. President's Commission on Law Enforcement and the Administration of Justice, *Task Force Report: The Police* (Washington, D.C.: U.S. Government Printing Office, 1967), p. 7.
10. President's Commission on Law Enforcement and the Administration of Justice, *Task Force Report: Corrections* (Washington, D.C.: U.S. Government Printing Office, 1967), p. 2.
11. Federal Bureau of Prisons, *Biennial Report 1970–71* (Washington, D.C.: U.S. Dept. of Justice, Federal Bureau of Prisons, 1971), p. 1.
12. Ibid., p. 24.
13. Herman Piven and Abraham Alcabes, *The Crisis of Qualified Manpower for Criminal Justice: An Analytic Assessment with Guidelines for New Policy* (Washington, D.C.: U.S. Government Printing Office, 1969) vol. 2, *Correctional Institutions*, p. 7.
14. Bureau of Prisons, *Report 1970–71*, p. 24.
15. Herman Piven and Abraham Alcabes, *The Crisis of Qualified Manpower for Criminal Justice: An Analytic Assessment with Guidelines for New Policy* (Washington, D.C.: U.S. Government Printing Office, 1969) vol. 1, *Probation/Parole*, p. 6.

Review Questions

1. Describe the *Police* component of the Criminal Justice System.
2. Describe the *Court* component of the system.
3. Describe the *Corrections* component.
4. In your own words, write a brief statement describing the three components as they constitute a "system."
5. What is the responsibility of the *Court* component of the system to the individual who is accused of a criminal offense?
6. What is the "dual role" of the probation officer as discussed in this chapter?
7. What five benefits does Whisenand refer to when discussing the applications of the systems approach to a police organization?
8. What is the legal source for "police power" of the individual states?
9. Does primary police power rest with state or federal government?
10. Draw a flow diagram depicting how the offender is processed through the Criminal Justice System.

2 Organization Principles and Practices

An organization is a system of relationships between things, people, jobs, groups, and processes arranged to accomplish a common objective.[1] "Organization is a pattern of ways in which large numbers of people, too many to have intimate face-to-face contact with all others, and engaged in a complexity of tasks, relate themselves to each other in the conscious systematic establishment and accomplishment of mutually agreed purposes."[2] Both these definitions characterize the organization as a systematic relationship of people and objects established to reach certain goals through common objectives. Whisenand defines the organization by also defining management and administration. His definition of *management* is "action intended to achieve rational cooperation in an organization," and *administration* is "organization and management."[3] As defined by Whisenand, "an organization is characterized by (1) goals, (2) a division of labor, authority, power, and communication responsibilities in a rationally planned, rather than a random or traditionally patterned, manner to enhance the achievement of specific goals, (3) a set of rules and norms, (4) the presence of one or more authority centers which control the efforts of the organization and direct them toward its goals."[4] Every agency of criminal justice that employs two or more people is an organization.

Certain fundamental maxims have been universally accepted as common to all organizations, regardless of size, purpose, or other individual characteristics. Some of these concepts have been so universally accepted that too rigid adherence "to the letter" might be more of a detriment than an advantage. They should be considered as general guidelines, with an awareness of the reality that there are certain occasions when the urgency of a situation makes it imperative that a rule be broken. For the administrator who makes a judicious application of these principles with sufficient flexibility, they serve him well.

SPECIFY GOALS AND OBJECTIVES

It is a fundamental necessity, before it can open its doors for business, that an enterprise identify and clearly define its goals and objectives. A police chief cannot hope to begin staffing the organization or planning divisional assignments without first deciding upon the methods that will be used to provide patrol coverage throughout the jurisdiction at various times of day. Whether to operate its own laboratory services or to contract with another department should be determined prior to construction of the laboratory and purchase of $50,000 worth of microscopes. William Newman in his text *Administrative Action* stated:

> Goals serve a multiple purpose in administration. They are vital links in the planning process, they aid in decentralization, they provide a basis for voluntary coordination, they become a focus for individual motivation, and they are also essential elements in the process of control.[5]

Goals for the Criminal Justice System as a whole include *ordered liberty in a society in which the people hold certain sacred constitutional rights, but waive certain rights by engaging in violent and unlawful activity,* and *fair and impartial administration of justice in a free society.* A police goal is to provide protection of life and property. A goal of the courts is to assure the accused of his constitutional guarantees in trials that are fairly administered. A goal of the corrections system is to aid the convicted offender in redirecting his life away from former criminal behavior patterns. *Goals* are defined in this context as those results that are effected through the accomplishment of the organization's missions, standards, purposes, and objectives.

Objectives are statements of plans of action which should prescribe how certain activities are to be carried out, under what conditions, and how well. No two organizations should be required to have identical lists of objectives; each will be distinctively different even if closely related to another organization with similar goals. Two neighboring county sheriffs' organizations may be identical in many ways, yet completely different in other respects. About objectives, Newman stated:

> Every enterprise needs a clear statement of its objectives as a basis for all planning. Plainly, for example, an airline must decide

whether its primary objective is to carry passengers or freight before it can lay out its program, select equipment, hire personnel, and begin to operate in anything other than a haphazard manner.[6]

Every organization will have a number of different objectives, which will require careful planning and development of a series of priorities. Divisions of administrative responsibilities and apportionment of work assignments will be directly related to the priorities. For example, if an objective of the probation department is to provide intensive counseling of small groups of clients as opposed to the larger case loads with a minimum of personal contacts, it will be necessary to employ a greater number of probation officers in proportion to the officer-probationer ratio. Whether patrol officers are to work in pairs or solo will have a direct relationship to the number of automobiles that must be purchased, and the maintenance staff to keep them operating must be manned accordingly. A policy that requires all arrests be approved by field supervisors prior to actual booking at the jail will make it necessary for the department to provide sufficient supervisors so that field officers will not have to wait interminable periods of time to have routine arrests receive a degree of attention that may or may not be necessary. A decision on which trials will be recorded and whether the transcripts will be provided free or for a charge will have a direct bearing on the court reporter staffing and financing. If deputy probation officers are to be required to carry weapons under certain conditions, provision must also be made for the purchase of the weapons, for initial training, and for continued practice. Facilities and supplies must be made available.

DEVELOP AN ORGANIZATIONAL PLAN

Many types of plans are utilized by an organization, and these show the organization's structure: among other things, the flow of authority and responsibility and the levels of the hierarchy, channels of communication, and relationships of the functioning units. Placement in the structure may indicate the degree of importance or attention given to a particular activity, which should be directly related to the objectives and goals of the organization. From a systems standpoint, a chart is necessary to delineate the flow of activities and information. The organizational relationships should be established to assure the most effective attainment of goals. Its design as a vehicle rather than a structure should be functional and as free as possible from unnecessary encumbrances.

In addition to the organizational chart, or table of organization, manuals of regulations and procedure should be prepared to establish guidelines for conduct and methods of operation that can be applied throughout the organization to assure continuity and consistency, with constant review to make sure that the organization continues to function in accordance with its goals and objectives. The regulations should clearly reflect the chief executive's expectations of the department members in the way of personal and professional conduct—both on and off the job if necessary. The general good reputation of the organization is important if its members are to be effective, particularly in the business of criminal justice. Any individual who functions in a professional capacity that involves regulation of, or interference with, another person's conduct must prepare himself for a life of careful scrutiny to make sure that he is "practicing what he preaches." As long as he is in public service he does not enjoy total privacy. The same principle applies to the organization, which functions as a public servant subject to constant surveillance by the people it serves.

ORGANIZE ACCORDING TO THE PLAN

Newman states that "the administrative process of *organizing* an enterprise or any of its parts consists of (1) dividing and grouping the work that should be done (including administration) into individual jobs, and (2) defining the established relationships between individuals filling these jobs."[7] May we hastily add that, once organized, the establishment should not be allowed to freeze into position, never to change whenever a change is needed. There are many vital questions that must be answered when carrying out the organization process. They include:

1. Do the proposed divisions of work correspond with the department's objectives? Are the proportions of personnel strength and degree of attention in harmony with the priorities that have been designated each of the objectives?

2. How should the organization be divided from the standpoint of management and supervisory activities? Are the supervisor-subordinate relationships clearly defined and the authority levels for different degrees of decision-making made known throughout the department? What are the lines of authority-responsibility and communications flow?

3. What line divisions and what staff functions should be established, and how will the relationships between line and staff be implemented?

4. What titles should be given to the several divisions, and what should be the rank structure within each division as well as the job titles of the people assigned to the various tasks?

5. What use will be made of specialists? For example, many police departments are now utilizing the legal advisor, an attorney who may not have had previous police experience, but who serves as an "in-house" advisor on matters of arrest, search, and seizure and as liaison representative between the department and the prosecutor's office. The coroner's

toxicologist may be a graduate chemist, or the probation department's training officer a teacher rather than an assigned deputy probation officer. The individual assigned to handle the fiscal matters of the organization might be an accountant rather than one of the individuals who has been transferred to the job on a temporary basis from elsewhere in the organization.

6. What will be the design of the table of organization? Very careful attention should be given to the physical arrangement of the chart which will accurately show the organization as it is intended to operate. For example, the traditional "military" model for a table of organization shows a relationship with the supervisor at the top and his subordinates in a row beneath him; a "colleague" model may show the same supervisor in the center of a circle and his subordinates appearing in a circle around him. The former creates the impression of authoritarianism with all of the authority flowing from the top to the bottom; the latter configuration stimulates the viewer to see the unit as a democratic group of individuals working together with the leader in a coordinating position. See figure 1. Looking at the matter practically, however, one must examine closely the individuals who are implementing the process, and the departmental policies regarding their relationships. Regardless of the appearance of a diagram the true test is the study of the results.

Relative sizes of the squares representing divisions of assignment or their location on the chart may cause the viewer to place greater or lesser

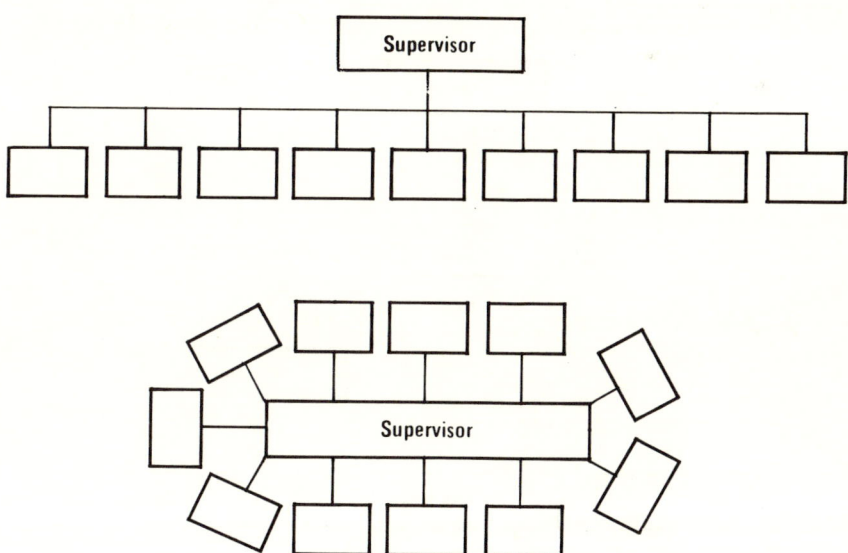

Figure 1.   *Table of organization: traditional model vs. colleague model.*

importance on a particular activity, whether the director of the agency and his staff intended it that way or not. Locations in the pyramid may also tend to indicate a difference in rank or power that unit may have in the organization. For example, consider the two models in figure 2 showing the training division. The same importance is to be placed on the unit in both examples, and the director and his staff hold the same pay grade. Since the unit in model B reports directly to the director, it unquestionably appears to be in a more prestigious situation because the unit in model A must communicate with the director through an intermediate-level executive. It appears that the director would generate less energy because he is farther from the

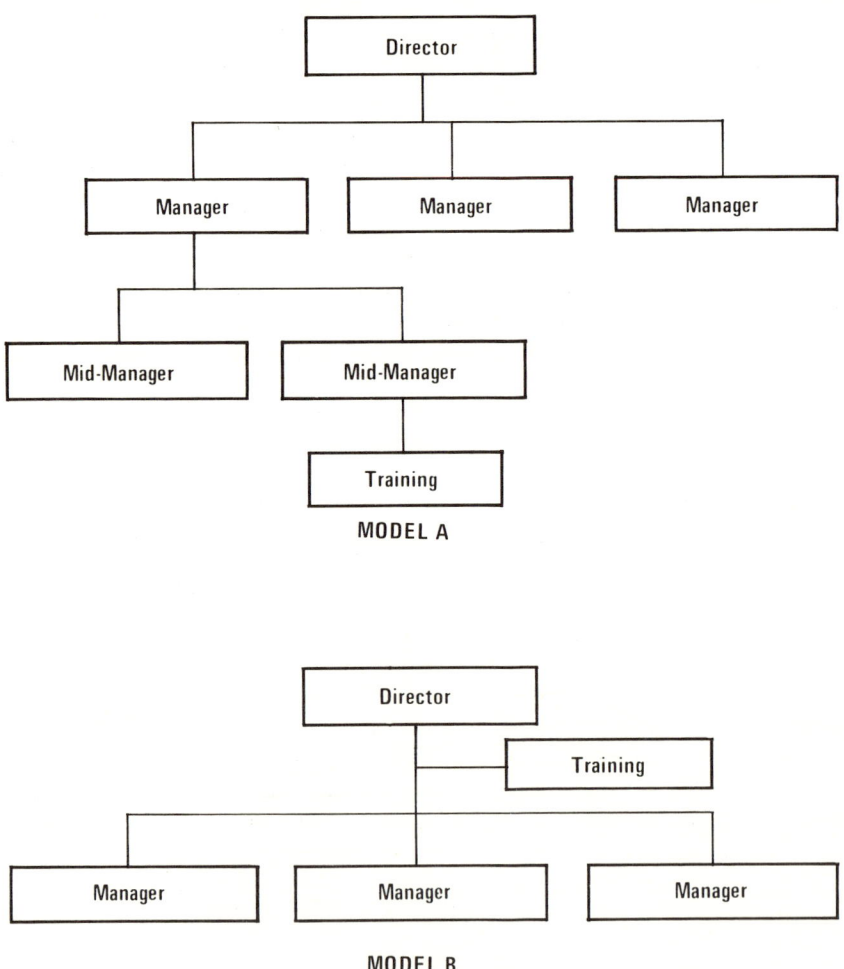

Figure 2. Two models of training division organization.

power source, and model A would consequently have less influence and lower prestige.

Newman lists six key considerations in the departmentation of any enterprise: (1) Take advantage of specialization; (2) Facilitate control; (3) Aid in coordination; (4) Secure adequate attention; (5) Recognize local conditions; and (6) Reduce expense.[8] Departmentation is also designed on the basis of these factors: (1) Purpose; (2) Process; (3) Clientele; (4) Area; and (5) Time. These factors as well as Newman's key considerations will be discussed in chapter 4, which addresses the problem of departmentation.

PRESCRIBE RELATIONSHIPS

Beginning with the highest level of management, the director, chief, or superintendent, the levels of authority and responsibility should be clearly defined and generally communicated throughout the organization. Ultimate responsibility for the organization's effective achievement of goals and objectives rests clearly on the shoulders of the chief executive. Each individual functions within his own sphere of responsibility for his personal performance, and he must have delegated to him an appropriate and corresponding amount of authority to carry out his assigned tasks. The authority structure is graduated according to the hierarchical structure of the organization, with lesser degrees of authority conferred on those in successively lower decision-making positions.

In the field of criminal justice, it is generally those in lower levels of the hierarchy who make a greater number of decisions regarding the actual objectives of the agency, yet progressively fewer decisions regarding the management and routine operations of the organization itself. For example, the district attorney in a medium to large size county with a heavy prosecution load serves as the administrative head of the organization and makes decisions regarding its management. At the same time, he is making fewer decisions in the day-to-day routine of prosecuting cases with regard to what charge to file on the information presented by an investigation officer, what agreement to make with the defense attorney in a negotiated plea for a lesser and included offense, or whether to recommend dismissal of a charge for lack of a substantial case. The chief of police makes the decisions about employment, promotions of personnel, divisional assignments, and other management decisions, but he may seldom make a decision regarding whether a suspect should be arrested for suspicion of burglary or assault with a deadly weapon. Keeping this dual decision-making process in mind, it is clear that the authority-responsibility relationship within an organization is held in the context of management decision-making.

Regarding the parity of authority and responsibility, Koontz and O'Donnell state: "Since authority is the power to carry out assignments and responsibility is the obligation to accomplish them, it logically follows that the authority needed to do this should correspond to the responsibility."[9] Professor Gourley makes this observation about levels of authority: "Authority to make decisions, to execute its responsibilities, should be delegated to the lowest practical level and persons to whom authority is delegated must be held strictly accountable for its exercise."[10]

Athos and Coffey address delegation of authority and nondelegation characteristics of responsibility:

> In all but the smallest organizations, managers must delegate some of their authority in order that the work may be divided and organizational objectives achieved. The ultimate responsibility for the achievement of the objectives is the manager's alone; this he cannot delegate. But he can delegate some of his authority to his subordinates to direct work that will contribute to the achievement of the objectives, and he can hold his subordinates responsible for those sub-tasks. The traditional principle of delegation has stated that managers should be given sufficient authority to command others in performing the necessary work.[11]

Koontz and O'Donnell explain the significance of authority to the role of the manager:

> Authority is the key to the management job. Since managers must work through people to get things done, management theory is necessarily concerned with a complex of superior-subordinate relationships and it is therefore founded on the concept of authority. In the manager of a company, division, department, branch, or section is vested power sufficient to force compliance, whether through persuasion, coercion, economic or social sanctions, or other means.[12]

Regarding delegation, Koontz and O'Donnell observe:

> The entire process of delegation involves the assignment of tasks, the delegation of authority for accomplishing these tasks, and the exaction of responsibility for their accomplishment. In practice it is impossible to split this process, since an assignment of a task without the authority to accomplish it is meaningless, as is the delegation of authority without a definition of the area over which the power is to be used. Moreover, since responsibility cannot be delegated, the delegant has no practical alternative but to exact responsibility from his subordinate for completing the assignment.[13]

Whenever any degree of authority is delegated to a subordinate and is going to have a direct and immediate effect on any other individual higher, lower, or at the same level in the hierarchy, it should be made known to all of those who will be affected to assure maximum coordination and cooperation. Sometimes an individual who has been conferred with an additional degree of power over that he previously held finds himself in an almost untenable position; others may believe that his so-called new power is self-assigned and they may not accept this new status. One important aspect of supervision is that the supervised comply and accept the supervision.

Delegation of authority is not as simple to practice as it is to state in theory. Certain tenacious administrators find it nearly impossible to "let go" and to delegate any authority to a subordinate. "The only way to get a thing done properly is to do it yourself" is a familiar phrase to virtually everyone. It means simply that the person holds the belief that his knowledge and performance are superior and only he can meet his demanding standards. True, other people, particularly less experienced and less knowledgeable subordinates, may come up with ideas that are not identical to those of their superiors. It does not necessarily follow that those ideas are inferior. The person who delegates must be receptive to the ideas of others, and he must allow for mistakes that are bound to be made while the actor is gaining his practical experience. The delegator must also be willing to trust his subordinate to get certain tasks accomplished and to be sensitive to needs and standards of his superior. One method of assuring that certain minimum standards will be met, or that a particular procedure is being used, is to develop certain controls in the form of written directions, or supervised performance prior to allowing the individual to perform "solo," and to develop a feedback system consisting of personal inspections and specific reports.

Delegation involves a direct-line relationship between supervisor and subordinate, a flow of authority, responsibility, and communications. Sometimes referred to as a *chain of command*, this line of authority is a regularly established channel designed for the purpose of passing the authority-responsibility relationship throughout the department within the hierarchy to assure a flow of communication and accomplishment of the work objectives. Henri Fayol, a French industrialist, described the chain of command—or scalar principle—as "the chain of supervisors ranging from the ultimate authority to the lowest ranks. The line of authority is the route followed—via links in the chain—by all communications which start from or go to the ultimate authority. This path is dictated both by the need for some transmission and by the principle of unity of command"[14] In large organizations, particularly government structures, this chain of command constitutes the red tape of bureaucracy and leads to "buck-passing."

In their classic text on management, Pfiffner and Sherwood explain the chain of command:

> Communications and orders flow "through channels;" that is, they do not skip levels or echelons. On the plus side this pattern strengthens the positions of subordinate commanders by assuring them that their own subordinates will not receive orders directly from someone on a different level, a very demoralizing practice. The requirement that orders and communications go through channels also makes for coordination because everyone on the chain of command will have seen the communication and thus be "in the know."[15]

It is absolutely essential that there be a clear understanding throughout the organization for proper organization functioning. According to Koontz and O'Donnell,

> Every subordinate must know who delegates authority to him, and to whom matters beyond his own authority must be referred. Although the chain of command may be safely departed from for purposes of information, departure for decision making destroys authority and undermines managership itself.[16]

Accountability for the accomplishment of certain prescribed tasks, often within time limitations, is passed on to the unit supervisor. He knows the capabilities of his subordinates as well as what they are doing, and can plan the work accordingly. The overall results could be far more damaging than any immediate benefits that might be realized if a supervisor from another division, or at some higher level, were to change instructions or reassign work to certain individuals in the group for some nondescript reason.

Responsibility, in relationship to the authority-responsibility concept, is an obligation that is a contractual arrangement between superior and subordinate, neither can abdicate nor can it be delegated. Koontz and O'Donnell sum it up in this manner: "While a subordinate is given authority to accomplish a service and the subordinate, in turn, may delegate a portion of the authority received, neither delegates any of his responsibility. Responsibility, being an obligation to perform, is owed to one's superiors, and no subordinate reduces his responsibility by delegating to another the authority to perform a duty."[17]

MINIMIZE DUAL ACCOUNTABILITY

Sometimes referred to as the "principle of unity of command," this concept holds the belief that one cannot serve two masters well. According to Newman, "One of the most widely recognized principles of organization is that a member of an enterprise should have only one line supervisor."[18]

Thus problems occur when an employee is not sure of where he stands in the organization; in his quest to please, he is inclined to vie for approval of everyone he believes to hold a higher position. Newman explains the dilemma:

> Aside from the fact that an employee is probably in a poor position to decide which orders should be postponed and which obeyed promptly, dual subordination is likely to lead to poor morale because the conscientious employee will feel frustrated if he cannot live up to what is expected of him, the indifferent employee will stop trying since he obviously cannot do all that has been requested, and all of them will sooner or later be reprimanded for failing to comply with instructions.[19]

When considering this concept, or principle, it is necessary to put it into context. There should be no absolute rule that an individual in an organization may answer to only one other person of a higher rank, or of equal or lesser rank in an advisory or staff relationship, to accomplish a particular objective. The organization should be established in such a way that each executive and supervisor is adequately informed of the scope of his authority and responsibility; this includes identifying the individuals who are to be assigned to him for direction and leadership. This way, the supervisor and his subordinates know to whom they are responsible and to what extent. If a supervisor is given the responsibility to accomplish a specific goal, then he must be given the authority to get the job done, which includes responsibility for the performance of the people assigned to him and the authority to require their accountability to him. For example, a police sergeant may have a team of officers assigned to him as traffic enforcement officers. Their objectives include concentration on a specific area of the city in which there have been several fatal and injurious collisions to locate and issue citations to traffic-law violators for the purpose of reducing the number of collisions in that area. The sergeant and his team meet at the beginning of each working day and discuss strategy. In his role as coordinator of activities the sergeant works out beat assignments and lunch and refreshment break times, and he may give each officer more detailed instructions. The officers are accountable to each other to accomplish the task, and the sergeant is directly responsible for the performance of his subordinates to his superior officer, who might be a watch commander holding the rank of lieutenant.

In the example just described, the team is operating and citations are being issued to the violators. Consider the results of that team's effort if another sergeant were to contact half of the men on the team and order them to leave their assigned districts and perform some other task. The officers tell him that they were supposed to work traffic enforcement, but he tells them that his orders must be followed. They comply because he holds a higher rank. What will be the result of the team effort toward the reduction of collisions if such an assignment lasts for more than just a very few minutes? Should the team's sergeant be held responsible for an increase in collisions because of this reassignment of his officers? Consider the results of the team effort if three of the eight officers were to decide that they did not like traffic enforcement and protested to the sergeant. Not being relieved of their assignment, suppose they then went to a lieutenant of another division, who told them to do whatever they wished and not to pay any attention to the unpopular sergeant. Certainly such an arrangement could not be tolerated. The "one leader" concept should not be restricted to a military-like organization. It must be applied to any organization in which people are assigned to do a job and are given the authority to get the job done.

One author states: "The principle of unity of command applies to those who are commanded, not to those who command."[20] He explains that a supervisor should not respect the principle to the extent that he will neglect to take action in emergency situations that require immediate supervisory attention or take some disciplinary action when an officer violates a law or rule. He also points out that superior officers should not make a practice of circumventing other superior officers and avoiding the "line of command." Gourley states it another way:

> It is as important for the chief to observe this principle as it is for his subordinates. If either the chief or personnel at the level of execution attempt to communicate by-passing the established chain of command, much harm will be done. Immediate supervisory personnel will have no knowledge of the communication and cannot, therefore, be held responsible for execution of the order or transmittal of the information involved.[21]

The purpose of strict adherence to the principle of single supervisors, says Gourley, is that police agencies operate in a climate of emergency "calling for strict discipline and an effective chain of command in order to meet the demands for prompt and decisive action."[22]

Koontz and O'Donnell state:

> The more completely an individual has a reporting relationship to a single superior, the less the problem of conflict in instructions and the greater the feeling of personal responsibility for results. . . . An obligation is essentially personal, and authority delegation by more than one person is likely to result in conflicts in both authority and responsibility. Moreover, unless a manager has total authority to hold his subordinate responsible, his position becomes undermined.[23]

In practice, there is a contradiction to the principle, although the contradiction does not negate the effects of the organizational concept providing appropriate allowances are made for the variations. An individual who is operating in a professional capacity in the Criminal Justice System holds a place in the organizational structure and functions in some type of supervisor-subordinate situation. And yet, in his respective position, he is an independent agent who makes decisions on the basis of an extensive series of "higher authority" relationships. First, consider the individual's heritage and background, which serve as his consciousness and basis for reactions to the many situations that confront him calling for decisions and value judgments. As a professional operant, the practitioner is responsive to the principles and ethics of the profession. His conduct may be dictated to a considerable degree by requirements of the profession rather than sometimes-conflicting requirements of an immediate superior. A prosecutor in the courtroom responds to orders from the judge, the judge acts in a manner prescribed by the U. S. Supreme Court and opinions of an attorney general. The police officer in the courtroom follows the strategies laid out by the prosecutor, has questioned a suspect according to rules set down by the Supreme Court, and collected evidence in a manner prescribed by the laboratory technician. An officer makes arrests on the basis of citizen complaints or perhaps at the direction of an officer from another division, he "books" the suspects according to rules established by the jail division commander, and prepares his reports to pass the careful scrutiny of yet another supervisor in the person of a records division sergeant. Other "supervisors" who have a direct effect on an individual's codes of conduct are spiritual leaders, or the precepts of a religion itself, codes of conduct of other organizations in which the individual holds membership, and his own conscience which aids in guiding him through his decision-making activities.

Obvious exceptions to the unity of command principle are those occasions when emergency situations require the immediate decision of a single individual who might be in the presence of members of two or more divisions of the same organization and occasions when disciplinary action is necessary to prevent misconduct on the part of an employee holding a lower level position or when urgently required punitive or disciplinary action cannot wait.

LIMIT THE SCOPE OF SUPERVISION

Most often referred to as "span of control," this phenomenon is a significant maxim of organization and management and is frequently listed as a basic principle. The reason for this emphasis is that it is an inescapable reality that it is physically impossible to interact on a continuous executive or supervisory basis with more than some optimum number of subordinate employees. Any argument with the concept is not with this fact, but with the claim by some experts that there is some sort of general rule with an established maximum in all cases. For example, V. A. Leonard, former police officer and professor emeritus at Washington State University, states:

> It is generally held that one individual can effectively supervise the activities of only from six to seven persons. . . . It is also generally accepted that as one moves upward through the levels of organization to the top of the enterprise, the number of subordinates supervised should be progressively reduced. Depending somewhat on the size of the department, it would be desirable for the Chief of Police to have only three supervisory or command officers reporting directly to him. In addition to observance of limitations on the span of control, this gives him the time and opportunity to give effective attention to the broader problems of management and planning. This, then, is the law of span of control.[24]

In their text *Police Organization and Management*, Leonard and his co-author state that the executive span should be not less than three nor more than seven subordinates reporting to a single executive, with the optimum number set at three.[25] Gourley addresses the same principle:

> In the field of management, there has been considerable speculation regarding the number of persons who should report to any one supervisor or manager. An extreme view is that the maximum number should not exceed five or six. Other authorities claim that the number can be considerably greater than this. *In American police departments in the past, there has been a tendency toward holding too large a number of persons answerable directly to the chief.*[26]

Pfiffner and Sherwood succinctly express their opinion on the subject: "There is perhaps no more hoary artifact of organization folklore than the notion of span of control."[27] It seems that when one makes the statement that a maximum number of subordinates should not be exceeded, there is an added attempt to prescribe some type of formula for arriving at the optimum number. The concept of numbers of supervisor-subordinate contacts also involves the formation of the organization structure and hierarchy relationships. The larger the organization, the greater the number of levels of supervision because of a mathematical formula that may be applied—such as, that first-line supervisors should not have more than seven subordinates, second-line more than five, and on up the ladder to the chief executive with an absolute maximum (and minimum) of three. Using such a formula would almost certainly assure the introduction of a new stratum of management with the growth of the organization to a succession of greater numbers. "It can do much to determine the number of levels in the organization pyramid, and in doing that it can impose a mushroom-like flatness or a cone-like depth of structure."[28]

Pfiffner and Sherwood explain the reasons why most American governmental institutions have such a large span of control:

> First, there is a tendency toward a large number of separate departments because the "empire-builder" type of department head wants to be answerable, if at all, only to the chief executive or governing body.
>
> Second, each pressure group desires its own pet administrative activity to be set up in an independent department rather than embodied as a bureau or division in another department.
>
> Third, every functional chief desires access to the seat of authority without going through intervening hierarchical steps.
>
> Fourth, each functional chief desires such access to the legislative or governing body as may pertain to the position of department head.
>
> Fifth, those interested in particular governmental activities fear that inept and dilatory handling of functional affairs may result if they are placed in what is merely one of the many units in a large department.
>
> Sixth, the sponsors of new administrative activities do not want to become units in an old department because they imagine that they will become stifled in the red tape of an organization which they believe already too large for effective action.[29]

The administrator should consider his own ambitions as well as those of many of the members of his organization in relationship to this matter of scope of supervision. The conscientious employee who works hard to justify the existence and the level of importance with which others should look upon his operation has a tendency to develop a feeling of universality when he looks around him. For example, the specialist whose entire lifetime is dedicated to his own small sphere of interest and control may be surrounded by a very small number of people who share his beliefs, but they are his only contact with the "outside world" on a daily basis. It might be difficult for him to comprehend how anyone else might not share his opinion of his own personal importance and that of his unit. The individual who is hopelessly captured at a static level in the hierarchy may attempt to have the unit upgraded, which will also cause his own status to improve both on a monetary and prestige level. There are certain privileges that go along with higher status in many organizations, such as bigger offices, more luxurious appointments, a private secretary, subordinates to do the work previously performed in a lower status, and membership in status-oriented subgroups within the organization.

The traditional view of organizational management, according to Sayles and Strauss,[30] is that the supervisor is responsible for coordinating the work of his subordinate and that control must be tight for efficiency. In order for him to perform in this environment, the supervisor's span of control must be very limited. The result is that the organization pyramid is quite steep, and they report that in some large companies it is not unusual to find ten levels separating the hourly employees from top management. Adding relatively large numbers of staff personnel and department heads to reduce the number of levels will result in organizational pyramids that bulge in the middle.

Criminal justice organizations are no exception to the supervision scope versus bureaucratic structure dilemma. The great danger in the creation of a multilevel structure is that the business of managing the structure becomes more important in the eyes of many of the management personnel than the actual goal-oriented activities for which the organization was developed in the first place. It is important to guard against the "organization maintenance" posture of devising methods to generate superfluous work and reporting requirements that do little more than increase the size of the organization and the number of levels of supervision without appreciably affecting any change in achievement of objectives. For example, a deputy probation officer prepares his probation report and may present it directly to the judge. After many years with this procedure resulting in the production of reports that are of inferior quality, the judge might require the probation officer to have a supervisor review all reports before they are submitted to the court. If the number of officers preparing the reports exceeds seven, it becomes necessary to create two supervisory officers whose sole responsibility is to pass on reports before they go to court. As the department grows, the number of supervisors at the first level grows to the point where it becomes necessary to introduce into the system another supervisory level with the responsibility to control and coordinate the first-line supervisors. The supervisors do not prepare any reports because their responsibilities involve supervision. Eventually, it may be possible with little effort to double the size of the department and only increase the actual output of the department by 20 to 30 percent. An unrealistic adherence to the so-called principle of span of control could easily lead to the justified criticism that a department had lost sight of its objectives. "Make-work time-waster" activities are the natural result of such organizations.

Sayles and Strauss maintain that the "flatter" organizations, or those that involve broader spans of control, are often desirable. Recent research, they state, indicates that "under many circumstances subordinates perform more effectively with limited supervisory order-giving and controlling."[31] The professional and paraprofessional nature of most of the criminal justice agencies, which involves a considerable amount of individual and colleague-type decision making at the operational level, tends to place them in the category of those organizations having broader spans of supervision.

There are certain considerations involved when determining the scope and nature of supervision in a criminal justice agency. There can be no formulas prescribed, but each of these factors should be taken into account.[32]

1. Personal qualifications of the executive or supervisor in relationship to his educational and work experience preparation and his supervisory background: The newly appointed first-line supervisor with no prior experience in supervision may have the ability to perform all the tasks that are performed by his subordinates but need time to mature in his supervisory capacity. He may have all of the supervisory skills but no knowledge of the tasks performed by his subordinates. Whatever the degree of skill or knowledge he has, each supervisor holds his own unique qualifications.

2. Actual decision-making authority and power to act delegated by the granting authority (the court, the city manager, the electorate) to the supervisor: Regardless of the position he holds in the hierarchy of an organization, the executive or the first-line supervisor will be impotent without commensurate authority and responsibility.

3. The expertise level of the individuals being supervised: The nature of their tasks, prerequisites for appointment to their respective positions with respect to education and experience, and personal qualifications all play a significant part in the type and amount of supervision each will require. For example, an investigator for the district attorney's office may be required to have five years' experience in criminal investigation prior to appointment, while an investigator for the local police department might be receiving his first actual criminal investigation experience (other than initial investigations) following his appointment to the position. The supervision required for each would be different. Another example might be that of a graduate chemist who is employed as a toxicologist for the coroner. Perhaps very little supervision would be required.

4. Authority granted to the subordinates to make decisions and to act on their own commensurate with their responsibility to accomplish certain specific objectives: If the subordinate must go to his supervisor to have his decisions made for him, or if he must have the supervisor approve each decision immediately following whatever actions he takes, he will require a different type of supervision and the assigned supervisor's span, or scope of responsibility, will be different. Police officers make arrests on the basis

of the laws, departmental guidelines, prosecution and court philosophy, and their own perceptual powers as well as personal judgment. If a supervisor must approve each arrest prior to the actual booking of the arrested persons, then the supervisor-subordinate ratio must be small. Attorneys working for the county prosecutor may operate with virtual independence except for being held accountable for the final dispositions of their assigned cases. The span of their supervisor may be quite broad, and he may handle a case load himself.

5. Amount of confidence the executive or supervisor has in his subordinates: The supervisor who cannot "let go" and let his subordinates exercise their own authority and perform on their own will find that he is curtailing the scope of his supervision and may be reducing his effectiveness. This is the type of executive who holds the view that the only way to get something done right is to do it himself. In extreme cases, one may find that the man is actually a 50-year-old patrolman in the chief's office.

6. Method of inspections and controls for measuring the quality and quantity (if applicable) of performance: There should be standards for the accomplishment of objectives and some means for ascertaining that such standards are met or exceeded.

7. Training and procedural outlines for task performance: Training should be thorough and constant, with periodic updating when necessary. If there are procedural manuals or guidelines for the routine and anticipated tasks with some consideration given to contingencies, there is need for continuous supervision of the routine performance by subordinates. Executives and supervisors who use a low-key approach to supervision, allowing their subordinates to carry out their duties without interference, and who participate or make decisions in the exceptional cases may find that their subordinates are more self-reliant, and thus their own scope may be broadened.

8. Morale among the employees and their compatibility with each other and their superiors within the organization: If the morale is low and there is constant bickering it may be necessary to provide closer supervision, although a closer look at the cause may indicate that the morale is low because the supervision is too close.

9. Physical facilities and working conditions: These are related to morale, as is the proximity of supervisors to the individuals they supervise. If close supervision is warranted and the people to be supervised are scattered throughout the countryside, the span will be closer than if they are all housed in one room sitting at desks.

10. Work requirements for the supervisor: The supervisor who must carry his own case load or perform a prescribed series of tasks in addition to performing his supervisory tasks may find that he is so bogged down with his work that he has no time for supervision. He must then either divest

himself of some of the tasks or consider a more limited scope of responsibility. As the supervisor progresses higher up the organization's structure, then his own work should be reduced. Staff assistance should be provided for the "busy work" requirements of his office. In many cases, the executive becomes little more than an office manager, and the only office he has time to manage is his own.

11. Accessibility of the supervisor to his subordinates: Is there a free flow of communications and can the employee with a question or a decision to be made at the higher level have immediate access to his supervisor, or must he go through an obstacle course and be subjected to interminable delays? Whether the supervisor intends it or not, the result of barriers being put between him and his subordinates will be either no decision at all or the subordinate making his own decision if he cannot find another supervisor who is accessible. In either case, the span must be reduced or the barriers set aside.

12. Nature of the tasks to be performed and the objectives: A service-oriented organization with constantly changing demands for new procedures and thus new procedures to be developed will require closer supervisor-subordinate working relationships than an organization whose policies and practices are constant and unchanging.

13. Time and energy required of the supervisor to perform in his decision-making and leadership role: There are physical limitations as well.

Organizational leadership involves a free flow of communications throughout the various organizational levels, sometimes calling for general staff discussions involving the several levels and the chief executive.
Courtesy: Police Department, Huntington Beach, California

14. Communications flow and comprehensibility throughout the organization: The goals and objectives of the organization should be clearly impressed upon all members of the enterprise, changes in procedure promptly communicated, and all aspects of the communications process should be free of interference.

15. Flexibility of the organization and its membership to allow exceptions from established policies and procedure to be made without undue delays.

16. Human and financial resources of the organization: Limitations on certain manpower or funds to purchase and maintain equipment and facilities may cause a supervisor's span to be broadened far more than under optimum conditions.

INTEGRATE AND COORDINATE THE FUNCTIONAL UNITS

Although the various functional units throughout the organization may have specialized methods of objective attainment, there are common goals and objectives of the organization as a whole. The principal function of management is to integrate and coordinate the various activities for the purpose of getting the best results with the minimum expenditure of human and financial resources. Formal relationships must be established and there should be a well-articulated and well-communicated procedure for the various activities to be integrated throughout the organization. As stated by Sayles and Strauss, "The purpose of any organization is to complete work: the production of goods or services. Individual task performance is only useful insofar as it serves to facilitate the attainment of the over-all objective of the enterprise. No matter how hard an employee works, his efforts are wasted unless they integrate with those of his fellow workers."[33]

Regarding coordination, Athos and Coffey stated: "As soon as any organization grows large enough so that work is divided and individuals and groups begin to specialize, coordination must take place. This coordination is achieved partially by establishing formal organizational relationships and by assigning the job of managing and supervising to specific people."[34] "Coordination is also partially achieved through the establishment of a formal hierarchy, which specifies who can tell whom to do what."[35] Koontz and O'Donnell point out the need for coordination in an organization:

> The necessity for synchronizing individual action arises out of differences in opinion as to how group goals can be reached or how individual and group objectives can be harmonized. . . . It thus becomes the central task of the manager to reconcile differences in approach, timing, effort, or interest, and to harmonize cooperative and individual goals.[36]

Quoting Mary Parker Follett:

> The principle of direct contact states that coordination must be achieved through interpersonal, vertical, and horizontal relationships of people in an enterprise. People exchange ideas, ideals, prejudices, and purposes through direct personal communication much more efficiently than by any other method, and, with the understanding gained in this way, they find means to achieve both common and personal goals. This recognized identity of ultimate interests then tends to bring agreement on methods and actions. . . . These principles indicate . . . that the method of achieving coordination is largely horizontal rather than vertical. People cooperate as a result of understanding one another's tasks, and the line officer's dictum "Coordinate!" is both unrealistic and unenforceable.[37]

Koontz and O'Donnell explain how the manager of an organization achieves coordination:

> He achieves it in two ways. First, he assures that the environment facilitates coordination by creating an appropriate organization structure, selecting skillful subordinates and training and supervising them effectively, providing and explaining the integrated plans and programs that subordinates will carry out, and establishing means to determine whether plans are being carried out properly and programs are on schedule. Second, he makes certain that his subordinates understand the principles of coordination and the importance of acting upon them.[38]

Every organization is made up of people, whose desires grow and change as they interact with other people; the objectives of organizations likewise change to meet the requirements of changed technologies, conditions, and changes in the needs and desires of those involved in the organization or those who are served by the organization. Rensis Likert pointed out that there must be a constant process of examination and modification of goals as well as consideration of the methods for achieving them. In his *New Patterns of Management* Likert made these observations:

> The objectives of the entire organization and of its component parts must be in satisfactory harmony with the relevant needs and desires of the great majority, if not all, of the members of the organization and of the persons served by it.
> The goals and assignments of each member of the organization must be established in such a way that he is highly motivated to achieve them.
> The methods and procedures used by the organization and its subunits to achieve the agreed-upon objectives must be developed

and adapted in such a way that the members are highly motivated to use these methods to their maximum potentiality.

The members of the organization and the persons related to it must feel that the reward system of the organization—salaries, wages, bonuses, dividends, interest payments—yields them equitable compensation for their efforts and contributions.

The overlapping group form of organization offers a structure which, in conjunction with a high level of group interactional skills, is particularly effective in performing the processes necessary to meet requirements.[39]

STAFF THE ORGANIZATION FOR MAXIMUM EFFECTIVENESS

Staffing the organization has a direct relationship to the objectives. The process of staffing involves filling, and keeping filled, the positions called for in the organization structure. After identifying the objectives of the organization and assigning priorities to such objectives, and while planning the organizational structure, it is necessary that critical decisions be made as to the characteristics and qualifications of the people who will give life to the structure. Although an organization cannot be changed at the whim or caprice of an administrator to fit the people within the organization, personal characteristics will necessarily change the structure of the organization because there are individual differences.

Task analyses for each of the positions within the organization should be performed and a listing made of performance standards and requisites as well as respective role expectations. Once the positions and their requirements have been described, the recruitment and selection of the individuals to fill the positions must be accomplished. In the Criminal Justice System, as in many other professions and occupations, many of the individual positions and ideal qualifications of the people to fill them have yet to be completely described. Considerable progress has been made toward a more scientific method of staffing for the several components of the system. The process is continuous, however, and there is little likelihood that anyone can state with authority that studies have been completed.

DEVELOP METHODS FOR CONTROL

The statement of objectives for an organization should be accompanied by provision for methods of control to assure accomplishment of those objectives. Effective controls are enforced through intelligent supervision of the personnel and implementation of a system of controls. Koontz and O'Donnell break down the basic control process into three steps: (1) establishing standards, (2) measuring performance against the standards, and (3) correcting deviations from standards and plans.[40] Using a systems approach to establishment and maintenance of controls, Norbert Wiener describes how—in the science he calls cybernetics—the system uses some of its energy in feeding back information that compares performance with the prescribed standards. This feedback points out errors and other discrepancies and causes the initiation of corrective action.[41]

Adequate controls must—

1. reflect the nature and needs of the activity.
2. report deviations promptly.
3. be forward-looking.
4. point up exceptions at critical points.
5. be qualitatively and quantitatively objective.
6. be flexible.
7. reflect the organizational pattern.
8. be economical.
9. be understandable.
10. indicate corrective action.[42]

If an objective of the organization is to maintain custody of sentenced prisoners there should be a method to inspect the security procedures of the institution to guard against escape. Any breach in security should be located and promptly reported to the unit in the institution responsible for maintaining the security at the point where the correction is indicated. In addition, there should be an indication as to the nature of the breach and subsequently provision of data to use for corrective action. Manpower deployment is a critical problem for virtually every police department. A control device should be instituted that would study patterns of called-for services and project manpower needs for specific times of the day and days of the week. An acute problem, such as pattern of burglaries occurring in a single location in the city, would be pointed out and then patrol supervisors could arrange for patrols to be increased in an effort to correct the problem by preventing additional crimes in the same area and possibly apprehending the culprit.

Forward-thinking and flexible characteristics of controls should be mandatory for any agency in criminal justice. Behavior patterns or demands for type of service may change; such trends should be identified as early as possible so that appropriate steps may be taken to address the problem. An example of such a changing need has been demonstrated during recent years with the tremendous rise in arrests for abuse of drugs and narcotics. So great has been the change, that entire institutions are geared for handling only drug offenders. This also illustrates control requirement 4 (above), which calls for critical problems to be pointed out. Management and supervision involves the exception principle, which means that normal and routine decisions are usually covered in procedural manuals, or in the laws or precedents, and require no unusual action. Only in the exceptional or unusual circumstances is there an immediate need for a decision to be made. Usually there is so much activity that the supervisor only has time to handle the exceptions.

Economy is a self-explanatory concept, although some types of control procedures might be considered quite essential and may be perpetuated by an organization for a number of years before the procedure is finally abandoned. An example of this is the reporting procedure involved in most agencies of criminal justice. Through complete reporting requirements the supervisors and executives of the organization have a means of evaluating the activities of their subordinates through a self-reporting procedure. In reality, the individual who prepares a good report may not necessarily be performing as well as his report might indicate. A careful analysis of the actual relationship of the various reports required by an agency to its stated objectives might reveal that the only reason for a specific type of report is "we have always done it."

Of prime concern is the objectivity of a control system. A "good" police officer may not necessarily be the one who makes the greatest number of felony arrests or issues more citations than any two other officers. An attorney is not necessarily doing a thorough job by getting a greater number of guilty pleas. He may be, but raw numbers tell us nothing by themselves. Once again, the control devices and techniques should be closely studied in relationship to the goals and objectives of the organization.

SUMMARY

An organization is a system of relationships. It consists of divisional units which are manned with people who must all function in some integrated and coordinated fashion for the purpose of accomplishing their common goals and objectives. In order to function effectively and economically it is necessary that the organization be developed and operated in accordance with certain guidelines, which include several concepts that are classically considered inviolable axioms of administration and organization. In this chapter we have explored those principles and their application in the system of criminal justice. They are:

1. Specify goals and objectives.
2. Develop an organizational plan.
3. Organize the department according to the plan.
4. Prescribe relationships.
5. Minimize dual accountability.
6. Realistically limit the scope of supervision.

7. Integrate and coordinate the functional units.
8. Staff the organization for maximum effectiveness.
9. Develop methods for control of the organization.

Whatever the nature of the organization, all criminal justice agencies are service oriented. Representing the established system of government and the people who are represented by that government—or more appropriately, governments—the administrator has the responsibility to organize and manage his segment of the system to best serve his constituents. As the needs of the system and society change, so should his organization so that it will more effectively achieve its objectives. Such change, however, should be responsive to demonstrated needs, not the whims or caprices of some vocal vested interest. Adherence to the basic principles of organization is necessary, but it is also necessary to maintain a constant flexibility to meet unusual and emergency needs for temporary deviations. The system should include controls and a well-designed vehicle for feedback of information so that the organization continues to function as it is intended that it should. Once the business of "keeping the store" becomes more important to the people who make up an organization than "delivering the goods" in the form of service, then the organization has outlived its usefulness.

Notes

1. John P. Kenney, *Police Administration* (Springfield: Charles C Thomas, 1972), p. 55.
2. John M. Pfiffner and Frank P. Sherwood, *Administrative Organization* (Englewood Cliffs, N.J.: Prentice-Hall, 1960), p. 30. All material from this book reprinted by permission of the publisher.
3. Paul M. Whisenand, *Police Supervision Theory and Practice* (Englewood Cliffs, N.J.: Prentice-Hall, © 1971), p. 71. All material from this book reprinted by permission of the publisher.
4. Ibid., p. 71.
5. William H. Newman, *Administrative Action, The Techniques of Organization and Management*, 2nd ed. (Englewood Cliffs, N.J.: Prentice-Hall, © 1963), p. 18. All material from this book reprinted by permission of the publisher.
6. Ibid., p. 18.
7. Newman, *Administrative Action*, pp. 143–44.
8. Ibid., p. 152.
9. Harold Koontz and Cyril O'Donnell, *Principles of Management: An Analysis of Managerial Functions*, 4th ed. (New York: McGraw-Hill, 1968), p. 27.
10. G. Douglas Gourley, *Effective Municipal Police Organization* (Beverly Hills: Benziger, Bruce & Glencoe, 1970), pp. 12–13.
11. Anthony G. Athos and Robert E. Coffey, *Behavior in Organizations: A Multidimensional View* (Englewood Cliffs, N.J.: Prentice-Hall, © 1968), p. 228. All material from this book reprinted by permission of the publisher.
12. Harold Koontz and Cyril O'Donnell, *Principles of Management: An Analysis of Managerial Functions*, 4th ed. (New York: McGraw-Hill, 1968), p. 59.
13. Ibid., pp. 67–68.

14. Henri Fayol, *General and Industrial Management* (London: Pitman, 1949), p. 14.
15. Pfiffner and Sherwood, *Administrative Organization*, p. 14.
16. Koontz and O'Donnell, *Principles of Management*, p. 74.
17. Ibid., p. 66.
18. Newman, *Administrative Action*, p. 191.
19. Ibid., p. 191.
20. N. F. Iannone, *Supervision of Police Personnel* (Englewood Cliffs, N.J.: Prentice-Hall, 1970), p. 19.
21. Gourley, *Police Organization*, pp. 13–14.
22. Ibid., p. 11.
23. Koontz and O'Donnell, *Principles of Management*, pp. 74–75.
24. From Leonard, V. A., *The Police Enterprise: Its Organization and Management*, 1970, p. 10. Courtesy of Charles C Thomas, Publisher, Springfield, Illinois.
25. V. A. Leonard and Harry W. More, *Police Organization and Management*, 3rd ed. (Mineola, New York: The Foundation Press, 1971), p. 69.
26. Gourley, *Police Organization*, p. 13.
27. Pfiffner and Sherwood, *Administrative Organization*, p. 153.
28. Ibid., p. 155.
29. Ibid., pp. 158–159.
30. Leonard R. Sayles and George Strauss, *Human Behavior In Organizations*, (Englewood Cliffs, N.J.: Prentice-Hall, © 1966), p. 351. All material from this book reprinted by permission of the publisher.
31. Ibid., p. 351.
32. Sources of information for this discussion of supervision span factors include William H. Newman, *Administrative Action. The Techniques of Organization and Management*. (Englewood Cliffs, N.J.: Prentice-Hall, 1963), pp. 256–64; Harold Koontz and Cyril O'Donnell, *Principles of Management: An Analysis of Managerial Functions*, 4th ed. (New York: McGraw-Hill, 1968), pp. 247–49; and Leonard R. Sayles and George Strauss, *Human Behavior in Organizations* (Englewood Cliffs, N.J.: Prentice-Hall, 1966), p. 352.
33. Sayles and Strauss, *Human Behavior In Organizations*, p. 395.
34. Anthony G. Athos and Robert E. Coffey, *Behavior in Organizations: A Multi-Dimensional View* (Englewood Cliffs, N.J.: Prentice-Hall, 1968), p. 43.
35. Ibid., p. 43.
36. Koontz and O'Donnell, *Principles of Management*, p. 50.
37. H. C. Metcalf and L. Urwick, eds. *Dynamic Administration: The Collected Papers of Mary Parker Follett* (New York: Harper and Row, 1941), p. 297.
38. Koontz and O'Donnell, *Principles of Management*, p. 53.
39. Rensis Likert, *New Patterns of Management* (New York: McGraw-Hill, 1961), p. 116.
40. Koontz and O'Donnell, *Principles of Management*, p. 640.
41. Norbert Wiener, *Cybernetics: Control and Communication in the Animal and the Machine* (New York: John Wiley and Sons, 1948), as quoted by Koontz and O'Donnell, p. 642.
42. Koontz and O'Donnell, *Principles of Management*, pp. 643–47.

Review Questions

1. In your own words, define "organization."
2. Define "goal" and give an example of a goal for each of the three criminal justice components.

3. Define "objective" as discussed in this chapter.
4. Draw a "colleague model" chart and explain the principle of this concept.
5. What is "chain command"?
6. According to Newman, why is dual subordination likely to lead to poor morale?
7. What are the consequences likely to be for the organization that functions under the leader who is afraid to "let go" and delegate authority to subordinates?
8. Specifically what is the purpose of having a "chain of command"?
9. What is Gourley's reason for why the chain of command should be followed?
10. How many individuals can a supervisor effectively supervise?
11. List and discuss some of the dangers inherent in the creation of a multilevel bureaucratic structure.
12. Name at least 12 of the 16 factors listed in this chapter which should be taken into account when determining the nature and scope of supervision.
13. What is integration?
14. What is the value of a task analysis when staffing an organization?
15. In the summary, nine principles of administration were listed. What are those nine?

3 Structuring The Organization

Once the objectives and goals of the organization have been developed and the priorities with which they will be achieved have been articulated and agreed upon, the organizational plan is developed. Using the plan as a basis, the next step in the organization process is the structuring phase. This is particularly important when one looks upon the organization as a system of relationships. Although it may have the appearance of a bureaucratic pyramid, the table of organization is a flow diagram for communications throughout the organization and for the transmission of feedback to the chief executive. The table shows authority-responsibility relationships, the scope of supervision at the various parts of the organization, the line or chain of authority, and the degree of importance placed by the executive on certain tasks. In this chapter the various factors that must be considered when structuring the organization are discussed.

DIVISION OF WORK

The organization must be designed to fit the tasks to be performed. In proportion to the relative volume of work to be performed by each separate unit and the degree of importance placed upon each unit, the design should begin to take shape. Even when the executive is confronted with an existing organization and he is evaluating its organizational structure, he should approach his study from the same viewpoint: as if the organization had never existed before. Principal considerations in the division process are the (1) major purpose of the unit, (2) methods or equipment to be used,

(3) specific functions or people to be served, (4) time—of day, week, month, year—on a regular or special basis, (5) geographical area to be served, and (6) special needs.

When discussing the major purpose of a division of an organization, the concept *line-staff* may be utilized to identify two of the basic styles of divisional work responsibility. Attributed to military science for its origin,[1] this concept generally defines the organizational units that are designed to provide the direct service as *line*, and those that provide support, advice, and services to those line divisions as *staff*. Sometimes a third classification is added, that of *auxiliary*, which are the reserve or support units to supplement the normal operations. In a police department, according to this method of classification, the line divisions would include patrol, traffic, investigation, vice, juvenile, and others that are dealing directly with the public as a police agency. Staff services would include such divisions as training, personnel, records, communications, laboratory, identification, and those units that provide services to the executives or line units of the department. According to Leonard, "The chief value of this distinction is that it gives proper location and status to the two major functions of police organization—preparation for the delivery of police service, and the delivery of police service to the people of the community."[2]

Athos and Coffey, on the other hand, tend to believe that such a separation is somewhat artificial and, in some cases, deleterious to the overall performance of the organization. They state: "This distinction became increasingly meaningless, however, as managers became aware that some of the staff departments were as essential as the line departments in achieving the company's objectives."[3] It appears that the major reason for the problem of definition is that somehow there are degrees of importance placed on one or the other category, and authority-accountability relationships are also injected into the argument. *Line authority* is defined as the direct relationship between a superior and his subordinates; *staff authority* is defined as advisory, or that type of supervisory relationship in which the individual with greater authority in the rank structure, but not in direct line on the organizational chart, may supervise only the task, but not the individual who performs the task.

Using different terms, Pfiffner and Sherwood approach it in this manner:

> Today it is more useful on many occasions to think in terms of two types of activity within the organization: (a) that which is substantive (direct) in its contribution to the organization's overall objectives, and (b) that which is adjective (indirect) in its contribution. Such a way of thinking removes some confusion and permits us to define staff in somewhat different terms. Staff should be thought of

> as a *process* occurring around the executive. This process involves thinking, planning, and organizing.
>
> The question of who gives the orders and who gives the advice becomes a matter of decidedly secondary importance. The advisor-authority concept does not really appear to be the keystone of the staff idea. It is much more appropriate to think in terms of the basic problem of extending the executive personality and the process by which it is done.[4]

An explanation of some of the causes for friction between line and staff is offered by Athos and Coffey:

> This friction often leads to delay and disagreement between some so-called line and staff departments. Line people sometimes believe that staff people tend to assume line authority, that some of their advice is "ivory tower" in nature, that some of them fail to see the whole picture (because they are too specialized), and that some try to steal credit for results. On the other hand, some staff people believe that line people tend to resist new ideas, that they are distrustful of staff and do not accept staff advice, and that the line people do not give staff enough authority and opportunity to help the line achieve good results. These kinds of feelings and the resulting confusion that exists over formal authority lead many managers to believe that line-staff problems are among the most difficult organizational problems they face.[5]

The axiom that no man can serve two masters in an organization has a residual effect on the line-staff controversy, whenever one arises. The chief executive of the organization transmits authority and responsibility to his subordinates while retaining ultimate responsibility for the end results of such delegation; this process is repeated successively down the hierarchical structure through the medium of a system of line authority-accountability relationships. There is a tendency in many organizations, particularly in the larger ones which have a greater number of supervisory levels, for directives, letters, and other forms of written or oral communications to be considered in respect to degrees of more or less authority. Likert explains the traditional concept and relates the same problem to the newer concept of addressing the problem:

> The traditional concept that the line has the authority and staff is only advisory is breaking down increasingly as technical processes and other problems become more complex. In many companies today, parts of the staff are exercising more influence than the line because of the great complexity of the technical processes and of the expertness of the staff. This often causes serious friction and conflict. The newer theory would suggest that the way to deal with the problem of line-staff relationships is to have the line build an

effective interaction-influence system involving multiple overlapping groups through which communication, decision-making and influence processes could occur. Staff would also help in building this overlapping group structure with much of the multiple overlapping provided by many staff and staff-line committees and work groups. This interaction-influence system would provide the mechanism to enable the organization to arrive at sound decisions, with all relevant parts of the organization contributing fully from their specialized knowledge and skills. The contributions of line and staff would vary with the problem and with the resources each possessed.

Under this concept of staff-line relationships, the line would not have the sole responsibility and authority to make decisions with staff advice. The line would have the authority and responsibility for building a highly effective interaction-influence system through which the best decisions would be made, with both line and staff contributing.[6]

The organizational chart that consists of line authority relationships only can be depicted as in figure 3. All instructions and downward communications go from supervisor to subordinate, and all feedback and reports of activities and results are transmitted upward from subordinate to supervisor. The staff-line relationship, which is prevalent in virtually all but the smallest organizations in the Criminal Justice System, may be depicted as in figure 4. The direct line authority-accountability relationship between supervisors and subordinate continues according to the plan, but there is an additional advisory relationship, such as from

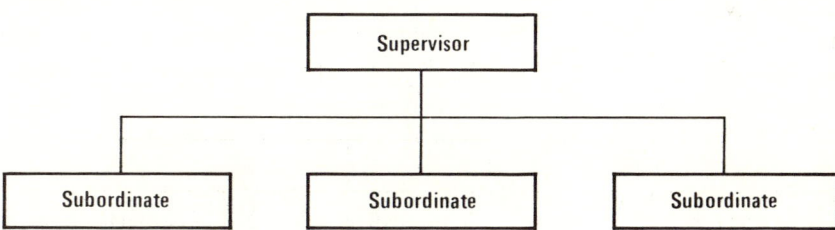

Figure 3.   *Organizational chart: line only.*

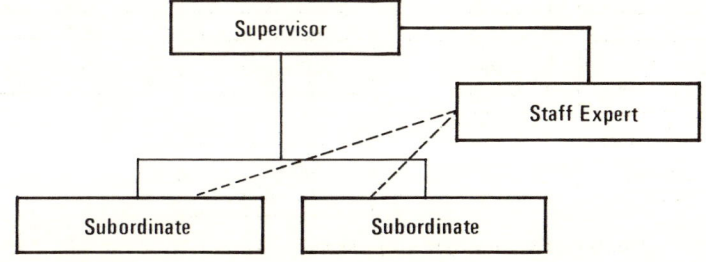

Figure 4.   *Organizational chart: line and staff combined.*

training or a legal advisor or a unit composed of technical specialists, through which the normal line supervision is by-passed.

Organizational charts showing divisions of work are illustrated in figures 5 and 6.

Departmentation of the organization according to methods or types of equipment to be used may be quite simple if the objectives and philosophy of operation are compatible. The criminalistics laboratory requires specially constructed facilities, including sinks and special exhaust fans, a lint-free environment, and the use of all types of special instruments. Closely related functions, such as the photographic laboratory, identification specialists, and toxicologists may also be assigned to the same division. In the very large department it may be necessary to have a different specialist (or more) for each type of analysis; in the smaller department it is not unusual for the specialists to work in two or more categories, such as photo technician and questioned-document examiner, or chemist-toxicologist-blood-analysis-ballistics expert. Certain office-centered work groups may be consolidated into a services division, and consist of records, clerical-secretarial pool, receptionists, switchboard operators, and duplicating-printing services. A police department may have a uniformed division instead of two separate divisions of patrol and traffic, because both operations involve routine patrol of the streets with heavier emphasis at certain times of the day or days of the week and both use the same kind of vehicles and wear the same uniforms. Probation and parole operations in some states are consolidated under a

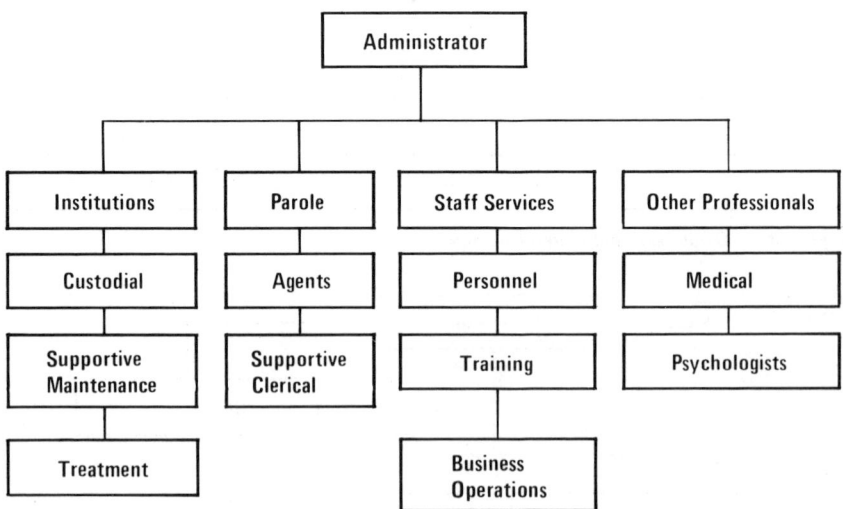

Figure 5. A state correctional system by function.

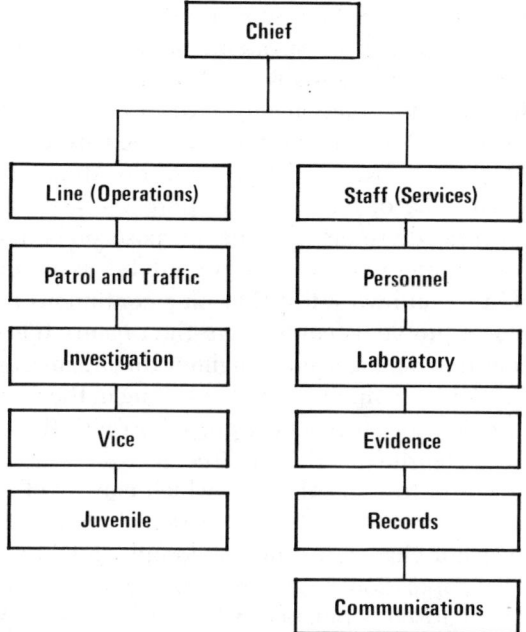

Figure 6. *A police department by function.*

single department because of the identical nature of the actual case work, although the legal status of the probationer and parolee may be technically different.

Special functions or people to be served (clientele) by the unit may necessitate a separation for practical and/or legal reasons. The philosophy of the adult and juvenile courts differs in that a juvenile is not actually convicted of a crime; rather, he is adjudged a deliquent and made a ward of the court for a period of rehabilitation. Juveniles have to be handled and housed separately from adults when they are placed in custody. Probation officers may be divided into adult and juvenile divisions. District attorney's departments may be separated into felony, misdemeanor, juvenile, major fraud, consumer fraud, nonsupport, intelligence, organized crime, and pornography divisions for the purpose of more effective prosecution of specialized types of offenses or special types of offenders. The purpose of the separation might be to allow the attorney to develop expertise in prosecuting specific types of very difficult or lengthy cases, or to cope with a particular philsophy, as with the juvenile court.

Divisions of a department by time are particularly applicable to those organizations that operate on a continuous basis. The unit that works a particular time of day might be a separate unit of a larger division, such as a patrol shift of a police department, or it may be a portion of the entire organization, such as a night court operation on a full-scale basis. Juvenile hall in a large jurisdiction may have an 18- to 20-hour full-service operation, or even a 24-hour operation manned by counselors, intake personnel, and clerks to handle the paper work. Although the operation for that particular time of day might require the assignment of representatives of several divisions, for the purpose of better supervisory-subordinate arrangements they might all be assigned to a single "team concept" unit and work together on a continuous basis.

Geographical problems confronting the organization might involve such distances in time and space throughout the organizational hierarchy that decentralization is complete—thus resulting in the establishment of a separate organization for all practical purposes, with the chief executive serving more as a coordinator than a director.

Special needs of the organization, which may be of a permanent or temporary nature, may necessitate the creation of a functional unit to meet those needs. A major change in court philosophy might cause significant changes in the jail population, case loads of probation officers, and possibly even a reduction in prison population. With the increase of probationers, it may become evident that a particular section of a city is represented by individuals who tend to commit similar crimes. A special "impact" team of probation officers may set up an office in the affected section and handle a minimum case load while working in the streets with street-corner groups in an effort to curb the crime and arrest rate. A sudden increase in major inmate disturbances in an institution will, no doubt, lead to the establishment of a specially trained unit to quell the disturbances through the use of special techniques and weapons. Many agencies throughout the Criminal Justice System have recently created research and development units as a result of the Safe Streets Act of 1968, which created a new source of funds for research among other purposes of the act. Consumer fraud units meet special needs of some prosecuting agencies, as do organized crime task forces, crisis intervention teams, airport security details, underwater rescue teams, or community services units of a parole agency. The possibilities are endless, limited only by the imagination of the administrator and the resources available to him.

SPECIALIZATION

A careful analysis of the organization's objectives will reveal certain tasks that can best be performed by people who have unique talents and specialized education and training to prepare them for performing certain sets of tasks with greater efficiency and economy. Specialization can be overdone, however, sometimes leading to the creation of artificial specialties. This reminds me of Parkinson's Law, which seems to be demonstrated in so many organizations, particularly police departments. In his book[7] Northcote Parkinson explains how the British Navy ships decreased by two-thirds and the number of military personnel by one-third from 1914 to 1918. Blue-collar workers who were employed to maintain the ships increased by about ten percent. Shipyard officials and clerks increased by 40 percent and the officials at departmental headquarters increased a whopping 78 percent. Parkinson's thesis is that an organization multiplies in size irrespective of the work to be done. It is not unusual for even the casual observer to see within an organization certain executives and supervisors create subordinate positions to enhance their own status and to see people in an expanding organization create unneeded tasks for each other. I recently observed an example of this phenomenon with the development of several local helicopter units. The senior pilot in one agency holds the rank of sergeant and the others who perform the same task hold the rank of policeman. In a budget request, the helicopter unit requested that the sergeant be relieved of regular flying activities so that he could supervise and coordinate the units from ground, and the request also called for an office with a secretary to assist the sergeant with his paper work. What a waste of the man's flying ability! And the paper work could quite easily develop into a great deal of statistics, reports, and other previously unnecessary "busy work," much of which would be for no other purpose than to justify the ground leadership position.

Continuing with the police enterprise as an example of what part specialization plays in an organization, Professor John Kenney recounts:

> Until the 1950's and 1960's the more common approach to structuring police departments was to create a specialized unit for each functional operation.... Special units were established for patrol, traffic, vice, detectives, juveniles, records, communications, property, and whatever other function appeared to be sufficiently large to warrant separation. Work was very segmented and management and supervising personnel proliferated.[8]

Traditionally, along these lines of specialization, the appropriate term would be *departmentation,* since the officers assigned to the various divisions had basically the same capabilities and training and their specialization was by assignment, a *pseudo-specialization.* In my personal experience as both policeman and administrator I have witnessed some ridiculous situations resulting from this skewed attitude of the so-called specialists. Patrol officers have witnessed flagrant violations of traffic laws, but dismissed the thought of taking action because, "that's a traffic problem." At another time a police unit made a midblock U-turn to avoid a traffic accident ahead, then one of the officers made an anonymous phone call from a telephone booth reporting the accident so that the "A-I" unit could do its job. Two motorcycle officers working in a patrol car on a rainy day encountered a nonbelligerent drunk and called for a patrol unit to make contact with him to determine whether an arrest would be made. Detectives discontinued an investigation and turned it over to juvenile officers because they found a set of small fingerprint smudges, patrol officers did not follow through with an investigation because it was the responsibility of the detectives or vice officers. Actually, this is not a problem of specialization, but a problem of supervision.

Kenney's "team concept," which is the principal theme of his book *Police Administration,* is an expansion and sophistication of the technique used by Vollmer more than 40 years ago:

> August Vollmer as Chief of Police in Berkeley, California from 1905 to 1932 developed a unique approach in organizing the department. He established the uniformed field officer as a "criminologist" responsible for the performance of all police functions on the beat. Ideally, each field officer was required (a) to be thoroughly familiar with all criminal and delinquency problems on his beat; (b) to be thoroughly familiar with resources on the beat and other resources available to deal with criminal and delinquency problems which did not require law enforcement action inserting individuals into the administration of criminal justice system; (c) to be capable of resolving criminal and delinquency behavioral problems with the help of available local resources without referral to agencies in the criminal justice system except when absolutely necessary; and(d) to be responsible for performing all of the essential field functions.[19]

Specialization has both advantages and disadvantages, which must be weighed in view of the organization's specific needs and other factors— such as available personnel to fill a position to augment or replace the staff once the unit is created and pay considerations that might not fit the existing pattern. It more than likely involves the employment of individuals with considerable education and experience, and their continued training is more costly. "Individual specialists . . . often work on depth-attention jobs, identify strongly with their work, and may even enjoy professional status," according to Sayles and Strauss.[10] Negative and positive considerations when making the decision whether to create a specialized position or division include the following:

Negative
a. Although essential to the operation of the department, the work load might not justify a full-time position.
b. Coordination and control of specialists and specialized units may be more difficult because of the independent nature of their work.

Specialists provide valuable services and leadership in their respective fields of expertise outside the normal line authority-responsibility relationships.
Courtesy: Federal Bureau of Investigation.

    c. Some specialists may be accomplishing little for the department objectives, yet keep busy on personal projects.

    d. There is a danger of duplication of housekeeping activities, separate filing systems, different reporting procedures, and the need for clerical staff to handle the work generated by the existence of the office.

    e. Two special units may work in competition with each other, and possibly at cross purposes with the rest of the department. There is sometimes hostile competition for staff, facilities, and equipment.[11]

    f. The specialist, although employed by the same organization, may develop an attitude that tasks of other units are of no interest to him and he will not take any action except in the area of his specialty.

    g. "Some administrators of specialist units become so obsessed with the need for developing ever higher skills through breaking down existing jobs and through more highly specialized techniques that they eventually produce an organism dependent upon expert operation in all its details."[12]

Positive
a. Specialization of nonprofessional tasks may reduce the costs of training because employees who concentrate on a single task may have less to learn.
b. There is a saving of time and energy if it is possible to keep an employee on a single task without having to move from one task to another.
c. Specialized equipment can be concentrated at one location, resulting in more efficient use of the equipment and saving the costs of duplicating the equipment at two or more locations.
d. Supervision of a specialized unit may be simplified if all of its members are well-trained and functioning correctly.
e. Costs may be reduced in salaries, because some specialties by themselves require less training and preparation than positions that call for diverse skills. For example, if stenographers are assigned to executives for the performance of secretarial tasks, they must all be able to take shorthand or operate a stenotype machine. On the assumption that each executive averages 15 to 20 minutes a day dictating his correspondence, the actual skills of a stenographer throughout the department may require only one stenographer, and other less skilled clerical employees can work in a pool. Another possibility is to use dictating equipment and specially trained typists who have no stenographic skills.
f. Attention is directed to a particular set of tasks, with specific responsibility and authority to carry them out assigned to a specialized individual or division.
g. "As each field of knowledge is advanced, constituting a continually larger and more complicated nucleus of related principles, practices, and skills, the individual will be less and less able to encompass it and maintain intimate knowledge and facility over the entire area, and there will thus arise a more minute specialization because knowledge and skill advance while man stands still."[13]

Bristow lists three different degrees of specialization: staff, functional, and divisional.[14] The specialist assignment is usually related to the size of the organization, but it can also be related to the degree of importance that must be placed upon the task or the extent of the need. The first type of specialization is by staff appointment. The staff specialist does not perform the task but has the knowledge, education, and expertise to advise those individuals in one or more other divisions on how to perform their jobs with respect to his speciality. The second type of specialist is the functional specialist. He is not separated from his original divisional assignment, but is relieved of his normal responsibilities when called upon to perform his specialized function. The third type of specialization is the separate division with its own internal structure and supervision and status designation in the organizational chart.

AUTHORITY RELATIONSHIPS

The chief executive of the organization never relinquishes his ultimate responsibility for the performance of personnel and the attainment of goals. He should establish the authority-responsibility relationships in accordance with the general guidelines covered in Chapter 2. Unless he is in a one-man organization, there is absolutely no way that he can do all the work or try to supervise all activities. A trite statement? Not really, in fact. One hurdle the new administrator must overcome is his desire to oversee all the operations and to do some of the work himself. His role is to accomplish the organization's objectives *through* other people. He must "let go" and delegate authority in large portions to correspond with the amount of responsibility he places on the shoulders of each subordinate.

The executive is the power source; it is imperative that he design the system of authority relationships so that the system functions successfully—communications flow in all directions must be fluid and constant and he must have adequate controls and a feedback system to complete the organizational pattern. With respect to operating and support units whether he designates them as line and staff, or by any other titles, the executive must provide for operating units to function without unnecessary interference but with appropriate support and assistance when necessary. Titles and ranks may appear artificial in theory, but in the real world of criminal justice management, the rank structure or "pecking order" of executives and supervisors is important. If two directors of major operating divisions hold equal ranks in the hierarchy, the communications are considerably different than if one ranks higher than the other. If the two are equal and some disagreement arises, there must be someone with a higher rank who has a direct line authority over them so that he may break the tie and make any arbitrary decisions that may have to be made. In a well-planned organization staffed with well-qualified professionals the likelihood of serious conflict is minimized, but many times decisions have to be made and there may be no time to hold an election to arrive at a democratic decision.

Koontz and O'Donnell describe the functions of the manager: "The most useful method of classifying managerial functions is to group them around the activities of planning, organizing, staffing, directing, and control."[15] Regarding the manager's organizing role, the same authors state:

> Whether he be president, sales manager, controller, or office manager, he will reflect the goals toward which he is striving by grouping the activities for which he is responsible, assigning some of them to subordinates, delegating the requisite authority to accomplish results, and providing for the coordination of these authorities.[16]

When organizing his department, the executive should consider these four major realities over which he has no control and which may directly influence the decisions he makes concerning delegation of authority and responsibility: (1) An executive's time belongs to everyone else. (2) Unless the executive changes it with deliberate action, the flow of events around him—not his own intentions—will determine what he is concerned with and what he does. (3) The executive is within an *organization*, which means that he is effective only if others utilize what he has to offer, and those include his superiors. (4) The executive is *within* an organization, which means that he sees the inside of the organization. He has to make a deliberate effort to see outside and grasp the reality of the world outside the organization.[17] Drucker makes this observation:

> An organization is not, like an animal, an end in itself, and successful by the mere act of perpetuating the species. An organization is an organ of society and fulfills itself by the contribution it makes to the outside environment, and yet the bigger and apparently more successful an organization gets to be, the more will inside events tend to engage the interests, the energies, and the abilities of the executive to the exclusion of his real tasks and his real effectiveness in the outside.[18]

ASSISTANCE FOR THE CHIEF EXECUTIVE

There are certain activities that the executive must perform himself or retain direct control of. There are two alternatives to the problem of the executive's personal responsibilities: appoint an assistant, or provide staff assistance. An assistant is for all practical purposes an alter ego and, in fact, becomes the chief executive. If he is in the direct line of authority, however, he is in an awkward "funnel" or "bottleneck" situation—or *he* is the chief executive and his superior becomes a mere figurehead. The better alternative to this dual leadership role is to provide staff assistance to the executive. Such people serve in an advisory capacity and are not in the direct line of authority, except with those in their own office.

Staff assistants may be individuals who have been promoted through the organization to whatever position they hold in their staff capacity, or they may be appointed directly to that position. Because they are not in the direct line of authority, their rank is secondary. Their pay grade may be directly related to other factors, such as decision-making responsibility, educational preparation, and other considerations that enter into any pay designation. According to Gourley, "These staff operations depend for their success on the ability, imagination, initiative, education, and training of their Directors. These are qualities which are not assured by the mere attainment of high police rank."[19] Newman states that the use of staff personnel is desirable when:

> 1. The duties of an executive exceed his capacity to fulfill them well, either because he lacks the necessary time and energy or because they require specialized knowledge that he does not possess; and
> 2. Relieving this load by delegation to operating personnel is not feasible because (a) uniformity or coordination of action in several operating units is particularly important, (b) economy or effectiveness can be increased by assigning the work to a specialist, or (c) operating subordinates lack the capacity (time or ability) to do more of their own planning or to work effectively with less supervision.[20]

Whenever the executive designates a staff position or unit, there are certain requisites that he must follow in order that the staff function will operate as it should. The prime requisite is that the executive make use of people. In order that they might function effectively it is necessary that they have frequent and intimate contact with him so that they might be in a position to anticipate his decisions and be able to carry on their activities with this knowledge. Communications between the staff people and other members throughout the organization should be free-flowing so that their expertise may be used to its full benefit. For example, if a police department employs a legal advisor who holds a law degree and is specifically assigned to provide certain legal advice in the department's operations, then the chief and other members of the department should use him or eliminate the position. The staff people should be able to function without being too closely fettered by the "red tape" of having to go through the line of command to operate in his advisory capacity, but the advisor should also do his work by advising and persuading others, as his direct line of authority is probably to the chief alone. A training division of any department should provide realistic training to meet current needs, but should not be in a policy-making position. The function is cooperative and reciprocating.

STAFF AUTHORITY

Pfiffner and Sherwood state: "The traditional concept of staff is aid to the executive, . . . presumably . . . without disturbing the formal command relationships in the hierarchy. Yet increasing specialization in the organization and growing pressures on the top executive have complicated this initially simple concept greatly."[21] This is an indication that the individuals who work in staff positions must be aware of their advisory capacity and should avoid assuming the posture—whether intentional or unintentional—of a commanding officer when performing their staff duties. His authority relationship is put in perspective by Koontz and O'Donnell:

> The basic nature of staff as an advisory relationship amply characterizes the nature of staff authority. Although the staff officer exercises line authority over the subordinates in *his* department, he has no other line authority. The information he furnishes of the plans he recommends flow upward to his superior, who decides whether they are to be transformed into action.[22]

LINE AUTHORITY

Dividing the work responsibilities in accordance with the goals and objectives of the organization involves identifying the major purposes and functions and designating the major operating units or divisions of the organization. The assignments of personnel should be proportionate to the needs and priorities of the various activities. Managers and supervisors should be appointed so that each operating unit has its own manager and supervisors. This assignment should be accomplished in such a manner that no supervisor is assigned more than that number of people believed to be optimum for the activity and the many other circumstances involved. The number can be adjusted—and should be—as needs change. As much as possible, no one should be in a direct line of supervisor-subordinate relationship with more than one supervisor, and each person should be informed of the relationship. The concept of line authority applies to this procedure, placing each individual in an organization under specific leadership consistent with his assignment.

COORDINATION AND CONTROL

Divisions within the organization should be grouped under common coordinating leadership according to the similarity and compatibility of their respective operations. For example, the police organization might group the various staff services under the overall direction of a single manager, the uniformed services under another, and the services that operate in civilian clothing under yet another. The probation department might designate a director of juvenile institutions to manage the overall operation and supervise the directors of the juvenile hall, the guidance centers, schools, camps, and various institutions. Another grouping within the probation department might be all probation services with divisions in juvenile and adult investigations and supervision. Administrative, fiscal, and clerical services might be the third major grouping. The relationships of the division may vary from one organization to another, but there is less difficulty in managing them if they are closely related in philosophy, methods, and geographical location. Because of one area that might be isolated, it may be necessary to designate one manager to direct all of the divisions at that location, in effect creating almost a separate organization with its own personality. In very large cities, each police precinct is more like a separate police department with its director the chief rather than an area commander.

Coordination is accomplished through leadership and supervision, as well as carefully defined procedures and general guidelines for all of the members of the organization to follow under prescribed conditions. The exceptions are handled by supervisors as they occur; then through the medium of meetings and conferences those exceptions that arise more often than previously anticipated are discussed and eventually covered in the procedures and guidelines. Control is accomplished through self-reporting procedures, which is the most common method of control in criminal justice agencies. Other controls are implemented through a system of examinations of results of activities, such as attorney's conviction rates, percentage of parolees released on their own versus those returned to the institutions, numbers of work units performed, percentages of cases cleared by investigators, and a variety of other reports. Inspections may also be utilized as a control technique. Actual observation of the individual employees either with or without their knowledge, conferences with them, and conferences with the people affected by their services. This aspect of management—controls—is an extremely important one to the effectiveness of the organization. Without feedback, the administrator has no way of knowing whether he is actually accomplishing the objectives of the organization.

APPROPRIATE ATTENTION

It may be necessary to create a special division as a basic operating activity or a special staff assignment and to designate an individual to assume responsibility for certain results that must be obtained. Until recently, many agencies in the Criminal Justice System, such as probation departments, district attorney's offices, or police departments, had no separate divisional assignment for community relations. Every individual in the organization from the chief executive to the newest inductee was responsible for community relations. This statement has always been true. But, it is almost impossible for some departments to successfully deliver their message about the many excellent benefits the community gains from their services unless a specific individual or unit goes out into the community disseminating the message. This concept may be similar to that of taking advantage of specialization, which may lead to the development of separate divisions within the organization.

Newman's chart listing the key considerations in departmentation for an organization[23] includes all of the considerations listed in this chapter, plus the additional consideration he titles "Recognize local conditions." By that he means that whatever the organization, the actual staffing of the various functions must be assigned to real people and the possibilities for diversification might be limited. For example, there might be a real need for a specialist of some category that simply is not available to this particular organization. What then? It might be necessary to forego establishment of the unit, contracting with a private company or arranging with another agency having such a specialist to take on the extra responsibility for this department. Promotions from within the organization might not yield the desired results. For example, one police department reorganized and created the position of captain, which had previously been nonexistent. The decision was made to restrict the applications to those sergeants and lieutenants within the department—for morale purposes. The written examinations were given, a few passed; then along came the orals. The examining board, consisting all of out-of-town administrators, *failed every single candidate.* Consequently, no captains were appointed that year. Instead of going outside the department, the decision was made to provide a "crash course" in police management and the following year two men were promoted to captain.

Local conditions also include informal organizations, or cliques, headed by indigenous leaders who have no supervisory designation on the organizational chart. Members of the organization might also hold membership in churches, fraternal organizations, bowling leagues, party groups, golfing clubs, alumnus organizations, or other affiliations that might call for greater loyalty than the allegiance expected of employees. These informal organizations within the formal structure must be taken into account whenever the executive is attempting to coordinate and control the operations of his organization to assure its accomplishment of objectives. Local conditions may also include the problem of not enough work for a particular division, although the executive believes such a division should exist. In that case, it may be necessary to consolidate two divisions into one. Pooling of resources may be mandatory.

ORGANIZATIONAL DESIGN AND RELATIONSHIPS

Now that the various divisions and functioning units have been identified, their respective tasks prescribed, the leadership selected, and the hierarchy or rank structure established, the next step is the organizational design. No small task, the design is extremely important. Exactly where a particular individual finds himself on the chart may have a direct and lasting effect on his self-image and on his performance.

Many innovative efforts have been made toward the physical appearance of the organizational chart, some for the purpose of showing work flow, others depicting "colleague models," "team concepts," and others that attempt to avoid the appearance of the hierarchy pyramid. Whatever the design, the lines of authority-responsibility and relationships between the various components of the system should be clearly shown on the chart so that everyone knows where he fits into the organizational structure. Professional autonomy in a criminal justice organization is a necessity at the operational level—the prosecuting attorney must have the personal authority to meet and confer with the judge and defense attorney and make decisions on the course of action he will take as a representative of his superior; the police officer in the field must have the authority to make a decision whether to fire his weapon in self-defense, or whether to arrest a suspect he observes in the commission of what he perceives as a crime. Both will later participate in self-reporting activities and will also be subject to continuous controls such as periodic inspections of their reports, but they are professionally independent. Organizationally, however, they cannot function independently. To do so would result in total anarchy and disorganization. Certain management principles and techniques must be employed in the operation of the organization. One of these is the organizational chart, which shows each individual where he is within the organizational structure and to whom he is responsible for what.

Relative Rank Structure

The traditional and most common model that depicts rank-ordering of personnel is the pyramid, or scalar model. Figure 7 depicts the pyramid. Figure 8 depicts a variation of the same concept.

Another variation of the hierarchical structure is presented by Sayles and Strauss in their discussion of "Management of Discretion"[24] and illustrated in figure 9.

Functional designations can be depicted in a chart as in figure 10.

Line and staff operations may be shown in several ways, depending on the relative relationships. See figures 11, 12, and 13 for some variations.

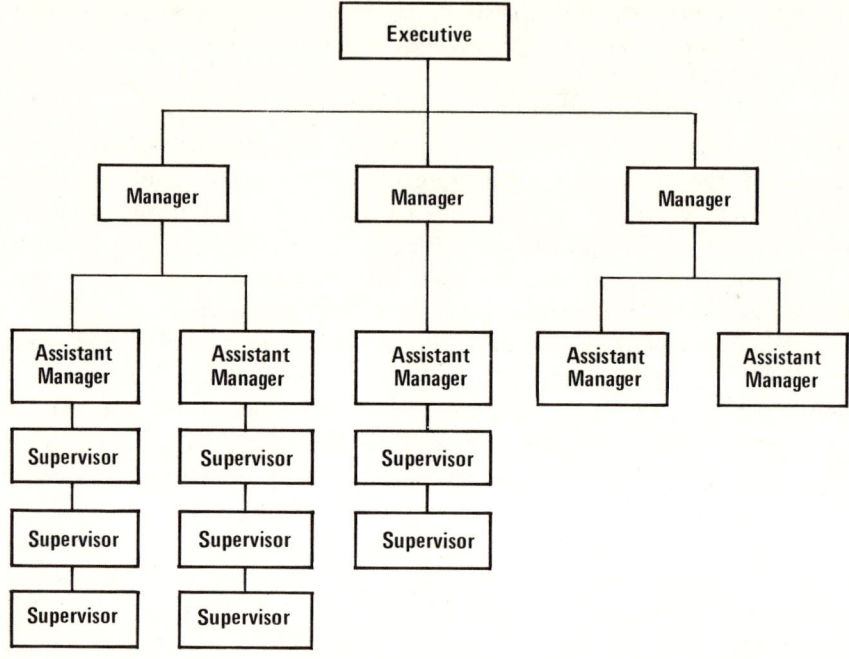

Figure 7. Rank structure: pyramid model.

Impact of Design

Although no attempt has been made in this text to draw variations of the basic designs for organizational charts, the innovative executive might wish to impress his superiors and constituents of his democratic and "generalist," or "colleague," approach, depending on the specific needs of the individual executive and the type of organization he directs. It is important, I believe, that the relationships should be shown clearly *as they exist* in practice, and each member of the organization should be impressed with his own importance to the success of its operations. However this can be done should be attempted by the executive who will probably prove most effective. According to Athos and Coffey, the design has a great impact:

> The way in which people and work are related through organizational design of structure has significant impact on behavior. Structural design influences such factors as freedom, dependence, and specialization, which in turn affect the degree to which people can determine and control their own behavior, exert their own initiative and creativity, and do significant work.[25]

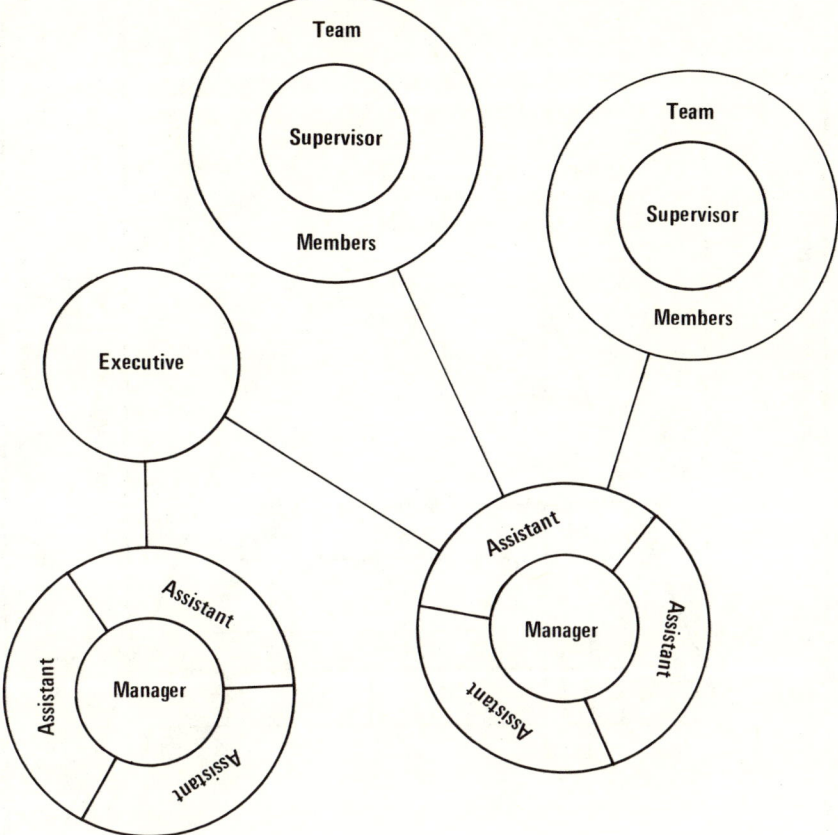

Figure 8. Rank structure: the camouflaged pyramid.

From one police point of view, consider what Iannone has to say:

> The line and staff type of organization is a combination of the line and functional types and is found in almost all but the very smallest police agencies today. It combines staff specialists or units with line organizations so that the service of knowledge can be provided line personnel by specialists such as the criminalist, the training officer, the research and development specialist, the public relations officer, the intelligence specialist, etc. Channels of responsibility and authority are thus left intact since the specialist's responsibility is to "think and provide expertise" for the line units which are responsible for "doing." The line supervisor must remember that he obtains advice from the staff specialist, not commands.[26]

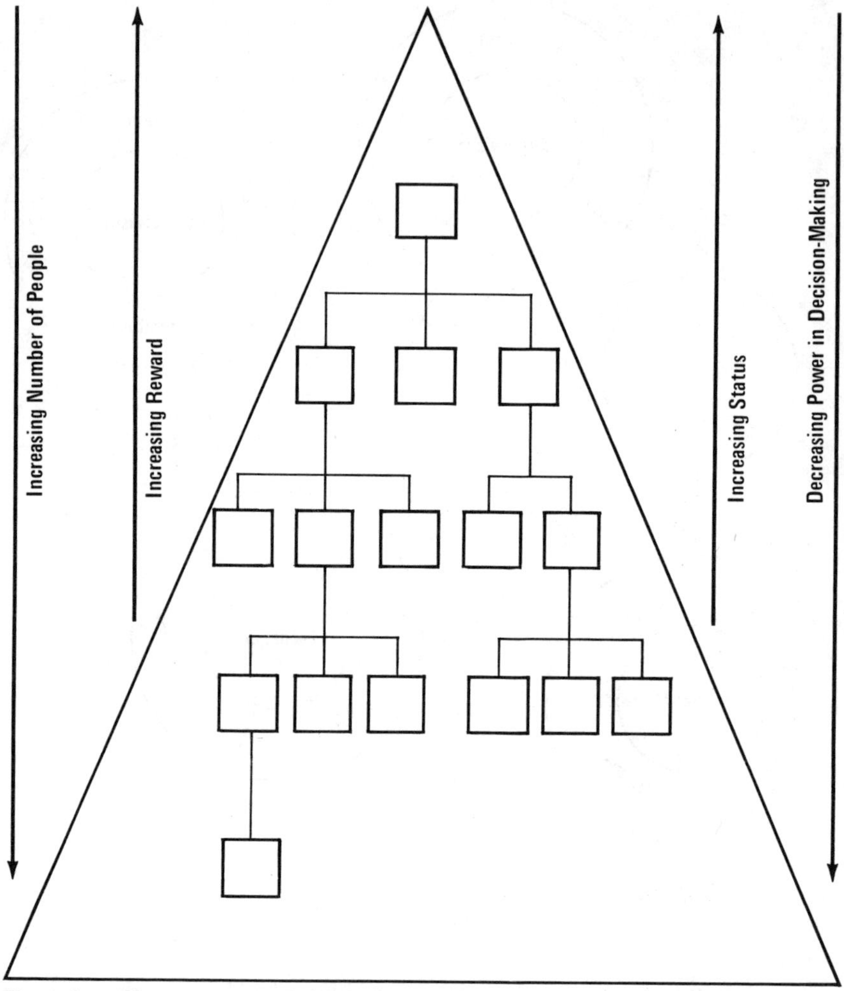

Figure 9. The organizational pyramid.
From Leonard R. Sayles and George Strauss, *Human Behavior In Organizations* (Englewood Cliffs, N.J.: Prentice-Hall,© 1966) Used by permission of the publisher.

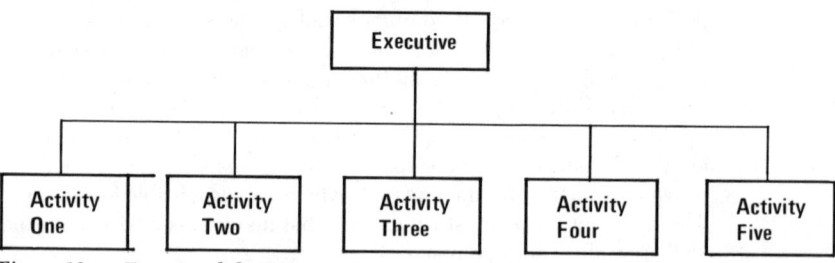

Figure 10. Functional designations.

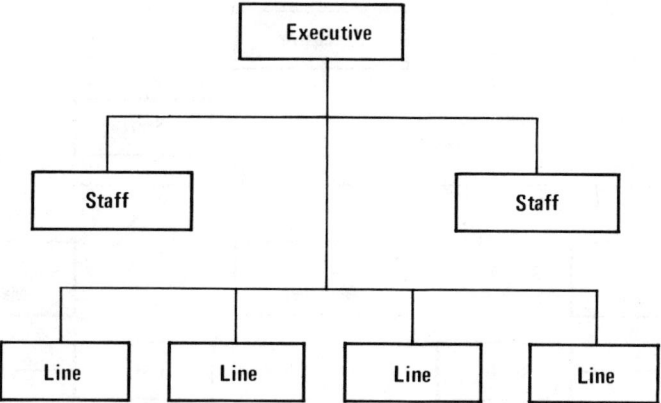

Figure 11.   Line and staff: variation 1.

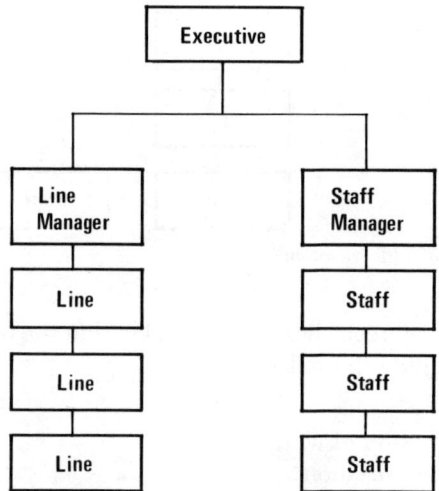

Figure 12.   Line and staff: variation 2.

SUMMARY

Structuring the organization is actually far more important than merely drawing a design for a chart to hang on the wall in the boss's office. It is a systems design which should reflect the actual plan of action for the entire organization. Certain considerations should be taken into account, not the least of which is the personal impression and self-image held by the

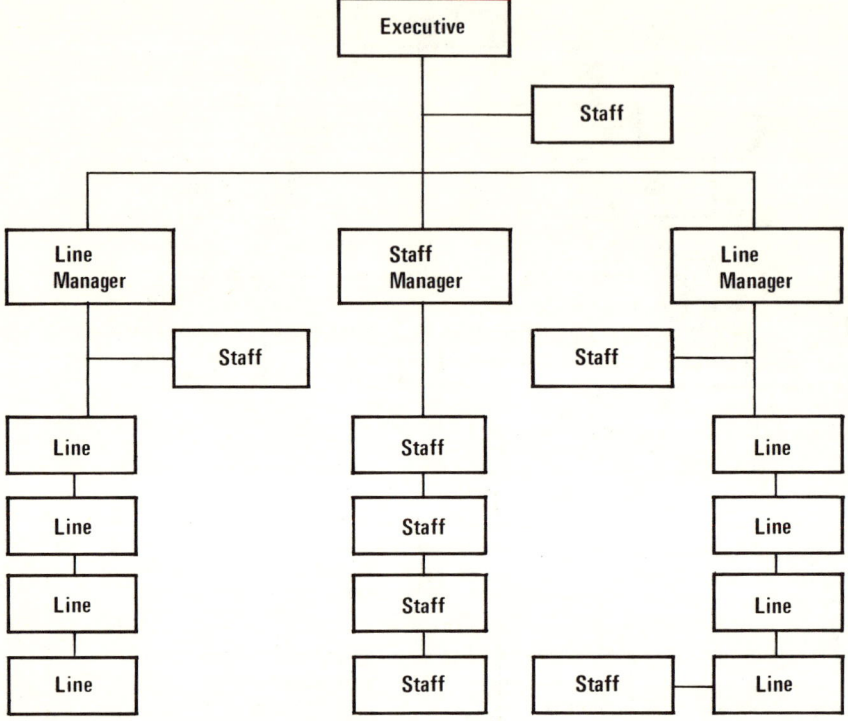

Figure 13.   Line and staff: variation 3.

individual employee, regardless of his level within the organization. Basic considerations include the following:

1. Division of work.
2. Specialization.
3. Authority Relationships.
4. Assistance for the chief executive.
5. Staff authority.
6. Line authority.
7. Coordination and control.
8. Appropriate attention.
9. Organizational design and relationships.

Once the chart is drawn and staffing is begun, specific local conditions must be taken into account and the actual organization put into operation.

Notes

1. From Leonard, V. A., *The Police Enterprise: Its Organization and Management*, 1969, p. 5. Courtesy of Charles C. Thomas, Publisher, Springfield, Illinois.
2. Ibid. p. 6.
3. Anthony G. Athos and Robert E. Coffey, *Behavior in Organizations: A Multi-Dimensional View*, (Englewood Cliffs, N. J.: Prentice-Hall,© 1968), p. 230. All material from this book reprinted by permission of the publisher.
4. John M. Pfiffner and Frank P. Sherwood, *Administrative Organization* (Englewood Cliffs, N. J.: Prentice-Hall,© 1960), p. 171. All material from this book reprinted by permission of the publisher.
5. Athos and Coffey, *Behavior in Organizations*, p. 230.
6. Rensis Likert, *New Patterns of Management* (New York: McGraw-Hill, 1961), p. 186.
7. Northcote Parkinson, *Parkinson's Law* (Boston: Houghton-Mifflin, 1957).
8. From Kenney, John P. *Police Administration*, 1972, p. 59. Courtesy of Charles C. Thomas, Publisher, Springfield, Illinois.
9. Ibid, p. 59.
10. Leonard R. Sayles and George Strauss, *Human Behavior in Organizations* (Englewood Cliffs, N. J.: Prentice-Hall,© 1966), p. 394. All material from this book reprinted by permission of the publisher.
11. International City Managers Association, *Municipal Police Administration*, 5th ed. (Chicago: International City Managers Assoc., 1961), p. 47.
12. From Bristow, Allen P., *Effective Police Manpower Utilization*, 1969, p. 14. Courtesy of Charles C. Thomas, Publisher, Springfield, Illinois.
13. Luther Gulick, *Notes on the Theory of Organization* (New York: Institute of Public Administration, 1937), p. 4.
14. Bristow, *Effective Police Manpower Utilization*, p. 12.
15. Harold Koontz and Cyril O'Donnell, *Principles of Management: An Analysis of Managerial Functions*, 4th ed. (New York: McGraw-Hill, 1968), pp. 47-48.
16. Ibid., p. 49.
17. Peter F. Drucker, *The Effective Executive* (New York: Harper & Row, 1967) pp. 10-15.
18. Ibid., p. 15.
19. G. Douglas Gourley, *Effective Municipal Police Organization*, (Beverly Hills: Benziger, Bruce and Glencoe, 1970), p. 41.
20. William H. Newman, *Administrative Action, The Techniques of Organization and Management*, 2nd ed. (Englewood Cliffs, N. J.: Prentice-Hall,© 1963) p. 203. All material from this book reprinted by permission of the publisher.
21. Pfiffner and Sherwood, *Administrative Organization*, p. 171.
22. Koontz and O'Donnell, *Principles of Management*, p. 299.
23. Newman, *Administrative Action*, p. 163.
24. Sayles and Strauss, *Human Behavior*, p. 349.
25. Athos and Coffey, *Behavior in Organizations*, p. 239.
26. N. F. Iannone, *Supervision of Police Personnel* (Englewood Cliffs, N. J.: Prentice-Hall, 1970), p. 17.

REVIEW QUESTIONS

1. What are the principal considerations in the division of the department into work units?
2. List the divisions that are usually classified as line units.

3. List the divisions that are usually classified as staff units.
4. What are some of the advantages of specialization? disadvantages?
5. What is the "team concept"?
6. Describe four major realities over which the executive has no control.
7. In what ways might an executive utilize a staff assistant?
8. How are staff and line authority different?
9. Describe some of the controls used by the executive to determine if the organization is functioning as it should be.
10. What are some of the purposes of organizational charts?

4 Administrative Communications

The general theme of this chapter is the process of communications as an administrative tool. Communications involves a complex system of information flow and feedback throughout the organization in all directions and by various means. Some of those means include orders, directives, policies, meetings, conferences, and every medium imaginable is used—radio, telephone, teletype, television, and the printed word. There is not only a formal system of communications, but also an informal one, utilizing similar means and media. The traditional concept of administrative communications flowing downward through the hierarchy of the organization within the strict confines of the chain of command and by formal means no longer fits the pattern of modern organizational operations. Many times the informal channels are more effective for some forms of communication, sometimes more desirable. Recent research shows, according to Sayles and Strauss, that "timely communication often requires bypassing certain steps in the hierarchial chain. Also, every organization needs an *appeal channel*, a mechanism by which subordinates can go over their boss's 'head' when they feel a serious injustice has been done to them."[1] Heresy? Perhaps 30 years ago, but not today. The age of specialization and the demands of society on the many agencies of criminal justice have changed the tenor of administrative communications. In this chapter we attempt to cover many of the concepts of modern organizational communications and their application in the administration of justice.

AUTHORITY-RESPONSIBILITY HIERARCHY

The most basic communications flow is that from the power source, the chief executive, through his immediate subordinates and on throughout the entire organization in sequential steps. The results of adherence to this system are described by Sayles and Strauss:

1. Nearly all contacts take the form of orders going *down* and reports of results going *up* the pyramid.
2. Each subordinate must receive instructions and orders from only one boss.
3. Important decisions are only made at the top of the pyramid.
4. Each supervisor has only a limited span of control; that is, he supervises only a limited number of individuals.
5. An individual at any level (but the top and bottom) has contact only with his boss above him and subordinates below him.[2]

This basic concept has undergone considerable modification during recent years. Contacts are between individuals whose work and merging responsibilities cause them to cooperate in their efforts and engage in continuous lateral communications, which are extremely important to the accomplishment of the organization's overall objectives as well as daily work goals. Sometimes referred to as informal communications because they are out of the chain of command, these contacts are very real and essential. Actually, informal communications are more on a social basis than a working one, although it may be difficult to distinguish between the two. Again quoting Sayles and Strauss, the work-oriented contacts include the following:

1. Work-flow contacts among people who must collaborate to get the job done.
2. So-called staff-line relationships, which can be envisioned as diagonal contacts.
3. Appeals to higher management by those on lower levels for modification of decisions made by their direct bosses.[3]

Pressures from peers and professional interaction among practitioners in the field of criminal justice may have more meaning to the individual than directions from a superior. Consider the prosecuting attorney and police officer combination in the courtroom. For the successful conclusion of a case, it is necessary for the attorney to direct the strategy and to prepare the officer for his testimony. The officer who disregards such directions would certainly find little success in presenting his testimony and seeing the fruition of his investigative efforts. Staff advisors, such as the legal advisor within the police department or the probation department, give advice that has a greater effect than that given during an informal contact. Although not within the line of command, such advice would probably have the effect of a direct command given by a superior, but in this case perhaps with greater authority because of the special role that the advisor plays. The third point made by Sayles and Strauss involves the appeals process that should be available to everyone in the organization. Certainly not to be employed in every instance when a superior-subordinate difference of opinion arises—a more or less routine supervision situation with some individuals—the avenue of appeal should be provided whenever the person on a lower level within the organization sincerely believes that he has a valid grievance. This is part of the feedback process in the communications system that is so necessary for the executive to assess the effects of his directions.

Professionalization of the many occupations within the Criminal Justice System has yielded interesting effects from a management standpoint. Although decisions as to the administration of the organization might be made more frequently by those in higher positions, actual working-policies regarding "discretion" decision making are formulated at the operational, or working, level. Educational and training preparation, plus rigid screening procedures designed to select only those self-reliant people who can take decisive action without close supervision, can have no other effect. Close supervision of the decision-making process involving probation and parole officers, police officers, and the many other professional people in the courts, institutions, and other agencies throughout the system is an absolute impossibility.

Guidelines and standards can and should be developed, but the actual evaluative process still involves personal value judgments. Consider this statement in view of the organization you may represent: "Today, organizations hire many managerial, professional, and technical personnel. Since they are often better informed on technical subjects than their superiors, the latter must abdicate certain key decisions to them."[4] Pfiffner and Sherwood propose that with the exception principle—leaving the routine decision making to the lower echelon except for unusual circumstances—and the modern concept of communications as a circuit rather than a pyramid "it is not necessary for a commander on each echelon to have seen and read every message, but only those which require his attention for the purpose of information or decision."[5]

Peter Drucker, author of *The Effective Executive* and consultant to some of the country's more successful enterprises, made the following observation in 1959:

> The business enterprise of today is no longer an organization in which there are a handful of "bosses" at the top who make all the decisions while the "workers" carry out orders. It is primarily an organization of professionals with highly specialized knowledge exercising autonomous, responsible judgement. And every one of them—whether manager or individual expert-contributor — constantly makes truly entrepreneurial decisions which affect the economic characteristics and risks of the entire enterprise. He makes them not only by "delegation from above" but inevitably in the performance of his own job and work.[6]

Although referring to the business enterprise, in practice these statements equally apply to the service agencies of the Criminal Justice System. Professor Kenney quite succinctly applies the newer philosophy to police service:

> The myth that administrative policy for the police department is made by the chief of police needs to be scotched. It is inherent... that policy is made at all levels of organization and in essence *all* personnel are ultimately involved in the policy-making process. Broad policies become formalized when approved by the chief of police. Policies relating to specific functions or operations may or may not require approval of the chief of police but may be formalized when approved by the appropriate command officer.[7]

From a personal standpoint, "Communications often involve *feelings* as well as *content* and how a message is sent, and to *whom,* is often as important as what is sent."[8] Since any organization is made up of people, then people-oriented approaches to effective management must be implemented. Consider this statement by Hanna and Gentel:

> Once the police administrator recognizes that implementation is the weak link to the success of the plan, he must familiarize himself with an administrative process which will be instrumental in achieving effective implementation. Perhaps no other process is as effective as *personnel participation.* Participation of those affected by decisions about their own welfare and working circumstances enhances compliance and commitment and reduces misunderstanding and resistance.[9]

BARRIERS TO COMMUNICATION

There are some authoritarian executives and supervisors who lack the ability to communicate or to stimulate the flow of communications among their subordinates. Many barriers get in the way and unless they are overcome the organization will fail. People who work at the operational levels of our criminal justice organizations are in a critical position to either make or break the organization. A supervisor is effective only if his subordinates allow him to be effective; they must accept him as a supervisor. The absolute dictator-type supervisor has no place in the modern criminal justice organization and must be replaced with one who is a diplomat and a master communicator. Here are some barriers to effective communications, and a few recommendations for overcoming them:[10]

1. An authoritarian attitude of the manager or supervisor is sometimes a manifestation of insecurity or lack of knowledge, or he may be on an "ego trip."

2. The individual's rank might impress him so much that he may set up barriers, such as dealing only with people of equal rank or higher, requiring appointments set up far in advance, and creating the problem of getting through an officious secretary or a requirement that the lower ranking person must first go through each step of the chain of command.

3. Unnecessary or unexplained delays in the communications process can result in complaints of bureaucratic red tape or "buck-passing."

4. An unreceptive attitude to and lack of understanding of the subordinate's position can be forgetfulness: the individual might have forgotten how it was when he was at the beginning level in the organization.

5. The executive indicates through his reactions that he only wants to hear good news; this results in a filtering or cover-up of real problems. The subordinates do not want to lose the favor of the boss by bringing him bad news and may find that rewards go only to those subordinates who have nothing but good news to report. So they may actually be "sitting on a keg of dynamite," but to their superior they are handling everything smoothly. Beware of the supervisor who has only good news to report while in a particular assignment, whose successor begins reporting an unusual amount of bad news.

6. Persons in subordinate positions may be less capable of expressing themselves than their superiors and fearful of looking stupid in the eyes of the individual who overwhelms them with his ability and his "charisma."

7. The supervisor may react to every suggestion for change or item of criticism as a personal affront to his skill or wisdom. This is a touchy situation when a sound proposal based on bona fide data proves that the boss's pet project must be abandoned.

8. An argumentative or "devil's advocate" position displayed by the executive or supervisor too early during the discussion can cause the discussion to end prematurely.

9. Favoritism toward information, reports, suggestions, and criticism offered by certain individuals who apparently can do no wrong in the

eyes of their superiors is often called the halo effect, and may also be applied to those individuals whose halo is in reverse.

10. There may be no avenue for legitimate grievances through which an employee may let off steam about real or imagined grievances.

11. "Machinery," such as department memoranda, bulletins, reports, and other means for communications, may not be available, or inadequately used. There might also be a problem in utilizing the means effectively for feedback from the operational areas to management.

12. Nonverbal communications might be much louder than those that are transmitted through the medium of sound. Facial expressions, lack of attention by the listener, other activities of superiors when allegedly receiving information, and other indicators of attitude change can effectively sabotage a communications system.

13. Explanations of orders, policy changes, and other information disseminated throughout the organization may not be clearly presented or may lack the necessary groundwork prior to the implementation of a change.

OVERCOMING THE BARRIERS

1. Listen. Many executives and supervisors have yet to develop the art of listening. We hear sounds, but never the meanings; the result is that we seldom receive the complete message. Instead of formulating an answer or some other "comeback" while the other person is speaking, the effective listener will ask questions and in every way possible let the speaker know that what he says is being heard.

Listen with a purpose: to gain information, an answer to a question, or to ascertain if the speaker understands what he is saying. This is particularly true when the conversation is a supervisor-subordinate contact and there are training or other supervisory needs to be identified *from what the subordinate has to say*. An important consequence of listening is that there should be some action, if indicated, to follow the listening to let the person know that what he had to say was heard, and heeded. There is no quicker way to sterilize the flow of communications than to do nothing.

2. Develop a communicating attitude. As one progresses to higher levels he gains a position of vantage from which he can see the organization and its activities with a broader perspective. It is important to remember that most of the employees can see only from a relatively obscured position.

3. Consider an open door policy. Many grievances should be handled at the operational level, between a supervisor and his subordinates. In a larger organization it is advisable to have a grievance committee, or board, to hear complaints from anyone within the organization who believes he has a legitimate grievance to air. The open door of every executive

and supervisor might serve the employees to get to know their managers on an informal basis, or to provide them with the knowledge that they have a last resort if all other grievance procedures fail.

4. Utilize a feedback method. Pfiffner and Sherwood discuss the concept known as cybernetics and its contributions to organizational theory. They point out that there are two major contributions, both related to the utilization of "information and control patterns of organizations to that of the new automatic machines."[11] First, management personnel develop the goals and patterns of the organization, but the machines monitor organizational activities electronically through a system of reporting methods. As long as the organization is operating within the tolerances prescribed as acceptable everything continues without incident. In case of exceptions to the tolerances, the decision makers—the managers—are alerted and they take whatever action they decide necessary. This is in accordance with the exception principle of management. The second contribution is analogous with biological factors. "The human brain is the planning and decision center which communicates goals and directives, through the nervous system to other parts of the body. These in turn communicate back their accomplishments which lead to new messages from the brain to continue, adjust, or discontinue the initial action."[12]

The cybernetics process as explained by Pfiffner and Sherwood is a circular process that involves goal-setting, communication and continuous review, modification, and feedback. The result, theoretically, is a smoothly functioning organization that adjusts to meet changing needs and brings back into line those activities that should remain constant. The method adopted, or the name by which it is carried out, is secondary to the importance of the actual need for such a process. There are other methods for feedback, which include self-reporting, inspections, meetings, brainstorming, and various informal procedures.

5. Have a systematic method of communications to disseminate information and maintain a continuous flow. For standardized regulations and procedures there should be current manuals and handbooks. General and special orders, instructions, bulletins, and other forms of written communications should accompany or supplement the spoken word to assure accuracy and a record of the information for later review and/or modification. Redundancy is good, say Sayles and Strauss: "If each word is crucially important, it pays to say the same thing in several ways. In giving complicated directions, for example, it is wise to repeat them several times, perhaps in different ways, to guarantee successful transmission."[13]

6. Recognize the informal communications system within the organization. One statement that I have heard from many administrators is that rumor-mongering is a bad practice that must be eliminated from the department. Rumors often travel much faster than official communications

because of unnecessary formality and the artificial need for certain communications to be passed on down through the channels of supervision, as if there were some magic attached to the supervisory power of knowing something before a subordinate hears it. In reality, because of such outmoded ideas, the grapevine transmits the information so that those who wait to hear through official channels are sometimes the last to hear about what is coming out of the executive's office. In my opinion, rumors are a good method of determining if the formal communications system is effective. If the grapevine is faster and more accurate, then the formal method had better undergo considerable modification; if the formal system is effective, the rumor-mongers will have little gossip to peddle.

In addition to the grapevine system, there are many informal organizations within any large organization. These groups may be formed for purposes of socialization of families, sporting events or participatory sports, fraternal or religious organizations, special hobbies, and common interests. There is nothing unusual for professionally oriented people to talk shop even during social gatherings. As a matter of fact, it would be unusual if the discussion in such a group did not migrate to their other common interest: their profession. Through these social contacts, there is considerable free exchange of information with little regard for the formal structure of the organization or for regulations that may require absolute silence outside the confines of the building.

Morale is dependent upon many factors, and good communications is high on that list of factors. Imagine the tremendous blow to a person's morale if he were to walk into the mail room or the coffee shop and discover that everyone there but him was aware that someone else received the promotion or transfer he was being considered for, or had reason to believe would go to him. That communications violation is flagrantly committed almost daily in many organizations. People who are to be affected by some management decision should be contacted directly and should be among the first to know of that decision.

7. Establish a reputation for integrity, honesty, and sincerity in keeping the communications flow constantly moving. Seek out the bottlenecks and detractors and design better methods for improving the system on a continuous basis. If the administrator adheres faithfully to this rule, his attitude is at least correct. What action he takes will either be made known through formal channels or through the grapevine.

MASS COMMUNICATIONS

Written directives, general orders, and types of communications *other* than the spoken word may be more effective than the spoken word in some cases. Some of the reasons may be that the information is of a technical nature and complete accuracy is more important than the extra time it might take to disseminate the information. There are difficulties associated with these means of communication, such as a lack of the personal touch with feedback and exchange of ideas between supervisor and subordinate and a reduction in the status of the supervisor. Techniques for overcoming these difficulties may include supplementing the written information with added personal messages or interpretations by the supervisors, prior dissemination to the supervisors to give them time to understand the material so that they can explain it to their subordinates, and encouragement of the people who receive the information to direct their questions or suggestions to their immediate superiors.[14] Once the organization begins to lose its personal touch through direct contacts, the cold, mechanical atmosphere may seriously affect the morale of the personnel and stifle the free flow of communications. Every effort should be made to prevent such a "freezing-out."

POLICIES

Formally speaking, a policy is a general rule for action prepared by management, although its origin may have been at the operational level. It is established "for the purpose of framing, guiding, or directing organizational activities including decision making," and is intended to provide a "relative stability, consistency, uniformity, and continuity in the operations of the organization."[15] The basic difference between a policy and a procedure is that a policy is eventually formalized and recognized by the chief executive of the organization; a procedure is more often a set of instructions related more to the actual performance of tasks. The delineation is not clear-cut in all cases, and may vary from one organization to another.

MANUALS OF RULES AND REGULATIONS

A very formalized method of presenting a series of relatively stable policies, and sometimes certain standardized procedures, is to publish them in book form in a manual. The recommended format is loose-leaf and if there is a numbering system it should be of such a nature that provisions are made for modifications, additions, or deletions. A working definition of a manual is that it is a printed and generally disseminated document that prescribes the rules, regulations, policies, and procedures which guide the systematic management of the organization. The following statement was made in reference to a police department manual, but has equal application in any agency of the Criminal Justice System that utilizes a manual:

> The manual in effect documents the administrative philosophy of the organization. It clearly defines lines of responsibility and authority, sets forth the organizational structure, and guides individual members of the department in the performance of their work. The manual serves the officer as the lawbook serves the judge.[16]

Several years ago, it was necessary to develop an updated manual of rules and regulations for the Santa Ana Police Department. During the several months of research and writing and an endless series of committee meetings, the document was completed and forwarded to the Chief of Police. Some years later, the constitutionality and general validity of several sections of that manual were challenged. A California appellate court decision explains the validity of certain restrictive portions of that manual:

> Although an individual can claim no constitutional right to obtain public employment or to receive any other publicly conferred benefit, the government cannot condition admission to such employment or receipt of such benefits upon any terms it may deem to impose. The government is not free to impose unreasonable conditions. (*Keyishian* v. *Board of Regents of U. of St. of N. Y.*, 385 U. S. 589, 605-606, 17 L. Ed. 2d 629, 87 S. Ct. 675, 685.) However, when circumstances inexorably so require, the government may impose conditions upon the public employee despite a resulting qualification of constitutional rights. (*Bagley* v. *Washington Township Hospital Dist.*, supra, p. 505.)
>
> When such a conflict does arise, the governmental agency seeking to impose restrictions on the exercise of an employee's constitutional rights must demonstrate that: (1) the governmental restraint rationally relates to the enhancement of the public service; (2) the benefits that the public gains by the restraint outweigh the resulting impairment of the constitutional right; and (3) no alternatives less subversive to the constitutional right are available. (*Bagley* v. *Washington Township Hospital Dist.*, supra, 65 Cal. 2d 499, 501-502.) In other words, a public employee may speak freely so long as he does not impair the administration of the public service in which he is engaged. (*Belshaw* v. *City of Berkeley*, 246 Cal. App. 2d 493, 497.) Similarly, a public employee may engage in political activity providing it does not affect the administrative functioning or public integrity of the governmental agency. (*Fort* v. *Civil Service Commission*, 61 Cal. 2d 331, 337-338.)
>
> Applying the Bagley formula to the rules and regulations of the Santa Ana Police Department, the limited restrictions on the policeman's conduct are valid. The paramilitary nature of a police force and the need for loyalty have long been recognized in California. (See *Cook* v. *Civil Service Commission*, supra, 178 Cal. App.

2d 118, 134: see also *State* v. *Steinkellner*, 247 Wis. 1 18 P.W. 2d 355, 358 .)

A department head has a right to exercise supervision to the end that discipline may be maintained so as not to disrupt or impair the public service. (*Hayman* v. *City of Los Angeles*, 17 Cal. App. 674, 679.)[17]

COMMITTEES

"A camel is a horse constructed by a committee." In many instances this adage might apply, but those are usually situations when a committee might not have the authority to make a decision or to take any kind of action. The problem might also be in the composition of the membership, or in weak support by management, or in any number of other circumstances that might render a committee ineffective. When used correctly, however, with the appropriate power to make decisions or to take action if necessary, strong support from management, and carefully planned membership, a committee can prove quite effective.

Professor William H. Newman points out that there are four occasions when committees are particularly useful: (1) when a wide divergence of information is necessary to reach a sound conclusion, (2) when the judgment of more than one qualified person is desirable, (3) when the success of a project depends on common understanding by many people, and (4) to enhance coordination.[18] Committees have advantages and disadvantages; whether one serves its purpose depends on whether its purpose is well-defined and appropriate for a committee's attention. Obviously committee meetings take time to organize and carry out; so when time is of the essence and a decision must be made immediately, perhaps it would be wiser to have an individual make that decision and have the task carried out. For an analysis of the results and a study to recommend future actions under similar conditions, a committee may be convened later.

Advantages of a committee are that the results are those of a group action and involve the input of many people. Sometimes when a difficult decision has to be made and the results will affect many people, the committee's group action and the "we did it" cooperative attitude of several people will have a salutary effect on the people affected rather than an abrasive effect. Of course, any decisions will be group decisions, and sometimes compromises and concessions have to be made to gain cooperation among disputing principles.

There are a few basic guidelines to follow for effective operation of a committee.[19]

1. Clearly define the purpose, the duties, and the authority of the committee.

2. Select committee members on the basis of the duties and responsibilities of the committee. If the anticipated action to be taken as a result of committee recommendations involves two specific units, it would be wise to have representation from those units, preferably someone who is in a position to make decisions and take action when necessary. Even when a consensus is desired, the committee membership should be kept small enough so that it is functional.
3. Provide the committee with sufficient staff assistance, including clerical, research, or technically qualified people who have the knowledge or expertise to do the tasks required of them.
4. Select the correct chairman, who will guide the meetings and set their tone; often the committee's success or failure will depend on his leadership.
5. Establish guidelines for the committee's operation, such as scheduling arrangements, agenda, summaries and reports, deadlines, result requirements (if appropriate), parameters within which the committee must work, and available resources.

Where to place the committee in the organizational structure depends on the purpose and function of the committee. If it is one that includes membership from several divisions in the organization, and its composition includes a variety of levels of management, supervisory, and operational level people, it would be most appropriate to place the committee in the category of a staff position. Having no authority of its own except in an advisory capacity, the committee would report its findings and recommendations to the chief executive or other administrator, who would exercise his own decision-making power and take whatever action he deems necessary. Another committee might be made up of members of the same division with its leadership identical to the organization's hierarchy. In that case, the committee might merely be an extension or a variation of the line function, with decisions made and action taken at the operational level.

MEETINGS

The larger and more complex an organization becomes, the more difficult it is for vis-a-vis relationships between supervisors, subordinates, and colleagues. Closed doors in an air-conditioned building, great distances from one office to another, obstacles such as the chain of command or secretaries and appointments, all interfere with the communications process. In order that information and directions may be passed on with personal interpretations and be free from distortion by intermediaries, it is necessary that meetings be used as a medium of communications. Of course, they should be meaningful, timely, and meet certain other criteria for effectiveness, such as having agenda disseminated in advance and follow-up reports of the meeting printed and distributed later. Drucker [20] describes an excess of meetings as a symptom of "malorganization." He states: "Meetings are by definition a concession to deficient organization. For one either meets or one works. One cannot do both at the same time."[21]

Too many meetings in an organization may be an indication that the individual who calls them has nothing else to do and that perhaps his particular position within the organization should be reexamined. Meetings are extremely time-consuming. For example, a meeting held away from an executive's office at ten o'clock in the morning means that he will not be able to start anything that morning, arriving and preparing for the meeting will probably consume the first two hours. The ten o'clock meeting might as well continue to noon, because lunch will interfere with any other activity and not until after lunch will the executive or supervisor get back to his routine. A well-organized executive who utilizes meetings for the occasions when he wishes to impart information or seek direct feedback, or to accomplish some other objective, will plan the meeting. He identifies his objectives and develops an agenda. He holds his meeting with a specific purpose. Drucker describes it as follows:

> The effective man always states at the outset of a meeting the specific purpose and contribution it is to achieve. He makes sure that the meeting addresses itself to this purpose. He does not allow a meeting called to inform to degenerate into a "bull session" in which everyone has bright ideas. But a meeting called by him to stimulate thinking and ideas also does not become simply a presentation on the part of one of the members, but is run to challenge and stimulate everybody in the room. He always, at the end of his meetings, goes back to the opening statement and relates the final conclusions to the original intent.[22]

Meetings may have an effect on morale, providing many of the participants with an avenue for open and uninhibited dialogue with their managers or other individuals in the hierarchy whom they might not otherwise see or be able to communicate with. Drucker states: "The frequency of work-group meetings, as well as the attitude and behavior of the superior toward the ideas of subordinates, affects the extent to which employees feel that the supervisor is good at handling people."[23]

What the executive and supervisor alike are looking for, it appears, is an appropriate balance of meetings when and where they would be most effective. They must be for some purpose and results should be demonstrated, otherwise meetings become "time-wasters" and demonstrate Drucker's concept of a poorly managed organization. As an example of types of material to be communicated which may best be transmitted through the medium of meetings, Likert states that there is

> cognitive material, such as: information or facts as to the current situation, problems, progress toward goals, etc.; ideas, suggestions, experiences; knowledge with regard to objectives, policies, and actions; and motivational and emotional material, such as: emotional climate or atmosphere, attitudes and reactions; loyalties and hostilities; feelings of support, appreciation, or rejection; goals and objectives.[24]

STAFF COMMUNICATIONS

Staff divisions, or units, and their members are often utilized in most criminal justice agencies. As discussed in chapter 3, the staff role is to serve in an advisory capacity, serving the organization, as opposed to the line functions, which are primarily designed to serve the public. In their advisory role, then, staff people gather data, issue reports, prepare directives (over someone else's signature usually), coordinate activities, provide specialized counsel, and perform countless other communication functions. Because of their unique position on the inside when plans and ideas are in the formulation stage, caution should be exercised that the staff unit does not overextend its own authority or develop its own power to the extent that it would interfere with the customary supervisory relationships. One of the problems developed in the area of staff activities may be that the information generated between staff personnel and executives and other management people is kept confidential unnecessarily. Some individuals may label some information "secret" for no other reason than to be able to maintain possession of information that no one else is supposed to have; then they can generate their own power by exchanging this secret information for special favors or other considerations within the organization. The best way to combat this phenomenon is to widely disseminate as much information as possible, keeping the contents of the secret file to an absolute minimum. In my own experience I have seen numerous occasions when so-called secret and confidential information held in tightly locked intelligence files may be learned in detail simply by reading the metropolitan newspapers and news magazines. Within an organization, when there are too many secrets, there is usually an excellent grapevine.

In the dissemination of information there are a few simple rules that should be followed, particularly by staff people, when the object is to avoid creating the impression that the report or bulletin is a directive from management to operational personnel:

1. Present the information in a factual and informative manner, without editorial comment that might be interpreted as supervisory chastisement or commendation.
2. Write to express, not impress.
3. Be direct and concise.
4. Illustrate points with charts and graphs, but not with meaningless or redundant material.
5. If the document is more than one page, consider the use of an introductory statement and synopsis on the first page for the benefit of those who scan the first few lines and then discard the material or set it aside for future study.

Inspections need not always be conducted in an authoritative manner. Feedback obtained through informal field contacts is often an extremely valuable means of administrative inspection.
Courtesy: Police Department, Greensboro, North Carolina

INSPECTIONS

Inspections serve many important functions in the communications process of an organization. Primarily, they serve as stimuli in the feedback sequence of communications flow. There are three types of inspections that are most frequently implemented in criminal justice management: authoritative, staff, and intelligence. The authoritative inspection is a method of supervisory control and coordination by direct contact and observation of performance; corrections are recommended or directed on a personal basis through the direct line of supervision. Staff inspections are indirect and advisory, with reports made to the chief executive or other manager. Staff personnel report the need for corrections in equipment or procedure, but they do not have the authority to direct the changes. Intelligence inspections may involve surreptitious investigation to determine the integrity of the organization and its effectiveness.

The first two types of inspection are generally accepted by employees as routine management techniques, but the third type may be the subject of grievances and, if improperly used, may lead to considerable hostility and poor morale within the organization. The administrator who utilizes intelligence inspections should make it known to the members of the organization that such investigations are conducted and should also explain their purpose. Only a few case studies should convince employee and supervisor alike of the value of all three types of inspection.

The authoritative inspection is continuously employed by the supervisor. Not only is it possible to point out errors and ways to correct them but also commendable performance will receive early discovery—a supervisor's compliments may reinforce good work practices as well as maintain a high level of morale. The staff inspection may serve as an excellent means to identify the employee who is engaged in misconduct, or who is not performing according to department standards, without making it necessary for his fellow employees to violate any code of loyalty that might exist between them. Rules call for personnel to report misconduct of colleagues, but from a realistic standpoint the administrator finds that such a report is more likely to be made in response to questions from a superior than on a strictly volunteer basis.

An example of an intelligence investigation that was instrumental in preserving the integrity of an organization involved a county parole board and a private attorney. Rumors were circulating quite freely that certain high-ranking individuals on the board were "on the take," and that parole could be bought. As a result of an investigation we determined that a local attorney was representing to his clients in jail that when he appeared on their behalf before the board two members of that board would be in a benevolent mood if they were given the "incentive." Taking the money his clients believed to be bribe money for his own use, the attorney would appear and the prisoners would be paroled. What the clients did not know was that their parole was assured even without the attorney's presence because of their own good conduct and other "good time" they earned in jail which cut down their actual time to serve. As a result of the investigation, it was possible to expose the fraud and encourage the attorney to practice elsewhere. There was no prosecution because of difficulties in gaining sufficient evidence, but the integrity of the parole board members was not compromised.

Some of the basic purposes for inspection as a communications tool in management are:

1. Through inspections it is possible to ascertain if the organization's objectives are being accomplished according to the methods of and in harmony with the philosophy enunciated by the chief executive and his staff. Reinforcement of acceptable practices may be accomplished through commendations and other means of positive discipline, and correction of unacceptable practices may be accomplished through supervision and negative discipline.

2. The effect of the activities performed by the organization, and whether there is need for any modification, can be determined by use of attitude surveys, interviews with people served in any way by the department, and other results of the actions taken.

3. It is possible to determine if all of the resources available to the organization are being utilized, and if they are, what their effect is.

4. Inspections stimulate the feedback process by encouraging people to communicate with one another in anticipation of various types of inspections so as not to be caught unprepared. Self-analyses and self-improvement often lead to an overall improvement in an organization's performance.

"Inspection does not create quality, but it does control quality, in that it provides the means for evaluating personnel, equipment, and operational performance. It embraces preventative measures which may be brought into play to prevent failure and raise the probability of success."[25]

APPEAL CHANNELS

Appeals on decisions, or what an employee may believe to be a legitimate grievance, serve as an excellent feedback system. Every organization should have some avenue for all of its members to take when they wish to appeal a decision or an action taken by a superior which may have caused some adverse effect on them. Sayles and Strauss list three reasons why they believe appeal channels are important for an organization:

1. Upper management cannot get additional feedback on the result of its own decisions and activities beyond that carried by the chain of command.
2. Individuals at lower levels who might feel oppressed and powerless to do anything about it gain a means of

protecting themselves, to a degree, from the arbitrariness of the hierarchy.
3. New ideas which might otherwise get lost may reach key decision-making areas.[26]

Although an appeal may first manifest itself in the form of a grievance and grow to serious proportions if not aired as soon as possible after it arises, it may actually lead to an exposure of the problem as little more than a minor error or a misunderstanding in communication. The result of most grievances correctly handled is a positive feeling on the part of the employee that his opinions and feelings are valued by the organization, and the matter is brought to a successful conclusion without incident. The alternative is a problem that swells to fantastic proportions until it finally boils to the surface and ends up as the cause of a belligerent confrontation and irreparable damage to the organization and the supervisor-subordinate relationship. It is not unusual in such situations for the actual cause of the confrontation to be forgotten; the confrontation itself does the damage.

INFORMAL ORGANIZATION

Although probably not officially recognized, the more dynamic relationships in an organization are through informal contacts. Sociometric in character, Pfiffner and Sherwood explain what they title the "social overlay," augmenting the design of the organizational structure with lines depicting relationships that exist in fact although not with official recognition. There is a pattern of relationships which is social in nature and exists because of a "net feeling of attraction or rejection."[27]

In many organizations there are certain individuals you can contact who are always able to get information for you, or cause some action to be taken, although their position in the table of organization may not appear to be that significant. Such people may be indigenous leaders who generate their own power by charismatic leadership ability or through strong informal relationships that span the entire organization, or they may be aggressive *people-movers* who are able to get the results they want by manipulative practices such as flattery, exhortation, or personal charm. Pfiffner and Sherwood refer to this phenomenon as the "power overlay";[28] they also refer to the "network of influence,"[29] which depicts on the chart the informal channel of communications which may or may not be superimposed over the formal table of organization. The administrator must recognize and understand these phenomena of group dynamics. To deny their existence and attempt to destroy them might not succeed. It might be the wiser course for him to recognize them and utilize them to his advantage or to develop his own networks, or overlays, within the organizational structure to assure department-wide integration and coordination.

SUMMARY

In this chapter we have briefly covered several facets of the fascinating study of administrative communications. The system of communications throughout an organization should be continuous and should operate in a complete circuit, from the chief executive to every member of the organization and then back to the chief as feedback. Informal organizations are in existence and should be taken into account when the formal system is considered. The most dynamic informal communications system that may exist is the grapevine; if it is operating effectively it should be considered as a signal that the formal system of communications has serious flaws and is in need of an immediate and complete overhaul.

Communications in an organization are a process of human and personal dynamics. Every legitimate means and media should be employed to assure an effective operation. In the next chapter I address the subject of personnel management, which is actually a continuation of communications, and an inseparable part of it.

NOTES

1. Leonard R. Sayles and George Strauss, *Human Behavior in Organizations*, (Englewood Cliffs, N. J.: Prentice-Hall, © 1966), p. 353. All material from this book reprinted by permission of the publisher.
2. Ibid., p. 349.
3. Ibid., p. 350.
4. Ibid., pp. 350-51.
5. John M. Pfiffner and Frank P. Sherwood, *Administrative Organization* (Englewood Cliffs, N. J.: Prentice-Hall, © 1960), p. 137. All material from this book reprinted by permission of the publisher.
6. Peter F. Drucker, "Long Range Planning, Challenge to Management Science," *Management Science* 5 (1959): 242.
7. From Kenney, John P., *Police Administration*, 1972, p. 47. Courtesy of Charles C Thomas, Publisher, Springfield, Illinois.
8. Anthony G. Athos and Robert E. Coffey, *Behavior in Organizations: A Multi-Dimensional View* (Englewood Cliffs, N. J.: Prentice-Hall, © 1968;, p. 233. All material from this book reprinted by permission of the publisher.
9. From Hanna, Donald G., and Gentel, William D., *A Guide to Primary Police Management Concepts*, 1971, p. 49. Courtesy of Charles C Thomas, Publisher, Springfield, Illinois.
10. Some of the material for this section has been adapted from Sayles and Strauss, *Human Behavior in Organizations*, pp. 371, 246-257.
11. Pfiffner and Sherwood, *Administrative Organization*, pp. 105-106.
12. Ibid., p. 106.
13. Sayles and Strauss, *Human Behavior in Organizations*, p. 255.
14. Ibid., p. 368.
15. Kenney, *Police Administration*, p. 47.
16. Report 206 Management Information Service, *Preparation of a Police Manual* (Chicago: International City Managers Association, March 1961), p. 1.
17. *Norton vs. City of Santa Ana*, 4 Civil 9646, 4th District Court of Appeal, Feb. 19, 1971.

18. William H. Newman, *Administrative Action, The Techniques of Organization and Management*, 2nd ed. (Englewood Cliffs, N. J.: Prentice-Hall, © 1960), pp. 246-47. All material from this book reprinted by permission of the publisher.
19. Ibid., pp. 249-51.
20. Peter F. Drucker, *The Effective Executive* (New York: Harper & Row, 1967).
21. Ibid., p. 44.
22. Ibid., p. 69.
23. Ibid., p. 69.
24. Rensis Likert, *New Patterns of Management* (New York: McGraw-Hill, 1961), pp. 26-27.
25. From Leonard, V. A., *The Police Enterprise: Its Organization and Management*, 1970, pp. 14-15. Courtesy of Charles C Thomas, Publisher, Springfield, Illinois.
26. Sayles and Strauss, *Human Behavior in Organizations*, p. 378.
27. Pfiffner and Sherwood, *Administrative Organization*, p. 20.
28. Ibid., p. 24.
29. Ibid., p. 23.

REVIEW QUESTIONS

1. What is an *appeal channel*? What is its value?
2. In what ways has communications flow within an organization changed in the last few years?
3. Give an example of an occasion when an informal exchange of information might have a better effect if the information went through formal channels.
4. At what level is policy formed in a criminal justice agency?
5. Several barriers to effective communications are listed. Please name at least five of those barriers and describe ways they may be overcome.
6. How is cybernetics applied to administrative communications?
7. Is there any good effect from a rumor?
8. Define "policy."
9. What are the four occasions when committees are particularly useful, according to Newman?
10. Under what conditions would you *not* utilize a committee?

5 Personnel Management

In the preceding sections of this book we have addressed some weighty problems regarding organization and management of the several criminal justice agencies: Goals and objectives must be clearly enunciated and agreed upon between the chief executive, his superiors, and his constituency; divisions of work in accordance with a master plan of operations and based upon the organization's objectives must lead to the establishment of various operating units to perform the basic tasks of the department and to serve the needs of the organization; lines of authority-accountability relationships must be drawn along with the channels of communication to assure a smooth-flowing system. Now that all these preliminaries have been attended to, the most important step looms into view—staffing the organization. Without people an organization is a lifeless skeleton; without careful and intelligent staffing, all that we have covered in the previous four chapters is meaningless rhetoric.

In this chapter we cover those aspects of personnel management which are more directly related to the responsibilities of the chief executive and his personnel staff: task analyses and position descriptions, selection of personnel, evaluation techniques, promotional procedures, and policy guidelines for personnel management. Supervision and training are personnel management topics too, and they will appear in the following chapters.

TASK ANALYSIS

Prior to staffing the organization it is essential to prepare a list of tasks to be performed by the incumbents in each position and to determine in advance which basic skills and academic proficiencies will be minimum prerequisites. Although certain modifications may have to be made as the positions are filled from all available sources, it is best to adopt a general policy that the individual should be adapted to the organization rather than the organization to the individual. If the objectives of the organization are realistic and each of the many positions are designed to meet those objectives, then it is reasonable to expect the individuals selected for the various positions to be qualified prior to their appointment. In *The Effective Executive* Drucker explains:

> One reason for this is that every change in the definition, structure, and position of a job within an organization sets off a chain reaction of changes throughout the entire institution. Jobs in an organization are interdependent and interlocked. One cannot change everybody's work and responsibility just because one has to replace a single man in a single job. To structure a job to a person is almost certain to result in the end in greater discrepancy between the demands of the job and the available talent. It results in a dozen people being uprooted and pushed around in order to accommodate one.[1]

Drucker presents four realistic rules for avoiding the trap of trying to build an organization to fit certain personalities. They are presented here in brief form, but discussed in greater detail in Drucker's excellent book. The first rule is to remember that no job is created by nature or by God; they are designed by fallible men and should not be such that successful performance is impossible. The test of an organization is to make common people achieve uncommon performance. The second rule is to make each job big and demanding, to enable a man to rise to the demands of the job. Third, the executives must know that they have to start with what a man can do rather than what a job requires. Drucker's fourth rule is, "To get strength one has to put up with weakness."[2]

The challenge of task analysis is taxing and time-consuming. An easy alternative is to visit another organization of a similar nature and adopt their successful ideas and practices for one's own. But each organization is not an exact replica of any other that might be serving the same purpose and a similar number of people. The first step is to designate a working title for the position to be studied and the specific objectives assigned to the task. If the position is not already in existence, then many of the procedures that follow will have to be anticipated in "brainstorming" or other types of sessions with small groups of people who will be performing and supervising the tasks. If the job does exist, in another organization or in the same one for which the study is being conducted, it should be borne in mind that a fresh approach with an objective point of view is absolutely essential.

Studying the Job

1. Each separate task should be described: what it is, when it is done and how often during the working period, how the task is performed and in what sequence, the minimum accuracy standard for successful performance, and the knowledge and skills required. Methods for ascertaining some of this information may include the following—some factors may have to be given arbitrary values by the individual performing the analysis: (1) Observe the task in person, by photographs and videotape or motion pictures, by use of a self-reporting log, or by listing them in personal discussions. (2) Ask questions of the person doing the job as he is performing it or by means of a questionaire. (3) Study the materials the performer uses while preparing for the task and while actually performing it; such as training materials, procedure manuals, printed forms, and tools. (4) Have the individual or a monitor (a secretary or assistant or student-intern) maintain a variety of logs at alternate times.

One log might require an individual to keep a running account of his activities throughout his working day in sequence. A requirement that exact times be used will produce some inaccuracy, however, because the 10-minute coffee break expanded to 23 minutes may show as only 20 minutes and certain times when the individual is daydreaming or engaged in other nonproductive activities may be deleted entirely—although many of those nonproductive activities may actually be critical to the task, such as trying to think of some way to successfully bypass step 4 in a 12-step process or actually thinking of some way to justify an argument against performing the task at all. (One of my favorite statements is that if there is no answer to your question, "Why?" either there might be a better way to perform the task or there might not be any legitimate reason why the task should be performed.) A periodic log requires the individual being studied to state specifically what he is doing at the moment an alarm is sounded or a specific time has passed, such as 15 minutes or half an hour. (One time a high-ranking officer was asked to maintain such a log. For some reason it happened that the alarm caught him either talking or doing nothing. His log showed "nothing" so many times that we listed the activity as "administrative long-range planning." In reality, we may have been correct. Another method of recording tasks is to assign a monitor to accompany the individual whose tasks are being studied, to make copious notes, and to devise an analysis from those notes.

2. The individual studying the task should perform the task himself, under the direction of one who regularly performs it, and tape-record the instructions or make notes. Many times the performer who is used to a task may not even be aware of what he is doing; when he is required to teach another person he reinforces his own proficiency.

3. The "critical incident" technique is quite appropriate for the many tasks in criminal justice occupations. There are certain factors that are extremely critical in the performance of tasks under emergency or stress conditions, or when a person's life and reputation are at stake and at the mercy of an individual probation or parole officer, or policeman. What makes a good employee in the eyes of his peers and supervisors may depend on critical factors, although they may not even be consciously taken into account. For example, the good secretary is one who can direct a persistent caller elsewhere in order to make it possible for her boss to finish writing a speech for the next day, and a good police officer is one who can make independent decisions on whether a crime is a felony or misdemeanor and—based on the knowledge that he has—whether or not to effect an arrest. A good prosecuting attorney must decide when to move for a reduction in the charge or a dismissal of the case. A good judge is one who rules correctly in view of the evidence that is constitutionally admissible and what he believes to be fact as opposed to fantasy.

Almost anyone can perform the routine; the effective people in our professions are those who can act and react with wisdom and justice in the exceptional situations. Specifically what the critical factors are for any given position must be determined in advance of the task analysis. Whether an employee performing a task or series of tasks is rated "poor," "mediocre," or "outstanding," may be determined by selecting jury-rated incumbents who fit into those categories and analyzing the specific reasons why they are so rated. Committees and conferences may also be employed to list and assign values to the critical incidents for this study. Although this procedure can also be used for personnel evaluations, the purpose here is to prepare a timely and accurate task list for each position to be studied.

4. A time and motion study should be made. With the aid of charts, diagrams, and a stopwatch each part of a task and the total operation may be timed and analyzed. How often a task is performed and how much total time is devoted to its performance may have a bearing on the skills and knowledge that the individual must demonstrate for placement on that specific job. Time and motion studies, when used in conjunction with flow charts, will show integration and coordination between tasks and the people who perform them in their respective positions. Interdependence of tasks may determine their placement within an organization, and their respective supervisors should be aware of the relationships. When using this procedure to study tasks, the analyst would take several sets of times under a variety of circumstances. Average times of average performers plus additional allowances for interruptions should be incorporated into standard task times.

5. Relationships should be identified. Interdependence of tasks is significant for coordination. Authority-accountability arrangements should

also be identified, such as a determination of which decisions may be made by the individual performing the task and which require another person to make them. The other person's accessibility for decision making would certainly have a direct bearing on the task under study.

Job Descriptions

Following a detailed analysis of the several tasks to be performed by each individual, job specifications should be prepared. General information should include: (1) title and definition of the positon, (2) placement in the organization and relative position in the organizational structure (assistant director, or assistant to—), (3) example of tasks to be performed, (4) distinguishing characteristics about the position, (5) minimum basic requirements (age, education, experience, skills), (6) desirable knowledge, skills, and abilities, and (7) financial remuneration.

Here is an example of a job specification for a secretary:[3]

DEFINITION

Under general supervision, performs varied and complex clerical and secretarial work involved in assisting a department head in the conduct of office details and performs such other related duties as may be required.

EXAMPLES OF DUTIES

Interviews and secures information from callers; makes appointments and introduces callers; represents the department on initial contact with public; relieves supervisor of unnecessary administrative details. Takes and transcribes dictation. Writes letters either independently or in accordance with oral and written directions. Assists in the preparation of budget estimates and checking of payrolls. Sets up and maintains files and card indexes. Assembles information and prepares reports; may take dictation and transcribe minutes of meetings. May supervise the work of a clerical staff and performs such other related duties as may be required.

DISTINGUISHING FEATURES OF THE CLASS

Employees in this class perform responsible and difficult clerical work which normally includes some minor administrative activities and responsibility for independent action requiring the exercise of judgment in making decisions in accordance with the policies and practices of the department. An employee in this class usually is immediately subordinate to a department head and may exercise supervision over one or more employees assisting with the more routine clerical details.

RECOMMENDED BASIC QUALIFICATIONS

Training and Experience: Completion of the twelfth grade, including courses in stenography, typing and office practice, and three years of experience in stenographic and clerical work, two of which must have been at the secretarial level, or some equivalent combination of education and experience.
Necessary Special Qualifications: Ability to take shorthand at 100 wpm and ability to type at a corrected speed of 50 wpm.

DESIRABLE KNOWLEDGE, SKILLS AND ABILITIES

Thorough knowledge of business English and spelling. Knowledge of business letter writing and business forms. Ability to perform difficult clerical work; ability to follow oral and written directions. Ability to deal tactfully, but effectively, with the public. Ability to effectively supervise and direct the work of others and to provide a neat and orderly personal appearance.

Figure 14.   Example of a Job Specification

Specific items of information that must also be available to the person responsible for filling the position include the following: (1) What tasks are performed by the individual? (2) How is each task performed? (3) How often—per hour, day, month—is the task performed? (4) How well must it be done for effective results? (5) What knowledge is essential? (6) What additional knowledge is desirable? (7) What basic skills are required? (8) What extra skills are desirable? (9) What are the prerequisites for this position as to age, physical ability, health, language proficiency, unique talents, and other desirable qualifications? (10) From a professional-vocational standpoint, where is this occupation now and where is it going to be in the future? (11) What are the critical factors that directly affect effective performance?

Most of the positions in criminal justice organizations are generally civil service positions. Lifetime, faithful, and devoted service are desirable characteristics of most type of government employment, or so it seems. Many organizations have their own retirement systems, which makes it impossible for the employees of one city or county government to transfer to another without forfeiting a considerable investment in time or money, or both. In keeping with this "closed shop" concept, it is most likely that many of the higher-level positions in an organization are closed to all but those who are currently employed and filling lower positions. The higher positions provide incentives to employees to remain on the job for many years with the ambition of someday receiving a coveted advancement. A more recent approach on the part of many agencies has been to recruit on an open basis, making it possible for well-qualified individuals to step directly into positions higher than entrance-level.

As the "lateral entry" concept has grown, so has the specialist trend. At one time, virtually every position within the police organization was filled with a sworn police officer. Property clerk, records clerk, jailer, communications operator, statistics clerk, personnel director, budget control officer, business manager, and most all of the positions were male police officers. Exactly why all positions were filled with police officers nobody seems to know—except that "it has always been that way"—but in some of the smaller departments, by having all employees be police officers there was a ready reserve on duty at all times in the event of some great need. Except in the very small organization of any type, whether probation department, correctional institution, district attorney's office, or police department, it is economically unsound as well as administratively foolish to perpetuate such a practice. Through careful task analyses it will be possible to identify the individual characteristics of each position within an organization and make a listing of essential and desirable qualifications. The next step is to select those people who are best qualified to fill the various positions. If this theory is carried into practice, it will no longer be necessary to have highly skilled deputy probation officers, attorneys, police lieutenants, or youth counselors performing such unrelated jobs as records clerk, radio dispatcher, or custodian of the school supplies in the storeroom. Each of those positions are also important to the effective operation of the organization and should be filled with the best-qualified candidates.

An example of a very extensive task analysis is a study performed for the Los Angeles Police and Fire Departments.[4] A careful evaluation led to their statement that "sixty-four assignments,...presently being filled by sworn personnel, were considered by the consultants not to require sworn personnel...."[5] Their list of the many positions calling for civilian (non-sworn) personnel included one captain, one lieutenant, and most of those at the policeman-policewoman level; the rest were sergeants or investigators. The positions list included: abandoned vehicle appraiser, jailer, property officer, analytical and personnel officer, parking lot supervisor, carpenter working foreman, metal shop foreman, supply commander, officer in charge of purchasing and receiving, most of the laboratory personnel, electronics technician, artist, forms analyst, and speech writer. A temporary or emergency assignment to any one of these positions would not be out of order, but there is no valid reason why police officers should fill those positions. As a police administrator myself, the response that I most often received whenever a discussion arose about "depolicing" (or "contaminating," in the minds of some old-timers) was that only a policeman understands the police operations and outsiders, or less-qualified people, should not be allowed to dilute the police strength. My response to that was that I had managed restaurants for several years and was able to operate efficiently without a single policeman on the payroll.

RECRUITMENT AND SELECTION

There are so many different professions, paraprofessions, and occupations in the various component agencies of the Criminal Justice System that it is difficult to illustrate examples without representing one particular occupation. Actually, little has been done to make any drastic changes in most of the positions throughout the system. Clerical and the myriad miscellaneous nonspecialized and nonprofessional positions are usually filled in about the same way as they have been for the past several decades. The same may be true of other positions in many jurisdictions.

Recruitment for each position, regardless of its place in the hierarchical structure or whether it is for the beginning level of clerk-trainee or for an especially qualified specialist, should be for the best qualified. The position should be attractive to the candidate, it should offer a challenge, an opportunity for growth and advancement, and a competitive salary commensurate with the position. Many positions in the Criminal Justice System have no comparable position in the business or commercial world; and any attempt to compare the positions with any other occupations is foolhardy and self-defeating. For example, one employee-generated newspaper decried the lack of support of police officers as "true professionals" and then went into a discourse on the disparity of pay, using as examples of the policeman's low pay the day wages received by electricians, plumbers, and cement masons. Although the policeman showed less pay per hour, the comparison itself was irrelevant. What position in private industry is equivalent to that of the parole agent? The attorney who works for the district attorney can surely demand a pay comparable to that of other attorneys in public service, but can hardly command a salary equivalent to that of F. Lee Bailey or Melvin Belli, or a legendary Perry Mason.

Should candidates be selected who are not residents of the local jurisdiction? This is sometimes the subject of a bitter city hall debate. The public servant who works for the county or city government is expected by some political representatives to reside in the community he serves. The reasons they give are: to keep them near their work, to assure their residence in the community, to keep their children in the community's schools, and to maintain their personal as well as professional interest in the community. The elected officials must reside within the boundaries of the city or county they serve and have the interests of their constituents at heart, including the unemployment problem. They are similarly concerned with the taxes generated by property owners and local purchasing, and all other types of expenditures that contribute to the prosperity of their community. If the government they serve pays them well, it would seem logical that the elected officials would expect the employees of that community to demonstrate some loyalty to the same community through their employment.

Personnel may be recruited through cadet programs or agency-sponsored clubs.
Courtesy: Police Department, Pasadena, California

However idealistic the concept, in practice it is unrealistic and archaic to expect all of the best-qualified candidates to reside within the governmental boundaries prior to their employment, or to expect them to move out of their homes after a specified period of time to comply with a required-residence rule. Many cities do not pay their employees enough money to expect them to buy property within the city limits. Other cities are so large that the employee will probably choose to move into the city to avoid spending four hours a day on the expressway. Selecting all candidates from within the local governmental boundaries may address the unemployment problem, but at the same time may not assure that community of the quality of service they should expect from the criminal justice agencies that serve them.

Recruitment should be carried on at the places where the qualified persons are probably located, but the local talent should not be overlooked. In order to favor home-town residents, it may be recommended that local residents be given precedence if all other factors are equal. Colleges offering courses in the disciplines most compatible with the needs of the agency doing the recruiting should be visited regularly and considered a constant source of candidates. Divisions of sociology and psychology as well as various administration of justice, corrections, police science, criminology, and allied fields should be continuously cultivated for candidate-referral, and the many other divisions of colleges and universities should not be overlooked either.

The military services have been an excellent source of candidates for the police service, not so much for the servicemen's background of regimented life as for their youth and good health. Young men and women emerging from military life usually have not committed themselves to career goals to the same extent as their counterparts who either have not served or had completed their service some time earlier. Competition is keen and we are all looking for the same men and women: young, intelligent, ambitious, healthy, willing to learn, and eager to embrace the many professions and occupations that we represent. All recruiters descending upon a source of employable men and women are competing in a buyer's market. What we have to sell is a lifetime of dedicated public service in exchange for pay that will make no one rich, working hours and conditions that are usually somewhat less than ideal, and stimulating lively interaction with the entire community in what is sometimes considerably less than a friendly and hospitable environment. In most of the situations involving arrest, prosecution, imprisonment, and control of the private lives of humans, at least one person is unhappy with whatever action we take. Yet, many aspects of the several occupations in criminal justice are very rewarding and more than amply compensate for what little inconvenience we may suffer. There is no type of human public service more essential to the safety and well-being of the nation's peoples than the Criminal Justice System. This is usually the criminal justice recruiter's sales presentation, used to attract candidates.

The original screening process should be conducted at the time of the initial application. The application form must comply with fair employment laws regarding nondiscrimination and certain questions of a personal nature must be respected as private, but the questionnaire must call for every question to be answered regarding qualification for the specific position to be filled. This is possible with a standard form if an instruction sheet lists the specifications for the position to be filled and lists the qualifications necessary for that position. Psychologist Henry Smith states that the application form, properly used, can serve as an objective personnel selection instrument.[6] His thesis is that a careful study of incumbents in the various positions will reveal requirements in those individuals whose performance and tenure, and other factors such as accident-proneness and productivity, are known. Weighting those factors on positive and negative scales may lead to the development of minimum point scores for employment with predicted success and long tenure. For example, if a married versus single status has historically had a positive or negative effect on performance, or if the number and age of the individual's children has some sort of effect, each of the factors would be assigned a designated weight. The total score would be the determining factor as to whether the candidate is likely to succeed on the job. To my knowledge, no criminal justice agency has utilized any such method for selection, at least not consciously, although the personal interview method is almost always certain to reflect subjective biases of the interviewers and usually does involve weighting in the process.

Personal Interview

Selecting interviewers at random, introducing them to each other for the first time just a few minutes prior to an oral board session, and then moving right into a series of interviews of several candidates has questionable validity. Selection of board members should be made with discrimination to assure a well-qualified board that will select those candidates best-qualified for the position. The board should be thoroughly oriented to the general needs of the organization and the specific needs in filling the position. Even though the oral board may consist of one or more members of the organization, it should not be left to chance to assume that the interviewers will know what qualities are essential to the job.

Oral interviews conducted on a casual basis are hardly any different than selection by chance. In a discussion by Smith on several oral interview programs studied at various times, "Did only 4 percent better than chance," "Was a big waste of time," and "No" were answers to this question: "Are the judgments he (the interviewer) makes with the interview more accurate than those he makes without it?"[7] Whether the interview serves any valid purpose actually depends on the selection and training of the interviewers. The application is designed to ascertain biographical information about the candidate. Written examinations and various personality or psychological tests are used to gauge his knowledge and emotional-mental qualifications for the position. The oral interview is left to serve the purpose of casting for the role to be filled. One of the principal questions the board answers, whether or not the members admit it, is whether the candidate fits the image, if his personal beliefs are at least compatible with those of the board members. The chief executive is looking for a self-image at least to some extent, because each employee is ultimately responsible to the executive and serves as his representative in whatever action he takes.

If the selection interview is utilized, as is the case in nearly all criminal justice agencies (required in many cases), certain guidelines should be followed: (1) carefully select and prepare the interviewers for their task; (2) substitute rankings of the candidates rather than numerical ratings, a process that involves rank-ordering the available candidates from most desirable to least desirable for the position; (3) have all candidates in the group from which the selections are to be made interviewed by the same interviewers; (4) rank all candidates according to some standards that all members of the board agree to and ask standardized questions for comparison purposes; and (5) require the interviewers to state the reasons for their decisions on the candidates, particularly those they rank at either extreme. If one interviewer ranks a candidate very high and another ranks the same candidate at the other end of the scale, it may be wise to have them discuss their differences in evaluation. They may not change their opinions but they will at least know on what grounds they disagree.

Stress interviews conducted by interviewers who are not qualified in making psychological evaluations may not produce valid judgments. It is not unusual for some candidates to sell themselves during the first minute or two of the interview and for others to "shoot themselves down" because they do not pass the attitude test. Interviewers should be careful to avoid directing the candidates into an impossible line of questioning that even the board members cannot answer intelligently, and then failing the candidate because he cannot glibly talk his way out of the corner. Objective value-judgments should be made on the basis of objective interview methods.

Psychological testing

Test batteries should be packaged for each position to be filled and should be considered both valid and reliable for the selection of people to fill the specific position. Interest tests may serve as a guide to both candidate and personnel technician as to whether the candidate is likely to be happy or contented to some degree with his choice of occupation. Along with tests to determine suitability for each occupation, it might be advisable to describe in realistic, nondramatized terms the actual tasks to be performed in each job. It is particularly important, I believe, that some of the myths about the glamorous criminal justice positions be dispelled to such an extent that the serious candidate will actually be able to look at the position in its correct perspective and then make his judgment accordingly. A man or woman who loves to be outdoors and shows an interest in working with people might find himself in an office working on statistics unless each position is described accurately and more care is given to the matter of filling each position with a more sophisticated placement procedure than is presently employed.

Aptitude and ability tests

Many civil service examinations are merely intelligence tests that serve at least two purposes. The first purpose is to identify those whose mental aptitude scores predict success on the job because of their superior ability to learn new concepts and procedures; the second purpose may be simply to reduce the number of candidates to only 2 or 3 times the number of openings that may exist at any one time. This second purpose may be as frequently employed as the first, because many civil service laws regulating testing provide that the personnel department may require a minimum score of 70 or some other raw percentage but may also adjust the scores up or down to meet existing needs, which may include too many or too few qualified candidates. A raw percentage score of 80 percent correct may be adjusted to equal 70 percent, or the scores may be adjusted upward.

Positions requiring certain basic aptitudes may call for specialized examinations to select those candidates who demonstrate the necessary skills. For example, an attorney may be required to show proof that he has particular knowledge of criminal laws and procedures in addition to his membership in the state bar and people who will be required to operate motor vehicles or aircraft should demonstrate refined skills in addition to general qualifications. Police officers who are expected to interpret their observations in terms of value judgments may be required to pass "situational tests," such as those discussed in the March 1966 issue of the *Journal of Criminal Law, Criminology, and Police Science* and studied by the Cincinnati Police Department.[8] The situational tests were "role-played," constructed situations of various types that the typical officer would encounter while on the job: missing persons reports, routine and unusual situations observed along a route of travel with objective tests given at the end of the tour, and "bull sessions" to determine attitudes, prejudices, and other personality characteristics that might affect the individual's later performance on the job, if selected.

Psychological screening of police personnel has been practiced at least since the early 1950s and on an experimental basis prior to that time.[9] The police officer's direct exposure to hostile people in times of severe emotional crisis has stimulated considerable research in psychological testing of police applicants. Some of the findings to date have been at least interesting and promise further study, even though nothing conclusive has been reported as to precise instruments for the measurement of police officer potential through psychological/psychiatric testing.

Stephen Nowicki reported that some tentative hypotheses have emerged from studies that "policemen are normal in adjustment, aggressive tendencies, and intellectual ability."[10] Quoting an earlier study undertaken by the Kansas Highway Patrol[11] Nowicki pointed out that "law enforcement has a facility for attracting disturbed applicants who see in law enforcement the opportunity to impose their will upon people by virtue of police authority."[12]

I suggest that this statement be quoted accurately, that law enforcement has a facility for *attracting* the type of person just described. There is no justification for any assumptions to be made from that statement as to the percentage of incumbent officers already on the job who may *possess* such undesirable propensities. It seems that this statement underlines the critical need for carefully screening through various means of psychological testing all candidates for positions of authority in the entire Criminal Justice System. The attraction would not be limited to the police ranks, but would possibly extend to any occupation or profession that involves the supervision or control of people. To make a statement such as "the police are emotionally disturbed" would be as injudicious as to say that "orthopedic surgeons are sadists" on the basis of a study that might show some medical students who had indicated a preference for orthopedic surgery had shown sadistic tendencies in psychological testing. The personnel technician should be advised of the types of individuals he should devise methods for identifying; he should develop test batteries and methods to screen out the sadist, the masochist, and those individuals whose personal deviations would be deleterious to their effectiveness as peace officers, prosecuting attorneys, guards, probation officers, or any other practitioner in criminal justice.

The Background Investigation

Prior to the employment of any professional specialist in the criminal justice components of *Police, Court,* and *Corrections,* many organizations routinely conduct background investigations on the candidates and those with whom they come into contact on a daily or regular basis. Under no circumstances should such an investigation take on the nature of a witch hunt, but an effort should be made to identify any behavior pattern, personality characteristic, or latent tendency on the part of the individual which would interfere with his effective performance on the job or damage the good reputation of the organization. In virtually all positions it is mandatory that a person with a record of one or more felony convictions be rejected. Behavior patterns of personality disorder, inability to get along with previous employers and fellow employees, unusual aggressive conduct, and other undesirable characteristics should be identified and taken into account at the time the decision is made to employ the person. Unlike the individual who maintains a private life, the public servant abdicates some of his privacy when he enters a public life.

For the purpose of determining the good character of the candidate and his abstinence from criminal conduct, the following people might be contacted during a background investigation: state and federal crime information clearing houses to determine criminal record, if any; police agencies at places of residence and employment; motor vehicle departments for driving and collision records; schools, trade schools, and colleges attended; employers and fellow employees; parents, relatives, spouse(s); a spiritual mentor; military leaders; a physician and other professional consultants; present and former neighbors; lenders and other financial affiliates; and social contacts. The investigator should avoid a personal meeting with the candidate prior to or during the investigation so that he might not form any personal opinions regarding the candidate which could in any way affect the investigator's objective reports of facts and opinions provided to him through a variety of sources.

Probation

Every employee, regardless of position or factors involved in his employment, should serve a probationary period, during which time his continuous appraisal will determine whether he shall gain tenure on the job. The exact amount of time varies from one department to another, but one year to eighteen months seems to be about average for probation. Actually, no employee should ever develop an attitude that he personally possesses the position, but he does need to have some assurance that he has tenure and is relatively free from the capricious or petulant behavior of some superior-ranking employee who might arbitrarily seek his removal from his position. Frequent evaluations and counseling sessions should be characteristic of the probationary period. If, during the probationary period, or at any time until the last day, there are serious reservations concerning the suitability of the employee, the decision should be made in favor of the organization. Continued tenure, even beyond the probationary period, should always be contingent upon continued high quality performance.

PERSONNEL EVALUATION

Employee evaluation serves a number of purposes for the benefit of the administrator and the individual being evaluated. The individual wishes to have feedback from his superiors on how he is performing, where he needs improvement, and under what circumstances he is meeting or exceeding the organization's minimum standards. "If you don't hear anything, everything is going well" is not an accurate statement. As a matter of fact, the employee who is doing well may receive frequent reinforcement and assistance from condescending supervisors and the employee who is not doing so well may be allowed to slip into oblivion and develop bad habits, compounding them to such an extent that there becomes no alternative but to provide him an opportunity to develop his bad habits elsewhere.

Evaluations should be valid, reliable, and reasonably frequent. They should measure what they are intended to measure: usually quality and quantity of performance, sometimes attitudes and reasoning ability. The instruments used should be designed so that they are consistent with respect to standards among employees, so that individuals may be compared with their own earlier performance and also with established norms so that accurate value assessments are possible. There should be frequent assessments, but too often or too seldom will have diminishing returns. Too seldom will lead to failure in any sort of follow-up system. If the employee is advised to improve in a certain category and is given some ideas how he might improve, the program is meaningless unless the follow-up is within a reasonable time so that reinforcement or corrective steps may be taken. On the other hand, if the evaluations are too close together the employee has no opportunity to grow and improve in his position; the evaluator will be repeating his advice seeing no demonstrable improvement, although it may be there, but slight. The *balance* is imperative.

Uses for a Personnel Evaluation System

Evaluation must have valid uses and be designed to correspond with the goals and objectives of the organization. The evaluation form design, techniques in filling in the required information, training of the evaluators, selling of the purpose and function of the system to the individuals being evaluated, and the actual business of managing the system (timing, distributing, collecting, counseling, and filing) all take valuable time and energy for everyone concerned. Some of the uses for evaluations are:

1. Aiding in the identification of training needs and development of training programs.
2. Screening and selecting employees for transfers of assignment and for promotions.
3. Determining minimum and average standards of performance for each job classification.
4. Providing the employee with a set of guidelines so that he knows where he stands in relation to the department's standards and expectations.
5. Giving the employee a method for seeing himself as management sees him.
6. Aiding in the determination of salary adjustments where merit is a factor.

7. Providing an evaluation scale on the employee in relation to his own prior performance and/or the performance of others in the same category.
8. Identifying strengths and weaknesses of the individual, of the supervisor in some cases, and of the organization in others.
9. Serving as a report to higher administration on the specific performance of individuals and the general performance of working units or divisions.

What Is Evaluated?

An evaluation should have a purpose. If each job classification has been accurately analyzed and assigned certain proficiency minimums, and if it has been determined what will be the minimum and desirable qualifications of the candidate for the position, then the evaluation of the individual filling that position should be used as a means of determining how he stands in relationship to the standard at the beginning of his career and later how he compares as he matures in the position. The management should know the qualities that are required and desirable for optimum effectiveness, but more important is the demand that the employee himself know what he is expected to be and to do. He must know how he is doing in his own eyes as well as in the eyes of his peers, and certainly he should know how he stands in the judgment of his supervisors.

Some of the qualities, or factors, considered in evaluations are:

KNOWLEDGE. A selection interview or some preliminary testing was probably conducted to determine whether the candidate for the position had the basic intelligence to comprehend the instructions he would receive while on the job and the adaptability to grasp the manipulative and performance portions of the job. Once employed, however, the employee is expected to gain certain levels of knowledge as he progresses. These include the language that is peculiar to criminal justice operations, the organizational structure and function, laws and procedures, regulations, policies, protocol, and the internal communications network.

SKILLS. Some positions may require no proficiency at the time of entry, many others may require the beginner to demonstrate a few basic skills. The management may have established certain standards for specific periods of time as the employee progresses; learning curves differ for individuals and some highly technical tasks may require longer periods of time to learn than others. Proficiencies may regress in the case of some employees; these should receive attention and some remedial effort.

COMPATIBILITY. Although some managers may heavily stress skills and knowledge as the most important factors to evaluate in an employee, probably a more critical factor is whether or not the individual can get along with his peers and supervisors on the job. Many errors can be overlooked and corrective efforts made if the person making the errors has the social sensitivity to apologize, express regret at having made the mistake, and visually demonstrate through unwritten communicative means that he is enthusiastic about improving in whatever area his peers and supervisors believe he should. Some attitudes of arrogance, disrespect, unconcern, or exaggerated selfishness may destroy an individual's value to an organization regardless of his knowledge or skills.

LEADERSHIP QUALITIES. Most criminal justice professional and paraprofessional positions require some degree of leadership—leadership of other employees and leadership of many of the people who are served by the organization. The job requirements include the direction or guidance of people under a variety of situations, many times under severe emotional stress.

PERSONALITY. The ability to cope with a multitude of situations and people with all sorts of cultural and social differences under as many different types of situations requires a certain type of personality. The evaluation of the employee in this regard should be as individualized as the particular position he fills in the organization. It may be wise to have those qualities desirable for each position be described by a personnel psychologist, who would explain the characteristics and the reason why each is important to the classification, plus some guidelines on how to evaluate them. Inexperienced and untrained raters may not be qualified to make judgments in this portion of the evaluation process.

SELF-RELIANCE. Most professional positions, and many of the related occupations in the Criminal Justice System, require self-reliance and independent decision making at the operational level. The individual is expected to carry out most of his routine activities on a continuous basis without close supervision. Many of the decisions he makes must be done under conditions that would be impracticable to require supervisory approval prior to action. The individual should be evaluated on his ability and willingness to make decisions and on the results of those decisions.

COMPLIANCE WITH SUPERVISION. Teamwork and coordination of activities are essential to criminal justice occupations as well as to most others. Self-reliance and willingness to act without directions are so strongly emphasized—as they should be—that a conscious effort must be made to coordinate one's own activities with those of others under the single leadership of a supervisor in special conditions. The employee should be evaluated on the basis of his ability to meet such changing needs.

SELF-CONTROL. Temper, prejudices, and personal problems may overshadow an individual's effectiveness if he doesn't have the self-control to operate effectively while keeping them in places where they do not cause interference with the job. The degree to which the employee can control his weakness should be included in a separate category, or it may be classified under compatibility.

APPEARANCE. Everyone is expected to dress and groom himself in accordance with the role that he plays.

QUANTITY AND QUALITY OF PRODUCTION. A medical doctor is not evaluated on the number of tonsils he removes during a given period of time, nor is a judge given a numerical score based on how many defendants he finds guilty or innocent. There are, however, certain occupations that involve some sort of production. Wherever applicable, the measurements should reflect quality along with quantity. A police officer may be evaluated on how he appears to succeed in family disputes by the absence of repeat calls rather than the number of husbands he books into the city jail. Two probation officers may handle an identical number of cases, but there is such a difference in the individuals under their supervision that one officer is able to effectively supervise every one of his clients, while his brother officer is overloaded and totally ineffective with nearly half of his clients. To say that one officer is doing a better job than the other without any other criteria for evaluation is totally worthless and would do an injustice to both of them.

Other qualities that might be found on evaluation lists, which are usually self-explanatory, are presence of mind, loyalty, industry, forcefulness, aggressiveness, physical fitness, dependability, punctuality, personal habits, maturity, job interest, expression, potential, overall value to the organization, understanding of human nature, and initiative. Whatever characteristics are included on the evaluation form, it should be a basic requirement that each factor be defined as well as listed; there should be examples or comparative scales for the evaluator to use to assure some uniformity and continuity in the evaluation system. The employee who is rated each successive time by a different supervisor, and who actually does show improvement in certain factors and/or lack of improvement in others, should be carefully evaluated so that there is an accurate picture of the individual for management to have when studying his progress.

The halo effect can easily influence the evaluator's own judgment ability and should be guarded against. To some supervisors there are certain individuals who seem to epitomize the ideal employee in all respects: superior knowledge, unusual personality, total mastery of required skills, and all other factors rated at the absolute top of the scale. At the other end of the spectrum there are those employees who can do nothing right, are totally stupid, and have no mastery of skills whatsoever. In both cases, the evaluator should be conscious of the fact that he might be the unsuspecting victim of a "snow job," or else his prejudices might be getting in the way of his vision. Each individual should be evaluated on the basis of separate factors on a one-at-a-time basis.

Another problem for management with the typical evaluation system is that supervisors are hesitant to rate the new employee too high, perhaps where he belongs because of his unusual talents and abilities, because there would be no way for them to show that he was improving over a period of time. With the rater who rationalizes in that manner, every employee would begin low and progress a little higher each time. In my opinion, this perpetuates mediocrity and is little different than the system that requires the employee to show some improvement in order to receive merit incentives or pay raises. If the employee were to perform immediately at maximum efficiency and meet all ideal criteria for the position he fills and then continue in such an outstanding fashion, his evaluation would show "no improvement," therefore actually penalizing him for starting out so well. Such a philosophy of improvement is false wisdom and should be abandoned in favor of a more realistic approach.

Evaluation Methods

Once the factors to be evaluated are decided upon, the standards defined, and the general guidelines developed for the relative values of the several factors in relationship with each other, the rating method should be determined. The method used is actually less important than the wisdom with which one uses that method. Managers and supervisors will find certain methods most satisfactory to their own operation and their individual personalities, but it would be advantageous to employ at least two different methods to assure a more accurate evaluation system. Although there are dozens of variations, the five basic methods of evaluation are (1) ranking, (2) rating scale, (3) essay, (4) check list, and (5) forced choice.

RANKING METHOD. The ranking method may be used for reasonably stable groups; the principal theme in the system is comparing each individual with his peers who are performing the same functions. One would imagine that seniority would be an advantage in this type of rating. It is, providing the senior employee is also of superior quality in the eyes of the supervisor. An overall ranking of all employees in one unit may be made, listing the most valuable to the least valuable. Then each of the several rating factors are handled similarly. The supervisor is forced to make a choice between employees and, if he is honest and objective, may find that he cannot be influenced by the halo effect and consistently rank one employee at the top of all of his lists. Although this method may have some value in identifying individuals with the greatest worth in certain categories in comparison with their peers, it should not be used as the only basis for individual evaluations. An employee ranking at the bottom of the list may actually be an excellent employee showing considerable improvement from one valuation period to another; but when compared with other individuals in his unit who may be slightly above him each time, his evaluation might not show any improvement at all. When compared with another group of peers he then enters an entirely different set of circumstances.

This method may be used by assigning a percentage score to each evaluated factor in comparison with an imaginary model, who would represent 100 percent in each factor. For example, in cases when volume of production might be a factor, the perfect score would require 100 units of work to be accomplished during a specified period of time. The employee producing 40 units would rate 40 percent, the one producing 18 units would earn a score of 18 percent, and so on. This scoring process might be complicated by a corollary scoring system involving the quality of completed projects. Although there should be no quota system in traffic law enforcement, some supervisor may consider a subordinate officer below average if he issues less than 30 citations per month. Perhaps all the officers on that shift are evaluated on the basis of their citation tally in comparison with this standard of 30. The difficulty in the system presents itself when one officer may issue 30 citations that eventually result in 16 convictions, and another officer issues 23 citations that result in 20 convictions. Which officer is the better of the two according to this particular system? There are many variables, such as whether the supervisor has access to the officer's radio log to find out what else he had been doing besides writing traffic tickets, statistics on convictions for citations issued, or the accuracy of each officer in filling out the citation forms.

An advantage in using this type of evaluation system might be in the selection of individuals for transfer or promotion on the basis of special interests or unusual skills. Another use of this method might be that of allowing the people being evaluated to know how they are rated in comparison with each other, thus creating a basis for competition, such as in the development of proficiencies in basic skills.

RATING SCALE. The rating scale is probably the most commonly used evaluation method. It is possible to evaluate an individual on the basis of his own progress since a previous evaluation or to rate him in comparison with some set of standards that might be created for the purpose of stimulating his improvement. Many variations of this method are used. One variation is the continuum, or the numerical scale, depicted in figure 15. Each item can be reduced to a numerical value, or a series of scores may be computed and totals compared with minimum or average standards. When this method is used, it is advisable that each point on the scale be described. For example, whether *outstanding* or *superior* would be considered as first and second, or vice versa, depends largely on the decision of the individual who designates their places on the scale. Variations of the rating method may consist of checking boxes or selecting from a multiple choice of from 3 to 7 (or more) items in rank order. For example, the choices might range from: weak, average, strong; or poor, below average, average, above average, excellent; or the choice may be in the form of percentages, such as lowest 5%, next 10%, next 10%, middle 50%, and so forth.

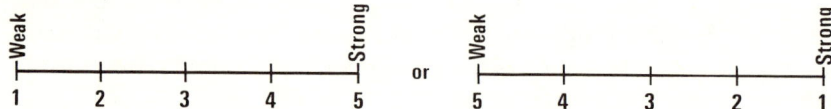

Figure 15. The continuum type of rating. A statement is made about a certain quality in the individual to be rated, such as "The person's loyalty to the organization is: (mark appropriate place on scale) or (circle one) _____."

ESSAY METHOD. The third evaluation method is that of requiring several supervisors who have had the opportunity to observe the individual being evaluated to write short essays on each type of activity they observed. The supervisor is required to describe what activity he observed, give his opinion, and write a critical appraisal of the employee's performance. When utilizing this method it is necessary for the supervisor to define his terms and to avoid the use of superlatives in favor of more descriptive and objective appraisals. He may be required to justify any extremely high or extremely low evaluation. When this is the case, careful attention should be paid to the supervisor who tends to rate all employees "down the middle" to avoid the extra task of writing explanations.

CHECK LIST. The fourth method of evaluation is the check list. A list of critical factors and routine tasks that must be performed in accordance with certain minimum standards may be merely checked off to show that the employee conforms to requirements. He may demonstrate proficiency in each of a list of skills and knowledge or the list may be designed to show that he performs his tasks in the correct sequence, when sequence is a factor. The check list may be designed in the form of a series of questions about various factors calling for yes or no responses. A question may ask if the subject being evaluated can perform certain tasks without direct supervision, or whether additional training in a certain subject is needed. Although this type of evaluation form might prove ineffective for purposes of comparing an individual's performance with a previous rating on the basis of scores or points earned, it may immediately point out deficiencies, strengths, and needs for training.

FORCED CHOICE. In the forced-choice method of evaluation the rater is confronted with a series of multiple choices from which he must choose one answer which most nearly describes the attitude, or ability, or performance of the person being evaluated. The choices from which the supervisor chooses may appear equally favorable, yet they have been carefully assigned different weights by a personnel psychologist who has studied the job being evaluated and determined those factors that are most critical to the successful performance of the incumbent on the job. The reason the values of each response are kept confidential and not disclosed to the raters is to prevent a supervisor's bias from being reflected in a high rating for a favorite subordinate. A supervisor might be giving an employee what he believes to be an extremely high rating, but he may actually be doing just the opposite. Of course, after one or two uses of the form, and after the reactions following receipt of the final scores, the form might outlive its usefulness. The key would be in the careful assignment of weights and the ability of the personnel psychologist to maintain the reliability and validity of the instrument. An accurate task analysis would be used as a basis for this type of format, plus a series of conferences with various supervisors and administrators to compile descriptive phrases of the various characteristics of each factor in their respective rank order.

Each of the statements on the forced-choice scale would be assigned a positive or negative value, depending on its importance in relationship to the task being evaluated. Values would change from one task to another; they may have no bearing at all in some cases and be critical factors in others. The weights would not be published, but would be computed and tallied in a series of major categories by the personnel technician. The supervisor and the person being evaluated would be advised of the total score. The major disadvantage of this type of evaluation would be that the supervisor could not discuss the rating with the subordinate because he would not know whether he was rating the subject high or low in each category; neither would the person being rated know where his strong and weak points were, because to tell him would disclose the weights assigned to each factor and then the secrecy of the different designations would be compromised.

For example, in these three questions, three statements such as the following may be assigned weights of 0, 1, and 2, respectively, although the rating supervisor may believe that he has chosen the highest by selecting the first one:

   _____a. Is very patient.
   _____b. Arrives at conclusions logically.
   _____c. Assumes responsibility for his own errors.

In the following example, the respective values might be 0, 2, and 1:

   _____a. Delegates work very wisely.
   _____b. Is exceptionally fair.
   _____c. Inspires his associates.

In this group, the rating weights might be 0, 0, minus 2, plus 2:

   _____a. Has a well-rounded personality.
   _____b. Lacks force and drive.
   _____c. Tends to be overbearing.
   _____d. Shows foresight.

One type of the rating scale method appears in figure 16. The second method, depicted in figure 17, utilizes a combination of rating and the essay.

Suggestions For Evaluations

Here are a few salient suggestions for consideration in the introduction and continued maintenance of a personnel evaluation system:

1. Use a jury method—having three or more supervisors—to rate the employee. This may not necessarily include his

PROBATIONARY OFFICER EVALUATION

_____   _____
Name and Badge Number   Date(s) covered

Rating Officer:
When marking this report remember that your life or well-being may someday depend on this new officer. An evaluation report, when conscientiously marked, becomes a valuable training aid in this individual's development.

Factors shall be marked on an objective basis with an explanation added on all categories listed as weak or strong. Rating boxes may be marked in ink but each report will require a typewritten summary.

		WEAK	AVERAGE	STRONG
JUDGEMENT	Actions based on sound reasoning.	☐	☐	☐
TEMPERAMENT	Proper self-control; calm in emergencies.	☐	☐	☐
MATURITY	Takes suggestions and criticism well. Profits from advice or criticism.	☐	☐	☐
APPEARANCE	Physical bearing and demeanor correct at all times. Uniform worn properly. Mannerisms generally acceptable.	☐	☐	☐
JOB INTEREST	Interested in all phases of police work. Questions well-directed.	☐	☐	☐
JOB KNOWLEDGE	Adequate ability and knowledge for time on the job. Applies previous experience to advantage.	☐	☐	☐
PERSONALITY	Poise that stimulates confidence; sense of humor; flexible. Pleasing habits and characteristics.	☐	☐	☐
EXPRESSION	Written and oral, clear and concise; uses proper grammar.	☐	☐	☐
INITIATIVE	Recognizes problems or situations that require police action. Displays normal curiosity. Active interest without continual prompting.	☐	☐	☐
AGGRESSIVENESS	Takes necessary action without hesitation.	☐	☐	☐
ATTITUDE	Maintains proper attitude toward superiors, fellow officers, the Department and the public.	☐	☐	☐
POTENTIAL	Ultimate value to the department.	☐	☐	☐

SUMMARY:

_____
Evaluating Officer

Figure 16.   Rating scale method.

INDIVIDUAL SUPERVISOR'S RATING

Instructions: Fill out the form in detail. This form will be completed on each employee during the last two weeks of each three month period that shall coincide with the shift change in patrol and other divisions shall complete this form in March, June, September, and December.

NAME:
POSITION:
BADGE#:
PERIOD OBSERVED:
SHIFT WORKED:

	Unacceptable	Below Average	Satisfactory	Above Average	Excellent	COMMENTS
1. Knowledge of Duties						
2. Report Writing						
3. Promptness						
4. Courtesy						
5. Appearance						
6. Firearms Duty						

7. Performs above average in (be specific): _____

8. Performs below average in and needs training in (be specific): _____

9. Specific items noted (give dates and be specific): _____

10. Overall performance rating and job attitude: _____

Signature of Rater: _____
Badge#: _____
Date: _____

Figure 17.   Rating and essay combination.

current supervisor if there has been insufficient time for the supervisor to observe the subject.
2. There should be a formal system for evaluations, with specified time periods between evaluations, and some provisions for continuity and uniformity in completing the evaluation forms and carrying on the counseling sessions.
3. Maintain a history of the evaluations so that the changes in an individual's performance may be reviewed. One question that should be answered and a policy established on that answer is: Should the evaluator see the previous ratings prior to completing his own evaluation or should they be available to him only for later comparison purposes?
4. Keep the system simple and uncluttered. The same rule should apply to the forms that are used for the evaluations.
5. The number of factors to be evaluated should be limited to a select few, and probably not more than will fill one page.
6. There should be a space for "not observed" to be indicated if such has been the case, and its use should be encouraged when applicable.
7. Try to maintain objectivity in preparing the evaluation format and in discussing the evaluation with the rated subject.
8. Discuss and review the evaluation with the subject; there should be no secrets about how he stands releated to the evaluation form.
9. Bear in mind that no one is indispensable. When the time comes that one believes an individual cannot be replaced, he himself should be, quickly.
10. The items to be used as the basis for the evaluation should be defined and uniformly applied throughout the organization to individuals in similar positions.
11. The raters should be allowed sufficient time to complete the ratings and hold the evaluation conference.
12. More than one rating system should be utilized to provide for error or halo ratings in one of the forms.
13. A good follow-up procedure to reinforce good practices and to correct incorrect ones should be in force on a continuing basis.
14. Avoid being unmercifully severe. There is a point of diminishing returns in any rating system.
15. Evaluations should serve a valid purpose.
16. There should be a channel for appeals on ratings that are challenged by rated employees.

PROMOTIONAL PROCEDURE

The more successful the selection program and the better good fortune in retaining well-qualified employees for long periods of time, the more challenging will be the task of promotions within the organization. There are two principal considerations of a promotional system: selecting the best-qualified persons for the higher positions and retaining the others who have not been promoted. "Best-qualified" should indicate how they are to perform in the higher position, rather than how they perform in the lower-ranking position. In virtually every occupation there seems to be a few people filling top administrative positions who were promoted beyond their capability to function effectively; the demands on them exceed their qualifications. Retention of those individuals who are not promoted, but who are equally as well qualified for the positions filled by the successful candidates, is extremely difficult and sometimes impossible. The realization that they have reached a dead end either results in their demoralization with a consequent reduction in efficiency, at least during a readjustment period, or they will move on to another agency where they have a greater opportunity to realize their goals.

Another challenge that accompanies promotions of successful candidates is convincing good employees that they were not selected because those who were selected are better qualified. The promotion policy and procedure should be based on valid criteria for promotion, decisions should be based on objective judgment as free as possible from office politics and patronage, and the promotional policy should be freely and frankly discussed so that all candidates for promotion are equally well informed on how they should prepare themselves for their candidacy to a higher position.

In the matter of promotions in the organization there are several matters that should be decided upon and made the subject of positive policy decisions:

1. Within the organization there should be a sufficient number of positions to which the promotable employee can advance. Although the hierarchy of an organization should not be expanded to such an extent that the number of levels from bottom to top is unrealistic, it is possible to develop systems of incentives within each rank. For example, the police department rank structure moves from policeman to sergeant, then to lieutenant, captain, and on up to chief. It would be feasible to develop up to four or five grades within each rank, depending on the individual's responsibilities, decision-making authority, independent operating capacity, and a variety of realistic proficiencies. Each rank could have grades, or ranks, within the traditional rank structure. In order to overcome the barrier sometimes caused by tradition, some agencies have abandoned the old titles in favor of such positions as agent, coordinator, director,

and supervisor. A deputy probation officer may merely carry the additional designation of I, II, III, or IV to denote his pay schedule as well as his relative position in the department.

2. A decision should be made on whether such barriers to promotion as minimum time in the next lower position, tenure on the job, and certain demonstrated proficiencies are valid criteria for promotion, or if they are mere hurdles to slow down the employee who is ambitious and tries to move too fast. The prerequisites should be developed to select the individual with the greatest potential for the position to be filled, rather than his qualifications for his present position. The greatest first line supervisor in the business might be just right where he is and totally inefficient once promoted to a level of inefficiency. Once there, he remains on the job until he retires from old age or emotionally-induced illness caused by his realization that he has been promoted beyond his capabilities.

3. Open versus closed promotions should be considered. Lateral transfer from one organization to another in the same classification has become more widespread during recent years. It would seem that true professionalism would demand of the Criminal Justice System that promotions be made from those candidates who are best qualified for the position to be filled. A promotion should not be a reward for an act of heroism or long years of devoted service so that the senile may fill the higher ranks to build up a greater retirement bundle. If there are members within the organization who are qualified for the promotion, and if they are given an opportunity to demonstrate those qualifications, then perhaps they should receive the promotion, provided all other factors are equal with another candidate who is applying from outside the organization. The closed system could perpetuate mediocrity and result in filling positions with the lesser of two (or more) evils, while a better-qualified candidate is "marking time" in another organization because he has to wait out the next few years for his own superior to finally decide to retire and make room for a competent replacement.

4. The method of testing for qualifications and other factors of promotability should receive careful consideration. Is a written examination a valid measurement instrument? If so, what should it test? When a written examination is used, it should test for potentiality of performance in the position to be filled. Oral interviews may lead to the selection of those candidates who are more proficient at salesmanship than at management of a large division consisting of 200 employees. If an oral interview is utilized, there should be some provision for the structuring of interviews and the establishment of guidelines to assure objective evaluation. Unstructured oral interviews may do little more than identify to the interviewers those self-images whose mannerisms and responses seem most likely to perpetuate their own attitudes and philosophies. As with the selection method

for entry-level positions, promotional positions should be the subject of task analyses and critical-factor studies, and the promotions procedure should be designed to select the best-qualified.

GUIDELINES FOR PERSONNEL MANAGEMENT

There should be a well-prepared and widely disseminated series of guidelines for the management of personnel matters in the organization. Personal and professional needs of the employees and their families must be provided for in the program. Although there should be no attempt to *direct* the private lives of employees, certain provisions should be made for their comfort and well-being in their activities away from the job. In the public service there is also a responsibility on the part of the employee to direct his own life in such a manner that his conduct and reputation do not in any way destroy the good reputation of the organization. As a consequence, there are certain rules he must follow both on and off the job; those rules should be published and disseminated as a part of the program for personnel management.

In addition to the organization's program of personnel management, guidelines need to be established and enforced for the following matters:

Standard compensation plan

Remuneration for the employee's services should be commensurate with educational preparation and skill and the various other criteria established for each position. The pay schedules should be competitive with similar positions in the private segments of the community. It is unrealistic to assume that a professional or paraprofessional individual will be happy to sacrifice the prospect of a high-paying position in private employment just so that he may join the "security" and "steadiness" of public service. Many people are not concerned with retirement in the distant future, nor are the confident and competent individuals whose professions are in wide demand likely to choose the position except as someplace to start. For example, consider the law school graduate who has just passed the bar. He may seek employment with the local prosecuting attorney for the purpose of gaining an almost immediate exposure in the courtroom with a heavy case load. He acquires a wealth of experience and makes many professional contacts, and soon finds out that to stay with the government position more than a year or two will lead to a tremendous financial loss. There are some attorneys, however, who choose to remain in spite of the lower income. Because there are some people who will remain for extended periods of time is no excuse for paying everyone in that job classification an inferior wage.

At several steps above the entrance level of each position, there should be pay incentives for tenure, demonstrated meritorious service, and professional growth. Independent of the promotional opportunities within the organization there should be provisions for noncompetitive advancement within the respective positions. If promotion is the only way an employee may advance, there are two major problems, as I see it: (1) many individuals who are doing quite well where they are must seek advancement to a higher supervisory or management position where their talents are lost to the organization, and (2) many individuals are likely to continue to receive promotions until they reach a level where their inefficiency precludes their further advancement and the organization suffers because of their inadequacies.

Health and accident insurance

At least a partial payment for the off-the-job injuries or illnesses of the employee should be an absolute minimum requirement to be included with a payroll package. There is a direct relationship to on-the-job attendance, and the insurance package should be designed to complement the sick leave privileges. Additional coverage for a spouse and/or other dependents should be available as well. Many organizations pay the full amount for employee and dependents as part of the fringe benefits to which their employees are entitled.

Credit unions

Many employees who work in some sort of government service contribute a large percentage of their income to a retirement program, which provides that they may withdraw their retirement funds upon termination from the job. If they find that their growing family and financial encumbrances may be appreciably offset by the receipt of those hundreds or thousands of dollars in the fund, it is not uncommon for an employee to terminate for some stated reason, draw his retirement money and pay off some of his bills, and then seek reemployment in the same organization or another of the same type to continue his "hardly interrupted" career. This problem could be offset to some extent if low interest, long term loans with flexible arrangements for repayment (such as payroll deductions) were made available to the employee, as they are through credit unions.

Benevolent associations

Most employee groups within organizations provide representation from within the lower echelons independent of the formal channels of

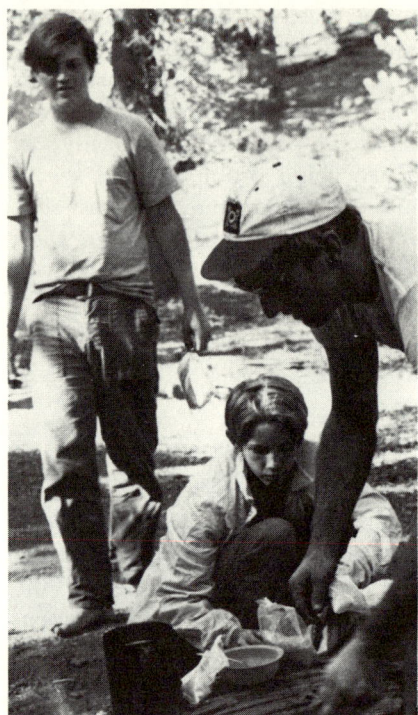 

Off-duty officer participation in community activities provides the officer with an opportunity to gain greater satisfaction while on duty. These photographs were taken while the boys and police officers were on a long hike and camping trip in the High Sierras.
Courtesy: Police Department, Westminster, California

communication and supervision. Membership in a trade union is an abrogation of professionalism, as it causes employees to be classified and handled as groups rather than as individuals and utilizes the strike as its principal means of inducing the employer to yield to demands for pay increases or other benefits. There should be some method for the employee to be represented in negotiations and/or conferences leading to improvement of working conditions. Benevolent associations and similar organizations provide such representation. At the same time such organizations might serve to provide social relationships and fraternal fellowship, and might participate in other such activities that promote the general welfare and morale of the organization's membership. The development and retention of benevolent organizations should be encouraged by management. In their absence, unionization and an increase in tremendously strong external influences might be felt.

Another problem of membership in a trade union is that such an allegiance might lead to partisan performance on the part of a public servant, an intolerable and unforgivable phenomenon in many circumstances.

Improved working conditions

Work schedules and assignments, days off, vacations, night pay differential, transfers, and the actual physical surroundings and equipment should be subjected to constant study and improvement for the benefit of the employee as well as for the overall better service that will result from such improvements. Seniority should not be overlooked, but neither should individual merit. The balance must be fair and impartial, and the two must be regarded in their own perspectives. Long years of continuous service should be rewarded in appreciation of the individual being recognized and as an incentive for others to likewise remain for long years; but long years of poor service is less valuable than a relatively short period of superior service.

Training and education

Educational efforts and professional improvement on the part of the individual should be encouraged and rewarded in the form of incentives and in-grade promotions. If at all possible without causing an adverse effect on the morale of the rest of the staff or the general performance of the unit, the employee should be allowed special consideration with his schedule so that he may continue his education. If such education is directly related to his occupation, it may be feasible to actually provide on-duty time for the employee to attend classes. In-service training should be continuous but actually relevant to the current demands of the individual's assignment and *never* for the sole purpose of training as an end in itself. Training should be designed and presented to meet specific objectives for the improvement of task performance and the increase of essential knowledge.

Discipline

Manuals and various other means of communication should be employed to articulate the organization's policies and standards for performance. Enlightened and capable leadership by the chief executive and his supervisory staff must be provided throughout each department, and discipline should be positive. If an employee knows what is expected of him under all of the different conditions of the job, he may positively discipline himself and know where he stands in relationship to what is expected of him. Negative disciplinary practices, when necessary to the performance and reputation of the organization and the employee, should be timely and fair. Exemplary punishment of an employee might deter others from committing similar acts of malfeasance, but at the same time might destroy the recipient of the punishment. Whatever the manager's decision in meting out negative discipline, he must be sure of its equity in relation to the violation. It must be consistent and free from favoritism.

Appeal system

Provision should be made for the employee to appeal any action affecting him that he believes should be reconsidered or reversed. No grievance should go unanswered, although many may be handled and resolved at the first line supervisory level. In any event, the employee should know that he has an ultimate appeal to the chief executive.

SUMMARY

No organization can function successfully for any period of time—except by accident or miracle—without some form of an organized personnel program. Since most administrators choose not to admit to accidental success, nor are they endowed with the power to perform miracles, they must resort to the more orthodox means of managing their organizations. In this chapter I have discussed the orthodox, nonmiraculous, approach. Policies and procedures for the routine guidelines that are used to direct the organization and its personnel are carefully promulgated, then widely disseminated. The next step is to enforce them, preferably through positive means, but as a last resort through the use of negative disciplinary measures.

Selection and assignment of personnel to the various units within the organization should be made only after the various tasks of each position are identified and described. Only then is it possible to establish criteria for selection and successful management of the tasks and the people who perform them. Selection of the individuals to fill the positions should be on the basis of their demonstrated capacity to perform. The method of selection should be chosen on the basis of its validity in appointing those individuals who are best qualified for the positions they are to fill. There are no foolproof methods for selection of personnel, but every method that promises any success should at least be considered. By the same token, current methods that prove invalid, which may include many of the testing and interviewing methods now employed, should be abandoned if and when it is discovered that the traditional way of doing things may not necessarily be the best way.

Evaluations should be conducted on the basis of performance and attitude requirements of the employee on the job he is currently performing, and promotions should be made on the basis of potential in the position to be filled. In both cases, it will be necessary for the administrator to carefully study the various positions within the organization with a view to their specific objectives, then to train the evaluators to pass judgment on the incumbents and to select for *potential* as well as on the basis of *demonstrated performance.*

In the next chapter we briefly cover the theories and general guidelines for supervision. Once the employee is selected and placed on the job, the next process is to lead and guide him in the performance of his tasks and help him develop an appreciation and understanding of the overall aspects of his job and of those whom he affects and who affect him in their professional or vocational interaction.

NOTES

1. Peter F. Drucker, *The Effective Executive* (New York: Harper & Row, 1967), p. 76.
2. Ibid., pp. 78-92.
3. Personnel Department, City of Santa Ana, California.
4. Report on Police and Fire Classification and Pay Studies (Chicago: The Jacobs Co., March 1970).
5. Ibid., p. 11.
6. Henry C. Smith, *Psychology of Industrial Behavior,* 2nd ed. (New York: McGraw-Hill, 1964), pp. 71-73.
7. Ibid., pp. 66-67.
8. Robert B. Mills, Robert J. McDevitt, and Sandra Tonkin, "Situational Tests In Metropolitan Police Recruit Selection," *Journal of Criminal Law, Criminology, and Police Science* 57 (March 1966).
9. The period following World War II produced many innovative techniques in psychological testing, with particular emphasis occurring in the 1950s. Reported by R. S. Seares, San Marino California Chief of Police: *Standards of Selection of Police Personnel Psychiatric Testing of Police Applicants,* a mimeographed report of a panel forum on selection and training of personnel, National (FBI) Academy Associates Retraining Session, November 4-8, 1957, Washington, D.C.
10. Stephen Nowicki, Jr., "A Study of the Personality Characteristics of Successful Policemen," *Police* 10 (1966): 39.
11. Nick J. Colarelli and Richard S. Siegal, "A Method of Police Personnel Selection," *Journal of Criminal Law, Criminology, and Police Science* 52 (1964): 281.
12. Nowicki, op cit., p. 39.

REVIEW QUESTIONS

1. Is it best to rearrange the organization to fit individuals, or vice versa?
2. List at least three good reasons for a task analysis.
3. How does one go about performing a task analysis?
4. What is the purpose of the "critical incident" technique?
5. Is the "lateral transfer" idea good or bad, in your opinion? Why?

6. What are the advantages to having nonprofessional persons replacing the professionals in certain "housekeeping" functions? Disadvantages?
7. What is the strongest argument you can present to support a view that candidates for a position should be taken from the public at large rather than limited to local residents only?
8. List the guidelines that the author recommends be followed in the utilization of the oral interview.
9. Discuss the type of personality necessary for each of the following positions: parole agent, police officer, judge.
10. What is the value of a probationary period?
11. List at least seven uses for an evaluation system.
12. Why is it important that the quality of compatability be stressed heavily?
13. Describe the "halo effect."
14. Of all the evaluation methods discussed in this chapter, which method do you believe most effective?

6 Supervision

Leadership, integration, and coordination are intrinsic to the successful management of any organization. In this chapter, I address those aspects of personnel management listed here under the generic term supervision. From the chief executive to the most recently hired employee at the operational level, the key to effective management is manifested in two parts: the supervision of subordinates, and the acceptance of supervision by those subordinates. Employees of any organization, no matter what their position, should not be treated as if they were indentured servants; they must be supervised through enlightened leadership methods. They are not to be driven or intimidated to respond to the rantings of tyrants. It is true that no employee, regardless of tenure, should consider himself the owner of any position, particularly in the public service, but neither should any supervisor operate on the assumption that he has God-given rights to *rule* his subordinates.

Kassoff[1] states: "Management involves people, people who must work together to achieve goals, and people who must receive direction and purpose." Quoting Peter Drucker,[2] Kassoff lists five basic operations that involve the manager in his supervisory role: (1) set objectives, (2) organize, (3) motivate and communicate, (4) establish and use measurement devices, and (5) develop people.[3] In previous chapters I have covered the first two activities. In this chapter, I address the latter three listed by Kassoff, plus leadership, direction, authority, coordination, and discipline.

LEADERSHIP

Koontz and O'Donnell list five basic managerial qualities: a desire to manage, intelligence, analytical ability, ability to communicate, and integrity.[4] The individual certainly must have the desire to assume responsibility for decision making and for taking the initiative to act without direction from a higher level of authority whenever the need arises. Desire alone will not qualify an individual to fill the position, however, but it will provide the appropriate attitude necessary to function effectively in a supervisory role. Perhaps intelligence should be restated as wisdom and judgment ability, along with the capacity to adapt to new situations and intelligently cope with them. The intelligence quality should also include the individual's mastery of knowledge related to the art of management and at least a moderate degree of knowledge about the various positions under his supervision. Although it may not adversely affect a supervisor's effectiveness if he cannot actually perform all the tasks his subordinates do, he should have some understanding of the tasks, their requirements, and their limitations.

Analytical ability is an absolute necessity for supervisory effectiveness: trouble-shooting and supervising according to the exception principle require a highly perceptive and astute individual. This principle should be applied at all levels; it prescribes that people performing under a supervisor's general jurisdiction should do so without having to be under his constant surveillance or having him give each matter his personal attention. The supervisor should have to handle only the exceptional cases. If a problem baffles a subordinate and he calls upon a superior to help him in making a decision on two or more alternatives, he should receive some guidance and perhaps a positive answer on which alternative to choose. A dilemma is created when the subordinate goes to the supervisor and states: "Boss, I have a problem. We have two alternatives: based on the evidence presented to me, we can either prosecute, or we can recommend dismissal on the grounds of insufficient evidence. What is your opinion?" If, after reviewing the information and examining the evidence, the supervisor replies: "You have a problem. You should either prosecute or move for dismissal," we now have a new problem—an indecisive supervisor. A keen analytical mind and the courage to make a decision are essential ingredients in the make-up of the true leader.

Communications skills are an absolute must in managerial qualities. Not only must the supervisor be able to write or speak what he has in mind, but he must also convey the same series of thoughts and concepts to the recipient of his messages so that the *meanings* of the messages are received as the supervisor intends for them to be sent. There is a great deal of truth in the old joke about the two psychiatrists who met on the street—as they approached one another, the first said, "Good morning";

as they passed the second said to himself, "I wonder what he meant by that." When the supervisor communicates, his method and style should assure a minimum of distortion. For example, a supervisor who is chastising a subordinate by stating "I don't want to ever hear of you making that mistake again" may be saying either that he wants the fellow to improve or that when such a mistake is repeated an effort should be made to see that it does not again come to his attention. The supervisor who vents his wrath upon people who bring him bad news and bestows kind words and recommendations for pay raises on those who bring him good news may soon find that he is receiving only the good news. His organization may be falling apart at the seams, but the only way he will discover the problem will be if he personally looks for it.

Integrity involves a personal commitment and strict adherence to a standard of conduct or a code of moral values. Along with this quality, it is important to effective management that the supervisor demonstrate a continuity in his enforcement of rules. Honesty and loyalty, plus many of the personal qualities frequently listed as desirable in a devoted public servant, may also be related to the quality of integrity.

Kassoff lists several characteristics that supervisors must have to exercise their decision-making talents which should be added to the list of managerial qualities. They include intuitive judgment (hunch ability), judgment courage (decisions in the face of uncertainties and frustrations), and open-mindedness (including the ability to listen).[5] Newman and Summer list five characteristics that are considered when appraising people for personnel development into leadership positions: (1) knowledge, (2) decision-making power, (3) self-reliance and self-assertion, (4) regard for others and social receptiveness, and (5) emotional stability.[6]

In searching for those elusive qualities that qualify an individual for the unique role of supervisor, we find that extensive studies have been made to isolate specific characteristics that might serve as guideposts to the discovery of the *qualified* supervisor. In their description of leadership qualifications, Hanna and Gentel make the following observations:

> One leadership skill stands out as highly significant. Vocabulary, precise use of the right words for the situation and the group, shows high correlation with leadership. The more precise the vocabulary is, the better chance the individual has to be leader of the group.[7]

Hanna and Gentel continue by stating that the leader is mentally and emotionally mature, that his interests lie in a wide variety of places, that he is effective in the social skills, and that he "relies on his administrative skills to a much greater extent than he does on any of his technical skills which may be associated directly with his work."[8]

In his excellent book on the subject of effectiveness in management, Drucker makes these observations:

> I soon learned that there is no "effective personality." The effective executives I have seen differ widely in their temperaments and their abilities, in what they do and how they do it, in their personalities, their knowledge, their interests—in fact in almost everything that distinguishes human beings. All they have in common is the ability to get the right things done.[9]

Although he disclaims any knowledge of personality traits, Drucker lists five "habits of the mind" that have to be acquired in order for one to be an effective executive. Effective executives (1) know where their time goes, (2) gear their efforts to results rather than to what work is to be done, (3) build on their own strengths and those of others around them, (4) set and work within priorities (concentrating on the few major areas where superior performance will produce outstanding results), and (5) make effective decisions. He concludes by stating: "What is needed are few, but fundamental, decisions. What is needed is the right strategy rather than razzle-dazzle tactics."[10]

The executive, manager, or supervisor may choose to operate with a style that works best for him under the given circumstances. He may exercise his leadership role in harmony with his personal qualities. Athos and Coffey describe the three basic types of leadership as autocratic (authoritarian), democratic (consultive), or laissez-faire (free-rein). Their definitions are:

> The autocratic leader mainly seeks obedience from his group by use of formal authority, rewards, and punishments. He determines policy and makes all decisions. The democratic leader draws ideas and suggestions from his followers and encourages them to participate in things that concern them. In some cases, he may let the group determine policy; in others, he may ask their advice but make the final decision himself. The free-rein leader plays down his role in the group's activities and acts primarily to provide information, materials, and facilities for the group in accomplishing its objectives. He exercises a minimum of control.[11]

Which one of the leadership styles a supervisor may use is usually a result of his own personal decision, but it may be a reflection of the leadership to which he is subject. In reality, there are occasions when all three of these leadership styles might be utilized by the same leader at different times. The wisdom is in making the decision when to use which style. Regarding the style of leadership, Likert makes the following observation:

> The high producing supervisors and managers make clear to their subordinates what the objectives are and what needs to be

accomplished and then give them freedom to do the job. The subordinates can pace themselves and can use their own ideas and experience to do the job in the way they find works best. Supervisors in charge of low-producing units tend to spend more time with their subordinates than do the high-producing supervisors, but the time is broken into many short periods in which they give specific instructions . . . .[12]

In his book *The Human Side of Enterprise*, Douglas McGregor presents an interesting discussion on points of view about employees allegedly held by two different types of managers.[13] Devoting two chapters (3 and 4) to the discussion, McGregor presents his Theory X and Theory Y managers. His imaginary Theory X model is an autocratic individual who holds the belief that the average individual dislikes work and will avoid it whenever possible. Because of this dislike for work, the average worker must be coerced, controlled, threatened, and directed constantly in order that the organizational objectives might be met. Manager X believes that the employee wants security above all, avoids responsibility, and actually prefers to be directed on the job.

McGregor's Theory Y manager model holds an extreme opposite view. He believes that the typical worker derives great pleasure from work and that he will exercise self-direction without external influence. This individual, in the opinion of Manager Y, will seek responsibility and develop to his full potential with little direction or control, because he knows that rewards await him upon successful accomplishment of his objectives. These are the two extremes we encountered previously under the titles of the autocratic, or authoritarian, manager (Theory X) and the laissez-faire manager. Having encountered this discussion in other texts and in management seminars, I feel that these two imaginary managers are introduced for the purpose of discussion, with the objective of leading into an acceptable alternative, which in many cases might be the democratic, or consultive, manager.

Since leadership directly concerns the acceptance of leadership, it is fundamental to consider the concept from the *follower's* point of view. Work and financial incentives are directly related. It is true that there are other considerations in human relations between management and the operational personnel, but economic considerations are important when one is considering the subject of leadership acceptance. Schein sees four conceptions of a rational economic man:

1. Motivated by financial incentives, a man will do that which yields the greatest financial gain.

2. Because economic incentives are under the control of management, Schein proposes that the typical employee is a passive individual who is to be manipulated, motivated, and controlled by management.

3. Personal feelings are irrational and the employees must not be allowed to let such feelings interfere with a rational calculation of self-interest.

4. Because of unpredictable traits in the individual, according to Schein, "organizations can and must be designed in such a way as to neutralize and control man's feelings . . . ."[14]

Taking these factors of rationality in seeking financial reward, the views held by the imaginary autocratic manager that an individual must be held in fear of his job, or the imaginary view that the individual will rise above all obstacles and perform well with no direction, Koontz and O'Donnell present their views on the nature of man from a manager's point of view[15] (parenthetical statements added by the author):

1. The individual is the primary concern of man. He wants to win, but he enjoys the success of others after he has personally achieved success.

2. The individual will work to satisfy the demands of his basic nature if the benefits exceed the costs. (He enjoys the work or whatever he is doing if it satisfies his needs.)

3. The individual can be led. (He responds to leadership, particularly when the leader's attitude and technique appeal to his basic desires.)

4. The individual wants to live and work in a social environment. (Informal organizations and other social contacts which may or may not be directly related to the work.)

5. The individual helps to create institutions to serve the needs of their memberships. (He needs a cooperative effort to hold his interest. A problem confronting him is how he can retain mastery of the institutions he helps create and maintain, and yet not become their slave.)

6. There is no average man. (Each is unique and has his own set of problems or challenges.)

7. The individual rises to the challenge of his full capabilities. (Another view sometimes presented is that an individual is likely to become what is generally expected of him.)

Leadership involves a very important challenge of assisting the individual in rising to his full capabilities, encouraging him by setting an example of how he might succeed in his present position, and guarding against the development of a cynical "loser's attitude." Seldom does one succeed without having to confront and overcome some adversity. Kassoff reminds us:

> It is important to recognize that it is the lowest echelon, or operational personnel, who actually help to reach the objectives. They must be made aware of the department's objectives and should be involved to some degree in determining them.[16]

MOTIVATION

Goal accomplishment involves effective management, or getting the job done with the greatest amount of cooperation and the least expenditure of time and resources. The manager must choose his style and methods, but whatever the style, motivation is of paramount importance. The employee is more likely to produce a better quantity and quality of service if he feels that he is understood, accepted, liked, and that his work is generally approved. The supervisor must develop and constantly utilize his talent for stimulating a desire in his subordinates to perform well because they feel that his needs for recognition and support are being met.

Motivation of employees is a phenomenon involving inner drives and goal-seeking activities. The motive, or "moving cause," for the employee may involve internal influences, such as a desire to achieve a goal, a challenge of overwhelming odds to be reversed—as in the case of physical or educational handicaps, or the internal drive that accompanies an attitude of professional dedication for accomplishment. The motive may also involve external influences, such as a promise of promotion or pay incentives, public approbation and respect for the accomplishment of certain tasks, or the leadership and encouragement of an inspiring leader. In the typical organization, the effective supervisor must consider all of these factors and coordinate the goals and objectives of the organization with those of the individual employees. He should employ as many methods of motivation as possible.

The employee has certain needs that must be satisfied: physical, social, and emotional. Some of these needs may be met, or a means to satisfy them may be provided, through the individual's employment. Most occupations provide at least a basic salary that make it possible for the individual to meet the first type of need, but even those appetites grow with satiation at a lower level. Social needs may be met both on and off the job. People are interdependent upon one another, and they are social beings. The job must be a pleasant place and the people must be compatible with each other.

Socialization in a comfortable working environment and during meal and refreshment breaks may be encouraged by a supervisor who realizes that individuals will produce better results when their social needs are met, providing that fair rules are enforced which prevent socialization to interfere with the organization's primary functions. One of the most effective methods of counseling a subordinate is during an informal refreshment break when there is no barrier, such as different size chairs on opposite sides of a big desk, between them. Social events sponsored by the organization, such as sports activities, bowling leagues, awards banquets, and

Socialization in a comfortable work environment is essential to a healthy organization.
Courtesy: Police Department, Pasadena, California

recognition of the organization's employee-operated benevolent associations, may aid indirectly in employee motivation.

Smith points out that supportive relationships within a group may be enhanced through the utilization of sociometry.[17] Although this particular concept may seem repugnant to an authoritarian-oriented executive, some consideration might be given the concept at least on an experimental basis. Sociometry was utilized in some studies by the navy during World War II, reports Smith,[18] and the results were favorable. The method of assigning a group of individuals to work together, as in the study cited by Smith, is to privately ask each person with whom he would rather work; he is asked to rank order them according to first, second, third choice, and so on. When used in the selection of personnel for a flying squadron, it was found that the effective squadron had no cliques, the men respected their superiors, had a closely knit organization, and preferred the members of their own group to outsiders.[19] Through this medium of personnel assignment the supervisor is creating a socially oriented group with work objectives.

Emotional needs of the individual also require the attention of the effective supervisor. Through the development of what Smith calls "supportive relationships"[20] the individual may feel his personal worth to the organization. Once employees are assigned to work together as a team, Smith suggests that they may produce better results if they are given group goals, then allowed to define individual tasks among themselves. Management representatives and members of the team of employees who are to actually perform the work meet to discuss the goals to be set for the group and to gain the group's acceptance of the performance goals. In this way, individuals will know that their contributions are important and that management is listening to what they have to say. Communications are open and free-flowing during such discussions. Smith states that "letting a group decide its own production goals is worker-management cooperation at its highest level," and "Whether managers are willing or not, . . . (to allow them to have this decision-making power) groups *do* make informal but effective decisions about their production goals."[21]

High morale (or whatever lesser degree of morale that may exist within an organization) is a result of satisfying the three basic needs we have discussed: physical, social, and emotional. There are other motivational methods that the leader may utilize, but they adversely affect morale and consequently have only temporary effectiveness followed by what might lead to organizational bankruptcy. Such motivational factors include coercion, paternalism, and excessive competition.

Leadership through the use of fear is not leadership at all. At its crudest level the technique is to constantly threaten to fire subordinates if they do not meet the supervisor's demands for production or service. The result will be a resentful employee who may seek ways to sabotage the effectivenss of the organization, a loss of his incentive to produce good results, and an overall tendency on the part of fellow employees to cover-up for each other. A group or clique may form to assure protection and at the same time it may develop methods for punishing "squealers" who jeopardize the safety of the group. Individuals who violate the "noncooperation compact" may find themselves the recipients of sometimes severe peer pressures.

Paternalism is a term used by Sayles and Strauss[22] which applies to the theory that if management is good to employees, the employees will work harder out of gratitude and loyalty. They point out, however, that paternalism may actually harbor resentment in employees who would rather do something for themselves than have it done for them. Another side effect is that soon the novelty of being given free handouts wears off and the employees begin to take them for granted.[23]

Excessive competition manifests itself in the form of unrealistic goals for the sheer purpose of producing *more* of some type of service than has been produced before, simply because the person stimulating the statistical growth is impressed by numbers. For example, a police supervisor may create excessive competition by pushing for a greater number of felony arrests or traffic citations. A court may process more arraignments or preliminary hearings, a prosecuting attorney may increase his case load, or a probation officer may prepare more reports for predetention hearings. Sometimes the competition is not among individuals but is a comparison of

Excess emphasis on competition among subordinates may prove detrimental to the organization. These officers have definite objectives in mind, but they focus principally on the safe flow of traffic with a minimum of injuries and property damage.
Courtesy: Police Department, Pasadena, California

one year's to the previous year's, or years', averages. Competition for the purpose of drawing impressive wall charts has no valid place in the general scheme of professional management.

A supervisor should work on the strengths of his subordinates, help them develop their unique talents and skills, and minimize their weaknesses. Peter Drucker strongly enunciates this technique: "A superior owes it to his organization to make the strength of his subordinates as productive as it can be. But even more does he owe it to the human beings over whom he exercises authority to help them get the most out of whatever strength they may have."[24]

Motivation may be stimulated if the people who will be affected in any way by some planned or anticipated action are both consulted and advised. Consultation on an important issue or the development of a new procedure should be sought from those individuals who have the knowledge essential to make value judgments on feasibility, costs, and other factors. If the new procedure is to be implemented by the individual from whom the advice or assistance is obtained, there is also a greater likelihood that he will cooperate to make sure the new procedure gets a fair trial when implemented. In all cases, when practicable, individuals who are to be affected by management decisions should be advised of the decisions and should be informed of the possible effect they might have. Reasons for the decisions should also be provided.

Employees should have the feeling that they are respected and trusted, and that they are expected to perform at a high level of competence. They should be assisted, but their work should not be done for them; they should be encouraged to strive for better performance, but perfection is not always possible nor should it be always expected. Careful attention should be directed toward their levels of competency and arrangements should be made to see that they have the essential training and necessary resources to function effectively.

MEASUREMENT DEVICES

Supervision of people and the various tasks they perform involves the utilization of some form of measurement device, like statistical computations. These should be used more for personal guidance rather than for general dissemination and quality of performance should be stressed as more significant than quantity. The particular device, of course, depends on the individual position being supervised. Performance, progress, improvement, and results should be key words in the development of any statistical control. In a paper presented on management systems, Lockheed's systems planning director Norman J. Ream had this to say:

> The types of performance measurement devised and their ultimate use determines what information will be considered relevant in the operation of a business. The results desired must be built into the management process in such a manner that one can determine whether or not expectations have actually been fulfilled, including a knowledge of the deviations. Otherwise, management cannot plan, for they have no information feedback and no precise control of their efforts.[25]

Management by objectives and goal-achievement or bit-by-bit itemization of individual activities of subordinates: whatever the method of measurement, it should directly relate to the organizational objectives. In the absence of careful control of any measurement system, the customary result is a proliferation of worthless time-consuming tally sheets and pages of reports that demonstrate only a superior ability to count.

DEVELOPMENT OF PEOPLE

Seldom is it possible to structure an organization and then staff it with people who are completely capable of performing all of the tasks required of each position. As pointed out in an earlier chapter, the people must be adapted to the organization. There are exceptions, of course, because of the unique talents of some individuals and the specific shortcomings of others who perform well in all other respects. An integral part of supervision is to get to know the strengths and weaknesses of one's subordinates. Encouragement and further strengthening of the individual's strong qualities should be an ongoing process, but equally as important is to help the individual identify and improve himself in those areas where he is weak and in need of development. V. A. Leonard presents an astute justification for the development of the individual:

> Individuals are tied together by ideas rather than coercive authority and control. Their capacity for productive and creative work, loyal self-sacrifice and enthusiasm for the job knows no limits when the whole man—body-mind-and-spirit—is thrown into the program. Administration by objectives rather than command fosters initiative, discretion and self-development. It is the men and not the organization chart who do the work.[26]

DIRECTION

Direction involves work assignments and the integration of the various individuals performing the work. Direction in an organization begins with orientation and/or indoctrination. In orientation the employee is introduced to the organization, its goals and objectives, its procedures, and its general expectations of employees. In the indoctrination process, an attempt is made to instill within the individual an understanding of all of those things covered in the orientation, and also to inspire the new employee to embrace its policies and attitudes as his own and encourage dedication and loyalty to the organization. Direction involves the guidance of the employee from that point throughout his membership in the organization.

Direction may be practiced in the form of management of individuals or groups through orders—written and oral, directives, information bulletins, training aids, and example. Close supervision of each task may be utilized, or an alternate style—inspection of the results to determine whether the person has performed well—may be employed. The method to be used by a supervisor may vary according to the distinctive personalities of the people being supervised. Some individuals work best when left to their own devices without close surveillance, others must work in groups to be effective, and still others are effective only when they are closely guided and reassured at every step along the way. The very astute supervisor will adapt to the individuals he is supervising and will employ a variety of techniques. Kassoff enumerates some guidelines for control, stating that they should: (1) reflect the nature of the activity, (2) report deviations promptly, (3) be forward-looking, (4) point up exceptions at strategic points, (5) be objective, not based upon personality, (6) be flexible, and (7) reflect the organization pattern.[27]

Not to overlook the individual's contribution to the organization, Athos and Coffey list these values:

> ... a belief in the dignity and the contribution of the individual, the need for opportunity for self-development, the willingness of the individual to commit himself to group effort and common purpose, a desire to be creative, a need for self-identification, and a willingness to accept responsibility and take risks.[28]

AUTHORITY

Authority has two distinctive and equally important parts: the right to command and the acceptance of command. An individual may possess power in his personal social universe, or he may possess power in the organization without the formally bestowed authority—charisma is a form of personal power that might convey an impression of authority. Authority is delegated from the chief executive down through the hierarchy of the organization, but in reality power that one is able to utilize is generated from the bottom of the hierarchical level in an upward direction. The ideal situation for a supervisor is to have both the authority and the power to supervise the individuals for whose performance he is being held responsible. With this arrangement the supervisor has the right and the capability to effectively direct the activities of his subordinate employees.

Individuals who have been indoctrinated in the idea that each progressively higher position in the hierarchical structure carries with it a greater authority and the real power to lead others in the same successive fashion may acknowledge such an idea. If this is the case with a majority of those being supervised, then the power-authority of the people who hold supervisory and management positions within the organization will be well balanced. Military-type leadership involves a continual indoctrination process in this concept. Each new employee is introduced to the policy that there is a hierarchy in authority and power and that they are concurrent. In order that personal feelings about the matter may be explained as irrelevant, employees are indoctrinated in the belief that the position or rank one holds—*what* he is—rather than *who* one is, determines authority.

For some reason, there are people in organizations who seem to believe that they have been given the divine right to lead others, that the power they possess along with their authority comes from some higher authority than the chief executive. Pfiffner and Sherwood discuss this idea and point out that Chester I. Barnard, one-time president of the New Jersey Bell Telephone Company, quite significantly attacked this "divine right" authoritarianism in American management philosophy in a series of lectures in the mid-1930s at Harvard University. Quoting Pfiffner and Sherwood:

> The essence of the Bernard thesis was that people differ in the degree of effort they will contribute to achieve the objectives of an organization. Hence, at any given time the individual members will be putting forth varying percentages of effort, with a consequent effect on their production. The organization must in some way secure their willingness to cooperate, and financial incentive is not the important way to do this. The degree of effective authority possessed by a leader is measured by the willingness of subordinates to accept it; and the acceptability of orders to the individual member can be graded on a time-point scale. There are those which are clearly unacceptable, those on which there is a mental attitude, and those which are unquestionably acceptable.[29]

In many criminal justice organizations, the terms *line* and *staff* authority are used in defining relative roles of the various managers, supervisory personnel, and operational personnel in the organization. The term *line* is generally used in this context as being that type of authority that a supervisor exercises in a direct supervisor-subordinate situation. *Staff* supervision is generally regarded as advisory or assisting, a supervisory control over the task or results of a task but no direct control over the specific activities of an individual of lower rank, who is not in the direct line of command. Sometimes the term *functional* supervision is used synonymously with *staff* supervision.

Authority may be delegated, originating with the chief executive, and is passed down to each successively lower position in the hierarchy. The delegation of authority accompanies, and should be commensurate with, the level of accountability assigned to each individual. In other words, when a supervisor is held responsible for the achievement of a specific list of goals and objectives, then it is imperative that he be delegated the authority to direct the activities of his subordinate ranking employees to a degree sufficient to be effective. Delegation is not only essential, it is highly desirable, because it extends the influence of a capable leader who is evaluated on the basis of the results he gets, not the unit amount of work he personally produces. Advantages of delegation are in leadership development and a general feeling of participation by employees throughout the organization.

COORDINATION

Coordination is accomplished through a careful delegation of assignments and the authority to carry them out, a continual process of communication to keep everyone within the organization sufficiently informed about the respective activities in relation to others, a continual series of inspections to ascertain if activities are being performed and objectives are being met, feedback and updating to make any indicated changes that may be necessary because of changing human or other circumstances, and taking whatever other steps are necessary to meet the deadlines and goals of the organization.

According to Kenney, coordination "may be viewed in terms of span of control, which refers to the number of persons the chief of police can supervise, or as a function of staff, which is an extension of the chief's personality, staff assisting him in performance of his command function."[30] "Control follows from coordination," states Kenney. "It has to do with the assurance that tasks are being performed and goals and objectives achieved through the process of a feedback of information from operational levels to top management which also facilitates the coordination process."[31]

Hanna and Gentel explain the coordination process:

> The police administrator must comprehend the role of the executive as one involved in a conceptual role, that is, involved in the comprehension of the organization as a whole and also as interrelated units with the objective of coordinating and forming a balanced team to cope with the basic objectives of the organization.[32]

Kassoff discusses coordination in terms of teamwork:

> Teamwork must be balanced. No one secondary objective can be made supreme over others, and it is management's task to maintain this balance of objective achievement. Periodic adjustments may be, and often are, needed as critical problems arise.[33]

Coordination is not possible without a high level of cooperation by various individuals who have been delegated authority and responsibility. It is impossible to supervise every task, and Sayles and Strauss propose

> that the process may be enhanced through goal-setting. By setting goals the manager can avoid the necessity for either making specific decisions or laying down detailed rules. This approach, which is in sharp contrast to detailed, minute-by-minute supervision, is often called "management by exception." It permits the subordinate to experiment, to adjust to novel situations.[34]

Coordination is achieved through a variety of methods in addition to those presented so far in this chapter. The specific style of coordination will depend to a great extent on the individuals being supervised and the personality of the supervisor. Other methods of achieving cooperation might include a shortening of the hierarchy—the number of levels one must go to have a question answered or a management decision made—or development of teams at the operational level who will be instructed to meet specified objectives but will be left to their own devices to decide how they are to go about accomplishing those objectives. Another method of coordination might be a "participative management" system in which committees and problem-solving teams are asked to study problems and to suggest programs to address those problems. This could result in broadened spans of control, because the teams would have greater autonomy; exceptions that would call for direct participation by the management would be fewer and farther between. Employment of specialists to meet sophisticated and highly complex demands for decisions at the administrative level might also serve to ease the problem of coordination.

DISCIPLINE

Positive discipline, that is, control through leadership and example and self-control by the participants in the organization, is by far the most desirable type of discipline. When the positive means fail, or lag, then it may be necessary to employ negative disciplinary measures. When employed correctly, even the negative disciplinary measures assume positive aspects. In this section, the discussion includes an explanation of the types of negative discipline and the purposes for their implementation.

Negative disciplinary measures that may be taken by the executive or any of the managers or supervisors at different levels within a criminal justice organization are usually very clearly delineated in civil service regulations. There may be prescribed infractions with a specified remedy or course of action that may be followed. In all cases when negative disciplinary action is taken there must be an avenue for appeal, either within the organization or through other lawful channels, or both. Since it is the executive's responsibility to manage the organization, any abrogation of his right to employ appropriate disciplinary measures, and to enforce them, would seriously interfere with his effectiveness. At the same time, it is essential that the interests of the individuals who make up the organization be protected in a legitimate manner.

The types of negative discipline include (1) oral reprimand with no written record, (2) recorded oral reprimand, (3) written reprimand, (4) point demerits or warnings which accumulate and lead to more stringent action, (5) forfeiture of days off or accumulated time, (6) fine, (7) suspension, (8) disciplinary transfer, and (9) removal from the service. Precisely which type or degree of punishment will be meted out for which violation of regulations or policy should be determined by the chief executive and his staff. Some agencies have printed lists or manuals of rules and regulations, and in some of those manuals are listed prescribed penalties for the various violations. Decisiveness and prompt response to violations with negative discipline is important to assure fair handling of the matter in consideration of the violator, and also for the general good order and morale of the organization. Whatever the system for disciplinary action, it must be fair, just, and as free as possible from favoritism or prejudice.

There are many purposes for the utilization of negative disciplinary measures in the management of people. Among them are:

1. To aid an employee in correcting a weakness, or to bring about a change in attitude or conduct to assure conformity to standards.
2. To dissuade others from committing similar violations — exemplary punishment with emphasis on the fact that infractions are met with punishment.
3. To demonstrate to the public that misconduct will not be allowed to go without appropriate attention.
4. To improve and maintain employee morale, reinforcing the acceptable conduct of the employees who adhere to the rules.
5. To maintain the prestige of the organization in the eyes of the public.
6. To supplement positive discipline with a supervision and training tool.

SUMMARY

Supervision is a critical human engineering activity of criminal justice management, as it is with the administration of any other enterprise. Basic supervision skills are universal and should be employed when directing a small unit within the organization or when managing the entire operation from the office of the chief executive. In this chapter, I have covered a few of the principles and techniques in supervision. Leadership and motivation involve supervision as an art: the process of accomplishing objectives through the effective employment of the skills, knowledge, and performance of others. Except for very short-term and unfavorable results, there is never cause to supervise by tyranny, and there is no evidence that criminal justice supervisors have been endowed with any "divine right" to lead others. The supervisory role is one that has been assigned and the boss delegates authority, but the actual power to supervise comes through the acceptance of the leadership by those individuals who are being supervised.

In order that we may effectively supervise on a fair and impartial basis, it is necessary that certain measurement devices be utilized to record and evaluate quantity and quality so the members of the organization may be realistically assessed. The methods of measurement must be directly related to the organization's objectives and overall goals and they should be designed and employed on the basis of their validity and reliability. People must be developed as individuals, but in an organization designed to serve the public it is necessary to develop the people to fit into their respective occupations within the organization rather then adapt the organization to the individual. There are exceptions, but those exceptions should be kept to a minimum.

Direction, authority, and coordination were also covered briefly. Coordination involves the direction of work assignments and the daily management of the organization's many activities through the judicious use of authority. In the discussion of authority, the two principal parts were described: the right to command, and the acceptance of command. Misuse of authority cannot be tolerated within any organization, and it is incumbent on the supervisor to employ authority correctly. The final part of the chapter was devoted to a brief explanation of the types of discipline and its purposes. The key to effective results through the utilization of negative disciplinary action is to use it for the primary purpose of strengthening the individual and the organization. Employed fairly, a department's disciplinary practices may cause the members and the public alike to recognize the organization and its members as ethical, honest, and dedicated to function in the public interest.

NOTES

1. Norman C. Kassoff, *The Police Management System* (Washington, D. C.: International Association of Chiefs of Police), 1967.
2. Peter Drucker, *The Practice of Management* (New York: Harper & Row), 1954, p. 343.
3. Ibid., p. 7.
4. Harold Koontz and Cyril O'Donnell, *Principles of Management: An Analysis of Managerial Functions*, 4th ed. (New York: McGraw-Hill, 1968), pp. 467–469.
5. Kassoff, *The Police Management System* pp. 23–24.
6. W. H. Newman and C. E. Summer, Jr., *The Process of Management* (Englewood Cliffs, N. J.: Prentice-Hall, 1961), pp. 220–221.
7. From Hanna, Donald G., and Gentel, William D., *A Guide to Primary Police Management Concepts*, 1969, p. 9. Courtesy of Charles C Thomas, Publisher, Springfield, Illinois.
8. Ibid., p. 9.
9. Peter F. Drucker, *The Effective Executive* (New York: Harper & Row, 1967), pp. 21–22.
10. Ibid., pp. 23–24.
11. Anthony G. Athos and Robert E. Coffey, *Behavior in Orgonziations: A Multi-Dimensional View* (Englewood Cliffs, N. J.: Prentice-Hall, © 1968), pp. 163–64. All material from this book reprinted by permission from the publisher.
12. Rensis Likert, *New Pattern of Management* (New York: McGraw-Hill, 1961), p. 9.
13. Douglas McGregor, *The Human Side of Enterprise*, (New York: McGraw-Hill, 1960).
14. Edgar H. Schein, *Organizational Psychology*, (Englewood Cliffs, N. J.: Prentice-Hall, © 1965), pp. 49–63.

15. Koontz and O'Donnell, *Principles of Management*, pp. 544–545.
16. Kassoff, *Police Management*, p. 11.
17. Henry Clay Smith, *Psychology of Industrial Behavior*, 2nd ed. (New York: McGraw-Hill, 1964), pp. 157–160.
18. Ibid., p. 159.
19. Ibid., p. 159.
20. Smith, *Psychology of Industrial Behavior*, p. 160.
21. Ibid., pp. 153–155.
22. Leonard R. Sayles and George Strauss, *Human Behavior in Organizations* (Englewood Cliffs, N. J.: Prentice-Hall, © 1966), p. 141. All material from this book reprinted by permission of the publisher.
23. Ibid., pp. 142–43.
24. Drucker, *The Effective Executive*, p. 92.
25. From a paper entitled "The Need for Compact Management Intelligence" presented at a symposium held in Santa Monica, California, July 29 through 31, 1959. Published in *Management Control Systems*, Donald G. Malcom and Alan J. Rowe, eds., (New York: John Wiley and Sons, 1960), pp. 78–88.
26. Leonard, V. A., *The Police Enterprise: Its Organization and Management*, 1969, p. 29. Courtesy of Charles C Thomas, Publisher, Springfield, Illinois.
27. Kasoff, *Police Management*, pp. 35–36.
28. Athos and Coffey, *Behavior in Organizations*, p. 251.
29. Reported on pages 77 and 78 of Pfiffner and Sherwood, *Administrative Organization*.
30. John P. Kenney, *Police Administration* (Springfield: Charles C Thomas, 1972), p. 96.
31. Ibid., p. 97.
32. From Hanna, Donald G., and Gentel, William D., *A Guide to Primary Police Management Concepts*, 1971, p. 12. Courtesy of Charles C Thomas, Publisher, Springfield, Illinois.
33. Kassoff, *The Police Management System*, p. 13.
34. Sayles and Strauss, *Human Behavior in Organizations*, p. 163.

REVIEW QUESTIONS

1. What are the five basic managerial qualities listed by Koontz and O'Donnell?
2. What is a supervisor's hunch ability?
3. Drucker lists five "habits of the mind" that have to be acquired in order for one to be an effective executive. What are those five habits?
4. Describe each of the following types of leadership: (1) autocratic, (2) democratic, and (3) laissez-faire.
5. According to the author, why is motivation so important to supervision?
6. What is an effective setting for a personal counseling session?
7. Describe the possible consequences of excessive competition.
8. What are the two different parts to authority?
9. Why must the amount of authority be commensurate with the degree of accountability of an individual?
10. What types of negative discipline may be employed in personnel relations, and what purposes would such employment serve?

7 Training and Education For Criminal Justice

In a few short years, skills training and education programs for the various criminal justice occupations have grown to substantial size and stature from somewhat meager beginnings. On-the-job training through mimicry and osmosis in a totally unconstructed setting throughout the country has become less common in many agencies during the past few decades. Although programs range from the quite crude to the sophisticated, there is valid reason today for every criminal justice agency to provide some form of organized training program. Home study materials, videotaped recordings—that can be televised via the nearest instructional televison station or by way of local commercial stations presented as a public service during low-viewer times—and a variety of other training media are available. Throughout the nation many of the federal, state, and local agency training programs are open to the smaller and less-advantaged agencies and provide training for their personnel. No longer is there a shortage of publications on the subject of police training; actually it is now a chore to cull out the better publications and decide what *not* to read because of limited time available. Academic programs for the preservice and the in-service student alike is available to an amazing extent at the many colleges, schools, and universities.

In this chapter we discuss the concepts of training and education, and attempt to show briefly similarities and differences in the two approaches to professional-occupational preparation. Then we present some guidelines for curriculum development in training and education. Various types of training currently utilized in criminal justice operations, and a review of

Officers from the Basic Law Enforcement Academy relax during a break at the Regional Criminal Justice Training Center, one of the first in the U.S. serving the training needs of all components of the criminal justice system.
Courtesy: Modesto Junior College, Modesto, California

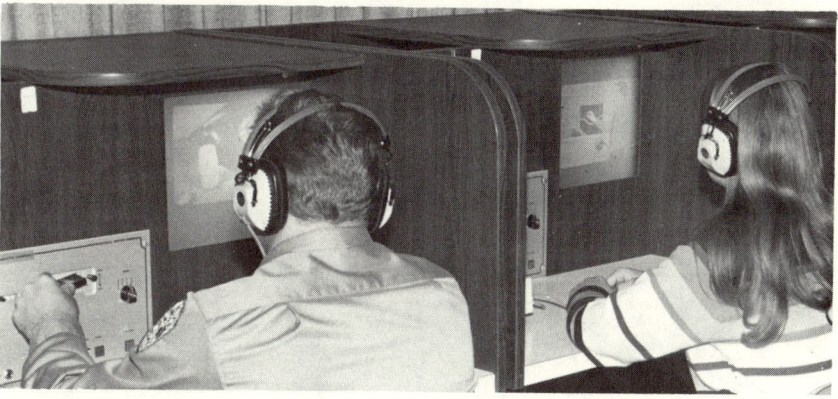

Basic Academy students involved in an independent study program through the use of multi-media in the resource center at the R.C.J.T.C., Modesto, California
Courtesy: Modesto Junior College, Modesto, California

the educational approach to both preemployment and postemployment academic programs round out the chapter, along with a report on recent studies and trends with some recommendations for both training and education. It is interesting to note that in 1960 there were only 40 two-year associate in arts degree programs available in law enforcement and only 15 baccalaureate and graduate degree programs in the entire United States; many states had no formal academic law enforcement programs whatsoever. In 1972, things had changed—515 separate institutions in virtually every part of the United States in addition to Guam and the Virgin Islands *reported* offering educational programs: 505 associate, 211 baccalaureate, 41 masters, and 7 doctorate degrees.[1]

Production of a roll call training sequence at the Center.
Courtesy: Modesto Junior College, Modesto, California

Members of the Basic Juvenile Hall Training Program and the Basic Law Enforcement Academy discuss mutual problems in the administration of justice at the Center.
Courtesy: Modesto Junior College, Modesto, California

Corrections education with that specific designation has emerged only during recent years to an appreciable extent. For probation and parole professionals there has been for many years a wide variety of educational options in sociology, psychology, or social work. In the Court component of the Criminal Justice System, the professional preparation for attorneys and the attorneys who move into judgeships has traditionally been through a basic college education followed by completion of law school. For the paraprofessional occupations of court aides and other court personnel, a specific educational program has yet to be developed. During the past few years the thrust of criminal justice education has been toward developing a core curriculum with a total system approach, a core of a few basic courses at the lower division college level which will be common for students who choose to pursue careers in any component of the Criminal Justice System—law enforcement, the courts, or corrections; then, students choose one of the several options and take specific courses in a particular interest area. This total system concept, we hope, will lead all practitioners to a greater understanding of the other components of the system in relationship to each other as well as to obtaining academic preparation for their specialized choice of occupations or professions. Later in this chapter, we discuss this core curriculum and the total system concept.

TRAINING AND EDUCATION

Skills development and indoctrination to the routine activities of the occupation are usually assigned the label *training;* the orientation to philosophy, theories, and concepts of the role through intellectualization are usually called *education.* Although it is virtually impossible to distinguish the two in many respects, recent attempts have been made in order that they may be handled differently. A simplified distinction might be to designate training as the process of instructing the individual how to do the job and providing him with basic information about the job, and *education* as the process of providing the individual with a body of knowledge on which he may base his decisions when performing his job. While training is generally directly related to the tasks to be performed by the practitioner, his education should be on a broad base so that he not only understands his own role in society but that of others who surround him and with whom he interacts. An educational program for a police officer, for example, includes courses in justice administration and aspects of law enforcement, but he is also required to take courses in political science for an understanding of the processes and agencies of government, English composition so that his reports may be intelligible and grammatically correct, speech and communications skills so that he may communicate more effectively, and sociology or a similar course to increase his awareness of the real world beyond his immediate "universe" of individuals with whom he works and who tend to share similar beliefs. Thompson S. Crockett and James D. Stinchcomb explain their concept of the need for education beyond the high school level:

> Underlying all of this unquestionably has been the ever-increasing search for a more attractive police image. Although this term means different things to different people it is difficult to foster pay, prestige, status in the community, and recognition as a professional within a system that makes few educational demands upon itself. The list of causative factors also must necessarily include: the increased recognition that greater knowledge is required in today's police operations; the wide array of social problems with which police officers are now confronted; the demands from community leaders for improved police-citizen contacts; mounting social disorders culminating in higher crime rates and, not surprisingly, the recent developmental experiences which other career fields have undergone.[2]

Charles W. Tenney, in a Massachusetts study covering the period from 1966 to 1969, defined training in this manner:

> A particular subject may be determined to be of the *training* variety if it is directed primarily to the mastery and application of particular rules, to the development of particular mechanical skills in the operation of particular items of equipment, or to the development of a skill in the performance of particular maneuvers concerning which little or no discretion is involved . . . . In other cases, the *manner* in which a course is taught and its *content* will determine its training character . . . . In either case, whether because of the nature of the subject matter itself or because of the manner in which it is taught, little attention is given to questions of policy, of discretion, or of alternative methodologies.[3]

Regarding the location of the training or the educational program, the same document contains this statement by Tenney:

> This issue of education versus training arises because many existing criminal justice curricula are heavily laced with training courses. But the question properly is not whether a course, a curriculum, or a program is "education" or "training." For both are generally conceded to be necessary, and there is no *logical* reason why either or both together should not be taught in college. There are, however, practical and empirical reasons why training subjects should be kept at a minimum or excluded altogether from the college curriculum. These reasons concern the nature of the subject matter, the instructors, and the institutions.[4]

The argument will probably continue for many years. In an attempt to give adequate coverage to both the educational and training aspects of the various components of the Criminal Justice System, here each is covered separately by arbitrary designation, although they should be virtually inseparable, as is the case in most professional colleges and universities. The doctor without internship and supervised medical practice or the lawyer without his apprenticeship as junior partner and courtroom assistant will never be able to demonstrate that they have acquired their education. The criminal justice professional and the paraprofessional need both educational and manipulative skills so that there will be greater likelihood that they will enjoy success when they engage in their jobs. Each preparation by itself is insufficient and neither is more important than the other in my opinion.

CURRICULUM DEVELOPMENT

Whether the objective is to develop a college educational program or an in-service training program, there are certain processes that appear to apply to both. In my experience as a training officer and as an educator, I have found the technique works equally well in either case, without compromising the philosophical orientation of one at the risk of diluting the other. Terminal performance objectives and demonstrable proficiencies must both be clearly defined and articulated prior to the actual preparation of either the training or educational course or program of instruction. As a matter of fact, from a realistic point of view, the curriculum developer must know the objectives to be identified and the degree of skill or knowledge to be demonstrated before he knows which of the two approaches should be employed. With only minor modifications, the techniques covered in this section of the chapter have been used for curriculum development of both training and educational programs.

Laundry List Approach

The typical approach to the training needs of a department of practically any size, including many of the more sophisticated agencies, is to use the technique sometimes called the *laundry list*. Utilizing this method, the individual who is responsible for the training function attempts to identify from supervisor's reports, overheard coffee shop complaints about training needs, brainstorming sessions, surveys and questionnaires, and virtually every possible source of information at his disposal, a list of the most important training needs for the organization. From this list, he plans principal topics that should be covered; from the many suggestions on how the material should be presented, he attempts to establish some sort of priority listing or sequential presentation of the various topics. Actually, an on-going training program designed for short and frequently convened in-house presentations might find this approach quite good, although of short-lived value.

The simple list of training topics may be adapted to a calendar for the month's training within the organization. From his own experience and with some research, the training officer may develop a course outline. Some organizations, such as the California Association of Police Training Officers, maintain extensive files of training bulletins and outlines for just this purpose.[5] One or two members of the organization might be particularly knowledgeable on the topic to be presented, which may lead to their assignment to prepare the course outline and possibly participate in the actual training program. Once the research has been completed and the raw data collected, the trainer adapts the material to the current organizational policies and procedures, and puts the program into action. The course outline itself may consist of a laundry list of points to be made during the lecture or the discussion.

The Systems Approach

Although the simple list method has seemingly been successful if one is to judge by the number of agencies that still utilize such a method, a far more valid method of developing a training program is through the systems approach to curriculum development. The method can involve either a great deal of sophistication or a simpler modified approach. Without at least some attempt to use a systems approach, a training program may look good on paper but is of no appreciable value to the overall effectiveness of the organization.

Instead of listing the topics to be covered in a particular course or complete training program, the training officer who utilizes the systems approach develops a series of *terminal performance objectives*. Stated in behavioral terms, the specific bits of knowledge and manipulative skills which the student is expected to learn from this program are described in understandable language. The statement includes the conditions under which the student will be expected to demonstrate what he has learned, specifically what he will do, and how well he must do it. If the training is intended to develop an understanding or appreciation of some idea or philosophy, there may be no way to teach the subject in the first place; if such a course were presented, how would you know if the objectives were met? A function of training is to cause the student to acquire knowledge or skill. The terminal performance objective of the training is to have the student demonstrate his acquisition of the knowledge and his ability to perform the task. For his test, the student will *do* certain things that he might not have been able to do at all, or as well as he did prior to his instruction. For example, the purpose of a training course is to qualify the peace officer in the mechanical skills of firing the revolver. The statement of objectives might be "Given a clean target at twenty-five yards, the officer will demonstrate his knowledge of the weapon by loading and unloading it without dropping the ammunition and in accordance with the posted range regulations, and within the prescribed time limits will fire a minimum score of 270 out of a possible 300 on the Standard American Target." The course is then designed to prepare the student to meet those performance objectives.

The training and objectives just described may be quite relevant to the agency's needs if the agency is a municipal police department. But of what value is the course if the agency is a probation department and the deputies are not required, nor are they encouraged, to carry firearms? Obviously, the first step in the systems method is to perform a task analysis of each position for which the training is to be designed, and eventually to instruct each individual in the specific tasks he is required to perform.

Robert F. Mager and Kenneth M. Beach, in their excellent guidebook *Developing Vocational Instruction*, stated that the systematic development of instruction "involves detailed specifications of the desired result . . . ; development of an instrument by which success can be measured; development of procedures, lessons, and materials designed to achieve the desired result; and steps to insure the continual improvement of course effectiveness."[6]

There are essentially three phases in planning a course of instruction: (1) Determine what you wish to achieve during—and as a result of—the lesson, and describe it clearly. (2) Spell out in the course objectives and in the outline what must be accomplished. (3) Check to see that the course succeeded in what it was intended to achieve.[7] In developing instruction, say Mager and Beach, this means: (1) Deriving and describing the objectives in meaningful form, (2) Developing lessons and materials designed to meet these objectives and trying out the course, and (3) Determining how well the objectives were achieved and improving the courses to improve the results.[8]

Initial Preparation

a. Describe the job. Describe specifically how the job is performed with particular emphasis on the tasks to be covered in the instruction. Define the individual's responsibility and authority for making decisions and the scope of his discretionary powers. The job description should also identify the individual and position within the hierarchy to whom the person and job under study is responsible.

b. Analyze the task. Describe the tasks separately and each of their sequential steps. Answer the questions, How often is the task performed? What is the difficulty level? How well must the task be performed to meet desirable standards?

c. Identify the student. List pertinent items that will be related to the level and methods of instruction, such as physical characteristics, education and prior training, experience level, motivation for taking the course, interests, attitudes, and biases. If the students are not known to the instructor, he may design a pretest to determine knowledge and skills which certain individuals may already be able to demonstrate. As a matter of practice, for some skills instruction, it might be wise to begin the course with pretesting and reduce the size of the class by excusing those people who pass the examination within desirable standards.

d. Determine the prerequisites. What must the student read, or perform, or what must be the entrance requirements for the course? Levels of instruction might be set for a specific course with the assumption that a certain lower proficiency level has been met.

e. Prescribe the course objectives. Specifically, upon completion, what will the student be able to do, under what given conditions, and with what minimum level of proficiency?

f. Write the examination. If the examination is to determine whether or not the objectives have been met at the conclusion of the instruction, then it is necessary to prepare the examination prior to the instruction. The examination and the instruction are inseparable, and in many cases making out the examination will be included in the list of objectives.

Course Development

a. Outlining this involves listing the major points to be covered in logical sequence and in order of importance. All the learning techniques should be considered when preparing the outline, such as the preparation, presentation, demonstration, and performance by student.

b. Sequencing. Should be logical, easy to follow, and arranged according to certain basic principles of instruction such as from simple to complex, and from familiar to unfamiliar.

c. Selecting content. Most critical, particularly for short courses of instruction. There seems to be more difficulty in determining what points *not* to include than in what *to* include in the instruction. When there is too much ground to be covered, the entire course may end in failure.

d. Selecting the instructional method. If the student is expected to demonstrate his ability to handle an intake interview at Juvenile Hall, the method of instruction might include a brief lecture to cover salient points, followed by a series of role-play situations and case-study discussions. A straight lecture would hardly be acceptable in this case. Variety in instruction methods may keep the students interested and stimulate learning. However, variety just for the sake of keeping the students entertained is a meaningless exercise. If the question of education versus training is to be addressed, this is the time to make the determination.

e. Preparing the lesson plan. A carefully prepared lesson plan, or instructional guide, will not only outline the key points to be covered, but will actually be more like a program with directions as to which method of instruction should be utilized at which points in the instruction. At certain points in the lecture, for example, the instructor might want to get feedback from the students about how much of the information they have absorbed. A script for specific questions to be asked during the discussion should be included in the lesson plan. Each new segment of instruction should list the objectives and the test items. As the instructor progresses through his outline, he will be reminded by the lesson plan to keep to the point and to be sure to prepare the students for the examination.

f. Trying out the course. Whether he chooses to practice with a live audience or not must be a decision left to the instructor. The course tryout should at least consist of reading through the material to determine that the time allotted and the material to be covered correspond in length, and to make adjustments in the outline prior to the actual presentation of the course material. Too often critiques of instruction, particularly in in-service training courses, erroneously report that the instructor did not have adequate time to present his course of instruction. The problem might be that he did not go through the tryout phase and simply tried to make four hours of material fit into two hours of assigned instruction time. With adequate planning, the instruction will fit the time provided.

Course Appraisal and Feedback

The true test of the instruction is in the student performance not only during the testing but on the job after he completes the course. If a small percentage of the students meet the terminal performance objectives, by scoring low on a written exam or failing to demonstrate a manipulative skill, the fault quite possibly lies with the inadequacy of the course or the instruction. Appraisal of a training program should include a study of the trainees in the actual performance of the tasks that they allegedly learned during the course of instruction. How the student performs during the examination will provide instant feedback on his learning skills, but how he actually performs the task after the instruction may well provide better feedback on the effectiveness of the instruction. During the evaluation process it is also possible to ascertain if the examination truly reflects the course objectives, and if the objectives are synchronized with the real needs of the profession. In a training program, it is important that the learned skills are the same as those utilized in actual practice. An educational course should likewise be relevant to current bodies of knowledge and theories. Keeping current may be accomplished through appraisal and feedback.

TRAINING OR EDUCATION REVISITED

Now that we have covered the steps of curriculum development, which include the actual instruction and feedback, perhaps a return to the argument of training versus education should be briefly considered again. Actually, it seems to me that in the systems approach to curriculum development it is only after we make a determination about the instructional content and the performance goals that it is possible to determine which approach would prove most effective. The time when a determination must be made about the instructional method also seems to be the most opportune time to determine what training approach will be used. Learning to use the firearm certainly involves a manipulative skill, but the educational approach is involved when we decide that some instruction should be included on the legal and moral obligations of the peace officer in his decision to use the firearm.

An example of a curriculum development program in which determinations were made about academic methods may be found in a study conducted by the University of Georgia in 1968.[9] In their effort to list the skills and knowledge essential to the several correctional professions and paraprofessions, the authors stated that the distinction between education and training is basically related to orientation. They added: "Education is considered to be a broad, general program of mental preparation in which the emphasis is placed on understanding and analysis. Training, on the other hand, is more narrowly conceived as techniques and specific skills for a particular occupational classification."[10]

In their study of the educational and training needs of the *corrections* component of the Criminal Justice System in the state of Georgia, Brewer and Blair broke down the occupational tasks performed by custodial officers into three categories: duties, skills, and knowledge.[11] They charted the areas of learning covered in preparing custodial officers for their duties into technical on-the-job training needs, skills, and conceptual knowledge. Their study showed a need for 21 technical on-the-job areas of training needs, 15 skills areas, and 23 areas of conceptual knowledge.[12] When applying the same method of task analysis to the jobs of probation and parole officers, the authors found that the educational background of the incumbents included at least baccalaureate college degrees, that many individuals had completed some graduate work, including several with masters' degrees. Brewer and Blair concluded that social casework, which comprises a large share of the methods used by probation and parole officers, requires graduate level education plus additional responsibilities of enforcing authoritative limits and standards on behavior. "Therefore," they stated, "it could be said that training for this field can be provided in the existing university setting and only on-the-job training in technical details needs to be provided."[13]

In their analysis of the tasks performed by probation and parole officers, using the same charting procedure, the authors listed 21 items in the category of on-the-job technical, 30 skills areas, and 33 items under the label *knowledge of*. While they stated that the training of custodial officers could be accomplished by simple on-the-job training, with some additional conceptual areas of knowledge,[14] they concluded that certain listed "skills training" items for probation and parole officers "can be taught by a university team to assure that basic conceptual knowledge is included."[15] This excellent study and its plan for action represents some of the most comprehensive work done on curriculum development for corrections education and training. It is interesting to note that the Office of Law Enforcement Assistance states in the preface: "Careful evaluation of these factors (a demographic survey of that state's probation, parole, and correctional personnel plus departmental policy and philosophy toward training) resulted in a realistic appraisal of the corrections *training* needs in the State—both immediate and long range. The Institute then devised a systematic plan of *education* to meet these needs" (italics added by this author). The defense rests . . . .

Moot court is an interesting and important part of preparation for the legal profession.
Courtesy: Pepperdine University School of Law, Santa Ana, California

THE COLLEGE AND UNIVERSITY ROLE IN CRIMINAL JUSTICE EDUCATION

A generous portion of the academic preparation for any of the criminal justice professions or paraprofessions should consist of liberal arts and basic educational subjects. A broad base in general knowledge and certain communications skills is essential to success, regardless of the specific occupation occupied upon completion of the academic exercises. Common to all major programs at the undergraduate level should be most—if not all—of the following subjects to meet the general academic base for advanced study in the major and in later graduate work: natural and/or physical science, political science or governmental institutions, American history (possibly with an emphasis on ethnic groups indigenous to the area in which the student will eventually seek employment), psychology, sociology or cultural anthropology, humanities (including the arts, languages, philosophy, or communications courses), English composition and literature, public speaking, and other electives which interest the student and may stimulate additional study to occupy his leisure time in activities that will provide a relief from the individual's professional activities.

Contrary to the beliefs of some uninitiated individuals who think that the entire law enforcement educational program is aimed at skills training, the typical program is heavily laden with general education and liberal arts courses with only a small percentage (from one-third to one-half) of the total program required in the major. Crockett and Stinchcomb state: "Unlike some occupational programs offered at the community college, the associate degree program in law enforcement has focused upon the need for a broad background of educational experience. It is designed to provide personnel with the knowledge and understanding necessary to operate effectively in a highly complex field of social control."[16]

Development of a curriculum in criminal justice education and an introduction to the academic institution involves considerable study and serious reflection. To prove the need for such a new program—which will result in claims of proliferation of courses or programs that will dilute the total academic program—will require some salesmanship and an intelligent approach to the matter when dealing with one's colleagues on campus. How can an estimate of potential students be made? From (a) A study of the employment needs in the area which identify hard facts about numbers of people already in the various occupations who will benefit from—and actively seek participation in—the new program, and (b) turnover rate, (c) recruitment projections, (d) trends in educational advancement, and (e) *professionalism movements* within the occupations. These students will also be taking advantage of the total college or university and its educational programs in addition to the specialized courses they must take in criminal justice.

Advisory committees should consist of leaders in the occupations to be served and also of community representatives who will be able to see the benefits gained from academic upgrading of the occupations. While advisory committees only advise, their influence on the academic institution can be overwhelming, particularly if the institution's goal is to serve the realistic needs of the community.

Development and introduction of an educational program new to the institution is challenging, yet rewarding. Dr. Peter P. Lejins, director of the Institute of Criminal Justice and Criminology at the University of Maryland, reported on the process and on his experiences while engaging in such a project.[17] This particular document is a must for anyone who finds himself involved in the process. Introduction of law enforcement curricula into the two-year and four-year colleges in California was, comparatively speaking, accomplished quite rapidly, in the two decades from 1953 to 1973, and with little resistance. In spite of the growth, few changes have actually been made once the programs were introduced. Only since about 1965 have the law enforcement programs been modified or supplemented to include corrections education at the lower division and undergraduate level. The principal thrust was given this movement by the several reports of the President's Crime Commission in 1967 and several subsequent studies funded by the Law Enforcement Assistance Administration and many private sources, which revealed the most urgent need for criminal justice education to upgrade all of the professions, paraprofessions, and related occupations involved in the administration of justice processes in the United States.

During the fiscal year of 1971–1972, a three-year study of the community college administration-of-justice academic programs was launched. The study reevaluated, and designed a core curriculum which would serve as a common base for educational programs leading to two-year degrees in the several different options in the field. A curriculum development task force was assigned to decide on the courses with an educational orientation (as opposed to in-service basic training programs) which would meet the academic requirements of four-year colleges and universities so that articulation would be desirable as well as feasible. I had the privilege to be included in the membership of that task force.[18] With permission of the committee chairman Mr. Bob Blanchard and of Mr. J. Winston Silva, consultant, California Community Colleges Chancellor's Office (the funding source for the project), excerpts are presented here to reflect the most current philosophy in California:

Task Force Statement of Education Philosophy

The many administration of justice agencies throughout the state and the nation have evolved from a variety of historical origins at different times and have developed into what we now see as conglomeration of professions, occupations, and paraprofessions with each requiring certain tangible and intangible skills and bodies of knowledge characteristic to their respective disciplines. The agencies within the administration of justice, in broad terms, consist of law enforcement, the courts, and corrections.

During the past several years, presidential crime commissions and numerous other segments representing a cross-section of interests have continuously concluded that education of Criminal Justice System careerists should be based on two primary theses:

1. Subsystems are no longer in a position to function in a vacuum of isolation from one another, lacking concern for the impact the operation of one subsystem has on the other; and,
2. It is of paramount importance that all system members have a deep sensitivity and understanding of human beings and the society in which they exist. This understanding should include the origin and styles of deviant behavior and current theories and practices of dealing with and treatment of these human weaknesses.

Historically, members of the administration of justice system have been educated and trained in an atmosphere of almost total segregation from their subsystem colleagues. Law enforcement, judicial and correctional personnel were educated individually with only a cursory coverage of the other member's subject matter. The segregation of the educational process has even included the almost total isolation of training facilities. Except for their sometimes concurrent attendance at an occasional college class, the members of each component were kept separate. They learned little of what the other members of the system were required to know, and the result had been what sometimes appears to be a total lack of knowledge and understanding of each other's respective roles in justice administration. Subsystem members, training for future involvement within the system, rarely had the opportunity to cross-pollinate ideas and theories on critical issues involving each of the segments. Generally, the first meeting of system members took place in the crucible of "real life," instead of in a laboratory meeting which offers a safer environment to exchange points of views and resolve difficulties. This isolationist attitude continues throughout the system in varying degrees today.

It appears inane to provide in-depth education for current and future practitioners in atmospheres of isolation and then to expect system members to magically work harmoniously in the "real world" of their constant interaction and overlapping responsibilities. The highly cooperative nature of each segment's interrelationships in the administration of justice requires more than a cursory orientation of the roles and responsibilities of the other segments. A common reservoir of knowledge would aid measurably in developing and maintaining this cooperative nature.

A common foundation of educational insights into the entire system would assist greatly in developing an understanding and sensitivity to the many difficult problems that face all members within the system. The educational approach needs to be handled on a system-wide basis. This committee has developed a core of five courses with the contents organized to include a "systems approach" to the entire administration of justice.

The committee feels that these five courses include a core of knowledge that is common to all segments of the system and will serve as a basic foundation in the building-block concept of the development of a totally integrated system. These courses have been developed with the thought of establishing a proper blend of the liberal arts and behavioral sciences with studies from the justice system.

The program for the administration of justice major in a community college should consist of a total of 24 units, including the five courses contained in this guide, which total 15 semester units. The balance of 9 units on a semester basis should be directed toward one of the sub-system components the student chooses as a specialization within the administration of justice program. Whether the student chooses law enforcement, courts, corrections, criminalistics, industrial security, or some other specialization will be determined by how he plans the balance of his schedule in addition to the five core courses. The core courses should be introduced at the lower division level in the college program. The five core courses contained in this project are classified as Part I of a multiphased master plan program. Part II will include a course outline guide of elective courses the student may take to complete his major requirements.

The committee does not perceive the five core courses as eliminating any elective courses or major courses within law enforcement, judicial or corrections. It views the core curriculum as a common starting block, logically leading into the many choices of elective courses.

In the past police science curriculums, as taught in most colleges, have been duplicated in varying degrees in most police academies. There appears to have been a high degree of overlap in the technical training courses and educational offerings. The academic approach seemed to take a back seat in favor of more traditional training methods and course content. The trend currently tends to avoid this particular approach; however, a relatively few institutions still maintain a somewhat parochial viewpoint on this issue. In some colleges, due to the alleged degree of comparable course content, transferable college units are offered for completion of a basic training academy. These units are not classified as elective credit, but part of the current block of required police science subjects.

It is the intent of the committee to establish a positive position on these controversial issues. In this light, the following points are set forth.

1. The course content as outlined in the proposed five core courses in this guide is academically developed and is not intended to include material which can be construed as training or technically related subject matter.
2. The proposed five core courses are designed to completely articulate to upper division status at 4-year colleges and universities.
3. Transferable unit credit for the five core courses should be granted only if completed in an academic college environment. Peace Officer training academies do not appear to fit this definition.
4. Transferable unit credit for the 9 (semester) units of elective work within the student's area of selected expertise should be awarded only if completed in an academic college environment.

Historical Development and Methodology. The genesis of the five core curriculum development had its inception from the 1970 Annual California Association of the Administration of Justice Educators (then known as the Police Educators Association of California). At that time, the five core courses were standardized and accepted as required classes for all police science majors. The membership adopted these courses with the proviso that the course content be revised and articulate to four year colleges. The project was funded through the California Community Colleges Office late in 1971, and established two major objectives:

1. To develop course content which provides for an academic approach and which is separated from training or vocationally oriented subject matter; and,
2. To broaden the approach to systematically include all system members within the Administration of Justice.

Reaching these objectives required the following revisions:

1. Restructuring and redesigning course content to be more palatable to all system members.

2. Restating the philosophical viewpoint to include other system members and the elimination of skill techniques or specialized emphasis in areas of interest to only one member within the system.
3. Retitling the courses to fit the system concept.

The committee met initially during October 1971, to establish the methodology of the project. A "request for help" letter went out to over 130 members within the educational field. This included a large percentage of community college educators and many four year college representatives. The request specified the need for current course outlines on the five core courses and more importantly, how they perceived these courses being taught to keep abreast of future changes and to include the entire justice system.

The returns from the field survey were reviewed, itemized, researched and consolidated and preliminary drafts were developed for each course by each committee member. Each course outline was then discussed at length by the committee sitting en masse and numerous changes were made. During March 1972, a package consisting of a rough draft of each course outline was sent again to the field asking for a critical analysis of each item contained in the courses. Mailings were sent to over 130 professional educators, training officers, and practitioners currently involved in the justice system. Evaluative comments with numerous changes were received from the field and each item was considered for inclusion in the final draft. Personal interviews were held with representatives from disciplines in the college community not associated with the justice system curriculum, practitioners within the justice system, professional educators and training officers. In May 1972, the committee met for an intensive two day course content review and preliminary final draft study seminar. At this time comments received from the field were discussed and necessary changes in the content were effected.

The course content, as now constituted, reflects the collective opinion of many professionals within the justice system. The committee recognizes the impossible task of "being all things to all people" and completely satisfying the numerous human opinions about every point within each course outline. However, during the entire project, the committee has been sensitive to the constructive evaluations from the field and made every attempt to properly and fairly resolve each issue.

The members of the committee have maintained an attitudinal posture which provided for inclusion of as many varying viewpoints as possible in the developmental phase of these courses. It is felt that this attitude of openness to suggestion and review has aided measurably the validity of course content and objectives.

Five Core Courses Redesigned The five core courses that were completely redesigned to meet what the task force agreed upon as a basic curriculum consist of (1) Introduction to the Administration of Justice, (2) Principles and Procedures of the Justice System, (3) Concepts of Criminal Law, (4) Legal Aspects of Evidence, and (5) Community Relations. Excluding the listed bibliographies for each of the courses because of variable local needs and/or desires, the course content and description of each of the five courses were presented as follows:

INTRODUCTION TO THE ADMINISTRATION OF JUSTICE

COURSE OUTLINE

LENGTH OF COURSE: 3 semester units or 4 quarter units.

COURSE DESCRIPTION: The history and philosophy of administration of justice in America; recapitulation of the system; identifying the various subsystems, role expectations, and their interrelationships; theories of crime, punishment, and rehabilitation; ethics, education and training for professionalism in the system.

COURSE GOALS:

1. To provide a knowledge of the various agencies encompassing the administration of justice system and the interrelationships between them.
2. To develop the ability of the student to recognize the administration of justice agency best suited to his or her talents and aspirations.
3. To develop an appreciation of the complexity of the total system and importance and dignity of being a part of the system.

GENERAL PERFORMANCE OBJECTIVES:

1. The student completing this course of instruction will be able to demonstrate his knowledge of the evolution of the administration of justice system, its objectives, role expectations, and trends through oral presentations and written examinations with an accuracy of 90 percent.
2. Completion of this course of instruction will develop an awareness of the crime problem. The student will demonstrate his knowledge of causal theories, criminal types, and

the implications of crime statistics through a term paper and written examinations with a 90 percent competency level.
3. Instruction shall provide the student with an overview of the organization and operation of administration of justice agencies. The student shall demonstrate his knowledge of the various agency organizational structures and their interrelationships through short essay assignments and written examinations with a 90 percent competency level.
4. The student completing this course of instruction will develop an appreciation of education, training, and professionalism in the administration of justice system. The student shall demonstrate his knowledge in this area through class discussion, research papers and written examination with 90 percent accuracy.

SCOPE:
I. The Need for Administration of Justice Agencies.
   A. ROLES AND OBJECTIVES WITHIN THE ADMINISTRATION OF JUSTICE SYSTEM.
      1. Law Enforcement
      2. Judicial
      3. Corrections
   B. EXPLANATIONS OF CRIME
      1. Causal Theories
         a. Evolution of theories
         b. Sociocultural factors
         c. Psychological considerations
         d. Political-economic implications
      2. Criminal Classifications
         a. White-collar criminal
         b. Organized crime
         c. Professional vs. causal
         d. Victimless crime
   C. SCOPE OF THE CRIME PROBLEM
      1. Implications of criminal statistics
      2. Volume and rate
      3. Crime related factors
         a. Human
         b. Time
         c. Environmental
      4. The correctional system and its relation to the problem
         a. Theories of punishment

        b. Treatment concepts
        c. Dynamics of recidivism
    5. The court system and its relation to the problem
        a. Time factors
        b. Sentencing procedures

II. Evolution of the Administration of Justice System

    A. DEVELOPMENT OF LAW ENFORCEMENT
        1. Early history
        2. Development of the English police
        3. Development of the United States police
    B. DEVELOPMENT OF THE JUDICIAL SYSTEM IN THE UNITED STATES
    C. DEVELOPMENT OF THE CORRECTIONAL SYSTEM

III. Overview of the Organization and Operation of Justice Agencies

    A. ORGANIZATION AND OPERATION OF LAW ENFORCEMENT AGENCIES
        1. Local
        2. State
        3. Federal
    B. ORGANIZATION AND OPERATION OF THE COURT SYSTEM
        1. Local
        2. State
        3. Federal
    C. ORGANIZATION AND OPERATION OF THE CORRECTIONAL SYSTEM
        1. Local
        2. State correctional institutions
        3. Federal
        4. Probation and parole

IV. An Analysis of Role Expectations in the Administration of Justice System

    A. LAW ENFORCEMENT
    B. JUDICIAL
    C. CORRECTIONS
    D. PRIVATE SECTOR

V. Education and Training

    A. COMMUNITY COLLEGE PROGRAMS
        1. Academic programs
        2. Technical training
        3. Academy training
    B. STATE COLLEGE AND UNIVERSITY PROGRAMS
        1. Academic

  2. Technical
   C. RELATIONSHIP OF PROFESSIONAL ASSOCIATIONS

VI. Professionalism
  A. CANONS AND CODES OF ETHICS
  B. RESPONSIBILITIES TO SOCIETY
  C. DISCRETIONARY POWERS

VII. Trends in the field of Administration of Justice
  A. CURRENT
  B. FUTURE

INSTRUCTIONAL METHODS:

1. Lecture and discussion
2. Guest speakers
3. Informational sheets
4. Demonstrations
5. Field trips
6. Transparencies, slides, films, audiotapes, and videotapes
7. Outside special projects and reports
8. Exploratory work experiences

EVALUATION METHODOLOGY:

1. Written examination
2. Special projects and/or report
3. Attendance
4. Class participation

MINIMUM STANDARD OF ACHIEVEMENT
Satisfactory achievement on all parts of the evaluation process.

SELECTED READINGS: (listed by the committee to reflect available current literature and texts)

PRINCIPLES AND PROCEDURES OF THE JUSTICE SYSTEM

COURSE OUTLINE

LENGTH OF COURSE: 3 semester units or 4 quarter units

COURSE DESCRIPTION: An in-depth study of the role and responsibilities of each segment within the Administration of Justice System: law enforcement, judicial, corrections. A past, present and future exposure to each subsystem procedure from initial entry to final disposition and the relationship each segment maintains with its system members.

COURSE GOALS:
1. To provide the student with a knowledge of the procedures involved in the justice system from arrest to release; and,
2. To develop skills in applying this knowledge to an understanding of the operation of the justice systems; and,
3. To develop an appreciation of the necessity for the justice system to operate as a cooperating entity so the most effective handling of cases can be provided; and,
4. To develop an ability to utilize the *material presented* in this course in making appropriate, discretionary decisions as to how to proceed while operating as a member of the system.

GENERAL PERFORMANCE OBJECTIVES:
1. When presented with the procedures involved in the justice system from arrest to release, the student will be able to demonstrate his ability to understand these concepts by passing a written examination with an accuracy of 90%.
2. After developing skills in applying knowledge of the procedures involved from arrest to release to an understanding of the operation of the justice system, the student will be able to give an oral presentation to the class that will demonstrate his understanding.
3. After developing an appreciation of the necessity for the justice system to operate as a cooperating system, the student will demonstrate his knowledge of his appreciation by writing a research paper describing his competency.
4. After developing an ability to utilize material in making appropriate decisions on how to operate as a member of the system, the student will demonstrate his knowledge of system membership by passing an essay examination with an accuracy of 90%.

SCOPE:

I. **Conceptualization**
   A. SUBSYSTEMS: FROM ARREST TO RELEASE
   B. ROLE IDENTIFICATION
   C. ROLE CONFLICT

D. SYSTEM OR NONSYSTEM
   E. THE CHALLENGE OF SUBSYSTEM COOPERATION

II. Legal Authorization for System
   A. U.S. CONSTITUTION
   B. CALIFORNIA CONSTITUTION
   C. CALIFORNIA PENAL CODE
   D. OTHER RELATED LEGAL PROVISIONS

III. Implications of Civil Rights
   A. ITS EFFECTS ON SYSTEM MEMBERS
   B. CONSTITUTIONAL GUARANTEES
   C. BILL OF RIGHTS

IV. The Police Process
   A. POLICE POWERS
   B. PROCESS OF ARREST
      1. Definitions
      2. Purpose
      3. Discretionary powers
         a. As last alternative
         b. Psychological and social impact
      4. Peace officer
      5. Private person
      6. Warrant
      7. Citation
      8. Responsibility of arrestee
   C. INITIAL CONFINEMENT
      1. Why jail?
      2. Alternatives
      3. Process of bail
         a. Historical aspects of bail
         b. Purpose
         c. Injustice
         d. Reform

V. Coroner—Medical Examiner
   A. HISTORICAL AND LEGAL CONSIDERATIONS
   B. RESPONSIBILITIES OF THE OFFICE
   C. THE INQUEST PROCESS

VI. Prosecuting Attorneys
   A. TYPES
      1. Attorney general
      2. District attorney
      3. City attorneys

B. FUNCTIONS
  1. Role and responsibilities
  2. Legal authority—discretionary powers
  3. Organization/staffing
  4. Relationship to city, state, federal prosecution
  5. Political implications
  6. Strengths and weaknesses
  7. Contemporary issues

VII. Defense Attorneys
A. PUBLIC DEFENDERS
  1. Role and responsibilities
  2. Legal authority
  3. Organization/staffing
  4. Political involvement
  5. Fees
  6. Relationship with system members
B. PRIVATE COUNSEL
  1. Politics of defense
  2. Fees
  3. Manipulating the system
     a. Continuances
     b. Jury selection
C. LEGAL AID SOCIETY
  1. Purpose
  2. Historical development
  3. Fees
  4. Organization/staffing
  5. How supported
  6. Political problems

VIII. State and Federal Regulatory Agencies
A. ABC
B. PUBLIC UTILITIES COMMISSION
C. F.C.C.
D. F.A.A.
E. FEDERAL SECURITY
F. CONSUMER AFFAIRS COUNCIL
G. LABOR COMMISSION
H. STATE COMPENSATION
I. DMV

IX. Courts
A. COURT STRUCTURE AND JURISDICTION
  1. Justice

2. Municipal
3. Superior
4. State appellate
5. State supreme
6. Federal district court
7. Federal appellate court
8. Federal supreme court
B. MAGISTRATE AND REFEREE
1. Historical significance
2. Responsibilities and duties
3. How selected
4. Qualifications
5. Political implications
6. Discretionary powers
7. Tenure
8. Removal
C. COURT APPEARANCES AND PROCEEDINGS
1. Purpose—rights of defendant
2. Arraignments
   a. Types of pleas
   b. Negotiated plea
3. Preliminary examination
4. Grand jury indictment
5. Trials
6. Appeals
7. Sentencing hearing
8. Court role of probation officer
D. THE VERDICT
1. Instruction to jury
2. Deliberation
3. Types of verdicts
E. SENTENCING PROCESS
1. Probation review and recommendation
2. Diagnostic research
3. Definite/indeterminate sentence
4. Sentence as prescribed by law
5. Granting probation
6. Inequity of sentences
7. Adult authority
   a. Responsibilities
   b. Constituted authority

XII. Correctional Concepts
A. GENERAL PHILOSOPHY
1. Stated objectives

2. Success factor
B. PROCESS UPON SENTENCING
1. Reception guidance centers
a. Classification and assignment
2. Role of adult authority
a. Determination of sentence
b. Assessment of rehabilitation
C. SECURITY FACILITIES
1. Maximum
2. Medium
3. Minimum
4. Locations
D. REHABILITATION—REALITY OR MYTH?
1. Purpose
2. Models
3. Contemporary issues
E. PRESENT CONCEPT OF TREATMENT
1. Community treatment centers
2. Model centers for treatment
a. Prisons without walls
3. Responsibility of educational institutions
F. THE FUNCTIONS OF PAROLE
1. Objectives
a. Rehabilitation under supervision
b. Social reintegration
2. The parolee
3. Role of the parole officer as a change agent
4. Case load
5. Success factor
6. Conditions of parole

XIII. Community Service Organizations
A. PURPOSES
1. Reason for development
2. Relationship with the justice system
3. Objectives of service
B. ORGANIZATIONS
1. Teen Challenge
2. Youth centers
3. Free clinics
4. Narcotics rehabilitation homes
5. Alcohol rehabilitation homes
6. Suicide prevention centers
7. Crash pads

INSTRUCTIONAL METHODS:

    1. Lecture
    2. Seminar style discussion
    3. Guest lecturers
    4. Demonstration
    5. Case studies
    6. Community based field trips
    7. Resource texts
    8. Correlational readings
    9. Special projects or papers presented for class evaluation

EVALUATION METHODOLOGY:

    1. Essay examination
        a. Quizzes
        b. Mid-term
        c. Final
    2. Active participation during class discussion
    3. Special project, paper or case study presentation to class
    4. Attendance

MINIMUM STANDARD OF ACHIEVEMENT:

    1. Satisfactory completion of all stated performance objectives. A minimum score of 70% out of a possible 100% on all examinations, papers, presentations and special projects.

SELECTED READINGS: (listed by the committee to reflect available current literature and texts)

CONCEPTS OF CRIMINAL LAW

COURSE OUTLINE

LENGTH OF COURSE: 3 semester units or 4 quarter units

COURSE DESCRIPTION: Historical development, philosophy of law and constitutional provisions; definitions, classification of crime, and their application to the system of administration of justice;

legal research, study of case law, methodology, and concepts of law as a social force.

COURSE GOALS:

1. To provide the student with a knowledge of the historical development of law and the philosophy of law.
2. To familiarize the student with the United States Constitution and to integrate constitutional provisions with the fundamentals of law.
3. To introduce the student to basic legal definitions and concepts which provide a foundation for law.
4. To develop within the student an appreciation for the value of case study and legal research as a means of interpreting court decisions in relation to the written statutes.

GENERAL PERFORMANCE OBJECTIVES:

1. When presented with an historical perspective of law, the student will be able to give an oral presentation to the class that would demonstrate his understanding of the cultural evolution of law. Each student will also be able to answer questions in a written examination pertaining to the philosophical and historical development of law with accuracy of 90%.
2. When confronted with a legal problem, the student will be able to associate appropriate cases and exercise sound discretion based upon legal research methodology and will be able to write briefs concerning decisions rendered in these cases that will demonstrate his understanding of the application of legal research.
3. When confronted with constitutional amendments, the student will develop a perception of contemporary issues relating to the administration of justice and will be able to demonstrate his knowledge of the legal concepts examined in class by writing a term paper describing these concepts.
4. When introduced to the basic legal definitions and concepts of law for nonlawyers, the student will develop the ability to cope with operational experiences by applying these definitions and concepts to the relevant legal codes in the administration of justice. The student will be able to demonstrate his ability to understand legal definitions and concepts by passing a written examination with accuracy of 90%.

SCOPE:

I. Legal Research and Methodology
   A. RAMIFICATIONS OF LEGAL RESEARCH
   B. ORIENTATION TO CASE CITATIONS
   C. OUTLINE OF THE LEGAL BRIEF
   D. USE OF THE LAW LIBRARY
   E. ATTORNEY GENERAL OPINIONS

II. Philosophical and Historical Development
   A. GENERAL AND SPECIFIC SOURCES OF LAW
   B. DEVELOPMENT OF COMMON LAW
   C. THE CONCEPTS OF STARE DECISIS
   D. PREEMPTION
   E. REPEAL
   F. MALA IN SE VS. MALA PROHIBITA CRIMES
   G. CRIMES WITHOUT VICTIMS
   H. FEDERAL CONSTITUTIONAL PROVISIONS
   I. POLICE POWER
   J. SUBSTANTIVE VS. PROCEDURAL LAW

III. The Nature of Criminal Law
   A. THE DEFINITION OF CRIME
   B. THE PURPOSE OF CRIMINAL LAW
   C. THE LANGUAGE AND CONSTRUCTION OF PENAL STATUTES
   D. CONFLICTS BETWEEN STATUTES
   E. DISTINCTION BETWEEN CRIMES AND TORTS
   F. CRIMINAL AND CIVIL LIABILITY
   G. JUDICIAL REVIEW

IV. Classification of Crimes
   A. DISTINCTION BETWEEN FELONIES, MISDEMEANORS, AND INFRACTIONS
   B. PUNISHMENTS
   C. PRIOR CONVICTIONS
   D. LESSER AND INCLUDED OFFENSES
   E. DOUBLE JEOPARDY

V. Corpus Delicti—Elements of Crime
   A. ROLE OF CORPUS DELICTI
   B. ACT AND INTENT—NEGLIGENCE
   C. PROXIMATE CAUSE
   D. GENERAL INTENT
   E. SPECIFIC INTENT
   F. TRANSFERRED INTENT

VI. **Capacity to Commit Crime**
   A. EXEMPTIONS TO CRIMINAL LIABILITY
   B. DIMINISHED CAPACITY
   C. CAPITAL CRIMES
   D. MALICE
   E. MOTIVE
   F. INTOXICATION
   G. PARTIES TO A CRIME
   H. ATTEMPTS
   I. CONSPIRACY

VII. **Overview of Specific Crimes**
   A. CRIMES AGAINST THE PERSON AND PROPERTY
      1. General application of segments V and VI
   B. CRIMES AGAINST PUBLIC DECENCY, MORALITY AND THE PUBLIC PEACE
      1. Historical development
      2. Constitutionally related discussion
      3. Community standards
   C. RELATED ENFORCEABLE LAWS
      1. Health and safety
      2. Business and professions
      3. Welfare and institutions
      4. United States code
      5. Fish and game
      6. City and county ordinances

INSTRUCTIONAL METHODS:

1. Lecture and discussion
2. Case study of recent court decisions
3. Students to brief and discuss case and its implications to the administration of justice
4. Field trip to county law library
5. Handouts
6. Texts and supplemental resources

EVALUATION METHODOLOGY:

1. Written examinations
   a. Quizzes
   b. Mid-term
   c. Final

2. Active participation in class discussion
3. Presentation of research papers to class
4. Attendance

MINIMUM STANDARD OF ACHIEVEMENT:
Satisfactory achievement on all evaluation methods, with a minimum score of 70% on a possible total of 100%.

SELECTED READINGS: (listed by the committee to reflect available current literature and texts)

LEGAL ASPECTS OF EVIDENCE

COURSE OUTLINE

LENGTH OF COURSE: 3 semester units, 4 quarter units

COURSE DESCRIPTION: Origin, development, philosophy and constitutional basis of evidence; constitutional and procedural considerations affecting arrest, search and seizure; kinds and degrees of evidence and rules governing admissibility; judicial decisions interpreting individual rights and case studies.

COURSE GOALS:

1. To provide the student with a working knowledge of the rules of evidence, the various kinds of evidence, and the admissibility of evidence.
2. To develop in the student the ability to evaluate the various kinds of evidence available in a given case in order to determine its admissibility in court.
3. To develop in the student skill in handling case material so that evidence admissibility will not be destroyed by improper techniques or procedures.
4. To develop in the student an appreciation of the value of all kinds of evidence and the need to use proper procedures and techniques so as to maintain the value and admissibility of evidence.
5. To impress upon the student that legally admissible evidence is the end product of all the work and effort of the

crime investigator, and that it is essential that he possess a sound knowledge of the rules of evidence.

GENERAL PERFORMANCE OBJECTIVES:

1. The student will be able to demonstrate a working knowledge of the rules of evidence, the various kinds of evidence, and the admissibility of evidence by passing a written examination.
2. The student will be able to evaluate the various kinds of evidence available in a given case and will demonstrate this ability by writing a term paper concerning its admissibility in court.
3. The student will demonstrate his ability to use proper procedures in maintaining the value of evidence by performing satisfactorily in a role-playing setting, involving a hypothetical case.
4. The student will demonstrate that he knows how to relate legally admissible evidence to the corpus delicti of the crime under investigation by passing a written examination.

SCOPE:

I. **Evolution of Evidence**
   A. WHAT IS EVIDENCE?
   B. PROOF AND BURDEN OF PROOF
   C. REASONS FOR RULES OF EVIDENCE
   D. THE EVIDENCE CODE
   E. APPLICATION OF RULES OF EVIDENCE
   F. DOCTRINE OF JUDICIAL NOTICE
   G. PRESUMPTION

II. **Detention and Arrest**
   A. CONSTITUTIONAL AUTHORITY
   B. PROCEDURES—PROBABLE CAUSE
   C. EVOLUTION OF CASE LAW
      1. *Weeks*
      2. *Cahan*
      3. *Rochin*
      4. *Wolf*
      5. *Mapp*
      6. *Miranda*

III. **Search and Seizure**
   A. HISTORY AND DEVELOPMENT—CASE LAW

B. THE EXCLUSIONARY RULE—DEFINITION
C. DEFINE
   1. What is search
   2. What is seizure
D. SEARCH WARRANTS
E. SEARCH INCIDENTAL TO ARREST
F. CONSENT SEARCH
G. SEARCH AND SEIZURE INCIDENTAL TO ARREST
   1. Cursory search
   2. Temporary detention
   3. Stop and frisk
H. SEARCH OF
   1. Houses
   2. Vehicles
   3. Other places

IV. **Discovery**
   A. REPORTING AND DISCOVERY PROCEDURES
   B. WHAT IS THE RIGHT OF DISCOVERY
   C. IMPORTANCE TO INVESTIGATOR
   D. PRE-TRIAL DISCOVERY
   E. RIGHT OF DISCOVERY THROUGH PRELIMINARY HEARING
   F. PROSECUTION'S RIGHT OF DISCOVERY
   G. UNAVAILABILITY OF ORIGINAL NOTES

V. **Types of Evidence**
   A. REAL EVIDENCE
      1. Defined
      2. Examples
   B. DIRECT
      1. Defined
      2. Examples
   C. CIRCUMSTANTIAL
      1. Defined
      2. Examples
   D. PREJUDICE
   E. SPECIFIC KINDS
      1. Character
      2. Manner of proof
      3. Character of victim
   F. SIMILAR OR RELATED ACTS OR CIRCUMSTANCES
      1. Possession of recently stolen property
      2. Sudden affluence
      3. Flight or other evasion

4. Complaint in sex offenses
5. Threats and prior difficulties

VI. **Witnesses—Competency**
   A. DEFINITION
   B. GROUNDS FOR QUALIFICATION AND DISQUALIFICATION
   C. ANALYSIS OF STATUTORY GROUNDS

VII. **Privileged Communication**
   A. BASIC STATUTES—EVIDENCE CODE
   B. GENERAL
   C. ATTORNEY AND CLIENT
      1. Nature of privilege
      2. Requirements
      3. Exceptions
   D. HUSBAND AND WIFE
      1. Privilege not to testify against spouse
         a. Nature of privilege
         b. Requirements
         c. Exceptions
      2. Privilege for confidential marital communication
         a. Nature and purpose
         b. Requirements
         c. Exceptions
   E. PHYSICIAN AND PATIENT
      1. Nature of privilege
   F. PSYCHOTHERAPIST AND PATIENT
      1. Nature of privilege
      2. Requirements
   G. CLERGYMAN AND CONFESSOR
      1. Nature of privilege
   H. IDENTITY OF INFORMER
      1. Nature of privilege
      2. Disclosure necessary for fair trial
      3. Where disclosure not required
   I. NEWS MEDIA
      1. Nature of privilege

VIII. **Self-incrimination and nontestimonial compulsion**
   A. BASIC STATUTES—EVIDENCE CODE
   B. NATURE OF PRIVILEGE
   C. DISTINCTION BETWEEN DEFENDANT AND WITNESS PRIVILEGE
   D. SCOPE OF PRIVILEGE
   E. GRANTING IMMUNITY AND EFFECT
   F. WHAT CONSTITUTES COMPULSION TO TESTIFY

G. NONTESTIMONIAL COMPULSION
H. BRUTAL BODY EXAMINATION
I. REASONABLE BODY EXAMINATION

IX. The Opinion Rule
A. BASIC STATUTES—EVIDENCE CODE
B. NON-EXPERT TESTIMONY
C. EXPERT OPINION
   1. Common knowledge

X. Impeachment, Corroboration and Refreshing Memory
A. BASIC STATUTES—EVIDENCE
B. IMPEACHMENT
C. CORROBORATION
D. REFRESHING RECOLLECTION OF MEMORY
E. PAST RECOLLECTION RECORDED

XI. Hearsay
A. DEFINED
B. DYING DECLARATION
C. SPONTANEOUS OR CONTEMPORANEOUS STATEMENTS
D. STATEMENTS AGAINST INTEREST
E. MENTAL STATE
F. BUSINESS RECORDS
G. OFFICIAL RECORDS
H. FAMILY HISTORY

XII. Confessions and Admissions
A. BASIC STATUTES—EVIDENCE CODE
B. STATEMENT OF CONSTITUTIONAL RIGHTS
C. *Miranda* WARNING
D. CASE LAW AFFECTING INTERVIEWING

XIII. Documentary Evidence
A. BASIC STATUTES—EVIDENCE CODE
B. BEST EVIDENCE RULE
C. RECORDINGS
D. OFFICIAL WRITINGS

XIV. Photographic Evidence
A. PHOTOGRAPHS AS EVIDENCE
B. FIRST RULE OF ADMISSIBILITY—RELEVANCY
C. SECOND RULE OF ADMISSIBILITY—ACCURATE REPRESENTATION
D. INDENTIFICATION OF A PHOTOGRAPH
E. POSED PHOTOGRAPHS
F. GRUESOME PHOTOGRAPHS

G. NUDE PHOTOGRAPHS
H. MOTION PICTURES AS EVIDENCE
I. COLORED PHOTOGRAPHS
J. PRINTS TO BE USED AS EVIDENCE

XV. **Introducing Evidence at Trial**
   A. PROPER HANDLING OF EVIDENCE AND MAINTAINING CHAIN OF EVIDENCE
   B. CONNECTING EVIDENCE WITH ISSUES OF TRIAL
   C. TACTICS OF DEFENSE TO DISCREDIT EVIDENCE

INSTRUCTIONAL METHODS:

1. Lecture—Discussion
2. Demonstration
3. Guest Speakers
4. Information Sheets
5. Transparencies, slides, films, and video tape
6. Moot Court (Role-playing)
7. Field trips to a court in action
8. Special projects or case study and report

EVALUATION METHODOLOGY:

1. Written examinations
   a. Midterms
   b. Final exam
2. Written project or case study report
3. Attendance
4. Active class participation

MINIMUM STANDARD OF ACHIEVEMENT:

1. Satisfactory completion of all stated performance objectives. A minimum score of 70% out of a possible 100% on all examinations, papers, presentations and special projects.

SELECTED READINGS: (listed by the committee to reflect available current literature and texts)

COMMUNITY RELATIONS

COURSE OUTLINE

LENGTH OF COURSE: 3 semester units or 4 quarter units

COURSE DESCRIPTION: An in-depth exploration of the roles of the administration of justice practitioners and their agencies. Through interaction and study the student will become aware of the interrelationships and role expectations among the various agencies and the public. Principal emphasis will be placed upon the professional image of the system of justice administration and the development of positive relationships between members of the system and the public.

COURSE GOALS:

1. Acquire a broad base of information regarding the social and ethnic structure of the community and the variety of cultural influences.
2. Develop an awareness of the many real and/or imagined problems of the various segments of the community in relationship to the Criminal Justice System. This shall be accomplished by means of an opinion survey, survey of available literature, lectures, and guest appearances.
3. Participate in discussions and group projects to acquire an awareness of the social and personal needs of the various individuals and groups of individuals in the modern society that may have previously been foreign to the awareness and experience of the students.
4. Identify conflicts in principles and philosophies of individuals and groups of individuals that contribute to confrontations and physical conflict with different segments of the Criminal Justice System.

GENERAL PERFORMANCE OBJECTIVES:

1. The student will demonstrate his fundamental knowledge of police procedures and philosophy and ability to explain them in informal dialogue session in real and simulated sessions. He will be rated by his fellow students on a five point chart and will meet the minimum standards agreed upon by the rating group.
2. Each student will participate in a group project consisting of one of the topics decided upon during the first three meetings of the course. He will perform according to the minimum standards decided upon by the project team, and

the final product of each group must be acceptable according to the requirements of a chief of police, probation officer, judicial process representative, or department head or his designee whose agency has the need for such a project. (This is determined by the instructor prior to the beginning of the course.)
3. The student will prepare a report or critique that reflects his critical evaluation of class activity or guest appearance. He will describe the activity or guest appearance. He will describe the activity, evaluate it in terms of relativity to the course objectives, and will make positive recommendations for future activities of a similar nature. The critique will meet the requirements of the form.
4. In simulated and actual situations, each participant will demonstrate his ability to engage in dialogue with people from a variety of backgrounds and different points of view, and will explain the justice system and policies to the satisfaction of a team of his peers serving as evaluators with a score of at least seventy out of a possible one-hundred points.

SCOPE:

I. Lecture Outline
   A. HISTORY OF CHANGE IN COMMUNITY RELATIONS IN THE ADMINISTRATION OF JUSTICE.
      1. "Public" vs. "Community" Relations
      2. Agency Responsibility to the communities they serve
   B. AGENCY BASED COMMUNITY RELATIONS PROGRAMS
      1. Description and Discussion of on-going programs
      2. Police—Courts—Corrections
   C. HUMAN RELATIONSHIPS AND CULTURAL CONSIDERATIONS
   D. COMMUNICATIONS
      1. Verbal
      2. Nonverbal
      3. Listening
      4. Blocks to effective communications
      5. Overcoming the blocks
   E. DYNAMICS AND MEDIA
      1. Criminal Justice–Press Relationships
      2. Policies and Procedures of agencies
      3. Agency-Community Relationships
   F. MILITANT AND DISSIDENT ORGANIZATIONS
      1. Current trends

2. Identification of organizations and leaders
3. Philosophies and methods utilized by the organization
G. STUDENTS CULTURE AND JUSTICE SYSTEM
1. Relationships
H. DISCRETIONARY DECISION MAKING
1. Alternatives
2. Psychological impact
I. THE SYSTEM IMAGE
1. Law enforcement
2. The courts
3. Corrections

II. Role Play and Actual Dialogue Sessions

Suggested topics. Guest speakers, and simulated representatives chosen from the class or elsewhere, should be utilized to expose the student to a wide variation of points of view.

A. CURRENT TOPICS FROM NEWS ITEMS
B. LAW ENFORCEMENT
1. The Police and civil rights
2. Local minority group–police relationships
3. Police policy on when to shoot
4. Probable cause for field interviews
5. Police responsibility at family disturbances
6. Police weapons, are they humane?
7. Too much "police protection" of certain neighborhoods
8. Officer powers of arrest and search
9. Prejudicial-preferential treatment by police
10. Lack of uniformity in law enforcement
11. Traffic control and law enforcement
12. Unpopular narcotics laws and enforcement
C. COURTS
1. What is the value of the Bartered Plea?
2. Why do the courts let arrested criminals off on technicalities?
3. Discussion of equity in meting out sentences
4. How do judges determine length of sentence?
5. Is the Supreme Court exceeding its authority?
6. Describe the role of the district attorney
7. Why does an attorney defend a client he knows is guilty?
8. Is there a value to the public defender system?
D. CORRECTIONS
1. Why give 72-hour passes to criminal convicts?
2. What factors determine a good probation risk?

3. What types of punishment are administered in prisons?
4. Does parole fail?
5. Community centered treatment programs
6. Parolees as parole officers
7. Is the prison system working as it should?
8. Is probation better for rehabilitation than imprisonment?

III. Group Projects

Topic and procedure for study and development to be determined by the instructor and the class. It should be related to the lecture topics and a group presentation may take the place of a lecture.

INSTRUCTIONAL METHODS:

1. Lecture
2. Seminar Style Discussion
3. Guest Lecturers
4. Demonstration
5. Case Studies
6. Community based field trips
7. Resource texts
8. Correlational readings
9. Special projects or papers presented for class evaluation

EVALUATION METHODOLOGY:

1. Essay examination
   a. Quizzes
   b. Midterm
   c. Final
2. Active participation during class discussion
3. Special project, paper or case study presentation to class
4. Attendance

MINIMUM STANDARD OF ACHIEVEMENT:

1. Satisfactory completion of all stated performance objectives. A minimum score of 70% out of a possible 100% on all examinations, papers, presentations and special projects.

SELECTED READINGS: (Listed by the committee to reflect available current literature and texts)

University of Maryland Law Enforcement Curriculum

The law enforcement curriculum adopted by the University of Maryland reflects a strong orientation in general education and liberal arts.[19] Out of a total of 124 semester units listed, only 30 units or a total of ten courses in law enforcement are listed as required. That curriculum includes the following courses: (1) introduction to law enforcement, (2) criminal investigation in law enforcement, (3) criminal law, (4) criminal procedure and evidence, (5) advanced legal problems, (6) law enforcement-community relations, (7) advanced law enforcement administration, (8) law enforcement personnel supervision, (9) security administration, and (10) directed independent research.

Dr. Tenney lists three models for law enforcement curricula, one for the two-year preservice and in-service (line) program, one for the two year in-service staff program, and a four-year program.[20] In addition to the essential courses in human relations (an integrated study of the social and behavioral sciences,) English, humanities, and science, Tenney lists for the preservice and in-service (line) program the following courses in criminal justice: (1) introduction to criminal justice I, (2) criminal law and procedure, (3) introduction to criminal justice II, (4) police operations, (5) evidence and (6) skills development, or skills training. The program includes 24 semester hours in criminal justice courses out of a total of 61 hours. The two-year model for in-service (staff) includes 24 semester hours out of a total of 60 in the following courses: (1) police organization and administration, (2) personnel management, (3) two semesters of police operations, (4) police-community relations, and (5) eight units of skills development or training.

In his model for a four-year college program, Dr. Tenney again strongly emphasizes the essential general education and liberal arts courses with a total of 53 semester hours in criminal justice courses and 15 in electives which might include criminal justice courses. The courses listed in this model include (1) two courses in introduction to criminal justice, (2) criminal law and procedure, (3) evidence, (4) police-community relations, (5) police organization and management, (6) the patrol function, (7) criminalistics, (8) the investigative function (9) police-juvenile problems, (10) the traffic problem, (11) comparative police systems, and (12) skills development.

University of Long Beach Law Enforcement Curriculum

Dr. Guthrie, then chairman of the Department of Criminology at California State College (now university) at Long Beach, outlined what he believed to be a comprehensive and workable program for law enforcement education at both two- and four-year institutions. Recommended curricula for four-year programs were:

Lower Division (first 2 years of college)
  Lower divison objectives:
    a. Liberal arts background (general education and required courses)
    b. Occupational training at performance level (full-time students and officers attending part time)
    c. Provision of a basis for upper division work
    d. Provision of a professional career preparation at entrance level
    e. Service courses to other college disciplines (business, engineering, government, journalism)
  Criteria for placement at lower divison level
    a. Orientation
    b. Broad liberal arts background
    c. Tool or technique type for practitioners
Upper Division (last 2 years of college)
  Objectives:
    1. Broad liberal arts background
    2. Education in theory of supervision and administration
    3. Amplification of lower division work through specialized courses
    4. Professional career preparation for supervisory and administrative assignment
    5. Teacher preparation for academic, state legislated training programs, junior colleges, colleges, and universities
    6. Background for graduate work
    7. Opportunity to participate in research
    8. Service courses for other disciplines
  Criteria for placing in upper division
    a. Advanced or highly specialized
    b. Supervisory or administrative in nature
    c. Theory and policy courses needed by top-level managers
Recommended Junior College Transfer Curriculum
  A. General education requirements
  B. Major (includes following courses)
  Introductory or orientation course
  Law
  Evidence

Procedure
Criminal investigation
Patrol procedures
Traffic control

Electives should include typewriting, first aid, lifesaving, photography

Liaison between 2-year and 4-year institutions is recommended.
Coordination is necessary between junior colleges and 4-year colleges in these areas:
1. Relative to courses and units acceptable for transfer from 4-year colleges to 2-year colleges
2. Junior colleges acceptance of academy, institute, or other non-academic, non-accredited, law enforcement training. No transfer-accredited courses only
3. Relative to student counseling terminal versus transfer programs[21]

It seems to me that lower division college work in the four-year institution and in the two-year program at a community or junior college, which comprises the same first two years of college as the university or state college, should be similar if not identical. True, there are many students who do not continue beyond the community or junior college. The educational programs should be comparable. The students who transfer from a state university or college to a two-year institution should be able to do so as easily as the students who transfer from a community to a state college.

Rutgers University Law Enforcement Curriculum

In *Police Science Degree Programs*, Professor Jack A. Mark, Director of the Police Science Program at Rutgers University, New Brunswick, New Jersey, made these recommendations to the Office of Law Enforcement Asistance about the funding of educational programs through loans and grants to students:

1 . . . strongly focus on transfer and baccalaureate programs
2 . . . look at funded programs of a terminal nature
3 . . . encourage planning and development of a master plan which seeks to accomplish the following:
   A. Inventory of educational achievement
   B. Coordinated approach in development of programs in police science:
      leave no gaps and avoid proliferation.

C. A joint and coordinated development of programs in police science so that curricula dovetail and courses provide a logical sequence to one another and supplement each other well.
D. Standardization of course nomenclature, content, and treatment of subject matter to make possible improved course evaluation and student programming.
E. Close liaison between lower and upper-division colleges and their chairman, etc.
F. Reasonably high standards for the faculty, supporting facilities, equipment, and instructional materials.
G. Sharing of faculty and staff facilities where no conflict exists.
H. Coordinated participation of faculties of several schools offering programs in police science, offering specialized institutes and seminars, research cooperation.
I. High calibre work-study programs
J. Winnowing of terminal programs and support only if a "richer transfer program cannot meet the needs of the community."[22]

Summary of Law Enforcement Educational Programs

Based on a study of the material discussed in this chapter and of literally dozens of catalogs for two-year and four-year institutions that present undergraduate educational programs in administration of justice, it appears that approximately one-third of the total program at lower-and upper-division undergraduate levels is in criminal justice; the balance of the educational program consists of a general education–liberal arts emphasis with strong recommendations for electives in the behavioral and social sciences. Specialized and professional courses may be offered within the institution's program, but their primary purpose is to serve as electives or to meet certain specialized in-service needs of the students.

Courses offered at various institutions at both upper and lower-division levels, and in some cases at graduate level, include the following.

Introduction to law enforcement (or administration of justice)
Introduction to corrections
Police administration (organization and management)
Police operations (patrol, traffic, other basic operations)
Criminal justice administration
Police role in crime and delinquency
Juvenile delinquency prevention and control
Concepts of criminal law
Criminal codes of the state
Legal aspects of evidence

Principles and procedures in the justice system
Community relations
Criminalistics (introductory and advanced)
Crime scene investigation
Defensive tactics
Firearms (or gunnery)
Investigation principles
Counseling and interviewing in corrections
Legal problems in corrections
Institutional (or jail) procedures
Civil procedures for court officers and bailiffs
Contemporary treatment concepts
Traffic control
Collison investigation
Business and industrial security
Police patrol techniques
Narcotics investigation and enforcement
Operational intelligence and vice control
Organized crime
Work experience (or skills development)
Internship or cadet orientation
Fingerprint technology
Questioned document examination
Supervision
Auxiliary services
Records and report writing
Virtually any course that a curriculum committee and college faculty agree meets educational criteria and can be presented at college level.

Correctional education is unique in some respects, according to Montilla. He states:

> Correctional agencies, along with all correctional programs, are part of society's system for the administration of criminal justice (which has its own local, state and national dimensions) in which the primary goal is public protection through crime and delinquency prevention and control. Within this system, correctional agencies and programs are associated with police, prosecution and the courts. But correctional agencies and programs are also part of society's "civil" machinery concerned with general health and welfare in which there is also a broad goal of public protection. Here correction is associated with the fields of medicine, education, social services and a variety of community institutions. The basic, and sometimes conflicting, differences

between the two systems are rooted in different orientations of the law: (1) that which relies on punishment of the offender for the purpose of retribution and as a possible deterrence to others, and (2) that which relies on the scientific method to help understand personality, group and environmental factors that influence human behavior so that these factors can be constructively manipulated to reduce disordered and deviant behavior.[23]

Those observations lend weight to our proposal that there be a common core of knowledge in the education of all criminal justice personnel. Beyond the core, then, there must be an entirely diverse array of courses that will be peculiar only to that criminal justice component for which the student becomes more specialized.

The meaning of "college level" instruction depends on the evaluator. It seems to me that, in order for a course to qualify for fully transferable college credit that will articulate with higher divisions and will stand by itself as a college course, the material should involve conceptual knowledge and be acceptable to the academic community as *college education*.

COLLEGE-AFFILIATED SEMINARS AND SPECIALIZED TRAINING COURSES

The college atmosphere and the expertise of professional educators who may be utilized in the development and presentation of seminars and courses on specialized subjects are conducive to the development of college-affiliated training programs. Clearly identified as technical training, no college credit should be granted, but a commensurate system of awarding of training points (1 point for every 20 hours, for example) in lieu of college credits would enhance the success of the programs. In pay incentive programs, the training points should be negotiable in conjunction with college credit. In California at the present time, all new training programs must be presented by, or in affiliation with, colleges or universities. It is possible to keep those seminars and short courses separate from the regular educational program by presenting them through a college foundation rather than through the instructional office. In some cases, the course may be presented as a part of the adult or continuing education program with no credit awarded.

Colleges have a major problem in affiliating with police academies, i.e., in order for the college to financially support an academy course it must be one that involves granting of credit. For many years, we have been pretending that some lower-division college courses and some academy courses have been identical. In some California colleges, transcripts show credit for attending courses listed in the catalog under the titles of Introduction to Law Enforcement, Police Patrol, and others, although the student attended an academy instead of any of those courses. In my opinion, that is a moral error, because I believe that those college courses and the academy courses are separate and distinct from each other. Academies should be clearly listed as academies; if such academies are granted the privilege of giving college credit, such credit should apply toward lower-division "terminal-degree" units. Those units should not, however, apply toward a baccalaureate degree. To allow such a practice would require a complete reconstruction of and an entirely different orientation to academy courses.

There is no valid reason why an academic institution should not actively take a leadership role in criminal justice training. Through separate funding resources—such as paid tuition that supports the housekeeping, instructional, and materials costs—the programs could be self-sustaining. An ideal "center of excellence" concept would be a conglomerate of academic and educational programs, institutes, seminars, and other activities designed to bring about an overall improvement in the various occupations and professions in the Criminal Justice System. Through consortia of several institutions, it would be possible to present noncredit training courses, upper- and lower-division educational courses, and even graduate courses in affiliation with a university.

Participation by colleges and universities in criminal justice training programs has increased particularly since the inauguration of the Safe

Official photograph, Los Angeles Police Department

Streets Act of 1968. Literally millions of dollars have been used to support students and programs in criminal justice training. The funding has been from federal sources through the Office of Law Enforcement Assistance. State funding is also used for similar purposes. For example, in California more than eight million dollars each year are assessed from traffic violators for the purpose of peace officer training. Although most of the money goes to the departments for reimbursement of wages while the officers are attending the training courses, reimbursement to the colleges for direct expenses of presenting specialized courses provides the financial support which makes such courses available. Among the courses which derive their support from federal and state sources are seminars in executive development, middle-management, and first-line supervision.[24]

IN-SERVICE TRAINING

Training for corrections personnel in the positions of custodial, probation, and parole officers has been systematically described by Brewer and Blair.[25] They listed a nine-part base of knowledge that should be common to all three categories of correctional people, regardless of their respective positions or prior academic achievements.

      I. Introduction to the system
     II. Concepts of the correctional system
    III. Communication
    IV. Dynamics of human behavior
     V. Personal and cultural norms
    VI. Mental and physical health influence on behavior
   VII. Influence of groups on behavior
  VIII. Change and the learning process
    IX. Resources[26]

A more detailed breakdown of the duties, skills, knowledge, and other pertinent data necessary to a comprehensive educational-training program were presented in charts in the same publication. A study of those charts (see figs. 18, 19, and 20) will reveal sufficient data to develop an extensive in-service training program.

Although probation and parole personnel have generally completed some college, and a large percentage have already attained at least the baccalaureate degree prior to employment, training on the job has probably not gone very much further than a short orientation-indoctrination series of meetings, and a brief understudy program of working with a senior officer in a variety of assignments. The institutional personnel in corrections have had considerably less education; most of them do not have

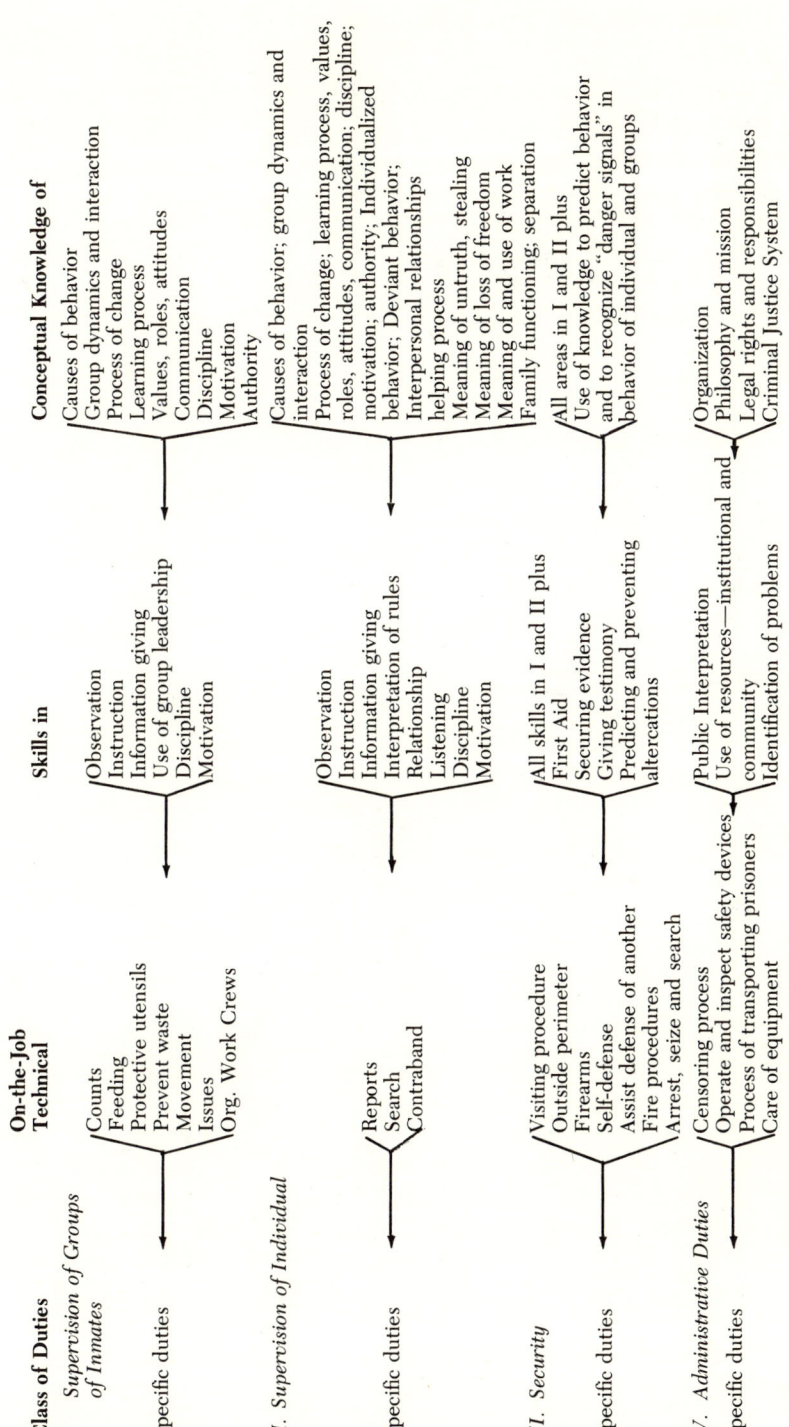

Figure 18. *Custodial Officers Duties, Skills, Knowledge*

Source: Donald D. Brewer and Carol Ann Blair, *In-Service Training for Probation, Parole, and Correctional Personnel: A Plan for Action* (Washington, D. C.: Law Enforcement Assistance Administration, 1968) p. 42.

Duties

I. Supervision of Individuals
A. Personal counseling for rehabilitation
  1. Employment counseling
  2. Personal problems, social, physical, emotional
  3. Training—education
  4. Marital and family
  5. Management—home, financial
  6. Social functioning

B. Enforcement
  1. Interpretations of rules and regulations
  2. Reporting systems
  3. Revocation procedures
  4. Dismissal procedures
  5. Follow-up procedures

II. Investigation
A. Pre-sentence (Probation)
  1. Collects information on
     a. Criminal record
     b. Employment, school history
     c. Family history
     d. Medical and psychological history
     e. Community reputation
     f. Collateral contacts and records
  2. Prepares report
     a. Organizes information
     b. Makes diagnosis and plan
     c. Makes recommendations

B. Parole report
  1. Collects information on
     a. Current family situation

On the Job Technical

Resource information
Referral procedure

Knowledge of rules and regulations

Location of records
Where information is available
Specific format of reports
Scope of content
Sample reports

See above

See above

Skills in

Interviewing
Recording
Organization of information
Establishing and maintaining relationships
Observations
Referral
Using community resources
Assessment—diagnosis
Prognosis—forecasting
Interpretation
Motivation
Information giving
Listening
Individualization
Empathy
Using authority
Communication—oral, written
Self-analysis
Problem solving

See above

See above

Knowledge of

Helping Process
Interpersonal relationships
Measuring of behavior
  normal   deviant
Personality development
Process of change
Basic learning theory
Social systems
Socio-cultural concepts
Values systems
Role theory
Family functioning
Group dynamics
Attitudes
Self-awareness
Authority—limit setting
Diagnosis
Social planning
Organization of community
Vocational guidance
Basic medical knowledge
Basic psychiatric knowledge
Behavior and illness
Narcotics
Alcoholism
Communication: written, oral, non-verbal

See above

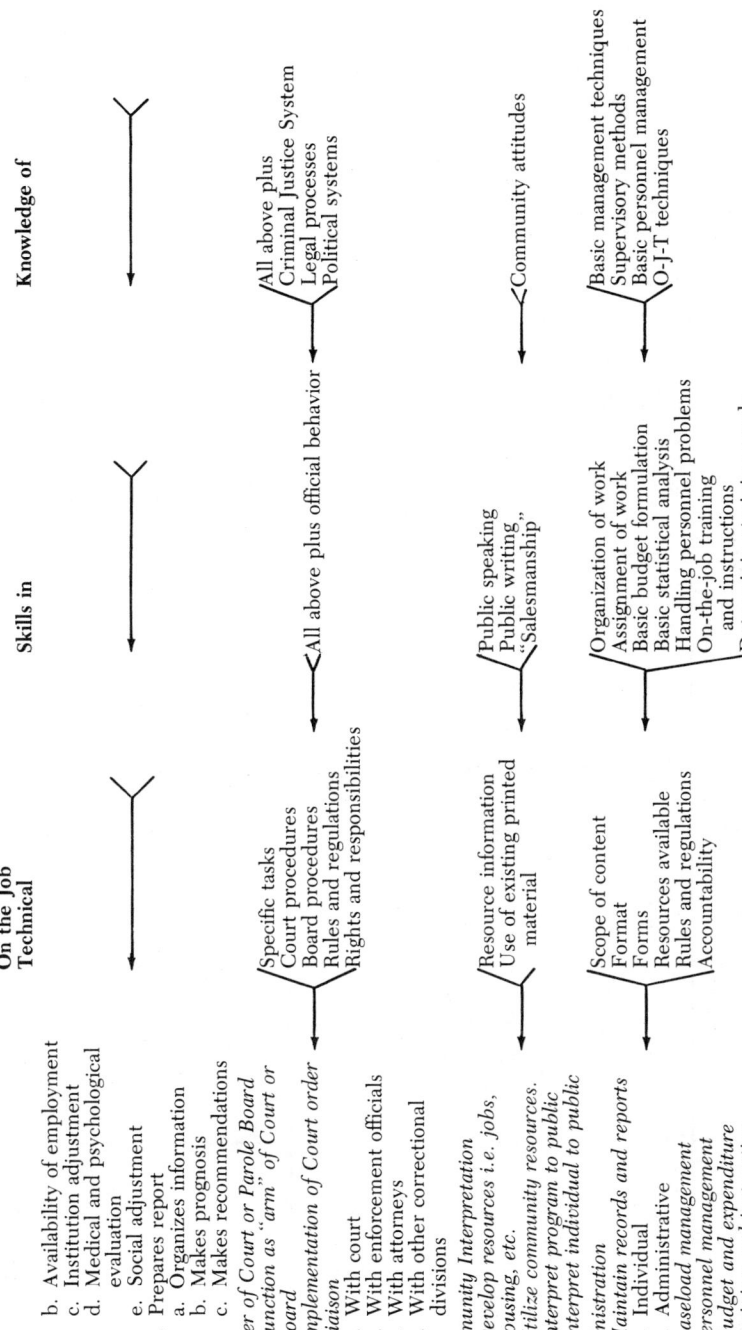

Figure 19. *Probation and Parole Officers Duties, Skills, Knowledge*

Source: Donald D. Brewer and Carol Ann Blair, *In-Service Training for Probation, Parole, and Correctional Personnel: A Plan for Action* (Washington, D. C.: Law Enforcement Assistance Administration, 1968), pp. 50–51.

Figure 20. Training for Probation and Parole Personnel

On-the-job-training Technical	Basic "floor of knowledge"	Skills Training	Institutes	Formal Education
Resource information Referral procedure Knowledge of rules and regulations Location of records Specific format of records Locating information Scope and content of reports Sample reports Court procedures Board procedures Rules and regs. of court or board Right to repeal of court or board Accountability	Introduction Concepts of correctional system Communication Dynamics of human behavior Personal and cultural norms Mental and physical health and behavior Change—the learning process Resources	Examples: Interviewing Referral process Recording Official behavior Public interpretation Case load management Problem solving techniques Training others	Examples: Narcotics Alcoholism Mental problems Guidance for Employment Organization of conventions	A.B. degree in Social Welfare-Corrections sequence Masters degree with field placement in corrections
This technical knowledge is always taught within the setting to which the employee is assigned.	This can be taught within the setting if there is the professional capability, It can also be taught by a specially employed Institution. This would also be the base for new employees.	These skills can be taught by a university team to assure that basic conceptual knowledge is included. Content will be based on the duties to which the skills relate.	These are thought of as periodic institutes within the academic setting with the goal of enrichment of the employee.	These are given within a properly accredited institution.

Source: Donald D. Brewer and Carol Ann Blair, *In-Service Training for Probation, Parole, and Correctional Personnel: A Plan for Action* (Washington, D.C.: Law Enforcement Assistance Administration, 1968), p. 56.

college preparation prior to entering their occupations. Corrections institutions have been well known, according to most of the literature available to date, for not having any sort of in-service training for their personnel. There are some exceptions, of course, but not enough.

In a single publication involving four projects for correctional training and manpower studies the following observation was made in the introduction:

> For a number of years leaders in the field of corrections have stated that one of the most demanding problems in the field has been that of training or more specifically, lack of adequate training for staff. Research has indicated that minimal training is carried on in the field of corrections and this tends to be concentrated in orientation or preservice areas. One of these studies (conducted by the Center for the Study of Crime, Delinquency and Corrections at Southern Illinois University) found that, not only was there little formal training in the field of corrections, but less than 25% of the correctional agencies had full-time training officers. This research completed in 1964 was replicated in 1966 with the same results. It concluded that, despite the recommendations of many authorities in the field that more training was needed, negligible increase in training activities had occurred.[27]

TRAINING THE POLICE OFFICER

Although in-service training programs for municipal and county police officers began early, the optimum program has yet to be developed. In 1970 Irving Slott, then acting director of the National Institute for Law Enforcement and Criminal Justice, wrote:

> The most critical period in the career of a policeman must be the one immediately following training, when he first assumes his duties as a full-fledged patrolman. The newly assigned recruit may feel insecure in his new uniform, with its significance for the role he is to perform and which distinguishes him from his familiar role of that of the citizen. He may adopt a variety of behavior patterns, many of which do not exemplify ideal police performance. His job performance is handicapped by emotionally charged situations which disrupt his academically learned procedures. Shortcomings in the latter emerge in the form of gaps which are those elements of job performance regarded by the instructor as either too trivial to mention or so generally known that he assumes the student knows them.[28]

In order that the gaps in the basic recruit academy be filled with some essential training, Slott recounts that the study team working on this

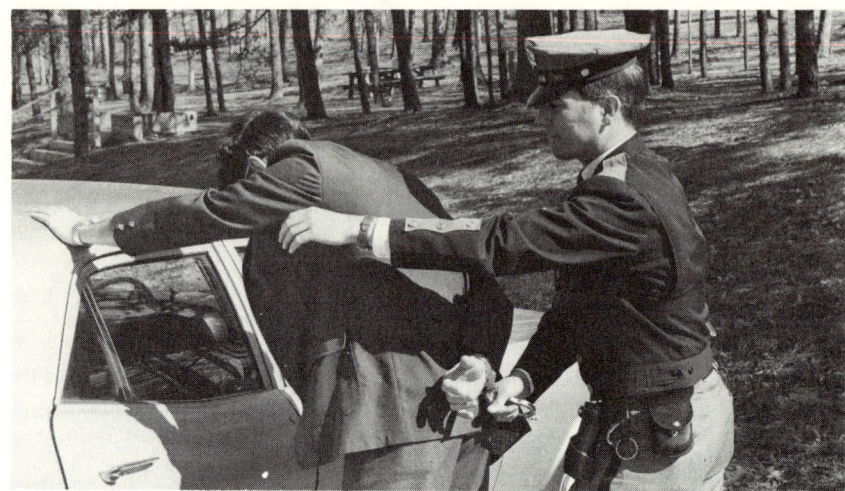

Field training involves refinement of basic skills in arrest and prisoner control, demonstrated by these officers.
Courtesy: Police Department, Greensboro, North Carolina

project recommended that the recruit who completes the academy be accompanied by an "escort officer," and that he perform his newly learned duties under the tutelage and guidance of the journeyman officer. This particular type of introduction to the police role may actually precede the academy in many smaller departments, in which the new officer is placed on the job and is allowed to perform under very close supervision until the next scheduled academy is convened. While in the academy, there may be single tours of duty or scheduled periods of time up to one month, during which the academy student is placed in the field as part of his academy instruction. If the academy is interrupted for such a field assignment, the officer works with a senior officer, in some departments called a *training officer* (separate and distinct from the officer assigned to the training division). Upon completion of his academy instruction and return to his field assignment, the training officer–journeyman arrangement may be employed. It is up to the senior officer to make the appropriate recommendation to the supervisor when he believes the officer has demonstrated in performance what he has learned in the academy or during his private tutorship. At some time agreed upon by the training officer and the supervisor, the new officer is released to perform as a "solo" unit in the field.

Because of its importance to the overall training of the new policeman, the academy is constantly undergoing study and revision. In California, the length of academies range from six weeks to six months, with the average time about 400 hours. Several studies are being conducted on this important matter but substantial recommendations that resemble uniformity are yet to be described. The basic course should certainly include many of the indoctrination-type courses to introduce the new recruit to the Criminal Justice System and his particular position within the system. A condensed and compressed program of instruction is a matter of necessity. A list of topics currently being presented in basic academies in California is listed here to serve as an example only. In my opinion, the optimum academy program has yet to be developed, and it may well be better defined when the reports on many of the studies currently under way have finally been completed.

The Basic Academy

The number of hours devoted to each subject has been established by Specification 3 (July, 1972) of Section 1005 (a) (1) of the Regulations of the California Commission on Peace Officers Standards and Training, but we have not included them in this text because the requirements will, no doubt, change before this book is published, and also because different conditions in various parts of the country will surely lead to the establishment of different hour minimums.

Sheriff's Deputies in training participating in physical fitness program
Los Angeles County Sheriff's Department official photograph

A. INTRODUCTION TO LAW ENFORCEMENT
   Criminal Justice System, Ethics and Professionalization, Orientation
B. CRIMINAL LAW
   Criminal Codes of the State, Laws of Arrest

C. CRIMINAL EVIDENCE
Rules of Evidence (Evidence Code), Search and Seizure
D. ADMINISTRATION OF JUSTICE
Court System, Courtroom Demeanor and Testifying
E. CRIMINAL INVESTIGATION
Assault, auto theft, and burglary cases; collection, identification, and preservation of evidence; crime scene recording, injury and death cases, interviews and interrogation; narcotics and dangerous drugs, preliminary investigation robbery cases, sex crimes, theft cases
F. COMMUNITY-POLICE RELATIONS
Discretionary decision making, general public relations, human relations, local programs, news media relations, race and ethnic group relations, role of police in society, role-playing demonstration (some department basic training programs include role training in some simulated patrol and investigation training problems)
G. PATROL PROCEDURES
Alcoholic beverage control laws, crowd control, disaster training, disorderly conduct and disturbance cases, domestic and civil disputes, field note taking, intoxication cases, mental illness cases, missing persons, patrol and observation, report writing, tactics for crimes in progress, telecommunications
H. TRAFFIC CONTROL
Citations: mechanics and psychology; driver training, drunk driving cases, traffic accident investigation, traffic directing, traffic laws, vehicle pullovers
I. JUVENILE PROCEDURES
Juvenile laws, juvenile procedures
J. DEFENSIVE TACTICS
Arrest and control techniques, defensive tactics, transportation of prisoners and the mentally ill
K. FIREARMS
Legal aspects and policy, range, special weapons
L. FIRST AID[29]

Field Training

In departments where field training is presented on any sort of an organized basis, a checklist or field training guide may be used to keep abreast of the individual officer's progress in the many different types of duties that he must perform. An excellent device for keeping a record of activities that the officer has performed, and others in which he has been instructed but has not yet had the opportunity to demonstrate, is a field training checklist. The individual who is being trained may maintain his own checklist and have the training officer or supervisor who is delegated the task of updating his checklist make the appropriate entries when applicable. The checklist should consist of specific duties that the officer must perform well, perhaps a listing of those tasks that might be considered critical to the success of the officer and the general reputation of the department. Categories may include departmental policy, duty manual, vehicle operation under emergency conditions, family crisis intervention, field interviews, traffic stops, personal searches, arrest, transporting prisoners, and handling of calls to name just a few. The list should be long enough to cover the most critical factors, but not so long that no one will wish to use the form.

The description of the task to be demonstrated could be followed with a series of spaces for initials and dates, one space for "instructed," a space for "performed," and a place for the supervisor or senior officer to indicate that the officer being oriented demonstrated in some way other than performance that he knows the information or could probably perform the task but that there was no opportunity to observe him in its actual performance. Upon completion of all of the items on the checklist, the officer's supervisor would review the list with him as a general review, then place the list in the person's file to satisfy the training audit that this phase of the training had been completed.

Roll Call Training

Fifteen to thirty minutes prior to the start of each shift, it may be possible to present an organized training program in the form of a constantly changing and currently timely series of training segments. Sometimes called *roll call training*, this method may be quite effective for those training topics that have occurred within the previous few days and that could have been handled better with a different approach. Short films or videotaped segments of instruction may be accompanied by a brief discussion of the material and sometimes a written or oral test for immediate feedback on the effect of the instruction. However, regardless of the expenditure of time and money or the content of the material, the system can become meaningless and its teachings quickly forgotten. The instruction must be relevant to the actual needs of the unit at the time the training is presented.

Training Bulletins and Home-Study Material

Carefully prepared, timely training bulletins may prove quite effective if they are easy to read and if there is some provision to assure that officers, for whom they are intended, study them. One method is to pass out an examination consisting of a few questions about the material in the accompanying bulletin. If the officer fills out the examination, there is some assurance that he is reading it. Another method of testing is to distribute the bulletins and then the examinations perhaps three or four days later. Without some stimulus to make the officer read the material promptly, some will discard or misplace the material immediately after they receive it, then claim later that they did not have sufficient time to read the material. A written test is not always necessary; as a matter of fact, task performance can be simulated or in actual case situations might more accurately reflect the effect of the training material.

Supervisor, Midmanagement, and Executive Courses

Professor John Kenney, of California State University at Long Beach, made the following observations regarding the training of supervisors and executive personnel in law enforcement:

> The training of supervisors is the key to the successful operation of most departments. The first line supervisor is in essence the principal department trainer. Persons in supervisory positions interact with other personnel in a manner that will produce the best results that relate to overall goals. It is they who really give direction to the achievement of goals and guide the role of the operational personnel in the performance of their jobs. Supervisors deal with the problems of personnel and perform a clinical role in problem solving.
>
> Middle management and executive leadership training for the police has only recently become a reality. It has long been evident however that one of the weakest links in the operation of a police department is in its management and leadership capabilities.[30]

The New York City Police Training Program is principally carried out by the first line supervisors, according to one report. Their sergeant training involves actual assignment to the Academy and back to the field on a rotating basis:

> The unit training program, essentially the only program providing regular in-service refresher training to the entire patrol force (aside from specialized training), will be improved and expanded. Therefore, priority will be given to unit training sergeants, who will be assigned to the Police Academy and detailed to field commands on a rotating basis. Training sergeants will participate in the production of unit training memos, telecasts and training bulletins, administration of the escort training program, and will accept greater training responsibilities. More training telecasts, more frequent training sessions and innovations in techniques of presentation are recommended. All members of the force will have access to printed materials.[31]

According to this New York plan, the unit training sergeants assigned to the academy should be rotated back and forth from the field so that their training would be more attuned to the "real world," actual field patrol work.

Three California courses, outlined by the Commission on Peace Officers Standards and Training, representative of many similar programs encountered in other states as well since the establishment of their respective standards commissions. The courses are the supervisory, the middle management, and the executive development courses. Aimed at the leadership of the law enforcement organizations, these courses fill a need previously left unanswered: training of managers for their supervisory and administrative tasks.

THE EXECUTIVE DEVELOPMENT COURSES. Recognizing the need for updating the executive on the current status of the profession and on basic management concepts, this course requires a minimum of 100 hours, which may include some time devoted to an administrative project.

A. **Introduction**
   Introduction and overview of the course, Challenge of Crime in Society, Role of Police in Society, Police Role in Crime Prevention, Total Community Commitment

B. **Internal Management**
   Personnel Administration (Management by Objectives, Police Manager Development, Motivation Techniques, Delegation of Responsibility, Training, Counseling and Interviewing, Performance Review and Evaluation, Grievance Procedures, Morale and Discipline, Improving Middle Management)
   Management Techniques and Aids (Planning and Research, Information Management and Automatic Data Processing, Police Legal Adviser, Use and Impact of New Technology in Police Management, Decision Making)
   Operations Management (Formulation and Implementation of Policy, Staff Inspections, Internal Investigation-Maintaining Integrity, Application of Science and Technology, Planning for Civil Disorders and Major Emergencies)
   Fiscal Management (Sources of Revenue, Budget Process, Preparation, and Presentation, Wage and Salary Administration, Inventory and Control of Equipment and Facility)

C. **Environmental Relationships**
   Inter- and Intra-governmental relationships, Urban Planning and the Police

D. Community Relations
Importance of Adequate Policy and Procedures, Community Relations Program Management, Processing Citizen Complaints, Group Information Media, Groups within the Community, Community's Role in Crime Prevention and Control, Evaluating and Maintaining Effectiveness.

E. Communications
Conference Leadership, Oral and Written Reports, Interagency Communication, Intradepartmental Communication (formal, informal), Effective Speaking and Writing

F. Individual Projects

THE MIDDLE MANAGEMENT COURSES. A 100-hour minimum in the following subjects is required:

A. Introduction
Course Orientation, Role of Police in Society

B. Organization and Management
Principles of Administration, Modern Police Organization (Line Functions, Administrative Functions, Auxiliary Functions), Role of Middle Manager

C. Motivation
Human Relations in Management, Techniques of Supervision, Psychology of Leadership, Effective Communication, Conference Leadership

D. Implementation
Research, Planning and Analysis, Deployment and Utilization of Personnel, Financial Planning, Execution and Control, Community Relations Program Management, Information Management, Training Program Management, Personnel Management, Planning for the Future

E. Examinations

F. Individual Projects

THE SUPERVISORY COURSE This course consists of a minimum of 80 hours, including the following listed subjects.

1. Introduction and Scope of the Course
2. Duties and Responsibilities of the Police Supervisor
3. The Supervisor's Relationship to Police Management
4. Communication Principles
5. Handling and Preventing Complaints
6. Motivating Employees to Work

7. Leadership
8. Psychological Aspects of Supervision
9. Morale and Discipline
10. Performance Appraisal and Rating Procedures
11. Supervisory Decision Making
12. Making Duty Assignments
13. The Supervisory Training Function
14. How People Learn
15. Job Analysis
16. The Four Steps of Teaching
17. Lesson Plans
18. Instructional Aids
19. Roll Call Training
20. Practical Application
21. Evaluation of Instruction
22. Written Examinations

ADVANCED OFFICER COURSES. Once the officer has completed his basic academy training and returns to the field for the beginning of his career, he is generally expected to continue his college education and to seek other special instruction on his own time and initiative. In fact, many officers amass literally hundreds of hours of time for their personal and professional improvement. There should be periodic required advanced officer sessions, for the officer to attend on duty time. These sessions should update him on such matters as arrest, search and seizure; community-police relations; new laws, and recent court decisions. This is required by law in some states, including California. In an effort to provide this updating and to keep the instruction relevant to the actual assignment of the officer, the Orange County (California) Sheriff-Coroner's Office in affiliation with Santa Ana College developed a series of advanced officer courses, each consisting of 40 hours of concentrated study. In addition to the above listed core courses, these minicourses include the following:

Investigator: Specialized courses include Case Preparation, Defensive Techniques, Development and Use of Informants, Firearms, Officer Conduct, Officer Survival, Related Investigative Agencies, Sources of Information, and Specialized Scientific Methods.

Patrol: Contract Law Enforcement, Defensive Techniques, Family Crisis Intervention, Firearms, Officer Survival, Patrol Officer as a Training Officer, Recognition of Explosive and Incendiary Devices, Report Writing, Sources of Information.

Jail: Defensive Techniques, Development and Use of Informants, Firearms, Jail Climate, Jail Discipline, Jail Operations, Jail Supervision, Report Writing, and Special Prisoners.

Civil: Bailiffs attend a class on Hazardous Devices Recognition while officers assigned to other civil duties attend during the corresponding time classes on Officer Survival and Handling of Mentally Ill Persons. In addition to the core courses, the specialized courses for this series include Defensive Techniques, Firearms, Narcotics Review, and Report Writing.

SPECIALIZED SHORT COURSES. Role playing is gaining favor as a learning device for many training programs. With careful preparation and strict guidelines for the actors to follow, it is possible to create realistic situations that require the officer-students to employ their judgment and discretionary prerogatives and to choose alternative courses of action. Special effects and props may be elaborately prepared on a sound stage, or most of the setting may be described to the players with the expectation that they will imagine their surroundings when imagining that the situation is real. Situations such as a search, mentally disturbed persons, and traffic violators make for good role playing.

Computer-assisted learning and multimedia methods may be employed as they are in the general academic environment. In order to keep the officer-students interested and motivated, the training program must be imaginative and creative. An excellent example of a participative training program, which includes realism and interest, is the Emergency Vehicle Operation Course. It requires the student to operate a motorcycle or automobile through puddles of water and inches of foam simulating ice and snow; hazard simulators create unpredictable situations that require immediate decisions and reflex actions.

SUMMARY

In this chapter we have covered a wide variety of approaches to the training and education for the various occupations within the Criminal Justice System. Throughout the entire chapter, many different types of techniques have been discussed, but there has consistently been a common denominator: the task analysis and instructional objectives concept. In order that any type of training or educational program may be termed a success, it is necessary that task analyses be performed; this analysis identifies precisely what must be covered in the instruction and how it must be presented for maximum results. Following the task analysis, the objectives of the instruction should be carefully prescribed. From that point on, the method of testing the instruction is decided upon, and the course outline is prepared. Through a systematized approach, it is possible to experience success in the operation of a program of criminal justice education or training or—what is more ideal—a combination of the two.

Notes

1. 1972–1973 *Directory of Law Enforcement and Criminal Justice Education*, prepared by the Professional Standards Division, International Association of Chiefs of Police, Gaithersburg, Maryland, p. 5.
2. Thompson S. Crockett and James D. Stinchcomb, *Guidelines for Law Enforcement Education Programs in Community and Junior Colleges* (Washington, D. C.: American Association of Junior Colleges, 1968), p. 6.
3. Charles W. Tenney, Jr., *Higher Education Programs in Law Enforcement and Criminal Justice*, PR 71–2 (Washington, D. C.: Law Enforcement Association Administration, 1971), p. 8.
4. Ibid., p. 6.
5. *See also* Thomas F. Adams, *Training Officers Handbook* (Springfield: Thomas, 1964), which is a collection of training bulletins.
6. Robert F. Mager and Kenneth M. Beach, Jr. (Palo Alto, Calif.: Fearon Publishers, 1967), pp. 1–2.
7. Ibid., p. 2.
8. Ibid., p. 2.
9. Donald D. Brewer and Carol Ann Blair, *In-Service Training for Probation, Parole, and Correctional Personnel: A Plan for Action* (Washington, D. C.: Law Enforcement Administration Assistance, 1968).
10. Ibid., p. 35.
11. Ibid., pp. 35–58.
12. Ibid., p. 41.
13. Ibid., p. 47.
14. Ibid., pp. ii, iii, 41–42.
15. Ibid., Fig. 5, p. 56.
16. Crockett and Stinchcomb, *Guidelines for Law Enforcement Education*, p. 9.
17. Peter P. Lejins, *Introducing a Law Enforcement Curriculum at a State University* (Washington, D. C.: National Institute of Law Enforcement and Criminal Justice, 1970).
18. The first-year task-force membership, under the chairmanship of Professor Bob Blanchard, Riverside City College, included Bob Ferguson of Saddleback College, Paul Howard of Bakersfield College and then president of the California Association of Administration of Justice Educators, Al Nottingham of Modesto Community College, and Tom Adams of Santa Ana College.
19. See Lejins, *Introducing a Law Enforcement Curriculum at a State University*, pp. 40–42
20. Charles W. Tenney, Jr., *Higher Education Programs in Law Enforcement and Criminal Justice*, pp. 29–33.
21. Dissemination Document Project 67–28 *Police Science Degree Programs: A Conference Report*, June 8–9, 1967 (Washington, D. C.: Office of Law Enforcement Assistance, 1968), pp. 46–50.
22. Ibid., pp. 66–68.
23. Robert Montilla, *Correctional Planning and Resource Guide* (Washington, D. C.: Law Enforcement Assistance Administration, 1969), p. 9.
24. Complete details on this California program may be obtained from the California Commission on Peace Officers' Standards and Training, Sacramento, California.
25. Brewer and Blair, *In-Service Training*.
26. Ibid., p. 49.
27. *Strategies for Meeting Correctional Training and Manpower Needs*, 4 Development Projects (Washington, D. C.: Office of Law Enforcement Assistance, 1969), p. 1.

28. George P. McManus (Project director), *Police Training and Performance Study*, New York City Police Department Project 70-4 (Washington, D. C.: Law Enforcement Assistance Administration, 1970), p. ii.
29. Titles of these subjects taught in academies should not be confused with college courses that have similar titles.
30. From Kenney, John P., *Police Administration*, 1972, pp. 101–102. Courtesy of Charles C Thomas, Publisher, Springfield, Illinois.
31. McManus, *Police Training and Performance Study*, p. vii

Review Questions

1. What is the distinction between training and education?
2. For what type of training program would you use the laundry list technique?
3. List a set of terminal performance objectives (TPO's) for this chapter.
4. According to Mager and Beach, what are the three phases of planning a course of instruction?
5. Why is the examination prepared during the initial phases of course preparation?
6. Of the many methods of instruction, which one do you believe is most effective? Why?
7. What procedure would you follow to ascertain what should be covered in a training program?
8. According to the task force statement of philosophy regarding the core curriculum, what is the objective of having all students take the core courses before branching out into their respective specialties?
9. List and discuss the content of the five core courses. Give particular consideration to the needs of the students currently attending your institution.
10. What, if any, are the advantages of having college-affiliated criminal justice training programs?
11. List basic training requirements for each of the following officer positions: police, probation, parole, custodial.
12. Why are supervisory courses so heavy in teacher training?

8 Research and Planning for Effectiveness

Organizational management involves some type of planning at virtually every step along the way, from the moment the objectives and goals are identified, to the recruitment of personnel and role assignments within the organization, to the organizational structure and the development of the building, and through to the everyday operations of the organization. Planning is involved in the building design. Anticipated tasks to be performed by each work assignment, their related activities, and the continuum of work flow throughout the entire organization all must be taken into account through intelligent planning when designing a building for efficient business operations. Before beginning as a service organization, the criminal justice agency must identify its long-range goals and objectives through planning and then the various tasks and work assignment to attain the goals—through the development of procedural, tactical, single-use, emergency, standing, long-range, and short-range plans. Many titles and definitions have been designated for the various types and functions of planning. Although there may be a variance on the words to use when discussing planning, there is a consensus that, whatever planning is, criminal justice administration cannot function without it.

In this chapter we shall identify planning, describe what it is and how it works, and discuss some of the applications of the process to the management of criminal justice organizations. We call it planning, although a more sophisticated approach would undoubtedly go into research design, survey research, and the more advanced forms and processes of planning. The latter will be left to the more comprehensive texts on the subject; this chapter approaches the subject from a general level.

PLANNING, DEFINED

For the purpose of this chapter, planning is defined as the gathering of facts, through research or diligent inquiry, which are relevant to a given problem that has been identified; the comparison and evaluation of alternatives; and the development of a procedure or model intended to facilitate the accomplishment of certain goals or objectives.

There are several types of plans, and as many varieties of the planning process. Probably the most essential is that of goals' articulation for organization. If the purpose or the mission of the organization is to provide protection for the community through effective management of offenders and redirection of their lives through enlightened leadership, then the initial planning for this probation department will involve an identification of the goals to complete the mission and the objectives to facilitate the accomplishment of the individual tasks that serve the needs of the organization.

Other types include procedural plans that cover the philosophy and operational practices within the organization; strategical plans that cover single situations or specific types of activities that may occur only occasionally rather than on a regular basis; and management plans which involve the development and staffing of an organization, articulation of goals and objectives, construction of buildings and other facilities, and the many other phases of organizational management.

A NEED FOR PLANNING

Planning is a viable process within an organization. Kenney states: "Within the department top management personnel will have to engage in a series of developmental, review and evaluation conferences with a continuous input of ideas, concepts and details from every facet of the department. There will be a need for identification and clarification of programs and a continuous review of operations."[1] Kassoff says: "The police organization is not immune from the need for planning. On the contrary, every modern police executive must use planning of various types if he would hope to achieve his department's objectives."[2] Wilson and McLaren make the unequivocal statement:

> The act of planning is an inseparable part of the administrative process. Successful police administrators plan continuously whether they realize it or not, since the function is necessary before any new program, system, or effort can be introduced. Planning is essential to the successful conclusion of any serious undertaking.[3]

The criminal justice agency, whether it is a probation department, corrections agency, law enforcement agency, or a court, operates as probably one of the largest service organizations in the city. The fiscal and personnel management and the maintenance of the physical plants for such an operation involve from thousands to millions of dollars in revenue. Planning for such an operation with efficient use of the money and with the accomplishment of the organization's objectives should be provided for as a prerequisite to the establishment of any new facilities or to the implementation of any new policy or procedure. Planning, which should involve in-depth research in many cases, should precede and accompany virtually every undertaking by the administrator and his supervisors.

Extensive research led to implementation of the helicopter in many jurisdictions.
Courtesy: Police Department, Costa Mesa, California

THE PLANNING PROCESS

Most of the various types of planning involve essentially the same general procedure. Beginning with the discovery or development of the need for the plan progressing to the data collection and evaluation, then going into the construction of a model document, and continuing through the process to the follow-up and feedback sequence, there are certain guidelines that should normally apply to the process.

1. Enunciation

The first step in any planning process is to identify the problem and to state specifically what it is to assure a common understanding from the outset. The problem may identify itself without study, perhaps out of necessity. The present building occupied by the department may have been quite adequate ten years ago, but now the department has grown to five times its size and legislative changes might have changed the objectives of the organization in such a way that not only is the size too small but the location is wrong. The problem might be stated as: a suitable site must be selected and a building designed that will meet current and future needs of the department, based upon past history and forecasts of needs for the next twenty years.

To merely identify a problem without clearly enunciating what it is and how it must be addressed may result in a worthless exercise in rhetoric. For example, a planning unit within the organization might anticipate a sudden overload on the agency through a change in law or procedure, such as one that will cause an almost immediate change in sentencing practice by the local courts which will double the load on the probation department and actually lead to closing of one of the correctional institutions. The problem might be simply stated in terms of more people to be supervised by probation and less inmates in the correctional system. The probation department must identify the problem as one which will cover all the implications and results of the drastic procedural change by the courts. Not only will there be more individuals to be handled on probation, but there will be need for restructuring of case loads, employment and training of new deputy probation officers, office and housekeeping problems, changes in the records volume and work loads, and quite possibly creation of an entirely new concept of case management through the development of decentralized offices strategically located in the neighborhoods where the anticipated probationers will be living. Forecasts, projections, and a great amount of educated guessing will go into the enunciation of this problem. What looked like a simple problem at first glance has now taken on the configuration of a whole series of interrelated problems.

2. Statement of the Objective

Once the problem has been identified and clearly enunciated in its various parts, the next step is to state the objective of the plan. Specifically what should result from the research and planning? Should locations for decentralized offices be listed? Should a procedural manual be prepared for new methods? What sort of training should be presented on short- and long-term bases? Will there be any changes in the organizational structure or accountability-authority channels? How shall communications be expedited in the most efficient manner possible? The statement of the objective, then, must be a straightforward articulation of the results that the planning units hope to attain.

The statement of the objective may include an historical account of what events have transpired to date and how this study's results will fit into the overall picture. It will prescribe what the department will do and under what conditions, with a statement of the desired results. It may also be advisable to forecast what might happen to the department or the community if the planning were not done and the desired objectives not met. For example, when presenting the objectives for the courts' new philosophy in sentencing procedures a brief account of the historical evolution of corrections shows that it no longer involves mammoth institutions, but instead emphasizes the development of community-based rehabilitation-oriented supervision (prisons without walls concept). Then the objective might be stated in terms of restructuring the probation department into decentralized units and new procedures for handling the tremendously increased case load. The result of no planning at all would be chaotic, it could be pointed out. For such a complex problem this series of planning activities would be stated in a series of objectives, each addressing a different segment of the problem.

When stating the planning objective on a specific problem, it is wise to anticipate that there will be a variety of reactions, from open resistance

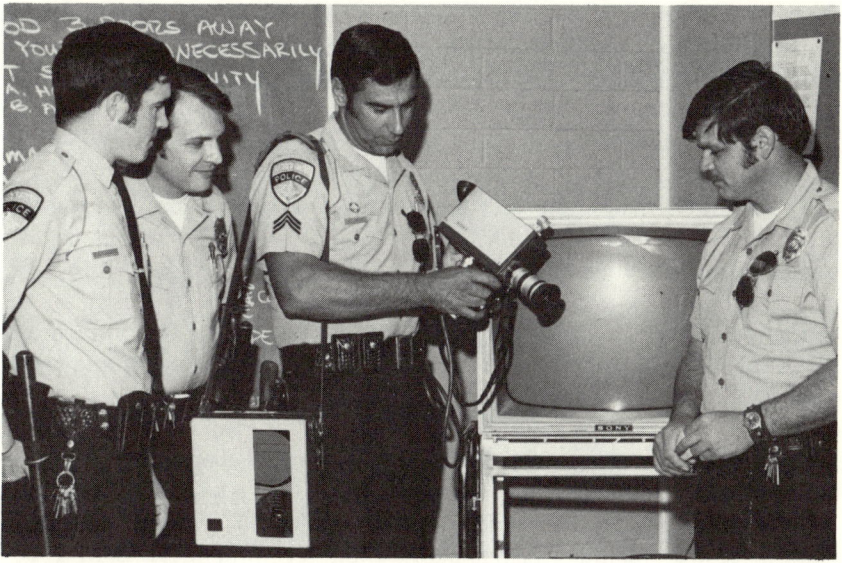

Videotape has become a standard training aid as a result of various types of experimentation.
Courtesy: Police Department, Garden Grove, California

to enthusiastic encouragement. Diplomacy is one of the most valuable qualities to demonstrate, particularly during the early stages when open minds and cooperative attitudes can make the task so much easier.

3. Exploration

Collect as much information as possible from every available source, including every point of view that has been expressed. When the researcher begins a study with a bias there is a strong possibility that the results of the study—no matter how "thorough" it may be—will reflect and/or reinforce that bias. Total objectivity should be demanded for every planning undertaking.

Methods of data collection vary with the type of study. Personal visits and actual on-the-scene observation of certain procedures in operation are essential when the study involves techniques. Equipment studies require collection of advertising material, news stories, personal interviews with individuals who have used the equipment, research to determine its legality and to be prepared to defend the use of the equipment in the case of anticipated litigation.

Exploration of a new type of equipment which will have an effect upon the public may include an opinion survey. For example, a local police department had outfitted its officers in "suntans" and plastic helmets for many years. Whenever the people saw one of their officers, or called for his services, they had grown used to seeing him with that characteristic appearance. Two members of the department approached me with a proposal for directed research they wished to undertake. For some time these officers had discussed the matter with fellow officers and some of the local citizens; they suggested that the officers discontinue wearing the helmets as a regular part of their uniforms, that they convert to the "soft cap," and at the same time they proposed that the department change to the traditional dark blue uniform more standard for the municipal police department in Southern California.

Their study of uniforms and helmets included pricing and estimates of changes in budget that would be necessary. But they also conducted a survey of all the department's members as well as a random sampling of the total community. The survey results reinforced their opinions that the change would result in an improved image in the community, increased morale, and more comfort for the officers who would abandon the helmets except for unusual occurrences. Armed with their completed study and recommendations for their uniform changes, the officers approached the chief of police and the city manager. Their recommendations were accepted. The changes might have been approved without the opinion surveys, but their inclusion in the study gave strength to the recommendations by providing an impact report on the anticipated reactions to such a change.

The utilization of aerosol tear gas by police officers and sheriff's deputies in the middle 1960s generated a considerable number of reactions running the entire spectrum of emotional involvement. People who became aware of its introduction to the police arsenal called it everything from "poison gas" to "magic sleeping potion." Rumors flew around about its deleterious effects and alleged lawsuits went rampant; some are still circulating. Extensive studies by many departments were conducted, which included exhaustive investigation of most of the rumors, of the officers in other departments who had used the gas, and of the subjects upon whom it had been used. Carefully documented research was necessary before a wise administrator would authorize use of the substance, and its eventual inclusion in the officer's standard equipment list was preceded by the development of a comprehensive training program. As a result of careful planning,, which included considerable exploration, the aerosol tear gas dispenser is a standard item of police equipment for many agencies.

The exploration phase of the planning process includes collection and analysis of the available data. At this critical point in the process it is extremely important that fact be distinguished from fantasy, and objective reasoning prevail over subjective. Alternative plans, products, or facilities must all be thoroughly explored so that they may be compared and evaluated before final determinations may be made on the most acceptable alternative.

4. Anticipation of Alternatives

Extensive exploration will undoubtedly reveal several alternatives which may appear equally acceptable. The next phase of the planning process is to project each of the more favorable alternatives as if it were the one that had been selected. Consider the cost effectiveness, the human relations factors, public relations impact, and the results in relation to the objectives of the study and the overall operation of the organizations or divisions to be affected. If a product is involved, it may be possible to conduct a "hands-on" experiment with two or more of the alternatives. Procedures may be tried out with an experimental group and a control group of employees to compare results of the alternative methods. Simulated exercises or role play may be made an official part of the manual of procedures or policies.

One method of testing a choice of alternatives is to utilize a devil's advocate, who Newman describes as a specific individual assigned the task of pointing out weaknesses or errors in a proposed action.[4] The advocate assembles the best negative arguments that he can. "If a proposal cannot withstand such an attack, action is postponed."

5. Choosing the Alternative

Most planning should indicate the alternative to be chosen and implemented, and should indicate a rank-order for the alternatives not selected. In the event that the first choice is not feasible, or if circumstances modify its desirability because of unforeseen occurrences, there should be a second, and sometimes a third, choice.

Once the choice of alternatives has been selected, the detail work begins again. Prepare a detailed, coordinated plan for action. If possible, every ramification should be considered and there should be little left to conjecture. There should be an explanation of the many considerations leading to this particular choice; the reasons for this choice should be explained. Visual aids, models, and supporting documents such as charts and diagrams all serve to reinforce the study and aid in the presentation to others so that they can understand and support the same plan. Projections of the plan into future operations of the department should be made so that the long-range as well as the short range effects of the plan can be studied with a greater depth of understanding.

Details of a plan for emergency mobilization and operations of a police agency during a time of a disaster or civil disturbance should include the following elements:[5]

(a) Statement of the problem. This statement should consist of some explanation for the plan, its background, and its importance to the overall objectives of the department.

(b) The department's objectives and goal on the occasion for which this plan is prepared. The police purpose during a time of civil disturbance is the restoration of order as quickly as possible with a maximum *assurance of personal safety* to the people and a minimum loss of property. The objectives for the accomplishment of the department's purpose include (1) containment of identifiable hazard areas, (2) dispersal of crowds and prevention of regroupings, (3) diversion of people away from the area, which may include total evacuation if necessary, (4) arrest of criminal law violators and efficient collection of evidence to assure conviction of the guilty, and (5) operations in accordance with certain priorities that are established during the emergency.

(c) Policies and legal requirements for operations during the emergency. It may be necessary to make an unequivocal statement that certain laws and policies shall continue without exception or modification, which include the restrictions on use of firearms and special weapons. Special laws to cover the emergency needs should also be discussed.

(d) Mobilization plans. The order in which the department is totally or partially mobilized and the procedures for notification of personnel should be detailed. Be ready to set in motion a decentralized telephone notification system which requires only one call from the department's communication center to an outside designee (such as a volunteer telephone answering service). The sequence of calling in off-duty and reserve personnel, those on vacation, and officers on special assignments should be preplanned. Continual updating of the call schedule to assure its accuracy at any given moment is just one of the many details to be worked out long before the real need arises. Provision for reporting payroll information and for assuring rest periods for the on-duty personnel, equipping them and providing them with means of transportation, and establishing auxiliary means of communication to accommodate the augmented department will be included in the detail work.

(e) Notification checklist. In addition to the management personnel already on duty, it will be necessary to call the chief executive of the department, ranking personnel with specific strategic assignments, government officials who should be apprised of the situation, the office of the governor if there is a possiblity that the situation will grow to a magnitude requiring state military forces, civil defense zone coordinators, the press and other media of communications, a judge who may wish to observe the situation in the event he is later called upon to issue warrants or to perform other judicial functions, the prosecuting attorney, a public defender, and whomever else should be notified in the event of a major civil disturbance. Not only should these individuals be notified, but there should be some means of recording the fact that they were called in the event that someone may later claim that he was deliberately or inadvertently overlooked.

(f) Logistics. Equipping, transporting, housing, feeding, and keeping track of the augmented department during emergency conditions will require considerable advance planning. Such a simple thing as eating may cause a critical problem when the need arises during a riot, an earthquake, or some disaster of major proportions.

(g) Strategies for specific types of activities including mass arrests, crowd dispersion, building protection, evacuation procedures, emergency housing of displaced persons, rescue of hostages, defense against sniper activities, bomb disposal, caring for wounded or injured people, and all of the many contingencies related to such a problem. It is impossible to predict what may happen under a given set of circumstances, but every possibility must be anticipated in the detailed plan.

(h) Public information. Not only must all of the press media be kept abreast of the department's activities, but there should be provisions for keeping the public informed on matters that may directly concern them. An information office and a separate communications system may be established to assure a free flow of information without interference with the other emergency operations. One consideration for establishing such an emergency communications network is to enlist the aid of a radio-dispatched fleet of taxicabs or trucking firm and to share their frequency, because all the public safety frequencies may be tied up with emergency broadcasts.

(i) Coordination of activities with operations of other government and nongovernment agencies. There is a need for harmonious cooperation among the many participating public safety agencies, road departments, public utilities, tow services, ambulance services, hospitals, fuel suppliers, air services, hotels and motels, warehouses, restaurants, recreation centers, and the many volunteer service organizations. It is important that all of the planning be done long before the need arises.

All contingencies should be studied when working out the details of the plan. It should be comprehensive, yet not unwieldy. In the words of Professor Kenney:

> Planning requires development of clearly defined goals and objectives. Simplicity, directness and clarity of concepts, and ideas are essential. Flexibility needs to be built into the process and there must be a possibility of achievement. Standards for operations should be provided, and there is a need for anticipation of the effects on future operations.[6]

6. Securing Consensus

An extremely well-executed plan may be sabotaged, it may be ignored, or it may be vocally rejected in a headlong confrontation, seemingly with no explanation. The trouble may simply be that one crucial step was overlooked: gaining a consensus. Everyone who might be affected in a direct or remote sense should be advised of the study and be encouraged to produce input into the study. Suggestions and critical comments should be solicited, and the individuals should be convinced that the final results will include their input as a part of the study.

An individual whose position may be affected in some way by a new procedure or item of equipment may fear that his own value to the organization may be in jeopardy. If his role will gain in stature because of some new procedure, or if there is a likelihood that he will be transferred to an equally important position elsewhere contingent on the acceptance of some new procedure, he should be informed. Let him know that someone is looking after his interests.

Other agencies whose operations may be involved in some way with a new procedure should know of anticipated or planned changes in procedures so that they can plan accordingly. The change may place an unexpected burden upon them that they cannot handle. The local prosecutor would certainly be an absolute must on the list of concurrences if the matter involves a legal question or a procedural problem involving evidence or any phase of the arrest or investigation process which might later be an issue. If radio procedure is involved, the central communications coordinator should be consulted. The telephone company should be consulted on tentative plans to change procedures involving telephone communications. The list could be endless, but the point is that none should be overlooked if at all possible. We are more likely to give it a fair trial and try to make it work if we had something to do with its development.

7. Rehearsal

If the plan involves construction of new facilities, it may be wise to build a model and to dry run through as many of the daily operations as possible. For example, your office will involve a considerable amount of walk-in traffic. Therefore, it should be easy to find when someone walks into the building; there should be provision for someone to greet the clients; waiting spaces should be adequate and comfortable; and the flow of people and work should be as smooth as possible. With a model it will be possible to "walk through" as many different types of situations as possible. One very impressive building I visit occasionally must be very confusing to a casual visitor. Although I have called on people there for about five years, I am still not sure where to find which office; there is neither a directory nor a guide to assist visitors. From a public relations standpoint, the building is a failure.

A proposed procedure or policy should be tried out with an experimental group prior to total department involvement, or it might be put into operation for a trial period, then fully implemented only after it has proven effective and any necessary modifications have been made to make the plan workable. A new accounting or budgeting procedure may be implemented for a 30-day period, given a fair trial, then introduced as the new procedure if it proves successful during the 30-day trial period. If the rehearsal proves that the plan needs more work, then the planning can continue while the existing procedure continues in force.

8. Implementation

Put the plan into effect. If the planning has been executed by a staff person or unit, the only thing left for the chief executive to do at this point is to sign the document which puts the policy into effect. There should be nothing more for him to do. Once the policy, procedure, program, or other action which emanates from the planning process is implemented, the follow-up work begins.

9. Follow-up and Feedback

Putting a plan into effect does not consist of mere proclamation that it will be done. Salesmanship comes in handy at this point in the planning process. An authoritarian leader may believe that he can order success, but the experienced manager knows that the secret to success in gaining acceptance of any new procedure or piece of equipment is in creating a feeling of participation on the part of the people who will be implementing the procedure. If the participants want to make something work it goes easily; if they have been led to believe that they must do it or suffer some punitive consequences, the system bogs down. It is entirely possible for an employee to present the impression that he is completely cooperative and willing to implement a new procedure while at the same time he is successfully sabotaging the program. This is one of the reasons it is so important to gain willing compliance on the part of those individuals who will be affected by the plan during the process. *Motivation* is a key word in the process.

Feedback is a continuous process, and a continuous flow of information about the successes or failures of the new procedure or plan should be encouraged. Any problems which arise should be carefully attended to and necessary corrections or modifications made as the needs arise. Planning is a viable, dynamic process, and when approached from that point of view there is a greater likelihood that there will be an overall improvement in the department's operations through intelligent research and planning.

VALUE OF PLANNING AS A MANAGEMENT TOOL

There is no doubt that planning is a valuable tool of management when effectively employed. No intelligent action is taken without some type or degree of planning. Harold Koontz and Cyril O'Donnell list four essential points which underline the importance of planning: (1) Planning offsets uncertainty and change; (2) it focuses attention on objectives; (3) loss and inefficiency are reduced; and (4) control is facilitated through effective planning while the future is also taken into consideration on a continuing basis.[7] Professor Gourley states that police planning serves many purposes:

> 1. It explains and clarifies policy by defining more accurately an immediate objective or purpose and by pointing out how this is to be achieved.

2. It serves as a guide both to timing and performance. It places responsibility for action and reduces the complexity involved.
3. It gives continued attention to the improvement of practice and procedure through assuring increasingly better performance.
4. It makes control possible by enabling accomplishments to be checked.
5. It assures the most effective and economical use of departmental resources of manpower and equipment.[8]

To the same point, from a business management point of view, Newman lists five benefits of advance preparation of one type of planning, the single-use plan:

1. Integrated and purposeful action is more readily achieved.
2. Crisis can be anticipated and delays avoided.
3. More efficient methods and procedures can be developed.
4. Delegation of authority to act is facilitated.
5. The groundwork for control standards is laid.[9]

Planning makes it possible to study alternatives and to select the more desirable course of action. Most of the routine activities of the organization, and many of the emergency activities, can be anticipated and committed to some sort of an organized plan of action. Problems can be anticipated and solutions worked out in advance of their actual occurrence. Then when the unforeseen circumstance does arise, it is possible to devote the major portion of one's time to unforeseen problems rather than to the routine and the already anticipated emergencies. Rather than management by crisis—with every other activity a crisis—it is possible to manage by exception. Efficiency and effectiveness in management both depend on research and planning.

SUMMARY

In this chapter we have briefly studied the management process of planning and its value to the organization's goal achievement, its need in the organization as a regular ongoing activity, and some of the techniques utilized in the planning process. In the criminal justice agency, as in any other organization, planning has always been carried out in some form or other. Only recently, since the enactment of the Omnibus Crime Control and Safe Streets Act of 1968, have we seen any substantial development of specific planning and research units in the criminal justice organizations. Most formal planning activities have been carried out by the chief executive or a staff member on an assigned basis whenever a specific need arose or whenever a new building was to be constructed. Since 1968, when many millions of dollars in federal grant program monies and many additional private sources began funding criminal justice research, we have witnessed the establishment of research and development or planning divisions in local agencies of medium and small size to follow the lead of the larger agencies, where planning has been a regular function for many years.

The basic procedure in the planning process consists of these nine steps: (1) enunciation, (2) statement of the objective, (3) exploration, (4) anticipation of alternatives, (5) choosing the alternative, (6) securing consensus, (7) rehearsal, (8) implementation, and (9) follow-up and feedback. Planning is continuous and no plan should be considered complete, particularly in the dynamic field of criminal justice.

Notes

1. From Kenney, John P., *Police Administration*, 1972, p. 106. Courtesy of Charles C Thomas, Publisher, Springfield, Illinois.
2. Norman C. Kassoff, *The Police Management System* (Washington, D.C.: International Association of Chiefs of Police, 1967), p. 10.
3. Orlando W. Wilson and Roy C. McLaren, *Police Administration*, 3rd ed. (New York: McGraw-Hill, 1972), p. 150.
4. William H. Newman, *Administrative Action, The Techniques of Organization and Management*, 2nd ed. (Englewood Cliffs, N.J.: Prentice-Hall, © 1960), p. 133. All material from this book reprinted by permission of the publisher.
5. Taken from Tactical Plan "A" prepared by the author for the Santa Ana Police Department in the summer of 1968.
6. Kenney, *Police Administration*, p. 107.
7. Harold Koontz and Cyril O'Donnell, *Principles of Management: An Analysis of Managerial Functions*, 4th ed. (New York: McGraw-Hill, 1968), pp. 92–93.
8. Douglas Gourley, *Effective Municipal Police Organization* (Beverly Hills: Benziger, Bruce & Glencoe, 1970), p. 16.
9. Newman, *Administrative Action*, p. 38.

Review Questions

1. What is the first step in the planning process?
2. Describe how you would go through the exploration phase of planning to make a change in a reporting procedure, to replace your current method.
3. What is the role of the devil's advocate in the planning process?
4. What are the nine steps in the planning process?

9 Fiscal Management

Fiscal management of a criminal justice agency involves intelligent planning and sound management procedures. From a fiscal standpoint, criminal justice is a large service industry. As a nonprofit operation, it is more critical that the program planning be evaluated on the basis of cost effectiveness and that the projected needs for the financial support of the department be accurate. The sources of income for the operation of a government-based criminal justice agency are fixed by legislative action each year and are dependent upon projected revenues in the form of property taxes, sales tax, motor vehicle licenses, fines, and levies of various types depending on the category of government: municipal, county, state, federal, or special district. From those sources, allocations are made to the various departments and subdivisions of organizations on the prorated basis of demonstrated need.

Once the budget has been established for the year, it has been all but cast in stone because of the strict limitations on revenue sources and the fact that there will be no more money coming in during the year. Contingency funds may be set aside for urgent unanticipated needs, but to think of them as potential sources of revenue would be futile. Departments are always in competition with one another because of the demands for their services and the perpetual fact that it is an absolute impossibility to satiate all of those demands. The budget must be agreed upon, funds allocated, and then the programs of the department must be managed with strict adherence to the department's objectives and activities in accordance with the budget.

Fiscal management of the criminal justice agency is a task of great magnitude.
Courtesy: Chief Eugene Camp, St. Louis, Missouri Police Department

In this chapter we discuss the basic functions of a budget, some considerations regarding maximum participation by the department's personnel, a discussion of the key points in the budgetary process, and a few guidelines on the challenging task of inventory control.

BUDGET, DEFINED

The budget is principally a management tool which expresses in numerical terms the programs essential to the effective accomplishment of the organization's goals and objectives. It is an allocating device because the government—although it has the power to tax—has limited resources which hardly ever meet the demands of the many executives for their respective departments.[1] As planning instruments, budgets are good because of their "specificness of expression, their ease of coordination beween one department and another, and their ready adaptability as control standards."[2]

Through the budget, the administrator must be able to demonstrate the need—the job to be done—in exact contrast to the almost infinite variety of other things that could be done.[3]

Executed correctly, a budget is a carefully devised plan which calls for the identification and articulation of goals, objectives, programs, priorities, time schedules, and which pinpoints the most efficient circumstances for the operation of the department within the financial limitations.

BUDGET AS A PLANNING TOOL

The organization was probably conceived on the basis of certain objectives, mandated by law in many cases. Using this foundation, the organization is planned to accomplish the objectives as prescribed. The needs are analyzed, the communications flow determined, and authority-accountability relationships established. The staffing is then accomplished, and determinations are made as to the types and levels of service to be provided. Priorities are established, and the entire operational philosophy and programs must be developed in terms of specific behavioral objectives.

The entire repertoire of the department's objectives are committed to a series of statements of performance objectives. Once that task is completed, costs for each of the programs are projected to cover all of the contingencies, and comparisons are made with the available resources. Since it is impossible to fulfill all the needs of an organization, priorities are designated, and judgments made about amended programs to provide the maximum quality service within the allocated funds. This is planning; the budget procedure involving this approach is sometimes labeled PPBS, Planning Program Budget System.

During the planning process, realism and practicality prevail. The total control of crime and the optimum level of performance for any of the criminal justice agencies is a physical impossibility. Programs are identified and priced, rank-ordered in accordance with the department's objectives and the expected results; then the overall operation is planned. It is often necessary to eliminate completely, or sharply reduce, the types and degrees of service that will be provided by the department. An interesting example of this system of reducing the services to the citizens occurred in Detroit; this city found that it had to sharply curtail its responses to called-for services and created instead the IMPACT center to screen out and refer calls to other public service agencies.[4]

When used in the manner described, the budget is one of the most significant tools in management planning. Every aspect of the plan involves some fiscal consideration, not only for the immediate future but for long-range projections. During the past few years, PPBS has gained some recognition as a budget-management tool, such as we have just described. We come back to a discussion of this system and others later in this chapter.

GETTING EVERYONE INTO THE ACT

If the fiscal management aspect is so critical to the complete operation of the organization, why not involve everyone in the operation at every step along the way? Is it "just something that management does to show us why we can't spend any money on a project that we need to do immediately,"? People in the lower echelon of the organization are inclined to believe so, unless they are personally involved in the process. Then they are knowledgeable about the concept of "cost-effectiveness" and keep the economic considerations of their functions in perspective when concerned with the emotional and professional considerations of that function.

The most valuable information that goes into the budget planning may come from the individuals who are actually performing the tasks. Management is usually informed about the broad, general aspects of the department's operations, but the low profile and virtual invisibility of the minute tasks at the performance level of many programs makes it necessary for the operational personnel to recommend expenditures at their level. They are using the equipment and the weapons, occupying the cubicle offices without windows, and operating the vehicles purchased from the lowest bidders. Their comfort, safety, and satisfaction on the job are directly related to their performance; in many instances, management has no way of knowing the true quality of that performance except through self-reporting methods.

Getting the management team involved in the budget planning sequence is relatively simple; it is just a matter of making the assignments and scheduling the meetings. They are expected to participate as a regular part of their daily responsibilities. Getting the entire membership of the organization so involved takes a little more ingenuity and a considerable amount of follow-up. Not only must everyone be involved, but it is equally important that everyone who does participate in the budgeting process be shown in a substantial way that their contributions are both heard and heeded.

Brainstorming sessions, debriefing personnel right after certain projects or activities are completed, committees of personnel representing more than one work unit, staff meetings with invited lower-ranking employee representatives, questionnaires and surveys, and personal interviews are all valid techniques for gaining participation. One procedure of questionable value is the suggestion box, which seldom receives a serious suggestion and which is usually ignored by management. If suggestions are aggressively and sincerely solicited from the operational personnel, such suggestions should be communicated in such a manner that further elaboration and negotiations with the originator may follow, and necesssary research may be intelligently conducted. Another important factor in the use of suggestions is that appropriate credit be granted to the creator of an idea.

When the budget is looked upon as a management tool rather than as an accounting necessity, it is easier to stimulate and cultivate all members of the department to consider it as a means whereby they may more effectively accomplish their objectives and goals. There should be a continual awareness of new equipment and improved methods to perform activities. On a year-round basis, every employee should be encouraged to submit recommendations for budgetary considerations. In a typical department which has not yet come to see the budget in its true perspective, the way it usually works is that there is a mad scramble for ideas, suggestions, and last-minute recommendations during the months of January and February. Then the department's recommendations are incorporated into the larger package that will enter a gestation period during which only top management will mull over the many recommendations and eventually produce a trimmed-down budget that the council or board of supervisors can trim down again to satisfy their interpretations of the needs of the various departments. Finally, the budget is cast in stone and becomes the rigid controller for the next fiscal year. Unfortunately, this method of budgeting is not effective, nor is it economical. The budget is not something to think of only once a year for a few short weeks, then to forget.

Budgeting is—ane should be in the mind of every member of the organization—a year-long activity. Recommendations should be solicited continually. Sometimes something that looked good a year ago is obsolete, and there is no valid reason why a reevaluation might not lead to a different program or purchase of different equipment than originally planned. Such modifications cannot be made irresponsibly nor should they become a matter of course; otherwise the budgeting system itself is obsolete. What I mean is that the process should be dynamic and vitally functioning as an essential part of the department's operation. Whenever an employee submits a suggestion for budgetary consideration, he should receive some recognition that his suggestion has been received and that it will be given consideration. His name should accompany the material, then when a final (or even tentative) decision is made concerning his idea, it should be a management policy to notify him as quickly as possible and to advise him of the action—or inaction—that will be taken on his suggestion. Some organizations stimulate considerable participation by engaging in a monetary incentive program. Rewards may be made on a token basis or an actual percentage of the amount of money saved by the employee's new method during its first year of operation. Every legitimate means possible should be employed to include everyone in the act of budgeting.

TYPES OF BUDGETS AND BUDGETING

In his book on *Government Budgeting*, Jesse Burkhead prefaces his discussion of classifications of budgets with this observation:

> Classification is the structural key to conscious and rational government budgeting. The manner in which the items of revenue and expenditure are grouped will be determined by, and also will determine, the character of the decisons that can be made in the budgetary process. These decisons result from a constant interplay of questions and answers among levels in the hierarchy of government. The purpose of budget classification is to help focus the questions and to clarify and detail the answers. The classification must not bracket the important questions; it must center on them.[5]

The type of budget utilized by the organization reveals quite a bit about the management. In this chapter we shall address three basic types of budgeting: function, performance, and line-item. Although an organization may actually use only one of these types, or all three, the emphasis on one type over the other two may reveal an overall philosophy quite distinctive from other organizations with a similar purpose. The *function* type of budget may reveal a somewhat flexible management system, in which general guidelines are provided for the operational supervisors and their daily expenditures are left to their discretion. The *performance* budget addresses itself more to programs and activities directed toward the accomplishment of specific performance goals. The *line-item* budget involves a rigid schedule of accounting operations in which activities are measured in terms of line-item or *object* expenditures, such as on paper, typewriter ribbon, payment of individual employees, household expenses, and other items. A closer look at these three types of budgets—and there are many more—reveals that each has an application and that they are likely to be used together; the principal difference among organizations is the emphasis.

Functional Budget

Each year the American people are presented with a summary of the national budget for the multitude of federal government departments and each of their many subdivisions. For the sake of time and space at the time the president delivers his budget message to Congress, and for the purpose of giving the citizens an opportunity to form intelligent judgments about the scope and content of government and its many activities, the functional type of budget is presented. The Justice Department budget is divided into its many subdivisons and their respective functions. Examples of the functional categories are the Office of Law Enforcement Assistance in the Department of Justice, or the civil rights activities of the same department. Using this system, it is possible to categorize most major government needs and vested-interest demands and, at the same time, study the many expenditures in comparison with each other.

At the local level, the functions of detective, vice, traffic, and patrol in addition to the many others within the police department may be categorized and treated separately within the police department budget. In the probation operation, functional designations may include field operations and its many subdivisions, institutions and their components, and the staff services. How the functions are to be classified and handled varies from one budget to another. Probably one of the simpler methods of functional classification is to design the budget to correspond with the department's organizational chart.

The advantage of the functional chart is that it requires the allocation of funds for overall fiscal management of the activity, but allows considerable latitude within each unit for expenditures. For example, the traffic unit of the police department consists of perhaps one-fifth of the total authorized officer personnel. That division may be charged with follow-up investigations of traffic collisions, selective enforcement of the more frequently vioalted laws statistically credited as the cause of a disproportionate number of collisions, traffic education and safety, school safety patrol, and parking meter enforcement. The functional budget provides for the overall activities of the traffic division, but may not allocate specific amounts to each of the acitivities. That portion of the allocation process is left to the discretion of the traffic division manager. He may determine that the majority of his unit's attention will be devoted to parking meter enforcement. His budget will reflect that emphasis. Of course, he will have to be able to justify his unorthodox system of priorities to his superiors, but he may spend the money in whichever way he sees fit if he is allowed operate freely within a functional budget.

Flexibility and freedom to innovate may be advantages of the functional type of budget, but the disadvantage may be that such a broad scope may lead to confusion and disagreement, or a laissez-faire attitude toward continuity in program management throughout the year. Many departments further refine the budget into a system known as performance budgeting, which requires much closer management and less flexibility throughout the year.

Performance Budget

Performance budgeting involves budgeting and planning by objectives. Fiscal considerations are based upon what it is that the department *does* rather than what it *buys*. According to Jesse Burkhead, "Performance budgeting shifts the emphasis from the means of accomplishment to the accomplishment itself."[6]

Utilized in conjunction with a function budget, the performance budget involves a series of accounting classifications based upon performance units. The department's objectives and goals are broken down into the functional divisions of the department. The various tasks which must be performed within each unit are analyzed in terms of unit costs, with the many units computed to show individual task costs in addition to the total program cost. Within the Department of Corrections the five-year plan may project a transformation to a certain community-based residential treatment center concept. Because of the experimental nature and social impact of this particular plan, the management decision is to make the transition slowly. Through the implementation of performance budgeting the total program cost for the five years is subdivided into units of capital expenditures for structural facilites, furnishings, and large items; operating expenditures for housekeeping, utilities, transportation, communications, personnel, and other units, then prorated on a year-by-year basis so that the budget for each item and for each year may be studied as parts of the total program. Through performance budgeting, individual tasks may be identified and considered in relationship to cost effectiveness, and to the priorities of needs. Several programs may be compared and management decisons must be made concerning feasibility and economic possibility in order to choose the most acceptable alternatives.

Performance budgeting is not new, reports Burkhead. It was actually tried in the city of New York for a 1913–15 public works project, but abandoned because it was too detailed and inflexible." . . . detailed classifications were devised for three public works functions—street cleaning, sewerage, and street maintenance. Each of these was divided into about ten subfunctions, called work classifications."[7] In 1934 the U.S. Department of Agriculture and the Tennessee Valley Authority began using performance budgeting by itemizing the budget according to the subjects of work to be done (Department of Agriculture) and in accordance with program and accomplishment (TVA).[8]

Burkhead, in his brief history of performance budgeting, also reported that municipal governments began using this system about 1939, when the Municipal Finance Officers Association presented a "model accounting classification, which emphasized activity classifications within functions." In 1946 the Navy Department presented its fiscal year 1948 budget on a program basis as well as on object basis. In its report on budgeting and accounting, 1949, the (Hoover) Commission on Organization of the Executive Branch of the Government stated: "We recommended that the whole budgeting concept of the Federal Government should be refashioned by the adoption of a budget based on functions, activities, and projects: this we designate a 'performance budget.'"[9]

Task analyses and unit costs are essential to performance budgeting. As a management tool, such a method of budgeting compels the manager to assess the value of the results of a task in relationship to the department's goals and objectives, and with a clear view of the costs attached to each task. It may well be that careful scrutiny of the individual activities will lead to drastic departures from tradition once it is discovered that the costs of many activities far exceed their effectiveness.

Line-item Budget

The line-item, or object budget is an accounting-oriented budget. Every kind of item—such as stationery and office supplies, maintenance and repairs to equipment, and salaries—is itemized within the many functional categories of the department. Grouped into different functions or activities or programs, the line-item budget ultimately involves the listing of specific types of items and total expenditures in fine detail. Through the use of the line-item budget it is possible to determine the total cost of paper and duplicating throughout the organization, for example. Although broken down into these categories within each function or program, the same accounting number is assigned and simple computations will yield totals, not only in one department but throughout the entire governmental operation.

According to Burkhead, the line-item budget is the most widely used form of classification for budget expenditures.[10] Elaborating on the scope of the object or line-item classification method, Burkhead stated: "The object classification is used in almost every state government in this country and in the vast majority of local governments, and is also used as a supplementary classification by the federal government."[11]

There are many advantages to the utilization of the line-item method, particularly from an accounting and statistical standpoint. Foremost is that it is possible to estimate in advance, and control during the year, the actual units of an item to purchase. This works in well with purchasing planning and in maintenance of a working inventory. Individual personnel and the costs for each is committed to the ledger. Accountability in purchasing and in use of supplies and equipment is facilitated through this method. Disadvantages also manifest themselves with such a system, such as an overattention to detail that might result if the administrator becomes its slave; it may also curtail administrative discretion in transferring funds from one object to another.

The objects are listed separately, except when a grouping is more feasible for some items not individually purchased. Objects listed separately might include—for personnel: salaries and wages, temporary wages, vacation relief, overtime pay, medical services, retirement, etc.; for utilities: gas, water, telephone, teletype and telegraph; for repair and maintenance: furniture and fixtures, automotive equipment, radio equipment. Objects that might be grouped together might include subscriptions and memberships, stationery and office supplies, printing and duplicating, and contract training services.

The arrangement of the objects in the budget may be incorporated directly into the functional and/or the performance budget. The possibilities of budget desin are limited only by the imagination of the developer. Principal among the considerations when developing the budget is the manner in which it will be used. Clear-cut policies should be developed along with the budget to assure utilization of the budget as a management tool to serve the organization rather than a rigid taskmaster that hinders rather than helps the management process.

PPBS (PLANNING PROGRAM BUDGETING SYSTEM)

Incorporating the function, object, and performance budget into a systems-type package, the more innovative approach to budget management is known as PPBS, Planning Program Budgeting System. It is essentially a program-performance–based budget with a systems application. Donald Hanna and William Gentel credit the Rand Corporation and former Secretary of Defense Robert McNamara with the development of the PPBS technique.[12] Professor Jack Kenney says that PPBS is actually nothing new but rather a conglomerate,[13] consisting of "innovations as well as tested practices in long-range planning, financial management, public accounting, performance budgeting, management science, and public economic analysis. . . . Primary credit for adapting these concepts for use by state and local governments is given to the State and Local Finances Project of George Washington University which was financed by the Ford Foundation."[14]

When applied to the typical criminal justice agency, there seem to be certain step-by-step procedures that should be followed in operating according to PPBS.

1. A careful analysis of the mission, or purpose for the organization's existence must be made. Objectives and goals of the entire organization and of its subdivisions must be spelled out in behavioral terms, that is, specifically what will the individual activities produce in the way of results?
2. The next step in the process appears to be that of structuring the decision-making process, and identifying how and by whom the different types of management decisons will be made.
3. Activities which the department will perform in order that they may most effectively and economically accomplish their objectives are worked out in the form of a series of programs. Some of the programs consist of alternative courses to pursue: it is the responsibility of management to choose the alternatives. Each program is studied in its entirety, over a period of several years in many cases, and costs are estimated for carrying out the program.
4. Each program's objectives should be described so that the results should be evident and measurable, when the objectives have been attained. It will be possible to weigh the results against the cost. Although some activities may be essential in spite of their costs, it may be necessary to abandon an activity or to choose an alternative which is more economical. The question to be asked during the frequent evaluation sessions is, Does the result justify the expense? In this system, several alternatives will have been identified, and management decisions will have to be made to choose those alternatives which produce the better results.
5. Single-year budgets are linked with multi-year budgets. Each year, and during the entire year, allocations for the programs are reviewed and management decisions made as to their continuation or modification for the following year. This, indeed, makes the budget a planning and management tool far more efficiently than many other types of budgets. A program is continued only when it can be

demonstrated that it is in fact attuned to the department's objectives and when measurable results may be used to document the necessary justifications. Future planning is more effectively related to past and present performance because the system demands that it be done that way.
6. The programs are interpreted in terms of objects so that the actual accounting function of the budget management may be carried out on the operational level.

The problems in utilizing a PPBS budgeting method may include overcoming the traditional view that the budget is nothing more than an accounting tool. PPBS forces all participants in the planning process to think of the department's activities in terms of programs specifically geared to attain some measurable and demonstratable objectives and to think of them in terms of their costs weighed against their effectiveness. Management decisions must be made in advance of their actual need, which calls for identification of alternatives and selection of the most favorable alternatives in terms of cost effectiveness. The more traditional approach is to let many matters take care of themselves as they occur. Experience has shown many managers that tradition may not always be correct, but it is generally the easier of two alternatives, and many decisions "make themselves," or are made by lower-ranking staff members when the time comes for them to take some action. The PPBS method requires more top-level management decisions based on projections, forecasts, and anticipated needs, and it takes much of the guesswork out of budget planning and management.

There are many advantages to using PPBS. One of the more significant is that it is possible to justify expenditures on the basis of logical analyses and demonstrated need. Cost-effectiveness studies may be routinely performed, and the most efficient utilization of manpower and other resources may be accomplished in a more systematic way and in a less emotional way. In the words of Kenney, the PPBS:

> . . . stimulates continuing analysis of existing and future programs. The resource allocation decisions. . . . require the development of information for the decision-maker on the costs, outputs, and benefits of existing as well as future programs. The use of output data in departmental management assists in the actual evaluation of programs. That is, actual relationships can be established between costs, outputs, and contribution of objectives.[15]

THE BUDGET PROCESS

Budgets, like any other governmental product of management efforts, are not developed in a vacuum. Because they are developed in a dynamic environment, this statement by Burkhead is worthy of consideration:

> The development of an adequate approach to decision-making in the allocation of public resources must recognize the interrelation of (1) the governmental machinery, and the administrator and legislator therein, in providing a mechanism for arriving at decisions; and (2) the influence of groups that are affected by public expenditures in shaping and molding the decision. Beyond these two, there is the influence of the facts—the measurement of specific benefits which have come and can come from specific expenditures.[16]

In his treatise on the budget, Burkhead points out that the administrator has a much greater influence on the size and character of his budget than one might realize, and he presents five characteristics that elucidate:

> First, it is evident that the administrator may have great leeway in determination of policy. The emphasis the administrator places on a problem, for example, may be used to shape public opinion or may create public demands for a particular style or amount of service.
>
> Second, the resources available to the administrator are not rigidly limited. He may create the demand for a program to such an extent that additional resources are devoted to his program. Such resources may be diverted from other governmental operations or they might be added by other means, such as a special revenue source.
>
> Third, the community does not have a set of values that determines the amount of resources which will be used for the different government functions. The values are determined—and continually in the process of being determined—by management.
>
> Fourth, the form in which the budget is presented and approved will determine the distribution of decision-making power between the administrator and the legislature.
>
> Fifth, budget-making provides the occasion for periodic review and reassessment of community needs and resources. Policy changes may be translated into operating programs.[17]

The Budget Cycle

The budget cycle is continuous. Preparation and feedback in many cases are synonymous and should be continually in progress throughout the year. Assuming that the process has to start somewhere, it is usually broken down into the following distinctive parts: (1) Preplanning at the operational-management levels, (2) management preparation and submission to the central budget control officer, (3) research and planning, (4) executive preparation and presentation, (5) legislative study and authorization, (6) execution, (7) audit, and (8) feedback. A brief discussion of each of those parts may further elucidate the process.

1. PREPLANNING. This budgeting activity is continually taking place. The goals and objectives of the department are being assessed and critically defined, and translated into performance goals and programs. When further broken down into the actual personnel to be assigned, it is necessary that a comprehensive overview—of the results to be obtained by the additional personnel or their reassignment—be presented as a valid justification for the change. Vehicles, equipment, support personnel, office and other working space, furniture, telephones, and supplies are all affected by the addition or subtraction of one individual from a functional unit within the organization. The same rule should apply to the purchase of equipment. A description of the item should be accompanied by a clear and concise explanation of its need and its application if purchased. Justification for purchases of items of equipment, or the addition of personnel, must be strong enough to withstand competition from other units within the department and from other departments within the same governmental structure; everyone along the way must see the demonstrated need.

2. MANAGEMENT PREPARATION. A single individual or office may be charged with the actual responsibility for budget preparation and management, but that is for accounting and accountability purposes. The budget is everyone's business. Supervisory and management personnel throughout the organization should coordinate all requests, justifications, and preparation of program descriptions. They should compile their budget packages in the form of programs and performance items with estimates of their total and individual costs.

3. RESEARCH AND PLANNING. Every proposal for the budget should receive study, some items more than others. Every conceivable alternative should be explored, social and economical implications subjected to scrutiny, and every possible ramification anticipated. A new technique that is going to be used by the department may lead to lawsuits or complaints to the press about the new "brutal" weapon. Surveys and various other means may be employed to sound out the temper of the community regarding certain procedures and equipment. Equipment should be tested, and consumer research should be handled by the vendor; it is only natural for the salesman to tout his product as the panacea for every problem the department has experienced during the past ten years.

4. EXECUTIVE PREPARATION AND PRESENTATION. This part of the process usually has a timetable, such as completion five or six months prior to the date that the budget is to be presented to the legislators for their public

hearings and legal action. By the time the individual proposals reach the office of the top-level administrators and the chief executive, they should have been completely prepared for all practical purposes. Armed with all of this information and supporting documentation, the executive can review what has been presented to him in light of the department's goals and objectives, and he plans the total operation by making a series of management decisions on the various alternatives presented to him. A well-executed budget recommendation from a middle manager in the organization should require nothing more from the chief executive than a decision whether to add the personnel or purchase the equipment. At this stage in the operation, there is considerable interchange of ideas and many meetings and conferences so that the management decisions may be made intelligently.

5. LEGISLATIVE STUDY AND AUTHORIZATION. This phase of the process usually has a firm date attached to it; again, there should be little left for the legislators to do but to choose from the alternatives and—by that action—determine the broad, general policies of the governmental jurisdiction in question. Through their control of the total expenditures it is often possible for the city council, for example, to mandate a philosophy. A resort community council may choose to have a somewhat lax police department, particularly in the area of vice laws. In a subtle manner, it is possible for them to withhold certain intelligence equipment and undercover investigation funds from the budget, making it difficult for the police chief to successfully pursue vice investigations and arrests. If the chief is to operate an organization that truly reflects the needs of the city and the community standards, his budget proposals should clearly reveal sufficient information to support his requests. Then the legislators cannot deny his requests, if they agree that the chief's views are valid.

6. EXECUTION OF THE BUDGET. This involves management and accounting if the budget is a performance budget and developed on the principles of the PPBS. Management on sound business practice principles should be the basic requirement.

7. AUDIT, AND 8. FEEDBACK. Performance and expenditures are compared with the department's objectives. Continuous inspections, evaluations, and other supervisory techniques must be utilized in order that an objective evaluation may be accomplished.

Budget Item Request Format

Usually the individual who initiates the original request for a budget item has a fairly accurate description of the item—quite possibly has had an opportunity to observe or participate in its use—and is in an excellent position to provide sufficient information for the manager to weigh its merit and to determine how it fits into his program plans. Following are a few of the questions that should be answered as a basic requirement for such a request:

1. Who wants the item and who will use it?
2. Describe the item (include photos, diagrams, etc.).
3. Specifically, what will be accomplished with its use that cannot be accomplished with something we already have, or that is available to us at no cost or inconvenience?
4. What is the cost of this item, and what is the projected cost of maintenance and repair?
5. What is the guaranteed life? estimated actual life?
6. Recommended source where this item may be purchased.
7. Is this item available for lease?
8. Was this item denied in the past? If so, what reason was given, and by whom, for not purchasing it?
9. Will the item replace something now in use?
10. If so, what do you recommend be done with the item being replaced?
11. Justify your request:
    a. What purpose will it serve and/or what program will it serve?
    b. What will be the result if this item is not purchased?
    c. Will it save money? Explain.
    d. Will it save man-hours? Where and how many?
    e. What are the benefits to the organization?

In short, the budget justification should clearly explain what the item is and how it will be used. Any arguments that might be used against its purchase should be anticipated and answered in a factual and objective manner. Each item will be weighed on its own merits and in comparison with all of the other recommendations that will be submitted, sometimes in competition with each other. Some of the traditional arguments that will be raised in opposition to the recommendation, whether valid or not, include the following:

1. It won't work because we tried it once before.
2. The boss won't go for it.
3. It is too radical.
4. It costs too much, or
5. We don't have the money.
6. We have never done it before.
7. Why change? What we have is good enough.

8. What are they doing in Chicago – Los Angeles – Berkeley – Miami – New York? (Choose one.)
9. Why don't we let a committee look into it?
10. It's against policy.
11. I don't like it.
12. You're ahead of your time.

Consider the Alternatives

Many of the arguments or questions raised will be valid, others may not be, although the individual raising them will consider them so. Years of experience may cause some seasoning on the part of an administrator who himself has previously submitted his own recommendations for change or improvement only to have them rejected. Change for the mere sake of change is meaningless and expensive: further it has a resounding negative effect throughout the organization. The addition or discontinuance of one form or one procedure may substantially modify an entire work unit's mode of operation. It is the responsibility of the person who offers the recommendation to consider every available alternative and to recommend what he believes to be the best based upon sound judgment and at least some preliminary research. If any more study is needed, the planning unit may follow up, provided the initial recommendation meets with a manager's approval.

The initial inquiry into the feasibility of a new product, as with a new procedure, is to determine what effect any change will have on the individual units within the organization and on the overall operation. What will be the financial and effectiveness impact? What will be the impact on morale and on the working conditions? The planning and research unit should follow up with a request for manufacturers' demonstrations, and quite possibly a period of comparative testing during which many alternatives may be considered.

When only one product, among several available, meets the rigid requirements of a particular need, then the competitors should be named and the reasons given why their product is not acceptable. This practice reduces the allegations of "cronyism" or that some other type of preferential treatment is given one vendor which might result in his monopoly of the market. One excellent example of good salesmanship and merchandising is the enviable position that an aerosol tear gas manufacturer holds. His product is one of many but it is so effective that police officers commonly refer to all such products by this trade name.

PURCHASING

Purchasing is often handled by a separate office in a central position serving the entire county or municipal government. That office establishes and operates according to certain legal and policy requirements. It is quite possible that the purchasing agent has little knowledge of special products or items of equipment necessary for a particular criminal justice agency. A few guidelines for the criminal justice administrator will expedite and simplify the purchasing process through the central agency.

1. Prior to preparing the requisition, investigate the products for suitability, availability, and actual cost. A cheaper price with a shorter life or without a guarantee may not necessarily be a more economical purchase.
2. Do the comparison shopping yourself. As sincere as they may be, vendors are hardly likely to extoll the virtues of a competitor's product.
3. Inquire into maintenance and parts replacement, and the availability of maintenance contracts.
4. Write clearly and succinctly, but descriptively enough so that the purchasing agent—who does not have your experience or knowledge—will understand your wishes.
5. Specify brand names of acceptable items, listing more than one if possible, and give your reasons why certain products that the purchasing agent might consider are not desirable.
6. Consider standardization within the organization and with other departments to allow for bulk purchasing, interchangeability, and greater flexibility in maintenance and repair problems.
7. Check products upon delivery, and reject inferior or damaged goods.
8. Document experience with the product that will provide later justification for its exclusive use, or for its elimination from the list of alternatives.
9. Check on the item after its purchase and determine if it is being used as intended, and according to the manufacturer's recommended procedures.
10. Attend conventions, demonstrations, and manufacturers' fairs to keep abreast of current and future methods and products.

INVENTORY CONTROL

Maintenance of adequate supplies and equipment is just as important to a service organization as it is to one which deals in manufacture and sale of products. The emergency nature of many criminal justice activities makes it imperative that an efficient inventory control system be instituted and maintained.

One method for keeping track of supply and equipment items in the organization is to maintain a set of itemized lists. For equipment, the items should be listed according to name, but there should be sufficient data on the list, or card file, to show the date of purchase, the estimated and guaranteed lifetime, warranty conditions, service contract information, and phone numbers of authorized and qualified maintenance people. It is also wise to keep a record of complaints about the item, and a history of repairs. A cost-effectiveness analysis may be accomplished with information from records such as these.

Supply items should be put on alphabetical lists that have columns in which the following information can be entered: (a) name of item, (b) location of inventoried quantities—personal stocks in the various offices and desks of individual personnel must be considered as expended or the inventory task will be an impossible exercise, (c) quantity on hand, (d) quantity used since last inventory, (e) six months' supply—estimate until a history is established, (f) date and quantity of most recent order and expected date of delivery, (g) comments regarding any future changes which might affect the item. A monthly or bimonthly inventory will be used for a continuous updating of the information. Although this list seems cumbersome, the entries can be quite brief and the value will far surpass any disadvantages that one might anticipate. The inventories should be kept—and used—for at least several months so that the total picture may be seen for budget purposes and to identify any seasonal fluctuations in use of some of the items.

SUMMARY

The fiscal management of an organization should be considered as one of the many ongoing processes of criminal justice administration. The budget and its many ancillary activities should be regarded as key management devices, and not relegated to some back-room and once-a-year activities to satisfy a legislative requirement. The budget is everybody's business and it is imperative that every single employee in the organization be encouraged to participate in the program. In this chapter we have briefly presented some thoughts on how this participation might be carried out.

The basic types of budget have been described in three categories: *function, performance, and line-item* or *object*. All three have applications in the criminal justice agency, usually within the same set of documents and their implementation programs. A concept of budgeting that has received considerable coverage during recent years—and a brief discussion in these pages—is the *Planning Program Budgeting System* or PPBS. This particular system is a conglomerate of all the various types of budgets, an eclectic approach in the systems method.

240 CRIMINAL JUSTICE ORGANIZATION AND MANAGEMENT

Along with an effective budgeting system must go the ancillary management processes of purchasing and inventory control. The fiscal management of the organization must assure the greatest cost-effectiveness of activities in direct pursuit of accomplishment of the department's goals and objectives.

Notes

1. From Kenney, John P., *Police Administration*, 1972, p. 111. Courtesy of Charles C Thomas, Publisher, Springfield, Illinois.
2. William H. Newman, *Administrative Action: The Techniques of Organization and Management*, 2nd ed. (Englewood Cliffs, N.J.: Prentice-Hall, © 1960), p. 22. Reprinted by permission of the publisher.
3. Kenney, *Police Administration*, p. 111.
4. For complete details, refer to "Impact-Detroit," in pages 322–29 of *Criminal Justice: Readings*, Thomas F. Adams, ed. (Pacific Palisades, Calif.: Goodyear Publishing, 1972).
5. Jesse Burkhead, *Government Budgeting* (New York: John Wiley & Sons, 1967), pp. 111–112. Copyright © 1967 John Wiley & Sons. Reprinted by permission of John Wiley & Sons.
6. Ibid., p. 133.
7. Ibid., p. 134.
8. Ibid., p. 134.
9. Ibid., pp. 134–136.
10. Ibid., p. 127.
11. Ibid., p. 128.
12. From Hanna, Donald G., and Gentel, William D., *A Guide to Primary Police Management Concepts*, 1971, p. 130. Courtesy of Charles C Thomas, Publisher, Springfield, Illinois.
13. Kenney, *Police Administration*, pp. 116–127. An excellent coverage of the PPBS budgeting concept is presented on these pages, for which Dr. Kenney credits the original author of the information, Richard A. Hughes, vice-president of Booz, Allen, and Hamilton, Inc.
14. Ibid., pp. 119–120.
15. Ibid., p. 122.
16. Burkhead, *Government Budgeting*, p. 45.
17. Ibid., p. 48.

Review Questions

1. In what way is a budget used as a management tool?
2. Describe how you would use the budget as a planning tool.
3. How does the PPBS compare with the line-item and the performance budget?
4. What is the benefit of the PPBS when compared with the more traditional types?
5. What is a functional budget, and how is it utilized?
6. Which type of budget involves budgeting and planning by objectives?
7. List the six steps in PPBS budgeting.

8. Describe a typical budget cycle for a criminal justice agency.
9. Prepare a budget request for an item you believe essential to the effective operation of one of the criminal justice agencies.
10. List some of the traditional arguments one is likely to hear when making a budget proposal and prepare a response to each one.

10 The Police Organization

Each law enforcement or investigative agency is distinctively different from all others because each has its own goals and objectives, d functions, philosophy, and methods of operation. The federal or state agency is usually charged with a specific investigating function (Secret Service, or Bureau of Narcotics) to the exclusion of almost all other criminal law violations or investigative responsibilities or the agency's jurisdiction may involve law enforcement activities related to the waterways (Coast Guard or Harbor Patrol), or the highways (Highway Patrol), or the Courts (Marshal). There are many similarities in these organizations as there are also dissimilarities, because of their uniqueness. Most of them, however, are organized in accordance with the basic principles outlined in chapter 2, and reviewed briefly in this chapter. The municipal and county law enforcement agencies are the most common type of police organization in the Criminal Justice System. For that reason, we outline and discuss an imaginary department that might be typical of either of those two agencies.

PRINCIPLES OF MANAGEMENT

Concepts or principles of management important in the police organization include the following:

1. Identify the organization's goals and objectives.
2. Develop an organizational plan.

3. Organize the department according to the plan.
4. Prescribe the various relationships throughout the organization.
5. Minimize dual accountability or the one-boss principle.
6. Realistically limit the scope of supervision.
7. Integrate and coordinate the functional units.
8. Staff the organization for maximum effectiveness.
9. Develop methods for control of the organization.

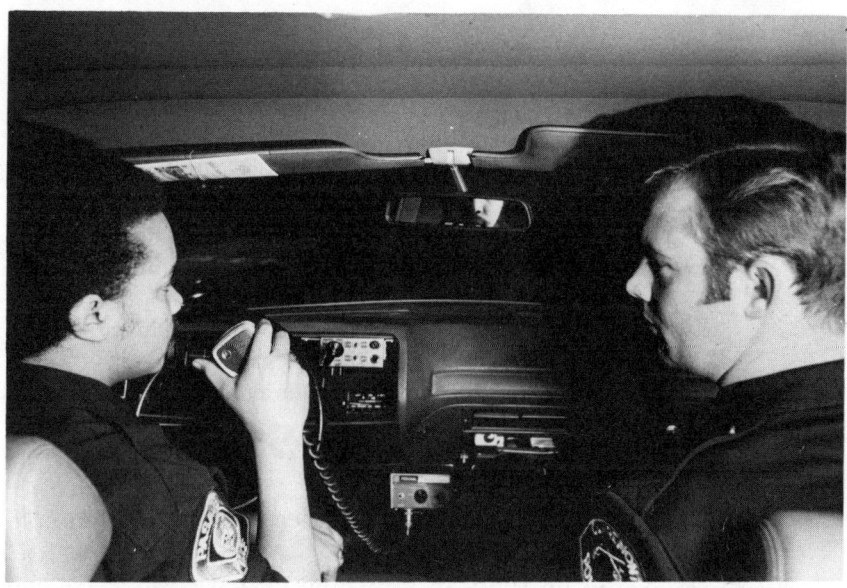

Courtesy: Police Department, Pasadena, California

Identification and articulation of the department's goals, or purposes for its existence, and the objectives intended for their accomplishment must be accomplished first. Once that task is done, then the objectives are rank-ordered according to priorities. How the many work programs and assignments are apportioned is in direct relation to the objectives. If the department's principal task is traffic control and enforcement, for example, then the principal division of work assignments and the greatest number of people will be assigned to the traffic division. If the principal task is to reduce the flow of illicit drugs, the emphasis will be on the narcotics division.

Work programs are divided on the basis of (1) purpose, (2) methods, (3) function to be performed or the people to be served, (4) time, (5) area, and (6) special needs. These factors must also be taken into account at the same time as the goals and objectives of the department. The police organization is a twenty-four-hour-per-day operation; its geographical jurisdiction must be apportioned into areas or subdivisions. In fact, when studying the typical police department, it is quite evident to the student that the department serves many purposes, utilizes many methods, performs a vast variety of functions, serves the entire community membership and almost continuously serves special needs of the people who call for its services.

Goals

The goals of the police department include the following:

1. Maintenance of an ordered liberty, which involves a fine balance between the rights and responsibilities of the citizens and their guests.
2. Fair and impartial enforcement of the laws of the nation and its political subdivisions, and the general administration of justice.
3. Protection of life and property through vigilant protective patrol and preventive maintenance.
4. Prevention and repression of criminal and destructive antisocial behavior.
5. Identification and apprehension of people who violate the law.
6. Recovery of stolen and embezzled property and return to its lawful owners.
7. Serving the courts by presenting evidence, witnesses, and by giving testimony.

To his list, the sheriff will add at least the following three goals:

8. Service to the court as bailiff.
9. Operation of the county jail.
10. Perform the functions of coroner, tax collector, or other responsibility designated by law; this varies from county to county.

Objectives

The objectives of the department, as we interpret them for the purpose of this chapter, include those listed below. But we hasten to add, there are many more that the individual administrator must identify and articulate; variables among departments are numerous.

1. Provide benevolent services in cooperation with other agencies and those not provided by other agencies, which include giving directions, counseling, rescue, providing for medical aid, and giving general assistance.
2. Mediate domestic and other disputes for the purpose of preserving peace and preventing crime.
3. Attend public gatherings and protect the rights of the people to assemble peaceably.
4. Investigate criminal offenses and take necessary steps to identify, arrest, and bring to a fair trial those persons who are responsible for those crimes.
5. Enforce the laws and ordinances enacted on government authority for the health, safety, morals, welfare, and convenience of the state and enforce the powers provided to the federal government by the Constitution and its amendment.
6. Investigate traffic collisions to compile and disseminate information essential for the needs of the participants and legally interested parties, and the prevention of collisions, education of the public, and assistance in street and highway engineering.
7. Investigate matters that may affect license and other regulatory matters as directed by the city (county) government regulations and laws.
8. Regulate vehicular and pedestrian traffic to expedite its flow from congestion and collisions.
9. Patrol the jurisdiction to observe and take effective action for the purpose of preventing and repressing criminal and antisocial behavior and to maintain the peace in the community.
10. Investigate complaints and calls for assistance in those matters which involve the legal and traditional responsibilities of the department.
11. Prepare reports and maintain records essential to the effective operation and management of the department.
12. Maintain a property and evidence storage facility for the safekeeping and return of lost and stolen property and control of evidence according to a system assuring procedurally correct presentation in court.
13. Early discovery of predelinquent and delinquent acts by children and youths, and effective disposition to deter development of criminal behavior patterns.

14. Assure an effective balance of vice control in accordance with the community standards through investigation and enforcement activities.
15. Interact with the various segments and individuals in the community to explain the functions of the department and its responsibilities in the administration of justice.
16. Act as master-at-arms in the court, maintain order, and provide other services as required by the judge.
17. Operate the county jail and provide related services.
18. Include other objectives not in this chapter. As stated earlier, the list must be individualized to serve the specific needs of the department at hand.

ORGANIZING THE DEPARTMENT

A study of the goals and objectives for the police organization indicates there is a need for major divisions of the department to accommodate the programs which will be carried out for the accomplishment of the objectives that have been identified. The divisions will include the functions of patrol, traffic, juvenile, investigation, property and evidence, records, and their subdivisions into work details and assignments. Although there are many different types of organizational structure, in this chapter the divisions will be classified under the broad, general categories of line and staff.

Although the distinction between line and staff may actually be an artificial one, the typical police organization is separated into at least two major categories: those activities directly related to the basic objectives designated as *line*, and those that are auxiliary to line, or supportive activities, which are designated as *staff*.

Line Functions

PATROL. The patrol division is the basic operating unit of the department; it is charged with the responsibility for performing all those tasks which can best be handled by a uniformed force of men and women assigned to cover the entire jurisdiction by various methods at all times of the day on a continuous basis. Except for housekeeping and other auxiliary functions, better handled by clerical and other support staff, and the management functions, handled by those in the hierarchy of the organization, the patrol division is responsible for the total policing and law enforcement responsibilities charged to the department. Holcomb states:

> The police patrol, whether on foot, or in an automobile, is the basic law enforcement method. . . . Careful patrol by intelligent

officers is the first line of defense against crime. The man on the beat does the day-by-day work that makes or breaks a law enforcement agency, that controls the vast majority of criminals and is the major basis of the police function of the protection of life and property and service to the public.[1]

An item analysis for the activities and tasks performed by the patrol officer would probably reveal most of the following as typical, although each agency has its own personal characteristics. The list has been compiled from several sources and generally applies to both the county sheriff and the municipal police department, except where indicated otherwise.

1. Routine patrol and observation. The purposes for this technique are many, including the mere presence of the officer in uniform and in a distinctively marked vehicle to create an awareness of his omnipresence. When they know a policeman is present, some would-be miscreants have a tendency to deter criminal or antisocial behavior. The officer attempts first to determine the "average" appearance of his district and the activities of the people; then, he addresses himself to those situations which appear out of the ordinary. What is average conduct for the officer's district may not reflect his own personal values because of the variety of cultures and individuals represented in that district. The officer questions people whose presence arouses his curiosity because of his responsibility for the peace and security of the district. He checks on the security of doors and windows, and looks after the safe conduct of people who are moving about.

2. Advise, direct, and provide information to the public. As the only visible representative of the local government, the patrol officer must be able to provide answers to questions concerning the history, geography, tourist attractions, food and lodging, entertainment, sporting events, and virtually everything worth knowing about the area.

3. Attendance at public gatherings to prevent unlawful acts. People have a right to assemble peacefully, to air their grievances, to seek entertainment, or to otherwise gather for whatever purpose they choose. They are entitled to those rights without interference from the thoughtless or lawless acts of others. The officer appears on the scene, determines that the assembly is a lawful one, makes his presence known for its deterrent effect on anyone who would convert the gathering into an unlawful one, and remains present until he determines that his presence is no longer needed.

4. Benevolent and community services. Ill and injured persons often call upon the police for aid or escort service to a doctor or hospital. The officer may administer first aid, attend a childbirth, revive a drowning victim, and take part in rescue operations. When invited, the officer responds to domestic quarrels and gives family and marital advice within the constraints of his legal responsibilities. Although they may not necessarily fall within the list of job specifications, the patrol officer performs

many services that are required of him by tradition and social custom. Such duties may include delivering death messages, making emergency deliveries of transplant organs and blood, and assisting people who have locked themselves out of their houses to mention a few. A complete list would be endless.

5. Preliminary investigations. According to Allen Bristow of California State University at Los Angeles, the preliminary investigation at a crime or collision scene includes the following steps:

> (1) Rendering aid and preventing further damage or injury at the scene; (2) Determining if a crime has been committed, the type of crime, and the identity of the suspect; (3) Arresting the suspect if sufficient cause exists; (4) Obtaining sufficient data about the identity of the suspect and taking steps to locate and apprehend him; (5) Preservation of the scene to prevent the destruction of evidence; (6) Locating victims, witnesses, and informants, and gathering information about the crime and the suspect; (7) Establishing in detail how the crime was committed or the incident took place; (8) Determining the availability of evidence, and estimating the extent of loss or injury; (9) Deciding whether evidence technicians or field investigators should be called to the scene; (10) The recording of this information in notes and/or on the appropriate report forms.[2]

6. Inspection services and aid to other agencies. Some miscellaneous inspections that an officer performs in addition to his regular responsibilities of inspecting for building and property security are to look for fires and hazards that might lead to fires, to check on building and safety code violations, to inspect alcoholic beverage control licenses, and to report on health hazards. He reports light and utility outages, wires down, broken water mains, holes in the streets and sidewalks, and a multitude of related activities; because of his continuous presence in his district, he can observe and report on any problems or discrepancies.

7. Responding to calls for assistance. Requests for the officers' assistance consist of many responses for which the officers will either handle themselves or refer to others. Such referrals include spiritual advice, marriage counseling, legal advice, financial aid, child guidance; officers are also asked to do something about unethical business practices, suicides and attempts at suicide, mentally or emotionally ill persons, improper trash collections and as many others as the imagination will allow.

8. Enforcing the federal, state, and local laws; issue citations and summonses; arrest the violators when reasonable cause exists. The patrol officer exercises a considerable amount of discretion when fulfilling this portion of his responsibility. Although he has the authority according to law to arrest someone for what he believes to be a criminal act committed in his

presence, or for felonies which were not committed in his presence, the officer must be reasonably sure that the person did actually commit a crime. Further, the officer must be able to substantiate the arrest with evidence collected through legal and constitutional means.

Regarding the exercise of discretionary powers of a police officer, a California Penal Code section states: "The rule of the common law, that penal statutes are to be strictly construed, has no application to this code. All its provisions are to be construed according to the fair import of their terms, with a view to effect its objects and to promote justice."[3] To further explain this "fair import" concept, the California Supreme Court stated in a 1964 case:

> When language reasonably susceptible to two constructions is used in a penal law, that construction which is more favorable to the defendant will be adopted. The defendant is entitled to the benefit of every reasonable doubt as to the true interpretation of words or the construction of language used in a statute.[4]

9. Expediting the flow of traffic and preventing collisions. The problem of prevention and reduction of collisions as well as the relief of congestion on streets and highways, which were designed and built to cope with the peak loads of many years ago, will usually be assigned to a separate division in a larger department. Whether a department is large or small, the patrol unit is responsible for routine enforcement activities and for handling the initial investigation of traffic collisions. Someone with traffic responsibilities, usually the traffic unit, compiles a list of the principal locations where collisions occur, identifies the times of day when there are patterns of common occurrence and the leading causes of the collisions. These facts are then disseminated to all officers. As a part of their routine patrol duties, the patrol officers will look for the collison-causing violations and will take appropriate enforcement action. At the same time they will assume responsibility for the task of directing traffic to relieve congestion at those times and places where problems arise.

10. Caring for animals. Separate agencies whose sole responsibility is to enforce animal control regulations and to care for animals and their problems operate in many jurisdictions. In those places where such an agency does not exist, or is operated only on a part-time basis, the police department is usually charged with the task on either a full-time or "some-of-the-time" basis. Issuing dog licenses, rescuing a treed cat, or retrieving a pet monkey are all typical activities performed by the police patrol officer.

11. Writing reports. Virtually every type of police activity requires some sort of a written record of the event, from a cryptic entry on a daily log to a very comprehensive investigation report. Written notes are necessary

because so many of the officers' activities require some later action, such as a follow-up investigation of a burglary by an investigator or legal action by the city attorney against a building code violator. The officer devotes from one-fifth to one-third of his total duty time to the preparation of records and reports, in my estimation. As stated in *Police Patrol: Tactics and Techniques:*

> Reporting is usually one of the least publicized tasks of the police officer, but it is actually one of the most important and time-consuming tasks that he is required to perform. The report is used as the basis for determining whether to charge an individual with a crime and, if so, what specific charge will be made. In many cases, the officer's report is the only criterion that his superiors have to evaluate his performance and decision-making ability. His report must be complete and accurate, since it is usually the only written record of what transpired.[5]

12. Testifying in court. The accused has a constitutionally guaranteed right to be faced by his accuser and to be assured a fair trial. It is most essential that the officer testify in court to those facts presented to him in the course of performing his duties. He must be objective and his testimony must be free from bias or prejudice, leaving the determination of guilt to the courts.

The traditional "beat patrol" consists of patrolling and fulfilling all the requirements of the preceding list within a prescribed section of the city. The officer may patrol solo or with a partner, depending on the area, the types of activities, and the policy of the chief executive. Some other methods of patrol, which either supplant or supplement the traditional method, include the San Francisco "S" Squad, Chicago's Task Force, Los Angeles Sheriff's Special Enforcement Bureau, and other variations of tactical deployment units. The purpose of these special units is to reduce street crimes—rapes, robberies, and thefts—through deployment of officers in civilian clothing in unmarked vehicles (including bicycles, motorcycles, and horses) in what amounts to a "saturation" of crime-plagued areas with police officers. Their task consists mainly of field interviews; they ask individuals to explain the legitimacy of their business in these high-crime areas. No doubt most of the people encountered are among the law-abiding who can quite adequately satisfy the curiosity of the officers, but some of them include the individuals who are responsible for the crimes.[6]

Two types of patrol frequently alluded to by administrators and supervisors who find that the standard patrol methods leave something to be desired, are the Aberdeen and the Salford plans. Rather than assigning individual beats to lone officers, teams of officers are used. According to Gourley and Bristow, the Aberdeen plan works like this:

> The crux of the Aberdeen Plan is the constable team. The number of constables making up a team varies according to the size of the patrol area designated to the team. Each team is commanded in the field by a sergeant. The team is equipped with a police car which is used to transport the men to their beat districts. The men do not patrol individually but as a team, with mobility provided by the radio car. The constables are encouraged to follow up all cases possible without calling for specialized assistance.[7]

The Salford Plan is also a foot-auto patrol based on fluid assignments. The principal difference is in the flexibility of districts, which vary in size with each shift and with each changing need. The areas requiring the greatest attention are saturated with patrols. Gourley and Bristow describe the function of the Salford Plan:

> The Salford police team is normally made up of a sergeant and nine constables. Each team is equipped with a radio car. The sergeant and the driver stay with the vehicle. The teams are informed of any special problems that have arisen since their last shift. The car is the focal point of the team; and, while it is used to patrol in conjunction with the foot man, the car is also used as a mobile station. Paper work, interrogation, etc. are carried on in the vehicle by the foot men, and the radio keeps them in constant touch with headquarters.[8]

Professor Kenney devotes a considerable portion of his book to the concept of team policing.[9] Team policing as it applies to the patrol function, according to Kenney, involves a more cooperative effort and supervision-free (relatively speaking) type of patrol activity. He explains its basis:

> Team policing is based on a phenomenon of accepting the premise that all personnel have a contribution to make to the policy and operational decision-making process. It presupposes that all personnel have a contribution to make to the operation of the department, are capable and motivated to make that contribution and that there will be acceptance, if worthy, of the contribution. It is a continuing process whereby involvement of all personnel takes place, a continuous input of ideas, suggestions and constructive criticism is fostered, and new ideas and concepts are ingested into the system.[10]

The precise model for the team concept is not described in Kenney's book, but he generally describes it as one in which everyone in each unit contributes to the planning and operation with equal authority as everyone else in the unit, that *peer control* is the rule rather than authoritarian control by a supervisor, and that the work of the group is oriented toward approaching activities from a program basis, that is:

... traffic control, investigations, community relations, and the programs as a foundational basis of departmental goals and objectives. The emphasis is placed upon work to be done rather than on the bureaucratic relationships of "who is responsible to whom." Dealing with specific situations replaces emphasis on command relationships. Elaborating on this issue, program goals become the principal focus of operation. Personnel work as a team in dealing with problems and situations rather than being concerned with the chain of command.[11]

Whisenand made the following observations about team policing:

> The work unit will become an integrated group of professionals (patrolmen, investigators, traffic, vice, and so on) engaged in tasks demanding a high degree of technical interdependence and group problem solving. Inklings of team policing can already be seen in some organizations. And, similar to his role in loosening communications, the part the police supervisor will play in extracting the advantages out of such an organizational arrangement is prominent. Briefly put, he will be more of a leader and less of a controller. Team policing, if it is to work at all, requires the very things that constitute the role of supervisory leader: (1) support-subordinate, (2) interaction facilitation, (3) goal emphasis, and (4) work facilitation. To fulfill this more complex role he will be furnished with new and sharpened tools. He will be more facile with systems analysis, program evaluation, manpower planning, operations research techniques, computer applications, and planning-programming budgeting systems (PPBS). And, of course, there will be new tools as yet unknown to us.[12]

The patrol function is the basic operating unit of the police department. Many departments utilize their patrol officers as generalists, charging them with the responsibility for virtually every facet of the department's total program. The other units have the responsibility for follow-up and specialized activities that cannot be handled by the patrol unit because of time and special considerations, such as the need to be away from the normal patrol duties for extended periods of time. The team policing concept employs an extension of the generalist approach, although perhaps with a different emphasis. The administrator must decide the extent of the patrol unit's responsibilities and the scope of their functions in relations to all of the other operating units in the department.

Deployment of the patrol force depends on the extent to which the officers will involve themselves in the many activities charged to their unit. Some of the policy determinations concerning distribution include the following:

1. Which calls for service will be handled completely by telephone, and which ones will require that an officer be sent to the caller's address?

2. Which calls will be "counselled out" by advising the calling party that the matter is not a police department matter and should be handled by another agency?
3. To what extent will the patrol officers become involved in neighborhood quarrels, family disputes, advising children regarding their school attendance, and other behavior patterns, giving advice in interpersonal relationships, and peace-keeping functions?
4. What portion of the crime investigations will be handled by patrol officers, and at what point will cases be turned over to the specialists?
5. What is the patrol officer's role in traffic accident investigation and traffic law enforcement? Will the officers be solely responsible, or will there be supplementary assistance and coordination by traffic specialists?
6. To what extent will the officers be responsible for building security in their districts that will necessitate their being away from their patrol units for extended periods of time?
7. How much of the public relations functions of the department will directly involve the patrol officer? Will he be required to visit school classes during the day? How much time will be required of him to visit buildings and "burglar-proof" inspect?
8. What will be the reporting responsibilities of the field officers? How detailed must their reports be? Where will they go to make the reports—to headquarters, to a telephone, or to a portable dictating unit in their vehicles? What type of forms will be used—all prose or the checklist type? Who types or writes the reports? How often must the officers visit headquarters to turn in their reports?
9. How will priorities be established to give certain calls precedence over others in case there are more calls for service than there are units to handle them at any given time?
10. How are the supervisors and administrators used for management of the field officers? Are they going to provide field supervision and leadership?
11. What types of forms and other documents must be maintained as supervisory control devices over the patrol officer: daily log, tally sheets, and others?[13]

Determining how to apportion officers to the different times of the day on a watch—or shift—basis, and how to provide the most effective type of patrol service, pose quite a challenge to the administrator. Agencies have used various types of formulas for patrol deployment. Many of them are based on numbers of crimes; a weight is attached to each crime based on a system of priorities related to the seriousness of the offenses or other action requiring police attention, the time involved in handling those incidents, and the time devoted to preventive patrol of the areas where those incidents occur in an effort to reduce their occurrences. Actually, this method of weighting has been criticized as ineffective. Bristow points out:

The theory of weighting the criteria selected for best distribution is based on two principles. First of all, certain police activities can assume more time or importance than others against the range in weightings and, secondly, by ascribing different weights to these criteria, their importance for preventive patrol may be stressed. For example, it is felt that a Part I crime is a very serious offense—hence, giving it a weight of 4 will cause any distribution formula to bring patrolmen to spend more time in the area where more Part I crimes are committed.

The theory is subject to criticism on several counts. First of all, a number of police departments have now observed that the seriousness of a given offense does not necessarily dictate the amount of time that is necessary to handle that offense.

The second criticism concerns the fact that police patrol is not a proven preventive factor in a variety of Part I type crimes.[14]

A more realistic method for determining the patrol strength necessary to meet certain performance levels is on the basis of actual need and "consumed time" for each activity. The seriousness of the crime has no direct relationship to how long it takes to complete the preliminary investigation when compared with investigation of a much lesser crime on any type of hierarchical scale. Also, there can be no relationship between types of crimes committed in a given geographical area and the amount of time devoted to patrol for the purpose of reducing the occurrences of certain crimes—many serious crimes cannot be deterred regardless of the expended patrol time. In tune with the same philosophy of personnel deployment on the basis of real need, the fluid patrol system has met with some favorable results.

Basically, the principle of the *fluid patrol* concept is to study the actual time consumed for the various patrol activities on an hourly basis and to develop a flexible district designation plan whereby the districts for patrol vary with the time of the day and the day of the week depending on need. The entire city is broken down into small reporting districts on a grid plan and a detailed analysis is continuously updated to show current profiles on the various types of activity for each reporting district. A reporting district may be a square block, a park, a single place of business, an intersection, or a larger area, depending on the people who design the program. Through careful analysis of the reporting districts, the officers and their supervisors may work out their field assignments and draw the district boundaries at the same time they prepare for the day's work.[15]

Additional factors which must be taken into consideration when determining how to deploy patrol personnel on the basis of real need include following:

1. Resident and transient populations, particularly in business and tourist centers.

2. Amount and types of crimes and arrests.
3. Locations of crimes and arrests.
4. Traffic accident statistics and patterns.
5. Locations of crime hazards, or "frequent incident" locations calling for extra police coverage.
6. Proportionate locations, or displacement of the population. Sparsely populated residential areas versus apartment-business areas versus industrial centers.
7. Socioeconomic factors. High-income families may have recreation diversions out of the city, while the less affluent may be captives of the neighborhood.
8. Zoning plan of the city. Relative locations of business, industrial, residential, and other types of zones.
9. Size of the city in square miles.
10. Geography and topography. Are there strips and islands of the city that must be patrolled? Mountains, bays, ravines, and other natural barriers may separate parts of the city and make them inaccessible although clearly within sight.

Courtesy: Police Department, Huntington Beach, California

11. Parks and recreational facilities. Locations, size, and proximity to residences and accessible roads.
12. Streets and highways. Total mileages and configurations, traffic flow patterns, state of repair and construction.
13. Locations and numbers of attractive nuisances such as rock quarries, abandoned wells, mines, deserted buildings, swimming pools, open holes, woods, sandpits.
14. Age ratios of the population. Juvenile versus adult, and the various age categories: preschool, adolescent, teenage, young adult, senior citizen.
15. Male-female ratios and married versus single.
16. Homogeneity of the ethnic and cultural backgrounds of the residents.
17. Modes of transportation, and locations of the transportation terminals.
18. Restaurants and theaters. Hours of operation.
19. Residence of persons convicted for various crimes.
20. Maximum number of officers actually available to do the job.
21. Amount of trust and confidence in the department, which may influence the frequency with which the people call for police service and advice.[16]

TRAFFIC. By 1924, the American motorists were involved in traffic incidents and collisions (most of these incidents are not "accidents"; note that we avoid the use of the word *accident*) that were killing approximately 20,000 people a year.[17] In 1924, as a result of the increase in automobiles then numbering in the millions (Henry Ford and his company alone produced more than 15 million of his "T" models by 1927), the extended highway system that was being developed as a result of the Federal Road Aid Act of 1916, and the phenomenal death rate, President Woodrow Wilson convened the first President's Safety Conference. That conference yielded a uniform vehicle code for the nationwide enforcement of traffic laws through the many thousands of local law enforcement agencies. As a consequence of the newly created codes, designed to bring about sanity and safety into the driving habits of a nation of people on wheels, many new state agencies were created for highway regulation and control and local police departments augmented their forces with the creation of new divisions charged with similar responsibilities in the cities and towns. The police traffic function was described by the National Safety Council in a "position paper" enclosed in the July 1966 issue of the *Police Chief* magazine. It contained the following statement:

The basic traffic functions generally recognized to be fully the responsibility of the police are:
1. Enforcement of traffic laws
2. Direction of traffic
3. Investigation of accidents.

The paper stated that to perform these duties the police must perform certain other activities, consisting of:

1. Maintaining comprehensive records
2. Compiling statistics and summaries for determining needs for future corrective action and for informing the public
3. Coordination with other agencies
4. At a state level and in large police departments, maintaining laboratory and technical aids for investigation
5. Conducting research and development

Additional ancillary services were presented as the police responsibility "which may or may not be incidental to the police traffic function according to the structure of the jurisdiction of the lack of the service being provided by other agencies." Those services were expressed as:

1. Public information and education
2. Traffic engineering
3. Cooperation with other agencies in related services[18]

Because of the need to have a single unit charged with the administrative responsibility for addressing the traffic problem in accordance with the overall goals and objectives of the department, a separate unit is usually operated as a traffic division. Although all of the uniformed patrol officers are also expected to handle the initial investigation of traffic collisions and to perform many of the routine traffic enforcement and control activities, the traffic division has the ultimate authority and accountability for the department's traffic programs. From an administrative standpoint, police traffic functions include the following:

1. The enforcement of traffic laws. Indiscriminate enforcement of the thousands of laws without some sort of direction or system would be impossible and would probably have little or no effect on the reduction of collisions or on the general improvement of traffic safety on the highways and streets. Many of the laws relate to vehicle configuration in the form of regulations on length, width, load, location of fenders or mud flaps, weight of the vehicle, weight per axle, and so forth. The majority of the laws

which the police officer of a local agency enforces involve the rules of the road: speed, unsafe turn, unlawful passing, and stop sign violations to mention a few of the literally thousands of laws that have been promulgated for the control of traffic during the past several years. A technique has been developed for systematic law enforcement of the collision-causing violations known as selective enforcement.

Courtesy: Police Department, Hartford, Connecticut
(*Hartford Times* photo by Ed Lescoe)

Selective enforcement, as applied to traffic laws, involves a comprehensive study of collisions and their causes in relation to violations of the laws. Through the use of pin maps, computers, or any other means, the traffic division statistician plots the many collisions throughout the jurisdiction. Each collision is located on the map, and is indicated according to time and cause. Collisions attributed to law violations are analyzed. Through this analysis, it is possible to determine which violations cause the collisions, along with their frequency and rank order; the times these collisions occur—the violations are presumed to be occurring at the same time; the critical locations of these occurrences are identified and charted. The result is application of *Selective enforcement* methods. When enforcing the traffic laws, the officers issue citations and make arrests on the basis of the rank-order of collision-causing violations. Enforcement activities are concentrated on the locations where the collisions are occurring, and efforts are focused on traffic enforcement during the times of day when most of the collisions occur. In the course of their regular duties, the officers address themselves to all law violations that occur in their presence, but they do so in accordance with a sequence of priorities.

The traffic division may employ automobiles, helicopters, STOL (short take-off and landing), fixed-wing aircraft, and two- and three-wheel motorcycles for their enforcement activities. The officers on duty as traffic specialists are usually assigned to principal streets and other locations where the greatest number of violations occur, and devote the majority of their time to the enforcement of traffic laws. This is in contrast to the patrol officer, who addresses himself to traffic problems as one of his many responsibilities. Gourley makes the following statement about the need for all officers to participate in traffic control:

> Traffic control . . . is no longer a new activity and has long since become too large to be effectively handled as a special practice by a limited number of personnel. Police methods of dealing with traffic problems are now well developed and all uniformed officers can, or should be, qualified to perform them.[19]

2. Direction of traffic. Expediting a smooth flow of motor vehicle and pedestrian traffic with a minimum of congestion tends to reduce the incidence of collisions and the resultant injuries and property damage. More life and property losses are sustained through traffic collisions than by means of criminal acts. Officers of the traffic division may be charged with intersection assignments to expedite the flow of traffic to supplement the signs and signals designed for that purpose, which sometimes require human assistance. Other officers may be assigned to work in cars and motorcycles to continuously patrol the heavily traversed streets for the purpose of speeding up or slowing down traffic on certain streets, diverting the flow away from congested areas that are bogged down because of a heavy load or because of a collision or other temporary barrier, and causing disabled vehicles to be towed away from the flow pattern.

Point, or intersection, assignments are quite often helpful as a means of relieving congestion. Sometimes the driver who has the legal right to *enter* an intersection does so but then cannot *clear* the intersection because of backed-up traffic. Sometimes pedestrians are inclined to enter the intersection ahead of the signal change, or linger there after entering with the knowledge that they have the right-of-way. A man or woman calling the movements of both pedestrian and vehicular traffic at those locations usually keeps the traffic moving smoothly.

3. Collision investigation. Few traffic incidents are "accidents." Most are "caused incidents." Initially, at the scene of a collision, the officer attends to the emergency needs of the injured and he takes immediate action to prevent further injuries or collisions. He calls for assistance to divert traffic away from the scene, places flares or signal devices, and administers first aid; usually all three almost simultaneously. Once the immediate needs are met, he then proceeds with the investigation.

The many purposes for the investigation include (1) determine the cause, which may be driver error, or driver violation; there may be physical causes such as engineering deficiency in channeling lanes or installing the wrong signs or signals; or there may be natural causes, such as rain, snow, fog, mud slides; or a combination of two or more causes. (2) Collect and preserve the evidence, question drivers and witnesses for the purpose of convicting criminal or traffic law violators. (3) Compile statistics essential to the traffic education and enforcement programs, including selective enforcement. (4) Write reports, which are essential to substantiate department actions and to provide the drivers and other interested parties and their lawful representatives with sufficient information for legal and/or financial reconciliation appropriate for the circumstances. (5) Aid the traffic engineer in compiling information essential to his functions related to traffic safety and control.

Except when the administrator believes that there is an advantage in having specialists perform the task, such as in a very large department where collision volume justifies assignment, the patrol officer should handle the initial phases of the investigation, including questioning drivers and witnesses and preparing the reports. A special unit may be delegated the responsibility for collecting and preserving physical evidence, taking photographs, and making a detailed follow-up investigation. The traffic division may have a detail of officers assigned to the follow-up function. Their responsibility is to continue the investigation on the next day for the purpose of securing additional statements from witnesses who may have left the scene, continuing further investigatory work to identify and locate hit-and-run suspects, and conferring with the prosecuting attorney for the purpose of initiating judicial proceedings against violators who have not been cited or arrested at the scene of the collision at the time of occurrence.

4. Education of present and future drivers and pedestrians. This set of activities charged to the traffic function includes preparation of news releases on new laws, collision causes, and statistics, plus seasonal reminders about driving habits peculiar to weather or other conditions. Another

form of traffic education involves participation in school and college educational programs at all grade levels, from preschool pedestrian travel through bicycle safety tests to special driver education courses. The teaching of court-imposed driver education courses, in lieu of fines or imprisonment, may also be assigned to the traffic division of a local police department or highway patrol. Education and training of all the department's officers assigned to traffic and other functions are also included in the responsibilities of this detail.

One of the principal goals in public education for traffic safety and for collision prevention is to gain cooperation and compliance. Attitude plays a critical role in driver conduct. If the driver wants to set an example by obeying the law and being courteous, the result hopefully will be a reduction in injuries, deaths, and property damage.

5. Traffic engineering. The police officer should not be expected to be a traffic engineer. That function requires special academic and practical experience and preparation, and may be delegated to the city's public works department, or some other department which employs various types of engineers. In some jurisdictions, the traffic engineer may be assigned

Courtesy: Sheriff's Department, Riverside County, California

directly to the traffic division of the police department. In either case, the traffic officers and their supervisors should continuously work closely with the traffic engineer to assure the greatest possibility of improving traffic safety and expeditious traffic flow.

INVESTIGATION. The structure and function of the investigation depend to a great extent upon the administrative determination of the degree to which patrol officers will carry out the initial investigations of crimes and other incidents calling for investigative work. In the very large department, it may be advisable to assign investigators to work around the clock throughout the city and to assume responsibility for the investigative function almost immediately, making it possible for patrol officers to resume their patrol duties.

The trend in modern police departments, and the more advisable arrangement from an administrative standpoint, is to have the patrol division retain responsibility for the initial investigation of all cases that occur during their tour of duty. This investigation should be carried out to a successful conclusion, if possible, and will include apprehension of the responsible parties as well as preparation of the reports. The beat officer discontinues his part of the investigation only when all leads are exhausted or when the investigation requires him to leave his district for a prolonged period of time.

The investigative function, as it operates in accordance with this generalist patrol officer concept, is principally responsible for the follow-up investigation. In more critical cases the administrators may determine that the follow-up begin almost immediately, but most cases are assigned to the investigator the morning of the next working day after the initial investigation. The investigative function, in departments utilizing this concept, has responsibility for the following activities:

1. Follow-up investigation. The investigators are usually assigned on the basis of types of crime—either a broad, general assignment of crimes-against-persons or crimes-against-property or a specific assignment within the broader category, depending on case loads, volume of crime, number of personnel assigned, and such other administrative matters including the extent to which a case will be investigated until it is eventually closed because of lack of leads and the volume of new cases to investigate. The assignments may be broken down into burglary—business and residential, theft, theft from auto,—forgery and checks, credit cards and fraud, assaults, sex crimes, arson, robbery, homicide, and as many other categories as necessary.

The investigator usually recontacts the victim and witnesses for additional information and whatever leads he can develop. He does not reinvestigate, but may visit the scene of the crime and use whatever his ingenuity and imagination, plus skill and available resources, suggest to solve the crime and to cause the persons responsible to be held to answer for the charges in court. He coordinates the evidence-gathering and related activities concerning the cases for which he is responsible, and his ultimate objective in each case is to successfully gain the conviction of the guilty. Although it is typically believed that a case is closed by arrest and recovery of the victim's property, a district attorney friend once stated to a graduating class of police recruits: "Please don't conclude your reports by stating that the case is closed by arrest; it is actually opened by arrest."

The investigator spends a considerable amount of time cultivating informants in a variety of occupations who have access to information which will aid him. He searches records and a multitude of information sources, and utilizes exhaustive methods of deductive reasoning. There is no magic to his work. The successful investigator who clears a high percentage of his assigned cases, is effective because he has a great deal of skill and experience—and the help of a little luck. Generally, that's how fellow officers feel about him, but the luck is usually man-made through the utilization of his talents and intuitive understanding of human nature.

Criminal histories of previously arrested individuals are studied for similarities in patterns to the cases under investigation; modus operandi files are studied to identify crimes that may have been committed by the same person, and to identify the responsible party on the basis of his personal behavior patterns and physical characteristics. Skillful interrogation techniques are employed to gain information, and various scientific techniques are employed to bring the cases to a successful conclusion. The purpose of the investigation is to identify the guilty party, to apprehend him, and to gain his conviction. Although it may not be stated in the job specifications for investigator assignments, it is equally important that the investigator clear the innocent when they have been wrongfully or circumstantially implicated in crimes.

2. Initial investigations in matters of a regulatory nature. The police department is usually charged with the investigation of applicants for special business permits such as pool parlors, bars, nightclubs, theaters, carnivals. The police also investigate a variety of other types of applicants for the police chief, the various commissions, the city council, mayor's office, city manager, and regulatory agencies such as the department of alcoholic beverage control. Discreet inquiries by non-uniformed officers are frequently necessary to assure the department that license and permit holders are operating within the regulations prescribed for them in such business as pawn shops, secondhand stores, auctions, charity events, and many places of entertainment and recreation.

3. Initial crime investigations discovered by investigators in the course of their own follow-up work, and those cases which call for non-uniformed investigation from beginning to end. Many investigations must be conducted with as much secrecy as possible, particularly those involving

vice, narcotics, or organized crime activities. The general application of this policy of non-uniformed investigations may be that uniformed patrol officers will not be involved in the investigation at any time when their action might compromise the intended objectives of the investigation.

4. Case preparation for court. Prosecution and conviction of the guilty is the end result intended. A close liaison with the prosecuting attorney is necessary so that the investigator may discuss the availability of witnesses and how their testimony will affect the case, may conduct additional inquiries in anticipation that the prosecution or defense may seek certain relevant facts during the trial, may report to the prosecuting attorney the results of laboratory examinations of evidence, and may coordinate necessary matters related to the investigation.

As a summary of the investigative function, consider this statement by Gourley:

> *The continuing investigation.* In order to successfully pursue a continuing or follow-up investigation, considerable specialized knowledge and techniques are necessary. Some criminal investigations are extremely complicated, including thefts perpetrated by fraud, arson, and premeditated homicide. Follow-up investigation requires the cultivation of sources of information, the application of sophisticated techniques of interview and interrogation, the application of science and criminalistics, and considerable knowledge of legal procedure and admissibility of evidence.[20]

Administrative decisions regarding the assignment of personnel to the investigative function involve the extent to which patrol officers will continue the initial phases of the investigation and at which point the investigators will assume the responsibility. Hanna and Gentel explain it this way:

> Although criminal investigation involves a maze of leads, legwork, long-distance calls, line-ups, and long hours, three basic factors must be considered by the police administrator. He must realize that (a) the mechanics of report completion, (b) the quality of preliminary investigation by the patrol division, and (c) case assignment criteria, all affect the quality of investigators required for assignment to the criminal and juvenile investigative effort in a law enforcement agency.[21]

The number of cases handled and the average time devoted to each investigation are among the criteria used for determining how many officers will be assigned to the investigative function. All crimes reported to the police cannot be worked through to total exhaustion of leads because of sheer volume. Most of the investigator's time is consumed by the most urgent or "hottest" leads, on several cases at once; one of his more difficult decisions is to choose priorities. Although no unsolved case is actually closed, many are set aside because of the continuous assignment of more recent cases that demand immediate attention. Out of this urgent rush to handle as many cases as possible and to work out some sort of solution to the majority of them, the investigator's role is constantly defined and redefined for him, and somehow he manages to accomplish his objectives.

THE JUVENILE FUNCTION. The prevention of crime or antisocial behavior that stimulates, or develops into, criminal conduct is one of the primary goals of the police department. The activities related to that goal generally involve the matter of delinquency prevention and control. Early discovery and prompt handling of predelinquent conduct seem to be among the more effective preventive devices available to the police. Therefore, specialists are usually assigned to the juvenile function. Although juvenile officers may not require a separate divisional assignment and may be a part of the investigative function, there should be certain officers within the organization designated as those who have the administrative responsibility for the entire department's juvenile programs, and who should set and control the department's general policies and procedures in all matters related to juvenile control.

Continuing the chapter with the original concept of generalist patrol officer assignments, the functions of the officers assigned this specialist role in the juvenile function usually include the following:

1. Follow-up investigations of cases involving juveniles (persons under 16 or 18, depending on the jurisdiction) as suspects, victims, or in some way directly affected by criminal or unusual social conduct. An investigator who identifies a suspect as a juvenile may call upon the juvenile specialist to assist him because of considerations peculiar to juvenile court or the department's juvenile policies. The initial assignment to a juvenile officer is usually made only when it is clearly established through evidence or eye-witness information that the suspect is a juvenile.

2. Maintaining liaison with the juvenile court, schools, youth service organizations and the various other agencies and organizations involved with youth and their many activities and problems. The purpose for the liaison is to maintain a favorable working relationship with those agencies and to serve the best interests of the youth in accordance with the good order of the community and the department's crime prevention programs. The juvenile specialists maintain a constant rapport with the community so that the administrative staff has sufficient information to make intelligent decisions regarding the department's juvenile control philosophy and policies.

3. Concentrated patrol of places of recreation and congregation by juveniles for the purpose of early discovery of delinquent and predelinquent acts and intensive counseling on a direct and personal basis for the

purpose of preventing incidents of juvenile delinquency. Because of the very close liaison that the juvenile specialists must maintain with the schools, it is wise to reinforce that relationship by extending preventive patrol activities to the schools as a complement to the in-house individuals who are responsible for the conduct of the students according to the education codes. Teams of men and women officers should prove most effective for this type of assignment to assure the most positive rapport with the students.

4. Actively participate in various community and public relations activities of the department to assure a broad community base of understanding of the department's juvenile control efforts and to seek a maximum amount of cooperation toward the accomplishment of its programs. A great deal of the juvenile specialist's effectiveness depends on his knowledge of the many youth programs available in the community and on his referral of youths to the appropriate agencies and organizations. The juvenile officers should have input into these organizations and should be continuously aware of their activities and ongoing programs.

5. The juvenile specialists and their supervisors should constantly review all the department's activities involving juveniles and how the department deals with them as a matter of policy and procedure. They should be responsible for assuming a leadership role in the formulation of department standards and procedures in matters of juvenile delinquency prevention and control and they should be involved in the continuous updating process. Because of their close working relationship with the juvenile court, the probation department, the schools, and all of the other youth-oriented agencies and organizations, they are usually the best qualified to participate in that capacity.

VICE INVESTIGATION AND ENFORCEMENT. "Crimes without victims" is a familiar term usually used to describe many of the acts classified as vice offenses. Unlawful gambling, alcoholic beverage control violations, prostitution, and some forms of sexual conduct forbidden by law are included in this broad category of vice crimes. Investigations of suspected vice violations must be conducted with a great deal of secrecy and information is gained in many cases through the use of confidential informants. Although against the law, many vice crimes apparently are not considered "wrong" by many, and others seem to regard such activities as none of their business. Unlike the armed robbery or aggravated assault or the grand theft, unlawful sexual conduct is hardly likely to arouse the ire of people willing to volunteer information about the miscreants. Their reaction is more one of a raised eyebrow and a comment to the effect "those people should get arrested."

Organized crime thrives on vice crime violations because some people appear to demand the goods and services forbidden by the vice laws and other people are ready and willing to provide those goods and services—even in violation of the law—for a price. "Taxunpaid" alcoholic beverages, or bootleg liquors, broaden the margin of profit for the bar owner who is willing to take the risk of dealing through illicit operators. Because of the greater margins of profit and the great risks involved, vice operators are willing to pay for protection in the form of bribes or other forms of payoffs and they use methods of force and intimidation to enforce silence.

From the administrator's point of view, the enforcement of vice laws is both sensitive and essential. Exactly where to place the vice function in the organizational structure depends on the type of community (residential or business versus resort or heavy itinerant population) and the history of vice activities in the jurisdiction. Another consideration may be related to the number of intermediaries the chief administrator wishes to have between the vice officers and himself. This is a factor in every decision the chief of police or sheriff makes when structuring his organization, but in vice it is probably more critical because of the secrecy that is necessary and the high risk—an unscrupulous officer may succumb to temptation and find himself on the payroll of a bookie or a call house madam. The vice function usually employs specialists who work nothing else during their tenure. Whether the unit is a separate function reporting directly to the chief or an integral part of the investigative function, it usually consists of men and women who are unquestionably honest and who are loyal to the chief to the extent that they keep him continuously informed about their activities and their progress—or lack of progress—on sensitive cases.

Narcotics and Dangerous Drugs. This function may be a separate entity, or it may be another of the many assignments already delegated to the vice function. Secrecy and the extensive use of confidential informants and paid or unpaid operants are characteristics of this function. Not socially acceptable in general, the traffic in narcotics and dangerous drugs is carried on without high visibility and the illicit users do so in secrecy. As a consequence, the investigators are forced to carry on their investigative activities in a surreptitious fashion with the aid of undercover and confidential informants in much the same way as the vice officers. The movement of illicit drugs is accomplished through ingenious and complex procedures and the task of narcotics enforcement calls for well-trained specialists who very closely cooperate with similarly assigned officers from contiguous jurisdictions as well as state and federal narcotics agencies.

JAIL. The municipal police agency that utilizes the jail on more than a short-time holding arrangement may include the jail function as a part of the patrol function because of the twenty-four-hour-per-day assignments. If there is a separate communications division, which would be responsible for manning the switchboards and radios in the headquarters building, the jail function and communications may be combined. In almost all large municipal police departments, and county sheriff departments, the jail function is a separate division or bureau.

Maintenance of the jail is a set of tasks which involves housing large numbers of itinerant residents with a turnover similar to that of a big hotel, but with the unique problems of maximum security and movement of persons within the complex of jail buildings and their transportation to court, the hospital, other jails, or prison. Most of the people housed in the jail are innocent; they have yet to go to court for a determination of guilt to be made, if such turns out to be the case.

Segregation of prisoners on the basis of sex, age, whether the charge is a felony or misdemeanor, and several other classifications is designated by laws and policies. Mail and visitors must be checked to prevent the ingress of narcotics or other contraband; the sick and injured must be treated; booking and bail procedures must be established and functioning smoothly; attorneys and clients allowed to consult in privacy, and a myriad of other details related to the operation of a custodial hotel service must be managed with efficiency.

The administrator performs two management roles: over the personnel of his division and over the prisoners in their custody. The challenge of such a responsibility is awesome because of the vast variety of techniques that must be used in such routine matters as motivation and discipline.

CIVIL DIVISION. The sheriff has a unique responsibility in contrast to the average police agency, that of serving the courts in a bailiff and noncriminal capacity. Maintaining order in the courts, serving subpoenas, and carrying out the mandates of the court requires a separate unit that functions almost independently of the other units of the department. The manager of this division must serve as the liaison officer between his own executive officer, the sheriff, and the various judges who are singularly responsible only to themselves in the administration of justice from their respective benches.

Staff Functions

Terms may vary, and organizational charts may take on different configurations, but most of the following activities are included among the staff functions of the police department.

BUSINESS OFFICE. Payroll, accounting, purchase requisitions and authorizations for payment, property and inventory, and the general management of the business operations of the department are handled by this division. The nature and extent of the activities and responsibilities of this unit depend to a great extent upon the general municipal or county government organization and management. Purchasing can be handled almost entirely by the city purchasing department, for example, providing that someone in the police department has carefully described precisely what type of equipment must be purchased so that only acceptable (or better) quality materials will be purchased. The purchasing agent cannot be expected to be an expert in all of the many departments for which he makes the purchases. All the personnel assigned to this function may be civilians, or "non-sworn."

COMMUNICATIONS. Radio, telephone, teletype, and all other forms of communication within the department and with other agencies may be performed by this unit. Administrative responsibility for this function may be placed with the patrol division in the smaller department. The reason for this assignment to patrol is to assure adequate supervision and continuous presence of command personnel who can make the necessary decisions for the effective operation of the total communications system. In the larger department, when continuous supervision may be provided within the unit itself, the more desirable arrangement is to separate this function from patrol, and to place it in a division by itself, or as a part of the records system.

RECORDS. Although each functional unit may maintain its own set of temporary or working records, all of the permanent records for the entire department should be maintained in a central location in the records division. This division is the central repository of all papers, files, and documents; it is the memory bank for the department. Some of the activities of this division include the following:

1. Maintain a central index of all the department's reports and documents related to its activities. Such indices should include an alphabetical card or computerized file which maintains a record of all persons, places, or objects that are related to matters handled by members of the department in their various duties and which should be retained for future retrieval and reference. Records and reports included in the various files referred to by that index include the following: persons arrested, complainants and witnesses to crimes and other police-related incidents, victims and suspects in criminal cases, wanted persons either on suspicion or by warrant, field interview records, persons involved in traffic collisions, identification files on persons processed through the department as arrestees or suspects, and modus operandi files. A detailed explanation of just which records should be maintained by the department is covered later in this chapter.

2. Providing a duplication service and furnishing to entitled persons copies of collision reports and other documents which may be released to interested parties.

3. Providing a clerical pool and stenographers to assist all other units within the department as a supplement to those clerical personnel permanently assigned to each division.

4. Compiling and disseminating statistical data on departmental activities.

5. Provide information services to the public by operating an information desk and assisting in maintenance of a complaint desk for the reception and referral of visitors to the department.

6. Perform other related clerical and service functions that will generally enhance the efficient management of the department.

An efficient records division serves as a catalyst. It is a rich storehouse of information for the department. The clerks perform a variety of services that assist in the clearance of cases, identification of suspects, recovery of property. The greatest challenge to the manager is to encourage complete utilization of the centralized system and to avoid the creation of separate systems throughout the department. There should be standardized procedures for filing and established policies for the release of information and its other uses.

Access to police records is an extremely delicate matter. Probably one of the greatest problems is in maintaining integrity and accuracy by assuring inclusion of all relevant information in reports and accompanying files and at the same time protecting the system's confidentiality. Contrary to the belief of many people is the fact that most of the records are not *public records*, which by law and public policy are available at any time for public inspection. Instead, most of the records maintained by the police department are *private records* of a public agency.

Much of the information contained in police reports is unconfirmed rumor; a report of a crime, for example, is not a verification of all the information it contains. It is merely a chronicle of what the officer has perceived, including what victims and witnesses have told him. It is not proof that there is any truth to any of the statements. Therefore, the report as a source of information is *hearsay*. Unverified slander may be recounted in a statement which may have been prompted by vindictiveness unknown to the investigating officer. For these reasons, as well as many others, only a very few of the police records are actually available to the public.

PROPERTY AND EVIDENCE CONTROL. This function is usually ancillary to the records function because of the close relationship and the storehouse characteristics of the operation. The property unit of the department is responsible for the supplies and equipment and the evidence control unit maintains custody of the evidence which is essential to the criminal prosecution o violators. Custody and control, under carefully guarded conditions and frequent audits, is important to the successful disposition of a criminal prosecution. Single-key systems are used whereby it can be established under oath in court that only one individual handled a specific item of evidence and that there was no possibility for contamination by other persons.

TECHNICAL SERVICES. This section of the organization may be designated a part of the investigative function, affiliated with records because the activities provide a service to all of the other functions within the department as does records, or it may be a separate division. It usually consists of the criminalistics and identification laboratories and closely related activities. The basic functions of technical services include the following:

  1. Field investigation of crime and collision scenes as a supplement to the patrol officers who may be charged with responsibility for the preliminary investigative duties, or on a continuous basis including preliminary scene investigations in departments not using the patrol CSI (Crime-collision Scene Investigation).

  2. Scientific and chemical analysis of evidence through the use of a wet chemistry laboratory, and a variety of instruments including microscopes, gas chromatographs, spectrophotometers, blood-alcohol testing devices; and other methods of scientific inquiry which include questioned document examination, the polygraph and photomicrography, and as many other avenues of exploration as are available.

  3. Processing and classification of fingerprints and other traces left at the scene of crimes and identification of suspects through search and filing techniques.

  4. Photographing and fingerprinting persons arrested for—or suspected of—criminal acts, or those persons who are applicants for various occupations requiring fingerprint searches for criminal histories as a part of the selection process.

  5. Photography: taking photographs of crime and collision scenes and other department-required photographic work, developing and printing services.

  6. Preparation of evidence for court presentation, and providing expert testimony on matters which fall within the purview of their expertise.

  7. Serving in an advisory capacity to all other units within the department and to other agencies in matters related to technical services.

  8. Assisting the training division in the development of field crime scene investigators and in all matters related to the collection, preservation, analysis, and presentation of evidence in court.

INTELLIGENCE FUNCTION. The intelligence function involves the integrity of the department and organized crime investigations. The extremely sensitive nature of these assignments usually requires that the workers report directly to the chief executive to keep him apprised of their activities. Organized crime involves alliances with community leaders, in many cases involving police officials. For that reason the chief must keep constantly alert to determine if any such alliance exists and to take decisive remedial action. Organized crime and organized vice are virtually always related. This unit may work in cooperation with the vice and narcotics units in many cases, but remain in the background and take no direct enforcement action themselves because of the confidential nature of their work and the importance that the officers remain anonymous. If their identity were to be generally known, or if their mere existence were too loudly proclaimed, their effectiveness would be lessened. One of the functions of the intelligence unit is to inquire into the effectiveness of the different divisions of the department—including vice and narcotics—by conducting their inquiries sub rosa. In order to determine if there any breaches in officer integrity or honesty, particularly in matters involving organized crime, some intelligence activities must be carried on within the department but without the knowledge of its members except the chief and the intelligence unit.

INSPECTIONS AND INTERNAL AFFAIRS. These two functions are direct arms of the chief executive. Periodic and unannounced inspections of the personnel and their performance is essential to the smooth functioning of the department. This inspection is not intended to supplant or to interfere with the normal supervisory and management functions, but should serve to assist them in the same manner as an occasional outside audit of the books assists a bank. An inspection system assures continuity in programs, and consistency in high-quality performance, while at the same time it locates deviations from standard performance and gross violations of department policies. The internal affairs function is usually limited to the investigation of complaints about the conduct of the department's employees alleged to be unlawful or in some way deleterious to the effective management of the department.

RESEARCH AND DEVELOPMENT. An organization stagnates if it is allowed to perpetuate itself with absolute unchanging policies and procedures in spite of changing needs. Every department is in need of some sort of system whereby all procedures and forms are evaluated in view of changing demands on the services that the department must provide. Even the smallest department must have at least one individual responsible for research and development. A grave mistake is made by many smaller departments that tend to copy a larger neighboring city on the basis of that neighbor's considerable success with a particular method of providing police services for their specific needs. The same administrators are shocked when they discover that their programs are not as successful as those of their neighbor. The reason is obvious: each department has an entirely different personality and no system can be copied exactly and be expected to work in precisely the same way.

The research unit is responsible for studying existing programs and materials, for researching new methods and materials, and for then providing management sufficient data to enable them to make appropriate decisions to assure maximum efficiency in accordance with the goals and objectives. The department research and development function includes the study of the following:

1. Administration and management procedures, and the system of communications throughout the department related to those procedures.
2. Department activities as they apply to the goals and objectives of the organization and its programs which are intended to achieve those goals and objectives.
3. Tactical and procedural plans.
4. Forms analysis, communications flow, and reporting procedures.
5. Crime and traffic collision analyses.
6. Supplies, equipment, and facilities used by the department.
7. Community relationships through surveys and special studies.

PERSONNEL. The city or county personnel agency should maintain certain basic records on the employees of all departments, but more detailed records regarding the everyday operations of the police department require that a more detailed set of records for supervisory, training, and other management considerations be maintained by the personnel division within the department. Recruitment, testing, and much of the processing work related to employment and separation of employees can also best be handled by the central agency. Intensified recruiting efforts aimed at achieving a one-to-one basis in the community may prove more effective if operated jointly with the department's personnel division. The final selection, after the series of testing and screening methods have been employed, should be made by the chief executive or his direct representative. To help the chief of police or sheriff make the decision whether to designate an individual a peace officer, a background investigation of the candidate's character and personal history should be conducted by the personnel division of the department.

Additional responsibilities of the personnel unit include maintenance of the personnel records, operating an evaluation program to determine the individual's suitability to perform on the job and to qualify for transfers or promotions. In addition, this department takes care of all other matters that the chief considers directly related to the improvement of a sound personnel program.

TRAINING. This department is responsible for management and coordination of all training activities carried on within the department, as well as other training programs in which the personnel participate. The coordination requirement is for the purpose of assuring a maximum of uniformity in training applications, which will affect the consistency of law enforcement and the response to different types of calls. Additional responsibilities include the maintenance of training and education records of all employees, educational counseling, and liaison with educational institutions which are attended by members of the department.

COMMUNITY RELATIONS The unit responsible for community relations in the department must design and operate a program for the total involvement of the department in maintaining an effective working relationship with all segments of the community. For a more complete discussion of this function, please refer to chapter 14.

POLICE RECORDS SYSTEM

Electronic data processing and various computer applications have been introduced to law enforcement in the form of police information systems. Storage and retrieval of information within agencies, and exchange of information among cooperating agencies, have been facilitated with beneficial results. Statewide and interstate computerized data banks of information concerning selected types of property (stolen automobiles etc.) and wanted felons have been operational for some time. The information contained within the computers of the National Crime Information Center is maintained by the Department of Justice in Washington, D. C. in cooperation with what will eventually include most of the major cities throughout the United States. Considerable space has been devoted to this type of information in more timely documents. Because of the rapid movement along these lines of systems designs for police information, we recommend that you refer to the most current literature available at the time and now we move on to the more basic coverage of records essential for the efficient operation of the average police department.

Master Alphabetical Index

This file maintained by the records center serves as the index to all other records and reports maintained by the police department, regardless of where they are stored. Card files or electronic files may be used, although by far the more common system is the 3 × 5 index card with an entry on the card representing each complaint or other type of record stored by the department. Examples of what type of information might be found in the "alpha" file include the following:

1. Wanted felons, as reported by teletype, FBI bulletins, and "escape" flyers from jails and prisons.
2. Complainants and reporting parties regarding police called-services which led to the preparation of reports of other department documents.
3. Suicides or attempts, witnesses, doctors, relatives, and other individuals named in the reports.
4. Names of deceased persons in which the police were called to investigate the circumstances.
5. Gun purchases reported by dealers, and registration of firearm ownership (required by law in some jurisdictions).
6. Licenses or permits to carry concealed weapons.
7. Witnesses to incidents, accidents, crimes.
8. Victims.
9. Suspects and arrestees.
10. Pawns and purchases by secondhand dealers (filed under the name of the person securing the loan or selling the item).
11. Field interview cards.
12. Bicycle licenses.
13. Nicknames ("monickers" or "running names"), cross-referenced to true names if known.
14. Vehicle repossessions (if repossessions must be reported in that agency's jurisdiction).
15. Warrants and other local "wants."
16. Persons involved in accidents, traffic and otherwise.
17. Owners of stored, impounded, or abandoned vehicles.
18. Registered persons who have been previously convicted of sex offenses, arson, narcotics violation, and other felonies, as required by local and state laws.
19. Identification cards on individuals who have been photographed and fingerprinted by the department for its permanent records for any reason. This list includes applications for employment, arrested persons, or any other purpose for establishing such a record. (The card includes the department identification number, physical description, and other identifying data.)

20. Vice activity files, which include cards referring to reports of certain types of vice activities filed according to the type of activity (gambling, liquor violations, prostitution, narcotics, etc.); and according to the names of persons and places allegedly involved.
21. Emergency telephone numbers and names of persons to contact in case of some urgent need during closed hours of business, industrial, and professional establishments.

Crime Card File

Containing information from crime reports, this file is indexed according to the crime classifications used for the state and federal reports. The cards contain the following information:

1. Case number
2. Type of crime
3. Date and time the crime was committed (estimated, if not known).
4. Description of lost property, and market value.
5. Location of the crime and a description of the type of property attacked, such as city street, business establishment, two-story house.
6. Name, address, occupation, and other information on the victim.
7. Modus operandi and trademark of the culprit.
8. Name and/or description of the suspect, if known.
9. Name of person(s) arrested and explanation of the property recovery, if any.
10. Disposition of the case.

The primary purpose of this file is to maintain a set of statistics on a current basis. It is a valuable aid for correlating crimes with similar modus operandi, possibly the same suspect, and is particularly adaptable to electronic data processing systems for statistical and investigative purposes.

SERIAL NUMBER FILE. This file contains cards filed in sequence according to the last two or three numbers (example: 7Z09253 would appear in the 53 or 253 file in numerical order) or in some similar retrieval system. Typical applications of the serial number file include the following:

1. Stolen and pawned objects bearing serial numbers.
2. Bicycle license numbers and serial numbers.

3. Handguns and other serially numbered weapons sold by local dealers.
4. License numbers of stolen automobiles.
5. Any owner-designated property numbers inscribed on property that has been reported as stolen.

STOLEN OBJECT FILE. This is another card or computerized file, indexed according to the type of object described in the crime report. It is usually checked by records personnel against pawned objects, property in custody of suspicious persons, and property that a suspect admits stealing but cannot remember where or when. A stolen object card should include the following information:

1. Case number.
2. Type of crime.
3. Date and time of the crime.
4. Location where the crime occurred.
5. A detailed description of the object, including numbers, if known.

PAWNED OBJECT FILE. This file is almost identical to the stolen object file and should be indexed in precisely the same manner. Filed according to the type of object, this file should contain cards on all identifiable objects which are pawned or sold to dealers in second-hand goods. It should be regularly checked against stolen object files and crime reports to match pawned objects with stolen objects

CRIME LOCATION FILE. Another card or computerized file, this index should show locations where all reported crimes and arrests take place in your jurisdiction. Each crime or other incident that the administrator decides should be included in this index will be filed according to the street names in alphabetical order, and in street-number sequence.

IDENTIFICATION FILE. This file is personalized to meet an individual department's needs, depending on whether it has a jail, is processing all persons within its own identification system, or if it employs another agency for many of those services. When such a file is maintained, it contains the following basic information about individuals:

1. Photographs and negatives of all persons processed through this identification system.
2. Criminal history forms received from the FBI and state bureau of identification, which is returned to the department in exchange for each new entry.

3. Fingerprints of persons processed through the system according to their fingerprint classifications.

BICYCLE LICENSES. Filed in numerical sequence by license number, this file may be included in the numerical file or be maintained separately. This file contains identifying data on bicycles and the names and addresses of owners.

INTELLIGENCE FILES. A must for any sizable department, this file contains information on persons known or suspected of participating in organized crime and vice activities, their associates, the "legitimate" businesses they use as a cover, and other pertinent intelligence information. Although much of the information in this file is gleaned from "official" and confidential sources, much is also gathered from newspaper and magazine clippings.

REPORT, OR COMPLAINT FILE. This document file contains the originals (or microfilmed copies which become the originals if approved by court order) of all reports and supplemental information concerning crimes, collisions, arrests, and incidents handled by the department and committed to some type of report form. The file is cross-indexed in the master "alpha" index and the several other manually operated or computerized files listed in the preceding paragraphs. If all incidents requiring the preparation of reports are assigned numbers as they occur, then this document file is similarly numerically sequenced. The numbering may be according to a single series, or more than one—such as a "crime" file, "traffic" file, and so on—but the single numbering series assures the searcher that there is only one file rather than a collection of different ones.

STATISTICS FOR EFFICIENCY AND EFFECTIVENESS

Feedback and evaluation of the department's programs rely heavily upon measurable performance. A department managed according to the concept of programmed planning to achieve specific objectives prescribes performance standards as a part of those objectives. The management task then becomes a function of management by results.

Management by evaluation of results is essential particularly for the larger departments where standardization of minimum quality performance can be monitored by keeping a close tab on the results. Numbers and percentages lend themselves well to many different types of interpretations and applications. The daily activities of officers in terms of the numbers of citations they issue, the percentage of cases they clear by arrest, the number of stolen automobiles they return to the owners, serve as thermometers to compare the officer's performance of one month or week to the previous corresponding period of time. Similar tallies may be used to compare entire shifts of officers against each other and against a standard.

The advantages in using numbers as the bases for making comparisons and evaluations are immediately recognizable, particularly to a production-oriented manager. Any change in numbers or percentages at any place on the charts will signal the need for a review to determine the reasons for the change. This variation of the "management by exceptions" concept calls for the manager's attention in matters which deviate from normal or routine.

There are pitfalls to this system, of course. First, to attach any sort of numerical standard to citations or arrests is a dangerous practice because it imposes minimum and maximum quotas, and many other factors are involved in determination of how many numbers an officer scores on a score card. Second, the end does not necessarily justify the means used to score high on the arrests and citations. There is a danger that the competitive-spirited officer may abandon protocol or legal requirements in order that he might make or top a record of some sort. The result is an overly aggressive officer, similar to the high-pressure salesman. Third, the officers whose numbers make a lower score are not necessarily the inferior officers. Quality and quality are not always on an equal level in the performance of all officers.

Keeping the advantages and disadvantages of the use of statistical controls in mind, the administrator and his managers at the various levels in the organization can use statistics to aid them in their management activities. Significant variations in percentages of case clearance may indicate an urgent training need, or may reflect a sudden change in the attitude of the courts, or any number of possibilities that require management investigation and decision making.

Following are a few types of statistical controls that may be utilized by the typical police organization:

1. Field functions, such as traffic or patrol, rely on specific numbers of tasks performed, the time consumed on each activity, and the results of those activities. Those activities include the following:

> a. Calls for service. Numbers of incidents handled and the average time devoted to each.
> b. On-sight activities. Numbers and types of incidents that are handled by the officer as a direct result of his own observation rather than in response to a call.
> c. Field interviews, both pedestrian and vehicles.
> d. Open doors and windows discovered and action taken such as an inspection of the interior or search for a possible burglar, and calling for the owner to secure the building.

e. Traffic citations and warnings, broken down into hazardous and nonhazardous categories.
f. Arrests, felony and misdemeanor by authority of warrants, or the result of the officer's on-sight observation.
g. Contacts with juvenile violators of bicycle laws and rules.
h. Vehicles, impounded, stored, or recovered.
i. Stolen and lost bicycles recovered.
j. Automobile collisions investigated.
k. Felony and misdemeanor crimes investigated.
l. Other activities that may be tallied for comparison.

These statistics are compared with time studies and averages of time required for each of the activities. Work schedules are also taken into account when comparing numbers and time consumed for the various activities; there are variations depending on the type of assignment or the district, and many other factors. Averages as well as totals can be determined.

2. Patrol and traffic divisions maintain statistical tabulations on total performance of the officers regarding traffic enforcement or control and any measurable items that may reflect the officer's effect on collision rates in specific locations or throughout the jurisdiction. Those indices may include:

a. Collision records, broken down into types of vehicles involved, locations of collisions, times of day the collisions occur, and the causes.
b. Crime occurrence files broken down into grids or districts on the map of the jurisdiction, the types of crimes, times of their occurrence, and other data that might aid in the apprehension of the guilty persons through patrol and surveillance techniques.
c. Pin maps, which may be separated into times of day and days of week, and which indicate the types of crimes reported and their locations. Each different colored pinhead represents a different type of crime. The pin map may also be used to plot traffic collisions by time, place, and cause.
d. Shift, or watch, assignment and deployment statistics.

3. Investigative functions, including criminal as well as juvenile, vice, and narcotics investigators, require a sustaining activity file. The cases assigned to an officer working a specific type of case accumulate and make up this sustaining activity file, or "open case" file. The cases under investigation are given varying amounts of time and attention, depending

on leads, information, and time available. Statistics for officers working these types of details include the following:

   a. Cases assigned (listed by type and by case number)
   b. Status, such as "cleared," closed, inactive because of lack of productive leads, or unfounded.
   c. Property recovered.
   d. Arrests, and convictions or other dispositions.
   e. Investigative time devoted to each case, and the average is updated to keep current investigation-time averages.
   f. Other assignments and activities in addition to investigative tasks.

4. Investigative records of overall activities and percentages and types of dispositions in relationship to the cases assigned. Basic records for efficiency include the following:

   a. Case assignments by detail (forgery, burglary, robbery) and by each individual officer.
   b. Percentage of clearance and other dispositions of cases, logged according to types of crimes.

Care should be taken to avoid comparing officers against each other, which places them in strictly a competitive setting. Sayles and Strauss emphasize just one of the problems that may be caused by department-imposed work standards:

> In most organizations there are other pressures at work "balancing off" the pressures exerted by the use of standards. As we have observed, the work group, unions, and colleagues have standards or norms of their own which may conflict with the requirements being imposed by top management.[22]

5. Department statistics for dissemination to other agencies and to the public may include summaries or other references to those various indices listed in the preceding pages. They may be released for crime prevention or public relations purposes by way of prepared press releases and annual reports. The principal reports prepared by the police department for general dissemination are the statistical summaries of traffic collisions for the National Safety Council, and the uniform crime reports for the Federal Bureau of Investigation, as well as similar reports for state agencies and other clearing houses for public data.

Each of these summaries is based upon crimes of collisions reported to the police, and neither represents a total number of occurrences. The reports and summaries are compiled in the department's statistical reports, which include the following:

1. Part I offenses known to the police. Part I includes (a) criminal homicide, (b) forcible rape, (c) robbery, (d) aggravated assault, (e) other assaults of a lesser degree, (f) burglary or breaking and entering, (g) theft of property valued $50 and over, (h) theft of property valued under $50, and (i) auto theft. Compilations include cases reported, and additional charts on the same offenses show percentages of those cases that have been cleared, property losses and recoveries, and persons arrested.

2. Crime Index. This index is a refinement of the part I category, and includes all of those reported offenses except misdemeanor assaults and thefts under $50. These offenses are not necessarily the crimes that one might consider the most serious in a legal or moral sense, although most of them certainly are, but they are more consistently reported. There are many very private types of serious crimes, such as child molestation or incest, that are less likely to be reported because of external factors—a family's wish to avoid the public humiliation, or further emotional trauma to the child, or lack of discovery. The crime index offenses are most likely to be reported because of the nature of the crime (homicide is seldom —comparatively speaking—overlooked; rape and robbery involve an outrage at the hands of strangers usually) or because certain external factors might require that they be reported (aggravated assault may require medical treatment and doctors and hospitals must report such incidents, thefts and burglaries as well as auto thefts require that a police report be made in order that the victims may satisfy an insurance claim). Consequently, the crime index represents those crimes most likely to be reported with measurable consistency.

3. Part II offenses for which arrests have been made. In contrast to part I and crime index categories, which include complete data on reports and dispositions, part II compilations for the uniform crime reports include data on the *persons arrested* only. The records section of the police department maintains comprehensive files on part II offenses —whether cleared or not—in the same manner as for part I and the crime index cases, but public dissemination of the total information is not feasible, largely because of wide variances between agencies and the tremendous volume of numbers that would have to be compiled on a national level.

4. Juvenile detentions and dispositions of cases handled by the department.

5. Citations for traffic offenses and their dispositions as reported back to the department from the courts.

6. Traffic collisions, classified according to types of vehicles involved, whether on a public roadway or on certain other locations, traffic and road conditions, and the presence or absence of certain types of traffic controls.

Statistical controls have increased with the increased utilization of electronic data processing methods and equipment. When used as an adjunct to sound management and supervision practices rather than in place of those methods, statistics are very helpful to the administrator. As with many other management devices, the secret to their effectiveness lies in maintaining the appropriate balance.

SUMMARY

The police agency is organized to meet a variety of specific community service-oriented goals and objectives. Although there are many such goals and objectives common to all police organizations, each department should be developed as a separate entity. The principles of management are not rigid rules, but they have proven effective as guidelines and they should be taken seriously when organizing and managing any criminal justice agency.

A typical organization may be separated into line units, which perform the basic tasks to meet the department's primary goals and objectives, and staff units, which provide the support and auxiliary services. Designation of which units shall carry out the line functions and which shall be considered staff involves a series of hard management decisions and rank-ordering of priorities. Most important, however, is the actual staffing of the organization to assure that its goals and objectives will be met with the greatest amount of effectiveness and economy.

In this chapter, we have reviewed the principles of management, which was followed by a discussion of the goals and objectives of a typical law enforcement agency. Using the line-staff type of organization, we then discussed the process of organizing and staffing the organization, pointing out many of the specific activities of each of the various units which make up the police organization.

It is important to bear in mind at all times in the managing process that the true effectiveness of the organization is best evaluated by the end results rather than the artistic design of an organizational chart.

Notes

1. Richard L. Holcomb, *Police Patrol* (Springfield: Charles C Thomas, 1971), p. 3.
2. From Bristow, Allen P., *Effective Police Manpower Utilization*, 1969, p. 27. Courtesy of Charles C Thomas, Publisher, Springfield, Illinois.
3. California Penal Code, Section 4.
4. *People* v. *Alotis*, 60 Cal. 2d, 698.
5. Thomas F. Adams, *Police Patrol: Tactics and Techniques* (Englewood Cliffs, N. J.: Prentice-Hall, © 1971), p. 18. All material from this book reprinted by permission of the publisher.
6. For a detailed discussion of these methods, see G. Douglas Gourley and Allen P. Bristow, *Patrol Administration* (Springfield, Ill.: Charles C Thomas, 1970), pp. 22–27.

7. From Gourley, G. Douglas, and Bristow, Allen P., *Patrol Administration*, 1970, p. 30. Courtesy of Charles C Thomas, Publisher, Springfield, Illinois.
8. Ibid., pp. 30–31.
9. From Kenney, John P., *Police Administration* 1972, pp. 74–93. Courtesy of Charles C Thomas, Publisher, Springfield, Illinois.
10. Ibid., p. 74.
11. Ibid., p. 75.
12. Paul M. Whisenand, *Police Supervision Theory and Practice* (Englewood Cliffs, N. J.: Prentice-Hall, 1971), p. 394.
13. Adams, *Police Patrol: Tactics and Techniques*, pp. 18–19.
14. Bristow, *Effective Police Manpower Utilization*, pp. 86–87.
15. Ibid., pp. 104–109. A detailed discussion of the fluid patrol concept and how it is employed by various departments.
16. From Adams, *Police Patrol: Tactics and Techniques, p. 20.*
17. Thomas F. Adams, *Law Enforcement: An Introduction to the Police Role and the Criminal Justice System,* (Englewood Cliffs, N. J.: Prentice-Hall, 2nd ed. 1973), p. 201.
18. *Police Chief* vol. 33, No. 7 (July 1966).
19. G. Douglas Gourley, *Effective Municipal Police Organization* (Beverly Hills, Calif.: Benziger, Bruce & Glencoe, 1970), p. 52.
20. Ibid., pp. 61–62.
21. From Hanna, Donald G., and Gentel, William D., *A Guide to Primary Police Management Concepts,* 1971, p. 47. Courtesy of Charles C Thomas, Publisher, Springfield, Illinois.
22. Leonard R. Sayles and George Strauss, *Human Behavior in Organizations* (Englewood Cliffs, N. J.: Prentice-Hall, 1966), p. 380. Reprinted by permission of the publisher.

Review Questions

1. List the nine principles of management, as a review of chapter 2 as well as this one.
2. Ten goals of a police department are listed in this chapter. List at least two additional goals that you consider important.
3. List and discuss at least five of the objectives of a police department.
4. Describe the steps of the preliminary investigations as presented by Bristow.
5. What are the Salford and Aberdeen plans? How do they compare with typical patrol plans in the city in which you live?
6. Describe Kenney's "team concept."
7. According to the National Safety Council, what are the police fully responsible for?
8. What is the principle of selective enforcement?
9. At what point in an investigation does the specialist take over and relieve the patrol officer?
10. Outline what you believe should be a department's attitude toward delinquency control.
11. What would be the advantage of making the vice unit directly responsible to the police chief?
12. Outline a list of those individuals and agencies that should have free access to the records of a police department.

13. What is the basic purpose of an intelligence unit?
14. Research and development may involve studies of what types of subjects in a municipal police department?
15. List at least three types of files that should be found in the records system, and explain why they are important.
16. What is the crime index and what criteria were used for selecting the crimes for this index?
17. If you were to measure the effectiveness of a patrol officer, what types of statistical controls would you use?

11 Court Administration*

Reference to *the Courts* is most often made without specific identification of precisely which court is the object of the discussion. Actually *the Courts* comprise a network of courts with a wide variety of jurisdictional boundaries responsibilities. From an organizational and management viewpoint, it is necessary to separate them and address each of the courts as a functional entity.

Traditionally, the courts have been managed by the dictates of the senior ranking magistrate, usually an astute and highly qualified attorney who is required to sit as a judge and magistrate in the courtroom and serve as senior office manager for the court in general. As prescribed by law in many instances, and by operational policy in others, the clerk of the court manages the ministerial and business matters of the court under the general direction of the judge. This leaves the judge free to concentrate on the more pressing matters of his office.

During recent years the clerk of the court has emerged as a more predominant administrator in the business management of the court. This is particularly true of the larger courts involving many divisions and up to hundreds of employees. A 1968 publication of the International City Managers' Association points up the need for professional court administrators:

*Material for this chapter is taken from unpublished writings of Mr. Richard R. Liberty, clerk of the municipal court, Northern Judicial District, South San Francisco, California. Reprinted with permission of Mr. Liberty.

Court Administration 287

Courtesy: Sheriff's Department, Riverside County, California

> The courts are one function of government which has neither appreciated the need nor implemented recommendations for professional administration. . . . This professional administration cannot be adequately provided by the judges; nevertheless, the administration of the courts must remain under the supervision of the judicial branch. What the courts need is an administrator. Even if the judges did have the time to devote to administration (which none of them do) they do not have the training in administration and management.
>
> The administrator's role in the judicial system is not decision making. Rather, the administrators' functions are to provide the judicial system with coordination, up-to-date statistical information, and internal housekeeping.[1]

As seen by those who recommend the position, it appears from the foregoing quotation, the court administrator is a business manager who is neither judge, attorney, or court clerk. In jurisdictions utilizing such a position, many of the duties and responsibilities would be the same as those currently required of the clerk of the court.

Judicial tribunals at the state level are basically creatures of the respective state constitutions. Many others are created to fill special needs, however, which are created by executive or legislative sanction. Such bodies include the Public Utilities Commission, Industrial Accident Commission, and the Federal Communications Commission. Under certain conditions, those agencies and others with similar responsibilities operate quite the same as the courts. The judicial tribunals created by the state constitutions include (1) the senate, which sits as a court of impeachment; (2) the supreme court; (3) district courts of appeal; (4) superior courts; (5) municipal courts; and other courts of inferior stature that may be characteristic of the several states.

Sound management principles must be applied effectively and intelligently in administration of the courts. Some characteristics of the court are unique, however. Probably the most obvious is that so many of the processes involved in the operation of the courts have tight time schedules, which require rigid adherence in order to assure the accused their rights to speedy trials and due process.

In the superior and municipal courts, the clerk of the court is generally charged with the duties and responsibilities as the chief administrative officer. His responsibilities include the following, which are prescribed by specific laws as well as other attendant factors:

1. Issue legal processes and notices as directed by the judge or judges of the court. Such processes as summonses, subpoenas, writs of attachment, writs of assistance, and many other processes.
2. Either the clerk or a deputy must maintain a register of actions, which contains brief notes on the proceedings of each case that comes before the court.
3. Maintain custody of evidence while trials are in progress.
4. Receive and distribute—according to various laws and ordinances—fines and other monies that the court receives in the normal course of business.
5. The clerk or a deputy attends each courtroom and assists the judge in keeping a permanent record of each case. Other courtroom responsibilities include administering oaths, drawing jury panels, and acting as a court reporter when one is available.
6. The clerk maintains records of all court proceedings and prepares them for appeals, when necessary, as well as reporting to the judicial council on all of the court's activities.

The National Association of Trial Court Administrators has identified a number of tasks and responsibilities which should be assigned to the court administrator:[2]

1. Personnel management services for trial court personnel.
2. Financial management services, including trial court budget development and execution.
3. Management of trial court physical facilities.
4. Information services to news media and other groups.
5. Assistance to the trial court in its relationship with other public or private agencies, including bar associations and appellate judicial administrative agencies.
6. Administrative services in selection and supervision of jurors.
7. Statistical management, including judicial statistics and other internal statistical reports.
8. Analysis of trial court administrative systems and procedures.
9. Case calendar management.

Economy and efficiency of operation are essential to the administration of the courts as much as they are to any of the components of the Criminal Justice System. Not only does it make good sense from a management point of view, but it is necessary in the interest of good *justice* management as well.

RECORDS AND REPORTING

Specifically what types of records and reports that are maintained by the courts are dictated by law, to a great extent? Each court action is assigned a number and additonally must be filed alphabetically by the names of the litigants, defendants, witnesses, and other participants in the actions. A review of the various court processes should illustrate the types of records and reports that are required of each process.

The Complaint.

In civil processes, the complaint initiates the action seeking remedy for some injustice suffered by the plaintiff. The relief sought for the injustice is usually interpreted in terms of some financial compensation. The original of the complaint is retained in a separate file with additional entries made on each individual named in the complaint. The original is assigned a number and placed in a numerical index. Other references to the complaint are entered into alphabetical indices. Additional information concerning the complaint are cross-filed in the several locations, such as the service of the summons, subpoenas, and other related information. If the defendant chooses to answer the complaint, which occurs in most cases, the answer is filed. If the defendant also chooses to file a cross-complaint, a new series of files are initiated.

Once the case has been adjudicated in trial or another manner, the action is recorded, then the judgment settled. Sometimes it is necessary to settle the judgment through a writ of execution, which is an order to the sheriff or marshal to locate and levy upon assets of the individual against whom a judgment has been awarded so as to satisfy the writ. The entire history of each case is entered into the several different files to reflect the chronicle of events as they develop.

TRAFFIC AND CRIMINAL COMPLAINTS. Citations are separated into traffic and parking citations and are filed in numerical sequence by category of offense and by the issuing department. As the recipients of the citation appear they post bail and the appropriate entries are made. In those cases when the defendant forfeits bail in lieu of returning to court to answer the charges, the case is closed at that time and the records will show the action taken. In the event the defendant chooses to appear in court—or if his presence is required by the nature of the offense and bail forfeiture is not allowed—an appearance date is set and the records will be made to reflect that action. If the defendant fails to appear in court at the scheduled date and time, he is notified by mail that a warrant is being issued for his arrest. He is given a few days to appear in some cases, but in all cases the warrant is processed and that set of records is opened.

Warrants are filed, then distributed to the sheriff, marshal, or another local law enforcement agency for service, which will lead to arrest and posting of bail and eventual appearance in court. At each step along the way, records are maintained. The warrant activity is accompanied by a series of communications, such as correspondence with the defendant, teletype communications to agencies who may assist in locating the subject of the warrant, and notification to the drivers' license agency to stop renewal of the subject's license until after the outstanding warrant has been taken care of.

Criminal Procedure

The accused is assured a fair trial in which he must be *proven* guilty, according to the Constitution. He has a right to counsel, and in accordance with the due process provisions of the Constitution he must be assured of appropriate adjudication of his case within some pretty closely spaced time frames. A speedy trial is included among the several rights provided for in the due process requirements. As with the several other types of processes previously discussed, each criminal action is assigned a number and a series-of-records entries are generated under the numerical and alphabetical filing categories.

Probation Reports

As an officer of the court, the probation officer files his presentence reports with the court. Although a court record, it is one of the several confidential files that is used only by the judge in his efforts to make a most judicious decision when passing on the sentence of the guilty.

The records system is designed to effectively serve the needs of the court with the calendar as an additional taskmaster. The activities of the court are closely coordinated with several other agencies of the Criminal Justice System that are interrelated by the nature of their respective roles in the system. Management of the records system of the courts, as well as the entire court operation, requires the skill of a professional business manager.

THE CRIME COMMISSION REPORT AND THE COURTS

The President's Commission on Law Enforcement and the Administration of Justice produced its principal report, *The Challenge of Crime in a Free Society*. and several accompanying task force reports focusing attention on the many problems and challenges confronting law enforcement and the many components of the justice system. Following are some excerpts from chapter 5 of the principal report that directly relate to the matter of courts administration and management.

The Courts

The criminal court is the central, crucial institution in the Criminal Justice System. It is the part of the system that is the most venerable, the most formally organized, and the most elaborately circumscribed by law and tradition. It is the institution around which the rest of the system is in large measure responsible. It regulates the flow of the criminal process under governance of the law. The activities of the police are limited or shaped by the rules and procedures of the court. The work of the correctional system is determined by the court's sentence.

Society asks much of the criminal court. The court is expected to meet society's demand that serious offenders be convicted and punished, and at the same time it is expected to insure that the innocent and the unfortunate are not oppressed. It is expected to control the application of force against the individual by the state, and it is expected to find which of two conflicting versions of the event is the truth. And so the court is not merely an operating agency, but one that has a vital educational and symbolic significance. It is expected to articulate the community's most deeply held, most cherished views about the relationship of the individual and society. The formality of the trial and the honor accorded the robed judge bespeak the symbolic importance of the court and its work.

Criminal Procedures

Even with their limitations the courts do not work perfectly, and never have. Hamlet considered "the law's delay" to be as deplorable a feature of the human scene as "the pangs of mispriz'd love," and the works of Charles Dickens are crammed with descriptions of the law's abuses, from the bumbling beadle in *Oliver Twist* to the unwieldy English Chancery in *Bleak House*. For as long as judges have had the power to determine sentences, there have been individual judges who have misused that power by sentencing too leniently or too severely. For as long as money

Courtesy: Pepperdine University School of Law, Santa Ana, California

bail has been used to insure that defendants appear for trial, it has discriminated against poor defendants. For as long as defense counsel have had the right to question and test the criminal process, some defense counsel have resorted to obfuscation and chicanery. Courts can be only as effective and just as the judges and prosecutors, counsel and jurors who man them. Protecting the courts against misuse, abuse, or simple operational inefficiency has always been a hard and urgent problem.

Court Scheduling, Management and Organization

From the beginning of the criminal process to its end, from police work to correctional work, there is a tension between efficiency —protecting the community from crime—and fairness—protecting the rights of individuals. If these opposing pulls are not kept in balance, the process tends to become either excessively arbitrary, perfunctory, and hasty or excessively deliberate, cumbersome, and dilatory. Every year both pressures are becoming stronger, and the effect of this on the courts is especially conspicuous. The volume of criminal cases is growing, and so cases have to be pushed through crowded courts. Decisions requiring intervention of defense counsel at early stages of the process are becoming more rigorous, and so the deliberation with which cases must be considered is becoming greater.

The commission is well aware that the preponderant, though not the entire, stress of the recommendations it has made for greater participation by counsel, for more careful procedures, and for fuller information relating to precharge decisions and plea negotiations is in a direction that will slow the process down. A chief purpose of this section is to discuss ways in which the countervailing pull can be strengthened, in which the process can be kept moving in the face of rising volume.

That all too often now it does not move is clear. There are courts in which the normal lapse of time between the preliminary hearing and action by a grand jury is 3 months, and in which persons charged with serious crimes normally await trial for over a year. Such courts make it a mockery of bail decisions. It is clearly unfair to a defendant to jail him for months without trial; it is clearly unfair to the community for a defendant charged with a serious crime to be at large for months without trial. Important cases are lost in such courts by attrition. Delay for the sake of delay is often in the interest of a defendant who is guilty and free on bail. If his counsel is allowed to procrastinate by making untenable motions and demanding repeated continuances, the process can be worn down to a point at which witnesses become forgetful or elusive, and the prosecutor may become so anxious to dispose of the case that he dismisses the charge or reduces it excessively in return for a plea of guilty. Such delay undermines the law's deterrent effect by demonstrating that justice is not swift and certain but slow and faltering.

In general, the courts in which these conditions exist are the overcrowded urban courts. Traditionally, the management of a court's calendar—the schedule of what cases are to be heard on a given day—is in the hands of the judge. In a court with a small caseload a judge has little difficulty in keeping track of every case and every defendant. He can remember what motions he has heard and how he ruled on them, how many continuances he has granted and for what reasons, which defendants are in jail and which are not. He can resist the pressure to delay that is brought to bear on him by defense counsel for tactical reasons, or by a prosecutor who has been slow to assemble his case. With no more than a sketchy set of records he can manage his calendar fairly and efficiently. In a badly congested court a judge, however elaborate and faithfully kept his records are and however fair and efficient he is, often cannot manage his calendar. And dividing the courts into "parts"—an arraignment part, a motions part, a number of trial parts—may increase the efficiency of individual judges by confining them to one judicial function at a time, but does not necessarily move cases through the process more promptly. Involving several judges in a case can make the case harder to keep track of. In order for crowded courts to manage their calendars well, they must conform to agreed-upon standards of performance, use up-to-date administrative and technological techniques, and be subject to central supervision.

A Model Timetable

A rigid advance schedule for the processing of a case is patently unfeasible. There are too many variables. Sometimes motions to suppress require that the legality of an arrest be examined at length; an elaborate search for evidence is justified; lawyers have conflicting engagements; witnesses fail to appear; a trial must be put off because another trial has been unexpectedly prolonged and there is no judge or courtroom.

Making allowances for needed flexibility, however, it is possible to establish standards that emphasize the court's ability to deal efficiently with its business, that distinguish between needless and unnecessary delay, and that provide a reference for court management.

In the report of the commission's administration of justice task force, a model timetable is set forth in detail. It is not intended, of course, to eliminate any traditional procedures from the process, nor is it intended to suggest that every case is the same as every other case or to remove from judges, prosecutors, or defense counsel any of the discretion it is necessary for them to have. The commission believes it is a fair and reasonable set of guidelines against which courts can measure their present performance. It proposes maximum intervals between specific steps in the process, for example, that the preliminary hearing follow the initial appearance by not more than 3 days for jailed defendants and 7 days for released defendants. It proposes that the period from arrest to trial of felony cases be not more than 4 months and that the period from trial to appellate decision be within 5 months—that, in short, the entire process take no more than 9 months. In chapter 11 of this report an experimental computer simulation of the workload of an existing court is described. This effort indicates the feasibility of the time standards described in the model timetable and shows the usefulness of this approach as a part of an analysis of court operations.

Court administrators should collect regularly reported information on the time the courts are taking to dispose of cases and should measure this experience against the standards. Delay may be met by a variety of measures including assignment of additional judges; calling extra or longer sessions of courts; special priorities for criminal cases; the public reporting of courts experiencing special delay; and, particularly when excessive delay is experienced between arraignment and trial, by the establishment of special parts and calendars in which particularly vigorous efforts may be made to deal with stalled cases. Establishment of the timetable by a court or court system can be by local rule, by calendar order, or, where rule-making power is totally lacking, by legislation.

THE COMMISSION RECOMMENDS: Courts and court systems should establish standards for the completion of the various stages of criminal cases. These standards should be designed to be within the capabilities of deliberate court consideration of cases, yet also should ensure that the disposition of cases shall be expeditious. Where existing court facilities are inadequate to enable cases to be disposed of in a reasonably short time, the need for greater resources and reform of procedures is demonstrated.

Technical Management

A requisite for the implementation of a timetable is that courts know at all times what the cases before them are and at what stages they are. In an age when new management techniques and business machines have revolutionized many business and government operations, the courts' business procedures have remained most places very much like those of a former age. The use of multiple long-hand entries, cumbersome dockets, and inefficient filing and indexing systems with limited retrieval capacity persists in many courts because the volume of cases has not been so great as to cause the system to break down. Increasing urbanization has placed great new pressures upon these courts, however, and has highlighted the inadequacy and obsolescence of the business methods used.

In some of the largest cities the volume of criminal court business has reached a point at which the use of computers and automatic business machines is being instituted to maintain an orderly flow of clerical business. While there does not yet appear to be a pressing need for the use of such elaborate equipment in medium sized cities, many of their courts do need to reorganize and modernize their manual clerical methods through better forms, filing systems, and indexing and scheduling methods. Modern technical management holds promise for enabling these courts to perform their job more quickly and cheaply by improving the retrieval of information, the scheduling of cases, and the maintenance of records.

The commission urges courts and court administrators to seek the advice and assistance of experts in business management and business machine systems in an effort to develop plans and forms for more efficient court business systems.

Central Supervision and Professional Administration

For cases to move expeditiously through a court with many judges and thousands of cases, it is necessary that all the cases and all the judges be centrally supervised. Central supervision of cases makes it possible to keep track of the status of every case, to shift cases from one judge to another according to their various caseloads, to set up special calendars for cases that inherently demand prompt action or that have fallen behind the normal schedule. Central supervision of judges makes it possible to assign judges appropriately, to set up work and vacation schedules that all judges are expected to conform to, and to press dilatory judges to act more speedily.

Of course, the supervision of calendars and judges is a judicial function. It could be performed by a court's chief justice, or by a small administrative committee of judges, or by an administrative judge appointed for this purpose. Whatever form central supervision takes, large and complicated courts need the services of professional administrators to assist the judges charged with administration. Some thirty states have provided for an administrative office to aid the judiciary by collecting judicial statistics, managing fiscal affairs, supervising court personnel, and performing duties in connection with the assignment of judges and scheduling of cases. In many of these states, however, the functions of this office are limited, and its potential has not yet been realized. By bringing men into courts with training and a primary interest in management, techniques of court management will be improved. Court administration is a developing field in which a clear understanding of techniques is evolving. There is a need for more experimentation and increased use of promising methods for ordering the business of the courts.

THE COMMISSION RECOMMENDS: States should provide for clear administrative responsibility within courts and should ensure that professional court administrators are available to assist the judges in their management functions.

Court Reorganization

While in some states successful court reform has created courts able to meet new demands, in many states the entire court structure continues to reflect an earlier age. There is a multiplicity of trial courts without coherent and centralized administrative management. Jurisdictional lines are unnecessarily complex and confusing. Each court and each judge within the court constitute a distinct administrative unit, moving at its own pace and in its own way. In a number of states courts not responsible to a statewide system nor subject to its management continue to be viewed as a source of local revenue, and criminal justice is seen as a profitmaking activity.

Modern management and efficiency can be promoted by putting all courts and judges within a state under a single, central administration with provision for the shifting and allocation of judicial and administrative manpower to meet changing requirements.

For this to be effective the judiciary must be given rule-making power over the methods used to handle its business. It is important that men continuously and intimately involved with court procedures be responsible for court rules. Legislatures cannot deal with the technical problems of court management and procedure effectively. In most states, the rule-making power is lodged in the supreme court, a judicial conference, or some other body of judges.

THE COMMISSION RECOMMENDS: States should reexamine their court structure and organization and create a single, unified system of courts subject to central administrative management within the judiciary. The commission urges states that have not yet reformed their court systems to draw upon the experience of those states and organizations that have made advances in this area. Central administration within the judiciary should have the power to make rules and shift manpower to meet changing requirements.[3]

SUMMARY

According to Mr. Liberty, the key to the efficient operation of the court is the extent to which the judge in each court involves himself in the actual management of the activities of the court and the amount of authority he confers upon the clerk of the court. The court clerk acts as administrator of court affairs of a nonjudicial nature, involving himself with schedules related to time factors attached to the various legal processes, the calendar of cases to appear before the judge or judges, and the management of the routine business of the offices of the courts.

Two major aspects of the courts are (1) to provide direct services to the judges in the operations of the courtroom activities, and (2) to carry out the activities of the related offices of the court involving records, evidence custody, and fiscal affairs. The vast differences that apparently exist among court operations—as indicated in the 1967 report of the Commission on Law Enforcement and the Administration of Justice as well as at this time several years later—seem to defy standardization, yet the many similarities in legal requirements seem to cry out for greater standardization. Court management requires cooperative efforts and intelligent application of sound management principles and procedures by the judges and professionally trained court administrators.

Notes

1. Municipal Court Administration, *Management Information Service* Report No. 292, May, 1968, p. 3.
2. Klein, Fannie J., "The Position of the Trial Court Administrator in the United States" *Judicature*, April 1967, p. 278 (recounted in supra).
3. President's Commission on Law Enforcement and the Administration of Justice, *The Challenge of Crime in a Free Society* (Washington, D.C.: U.S. Government Printing Office, 1967), pp. 125–57.

Review Questions

1. What is the relationship between the judge and the clerk of the court regarding management of the court's daily business operations?
2. Describe the function of the deputy clerk in the courtroom.
3. Is the word *court* a term used to describe the place where the activities take place, or does it refer to the individual sitting on the bench?
4. What is the legal basis for establishment of a municipal court?
5. Visit your local municipal and superior courts. Interview a court official, then draw an organizational chart for those two courts.
6. Describe the court system in your state.
7. List the various records and files that a court must maintain in order to record all of the types of information Mr. Liberty describes.
8. List and describe the merits of the president's commission's recommendations concerning the courts and their management.

12 Probation and Parole Administration

Having reviewed the general principles of administration in the Criminal Justice System, we will now relate these principles to the third major subsystem or output, the correctional process. In this chapter we explore probation and parole as subsystems. The goals and objectives of probation and parole are reviewed as are their relationships to the other justice system components.

Probation and parole are frequently seen as one and the same by the layman; in fact, they are two distinct phases of the correctional process. Understanding of the terms is further complicated because our justice system is bifurcated into a juvenile justice system and a Criminal Justice System. Probation and parole have significance to each, but their roles are quite different. The principal difference between probation and parole is that parole supervision and treatment occur after an offender has been incarcerated for an extended period of time, usually in a state-operated institution, and probation provides presentence sociological study to the court as well as supervision of the offender while on probation.

DEFINITIONS OF PROBATION AND PAROLE

Probation is the process by which society tries to provide corrective assistance to the individual in conflict with the law, at the same time affording protection to the community. It is not feasible, either socially or economically, to imprison all offenders; experience has shown that the majority of offenders can be better prepared for constructive lives without removing them from their family, job, community, and familiar surroundings. Some agencies prefer to reverse the order of the definition by indicating that the primary aim of probation is to protect the community by contributing to the rehabilitation of an offender through constructive control.[1] It is also significant that probation activities have been broadened to include prevention and diversion programs. The purpose of these programs is to stop potential offenders or persons who have displayed a proclivity toward criminal or delinquent behavior from entering the criminal or juvenile justice systems in a formal way. Thus, the output phase of the justice system becomes a subsystem which attempts to eliminate its own input.

Parole supervision resembles probation in methods and purposes. Parole is the process of continuing in the community the correctional program begun in the institution. It functions to assist the offender in adjusting to his freedom without placing the protection of the community in jeopardy.[2] While probation is granted by a sentencing court, parole is granted by an administrative board or agency on the basis of the inmate's prior history and readiness for release.

HISTORICAL DEVELOPMENT OF PROBATION AND PAROLE

Informal experimentation in the release of offenders to the charge of respected volunteer citizens marked the original concept of probation which continued for nearly 40 years in the middle of the nineteenth century. John Augustus, a Boston bootmaker, was the first citizen to begin this practice in 1841. By the late 1800s, states had enacted legislation permitting courts to suspend sentencing and later provided for paid staff to supervise and treat released offenders. Juvenile probation followed shortly after the turn of the century when states began to enact juvenile court laws which recognized a need to remove children from the criminal justice process. The basic philosophy of the modern juvenile court is to serve the best interests of the minor in order to divert him from entering the Criminal Justice System. By 1910, 40 states provided juvenile probation services. Nearly all these services were placed under the control of local governments. Formalized adult probation services evolved simultaneously and, by 1956, every state had statutory provision for adult probation services.

California has been a leader in the provision of probation services. Since 1903, when California first made provision for probation, there has been a tremendous growth and enrichment of services. By 1971, some 274,000 offenders were within the California correctional system. Of these, about 200,000 were probationers (112,000 adults and 88,000 juveniles). This represents about one-fourth of all persons on probation in the United States. Because the law provides for probation services at the county level, a wide variety of service patterns exist, running from a one-man or part-time operation to the Los Angeles County Probation Department, which employs over 2,000 professional staff. The extent and quality of probation service varies greatly not only from state to state but from county to county as well. Nevertheless, the use of probation as a dispositional sentence is an ever-increasing practice among courts in all jurisdictions. In California there was a significant increase in the sixties. In 1960, 44.4 percent of the superior court convicts were granted probation. By 1969, this percentage had risen to 65.6.[3] Similar increases have been observed in juvenile probation grants by the juvenile court.

Parole for juveniles has its historical foundation in "aftercare" associated with refuge houses for children in the late eighteenth century. The first official recognition of parole came in 1876, at New York's Elmira Reformatory. An early concept of parole was that it was a continuation of the prison sentence served in the community under prescribed conditions. Under this philosophy, the parole officer exercised broad discretionary authority. He could return the parolee to custody whenever he felt it to be in the best interest of the community. This kind of latitude in returning parolees to prison has been curtailed by court decisions and parolees are now guaranteed due process of law and legal counsel before they can be returned. More contemporary descriptions stress a community-based process with a shift of focus to rehabilitation rather than threat of return to custody.

Modern probation and parole organizations stress professionalism and the use of many behavioral science tools. Probation and parole officers must have a working knowledge of many disciplines including law enforcement, the judicial process, psychology, sociology, education, vocational training, counseling, recreation, and others. Officers serve as coordinators and referral agents in order to fully utilize the resources available in the community.

LEGAL FRAMEWORK—FUNCTIONAL AUTHORITY

Probation services are generally called for by statute; its two divisions can be broadly defined as investigative and supervisory. Both services are provided in the Criminal Justice System for adults and the juvenile justice system for persons under the age of 18.

In California the authority for adult probation services is found in Section 1203 of the California Penal Code. This code gives the powers and responsibilities vested in the probation officer. Included is the peace officer's power to arrest when taking a probationer into custody. The legal authority for juvenile probation is found in Article 7 of the Welfare and Institutions Code of California. These codes are quite precise in describing the functions of probation in California. Similarly, the parole function is precisely codified for adults and juveniles. Parole is a function of the State Department of the Youth Authority and the State Department of Corrections in California.

Legislation can significantly alter the roles, functions, objectives and volume of work flowing to the probation and parole subsystems. State probation-subsidy legislation can shift financial resources and alter the entire treatment approach from emphasis on incarceration to emphasis on community-based treatment. Correctional administrators must maintain a constant awareness of significant legislation. In some cases input from the agency administrator to the lawmakers is indicated. This is generally done either collectively through professional organizations or by individual efforts to persuade lawmakers.

TRENDS TOWARD NONINSTITUTIONAL CORRECTIONS

An attorney general's task force in California recently noted,

> The trend is, simply stated, one of reducing the number of criminal offenders who are taken into close confinement and reducing the length of time served by those who are held in custody. The orientation of the decision makers toward this trend, and the various available programs, work together to produce a single result, to wit, a steady reduction in institutionalization and a comparable increase in community-based handling of offenders. The trend is nationwide and is clearly manifested throughout the California Department of Corrections, the California Adult Authority, the probation departments of the various California counties, and the court system.[4]

Many question whether this trend serves the objectives of the justice system and they feel that it is contrary to public desire. The issue remains, How shall the system deal most effectively with the offender while maintaining acceptable protection of the community? The broad, ill-defined concept of the public interest is applicable; it would appear that decision makers have determined that ever-increasing numbers of criminals and delinquents will be dealt with at the local level of government and primarily through the auspices of probation and local correctional institutions.

Others feel that every effort should be made to retain the offender in the community to maximize his chances for successful reintegration into society. Proponents of this approach advocate incarceration only as a last resort. Many persons in custody can be effectively returned to their communities through the expanded use of probation and parole. A demonstration project was conducted in Saginaw, Michigan, over a three-year period ending in 1963. In that project, judges agreed to increase the number of persons placed under the supervision of trained probation officers. Prior to the beginning of the project, the judges used probation in about 50 percent of the cases; with the project's inception, they increased the use of probation to 80 percent. Despite the increase in use of probation there was no increase in the revocation rate (failure of probation) over the three-year period.[5]

One certainty in the future of probation and parole is that they will continue to play a significant role in the justice system. The output of the system is typically divided among the correctional components as follows:

Percentage of Correctional Population Served

	%
Juvenile Camps	1
Adult Jails and Camps	5
Parole	10
State Institutions	12
Probation	72

It is also important to see these subsystems in their proper perspective relative to the entire justice system. As can be seen in the flow chart below, the percentage of offenders who reach the probation or parole

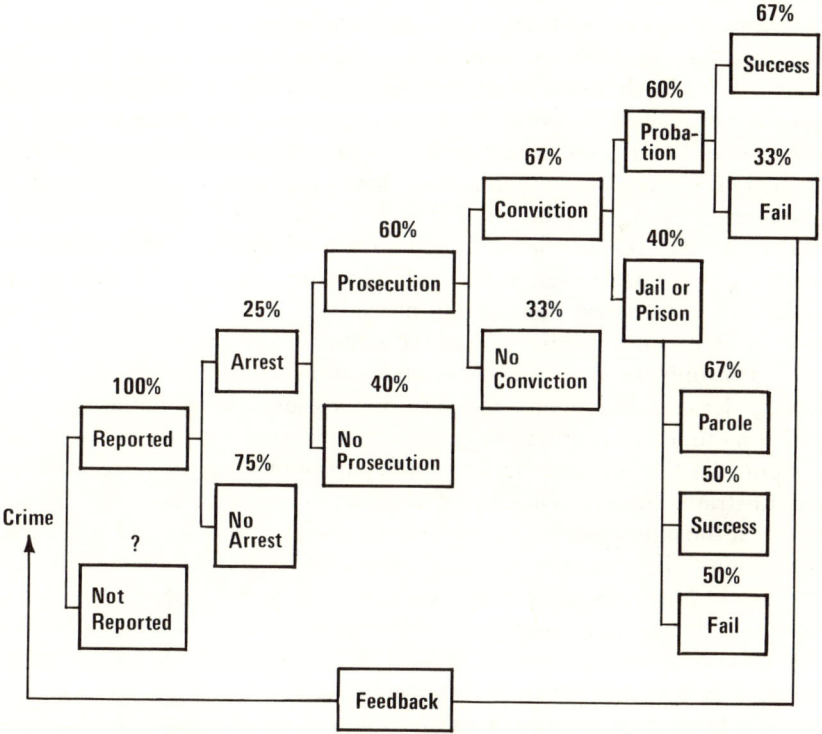

Figure 21. **Criminal Justice System Flow of Offenders**

Source: Robert M. Carter, A. W. Eachern, and Herbert Sigurdson, *The Uncertain Future of Criminal Justice"*. (Unpublished paper, University of Southern California, based on 1969 data.)

function is rather small when compared to the maximum potential. Using the percentages shown, for every 100,000 crimes there are only 25,000 arrests. Of those arrested, 15,000 are brought to court and only 10,000 are convicted. Of these, 6,000 are granted probation (25 percent of those arrested) and 4,000 are committed to jail or prison. Of the offenders committed, 2,000 are released on parole. Probation succeeds 67 percent of the time and parole succeeds in half the cases. Based on these data, probation and parole, the final effort at rehabilitation, is successful with one out of every five persons arrested. This information is the result of projected assumptions from a Criminal Justice System simulation study prepared by the University of Southern California and funded by the California Council on Criminal Justice.[6]

THE GOALS AND OBJECTIVES OF PROBATION AND PAROLE

Stating the Objective

While the definitions of probation and parole may be readily understood, the true objective of noninstitutional treatment can prove to be illusive, vague, and unclear. It is insufficient to rely on the specification of functions articulated in laws and codes, and it is unwise to assume that the objective is clearly understood, because it generally is not. Consider the question of success of probation. Is there success if the probationer commits crimes but of a lesser nature than before his probation experience? If probation is successfully terminated, how long must the probationer be monitored to assure he has not slid back into criminal behavior? Consider too the value of a clearly defined and understood objective when determining the expenditure of resources for delinquency prevention and diversion programs. To develop policies and procedures without an objective is to navigate without a rudder toward an unknown destination.

The objectives of probation and parole agencies can, at best, be loosely defined. Statements found in publications are incomplete, vague, and sometimes in conflict with each other or another part of the justice system. Yet the very foundation of a department's services, organization, administrative practices and proof of success must stem from these objectives. At the operating level there may be a wide divergence of interpretation about policy statements, legal requirements, and service objectives.

In order to operationalize a system, or as in the case of probation or parole a subsystem, it is essential to state an objective which contributes to the greater system's purpose or goal. Components or agencies cannot function systematically unless they can be arranged in relation to a general sense of mission or purpose. This then allows for each agency (probation or parole) to construct objectives with a common purpose. The primary objective of corrections is the protection of society (common to all parts of the justice system) by minimizing the probability of new illegal conduct. This being the objective of corrections, secondary objectives can be stated which include prevention, incarceration, rehabilitation, and reintegration. Each of these then is compatible and supportive of the corrections objective and the general mission of the justice system.[7]

In large organizations, bureaucratic weaknesses to a significant degree may divert the organization from its objective. Bureaucratic inertia, the doing of a task merely because it has always been done, technical expertise in isolation from the total organization objective, impersonality, and the difficulty of coordination and communication, all present major challenges for the administrator or manager who is attempting to navigate his organization toward an often ill-defined destination.

At the line level, a lack of uniform interpretation of what a probation department should be doing can be so pronounced that it is sometimes impossible to establish meaningful standards of performance. Take for example an individual probation officer who feels success when his probationer makes significant changes in his attitude even though the probationer continues to commit minor infractions. This change should not be measured as a success if the objective of the department is to protect the community by preventing the probationer from committing any and all further illegal acts.

As in all organizations, the integration of the organizational goal with the goals of individual members is a major responsibility of the administrator. Argyris has developed a major theme around the dichotomy of individual and organizational needs, states Harold Rush. He has pointed out that, traditionally, organizations and their individual members do not meet each other's respective needs and that both must do so more effectively in order to deter subversion of the organization's goals.[8] Unless the individual probation or parole officer has a personal stake in the success of the agency and unless the agency can meet his personal needs and goals, little success can be expected by either the individual or the organization.

In an organization where all, from administrator to first-line officers, have a clear understanding and personal interest in striving toward a common goal, much can be accomplished. In attempts to optimize this ideal, the administrator and the managers of an organization face many pitfalls. Formally stated goals are not interpreted the same way by each level of organizational membership. Further, the stated objective of the organization may be remote from its real objective. The implementation and interpretation of goal application is the key to integrating the system. The strength of a constitution rests on its ability to be interpreted, so do the formal statements of organizational objectives.

The quality of organizational output is rarely measurable against a formalized statement of objectives. To produce quantitatively, whether it be a product or a service, may have little relationship to the real objective of the organization. Thus, the first task of the administrator and the organization is to define the real objective, the genuine reason for the existence of the organization in qualitative terms. For a university to set as a goal graduating large numbers of students with little regard for the quality of education rendered is improper application of the principle of organizational goal setting. A rehabilitation agency must consider not the number of offenders processed through the agency, but rather the degree to which those offenders have modified their attitudes and behavior.

Organizational objectives are often value loaded and there should be an effort to make them legitimate and accepted by both the internal and external elements of the system. The objectives must fit in to the larger scheme of things to maintain a social balance. For example, if a correctional organization's objective is rejected by both the law-enforcement component and the general public, it is not legitimate, because it is not in balance with the organization's environment. The administrator must consider the very role of government itself when establishing the objective. The point at which a probation department can justifiably intercede in behalf of a minor child over the objection of a parent can be an issue of governmental control in a matter that might be considered private by some observers.

The administrator also needs to consider the perceptions of the members of the organization. The goal should be seen as difficult to achieve, but it cannot be beyond belief. A goal for probation and parole to rehabilitate every offender coming under its jurisdiction to the point of eliminating all recidivism would have little credibility in the eyes of the probation or parole officer. A better goal might be to maximize the opportunity for rehabilitation to minimize recidivism.

A much-overlooked aspect of goal setting is that goals should be in a constant state of potential change because organizations are affected by internal and external changes in environment. Administrators need to remain aware of the accelerated pace of these changes, and predict with some degree of accuracy the potential of factors that call for modification of organizational objectives. Too often objectives are reactive rather than proactive. Objectives should relate to future trends and events based on various indicators available to the administrator. The probation department should have, as part of its objective, a delinquency prevention function which justifies a program of drug education, while drug abuse is still significant. If reaction is slow, the drug education program may be implemented after the problem has become either too large or passé.

Effective goal setting is imperative for the carrying out of planning, budgeting, and management. The popular utilization of program budgeting and management by objectives has further emphasized this function of administration.

Probation Objectives

Management by objectives, an administrative model, is gaining acceptance in correctional agencies slowly because of a lack of management sophistication and because of conflicting societal definitions of the correctional objective. A growing demand for efficiency, especially in larger departments, has stimulated interest in this approach. Correctional administrators are beginning to combine management competence with correctional competence for the solution of pressing social problems. This method minimizes reliance on ideology, trial and error, and tradition while providing a rational guideline for ordering and allocating manpower, equipment, and fiscal resources. It eases decision making and gives direction to diverse operations.

A CASE STUDY IN DEVELOPING PROBATION OBJECTIVES. In 1963, an interdivisional task force of the Los Angeles Probation Department formulated their department's objectives as:

1. *Protection of the community*—to safeguard the community from repetition of offenses through the use of modern methods of diagnosis, control, and treatment.
2. *Prevention of crime and delinquency*—to identify and correct behavior likely to result in crime or delinquency, and assist in and support programs to alleviate social and economic conditions conducive to crime and delinquency.
3. *Rehabilitation*—to restore the offender to a useful and law-abiding life in the community through the use of modern methods of improving behavior and attitudes.
4. *Administration of justice*—to support enforcement of the law and provide full and objective information to the courts so that cases are handled appropriately.
5. *Protective services for children*—to provide protection and assistance, on the order and under the authority of the court, to certain dependent, neglected, abused, and abandoned children.[9]

What appeared to be a clear statement of objectives to the probation department managers was not so clear to a management survey consultant team. The latter pointed out that many terms used were vague: what, for example, is the precise meaning of rehabilitation? The team also noted that the stated objectives were not fully understood, uniformly interpreted, or consistently applied. Officers were given too little training about objectives, and the objectives were not translated into guides for action. Furthermore, the team found that these objectives were misunderstood and misinterpreted by key persons and interest groups outside the department.

A task force was formed to examine these criticisms. A thorough search of correctional literature for material relevant to objectives in probation proved fruitless. Discussions of philosophy, ethics, and principles were all that could be found.[10] The task force discovered a serious lack of knowledge and understanding of the probation function among people who should know. In an effort to rectify this, the task force reduced the department's objectives to four:

1. protect the community
2. rehabilitate probationers
3. further justice
4. protect children.

The prevention objective was eliminated because it referred only to broad activities with no focus or direction. The department was not actively involved with prevention of a nonclient population and there was no legal or budgetary mandate for the prevention activity. Certain elements of the original prevention objective were encompassed in the protection and rehabilitation objectives. Prevention was seen as a worthwhile activity of probation; it is economically sound but was not being effectively performed by other agencies or organizations and so the probation workload was affected. Probation was felt to be a logical agency to carry out broad prevention programs in view of the training and expertise of its staff.

In order to make these objectives more usable, the role of the department in striving for each of these objectives was articulated. A step-by-step guide for implementing these objectives through the management by objectives technique was prescribed and defined.

To Protect the Community
DEFINITION:
   To protect persons and property from illegal and antisocial acts by persons receiving probation services.
ROLE OF THE DEPARTMENT:
   1. Assess the nature and degree of danger presented by persons referred.
   2. Determine the course of action that will best protect the community.

3. Provide the courts with information and recommendations related to means of community protection.
4. Exercise such supervision and control of probationers as will be essential to protecting the community, taking preventive or corrective action when necessary.
5. Maintain and operate diagnostic, detention, and treatment facilities for juveniles.
6. Conduct research to improve diagnostic and predictive capabilities in relation to community protection.[11]

The protection objective is in this manner emphasized by citing the department's role in providing diagnostic, prognostic, planning, and control functions. This procedure gives reason for the department's activities in determining whether probation supervision can assure protection of the community. It involves assessing the available resources and making appropriate recommendations. At times a probation department must recommend probation to the courts as the best program available, even though it cannot realistically safeguard the community with full certainty.

Each of the other objectives was similarly defined and the department role was clarified in each case. This process was only the first step in beginning to integrate the objectives into the everyday activity of several thousand employees. The task force set a tentative plan of implementation noting that the elaboration and modification of this plan would be a continuing task of management as the implications, requirements, and potentials of management by objectives became better understood.[12]

Parole Objectives

Like probation, parole is not a single system but two systems, and it plays similar roles, one for juveniles and one for adults, in the greater justice system. In most states the two are separate departments although they may both be under a parent agency. Parole falls at the very end of the correctional continuum. It is the point at which criminals and juvenile delinquents are often presumed by the public to have been rehabilitated, but it is also the point where recidivism is highest. In parole, we find the offenders who have not yet profited from the handling of all other agencies in the system. Public reaction to parolees who endanger community safety can be most vehement. For all of these reasons, it is most critical that parole objectives be clear, understood, and well integrated into the parole agency through the individual parole officers.

Parole, as stated earlier, is the continuation of the institutional treatment process. It returns the prisoner to his community under specified conditions and with professional guidance directed at reintegrating him or her into society. The predominate objective of parole is to protect society by preventing or reducing the likelihood of further illegal behavior; simultaneously parole should help the parolee make a good adjustment to necessary social controls and should discover ways in which the parolee can put his abilities to self-satisfying and socially constructive use.[13]

There have been many innovations in parole over the past 30 years such as new techniques of supervision, expanded research, classification and diagnosis, and the use of paraprofessionals. Most writers and practitioners agree, however, that the basic principles and philosophy of parole have remained the same. The guidelines set by the 1939 National Parole Conference still stand as a model of progressive parole theory and practice today. The delegates to the conference, assembled at the request of the president, represented governors, the judiciary, law enforcement, the church, the community at large, and various correctional systems. The delegates recognized that nearly all prisoners are ultimately released and that parole, when properly administered and carefully distinguished from clemency, protects the public by maintaining control over offenders after they leave prison. The conference delegates declared that for parole to achieve its purpose, the following conditions should exist:

1. The paroling authority should be impartial, nonpolitical, professionally competent, and able to give the time necessary for full consideration of each case.
2. The sentencing and parole laws should endow the paroling authority with broad discretion in determining the time and conditions of release.
3. The paroling authority should have complete and reliable information concerning the prisoner, his background, and the situation which will confront him on his release.
4. The parole program of treatment and training should be an integral part of a system of criminal justice.
5. The period of imprisonment should be used to prepare the individual vocationally, physically, mentally, and spiritually for return to society.
6. The community through its social agencies, public and private, and in cooperation with the parole service should accept the responsibility for improving home and neighborhood conditions in preparation for the prisoner's release.
7. The paroled offender should be carefully supervised and promptly reimprisoned or otherwise disciplined if he does not demonstrate capacity and willingness to fulfill the obligations of a law-abiding citizen.

8. The supervision of the paroled offender should be exercised by qualified persons trained and experienced in the task of guiding social readjustments.
9. The state should provide adequate financial support for a parole system, including sufficient personnel selected and retained in office upon the basis of merit.
10. The public should recognize the necessity of giving the paroled offender a fair opportunity to earn an honest living and maintain self-respect to the end that he may be truly rehabilitated and the public adequately protected.[14]

A correctional system study in California in 1971 reported that its parole task force was in agreement with these principles, with only one exception. The task force noted the only point that does not fit a progressive model for parole today is number 7. It was noted that a modern statement of parole philosophy must remove the emphasis on prompt reimprisonment and replace it with a stress on releasing the offender on parole to the community as soon as possible, consistent with public protection, and make every effort to keep him there through effective rehabilitation and reintegration.[15]

The reader may find these statements at odds with each other. The question is one of emphasis. The 1939 statement is probably more in keeping with the general attitude of the public concerning the freedom of released offenders. The progressive statement is also concerned with public protection but this concern is given less emphasis in favor of an attitude of rehabilitation whenever it is possible without jeopardizing the safety of the community.

JUVENILE PAROLE OBJECTIVES. The foregoing description of the principles of parole refer basically to all parole, but they were written with the adult parole system in mind. We will now explore the objectives of juvenile parole and how it differs from adult parole.

In defining the objective of juvenile parole, we shall look to California as a model. In 1941, the Youth Authority Act spelled out the objectives of parole as follows: "To protect society more effectively by substituting for retributive punishment methods of training and treatment directed toward correction and rehabilitation of young persons guilty of public offenses."[16]

A briefer statement might be the protection of society and rehabilitation of youth. As one can see, when stated in its simplest form, this objective is basically the same as for adult probation. To some the concept of early release on parole demonstrates a weakness in the justice system, but it must be remembered that the ultimate goal is to reduce repetition of delinquent or criminal behavior. Rehabilitation of offenders to prevent their return to antisocial behavior is the most likely method of accomplishing this goal. Varying lengths of institutional care coupled with aftercare supervision and treatment in the community seems to be the best approach to this rehabilitation.

The *Parole Manual* of the California Youth Authority describes the dual objective of parole. It specifies that the parole agent serves two distinct yet compatible purposes in the treatment of delinquents: (1) Assisting wards in their rehabilitation and (2) protection of society. It goes on to state, he (the parole agent) must maintain the clear perspective of his duties so that the needs of his wards and the safety of the community are maintained in the proper balance, one not being met to the exclusion of the other.[17]

Parole supervision offers the released juvenile offender the guidance he needs to help him work out his problems while in the community. Parole is, as previously noted for adults a continuation of the overall correctional process. Its goal or objective is to provide the kind of individualized treatment that will enable the parolee to become self-sustaining, law abiding, and a contributing member of his community. To be effective, parole supervision should emphasize the parolee's emotional needs and his environmental situation. Parole supervision relies on casework principles and methods, including the appropriate use of authority and the sense of responsibility for community safety. The parole agent must employ the basic objective of parole when making critical casework decisions involving the parolee's freedom versus community protection. Unfortunately, there are no easy or simple formulas to be followed in order to assure that the proper decision is made in each individual case. The parole agent, his supervisor, and the department administration share responsibility in striving to make the right decisions based on education, training, and experience coupled with sound social science research.

Having determined the objectives of probation and parole, or at least expressed some models of objectives employed by departments of probation and parole, we will now continue to review the strategies by which these objectives may be sought. Objectives are meaningless until employed at the operational level. To accomplish the functioning of an agency toward its objectives, a number of necessary criteria must exist: organizational management, structure, staffing, training, communication, resource development, funding, and adapting to change are each critical to this end.

Perspectives on Community-based Treatment

In respect to the value of community-based programs (probation and parole), the Corrections Task Force of the President's Commission of Law Enforcement and Administration of Justice noted:

> A key element . . . is to deal with problems in their social context, which means in the interaction of the offender and the community. It also means avoiding as much as possible the isolating and labeling effects of commitment to an institution. There is little doubt the goals of reintegration are furthered much more readily by working with an offender in the community than by incarceration.[18]

A 1964 study by the California Board of Corrections found that, since the circumstances leading to crime and delinquency exist in the community, their cure also should be sought at the local level; this method allows the offender to be close to his family and to the important social ties that bind him to conformity in the community, presuming this conformity is desirable and in the best interest of society. The field supervision component of correctional services appears to have the greatest potential for delivering services at the local level.[19]

The community-based probation supervision services have been fairly successful when success is measured by offenders who have not had their probation revoked. One analysis has shown that in 11 independent studies probation succeeded in from 60 to 90 percent of the cases it handled. Corroborating studies in Massachusetts and New York, as well as in foreign countries, provide results with a success rate of about 75 percent. In California, 11,638 adult probationers granted probation during the period 1956–1958 were followed for seven years. Of this group, 72 percent were successful.[20] These studies tend to validate the data put forth by the University of Southern California simulation study.

Offenders can be kept under probation supervision at much less cost than in institutions. A national survey indicates the average state spends $3,400 per year for institutional care of one offender, excluding building costs, while probation supervision costs only about one-tenth that amount.

It is generally accepted that, in terms of human values or in terms of dollars savings, community-based supervision and treatment of offenders, incorporating community resources, is the most effective means of dealing with juveniles and adult offenders who do not pose a serious threat or danger to public safety.

Certain ingredients are essential for the construction and operation of adequate field supervision services. These are:

1. Clear designation of goals and policies and adherence to such goals and policies.
2. Adequate manpower, both in the numbers of field supervision officers and in the appropriate training of such officers.
3. Cooperation of key social institutions such as the family and the school.

4. Employment opportunities for probationers and parolees; inherent in this ingredient is the necessity for the development of a program whereby an ex-offender's past criminal misconduct may not constitute a barrier to employment.
5. Ongoing research to determine effective classification procedures (diagnosis for differential treatment), and to determine differential treatment practices which can be applied successfully to various types of probationers and parolees.
6. Public education about the problem of reintegration of offenders into the community in order to elicit the community's cooperation in carrying out specific field supervision efforts.
7. Improved administrative structure and practices.
8. Improved staff development through intra- and extramural training.
9. Expanded and improved diagnostic and mental health services for probationers and parolees.
10. Improvements in the law, particularly in respect to current statutory restrictions upon the granting of probation.[21]

Field supervision throughout the country varies enormously—from large probation departments that employ thousands and experiment with highly sophisticated programs to one-officer departments that serve at the wishes of a judge who also uses the officer to run his campaign for reelection. Field supervision has nevertheless improved in the past decade to a great degree and this improvement has accounted for an increase in using community-based treatment. As this trend continues, commitments to institutions especially at the state level will decline. Care must be taken, however, not to expect too much from field supervision; there will always be a percentage of offenders who must be treated in a custodial setting. Also, individual officer case loads can easily spiral to a size that does not provide sufficient time to effect significant treatment. In some states the financial savings realized by the increased use of probation has been returned to the local field supervision agency in order to reduce case loads and improve the effectiveness of the service. This probation subsidy will be discussed more fully in subsequent paragraphs.

ORGANIZATIONAL STRUCTURE

Theorists designate the general organizational structure of correctional components as the bureaucratic model which tends to emphasize:

1. *A structured hierarchy*—a pyramidal organizational structure with each unit or individual supervised and controlled by a higher one to the top or organizational administrator.
2. *Task specialization*—a principle which calls for employees chosen on the basis of their merit and ability to perform certain specified tasks.
3. *Specialized field of competence*—the tasks performed are the sole responsibility of the specialist.
4. *Standards of conduct*—organizational life is predictable and the organization is thus stabilized because individuals comply with statements of policy and procedure.
5. *Records*—maximization of record keeping concerning administrative acts, decisions, policies and rules also contribute to the organizational stability.

The principles of any bureaucratic structure include a chain of command structured along a pyramidal model, a well-defined system of procedures and rules for dealing with many contingencies, division of labor along lines of specialization, selection, and promotion based on merit and performance. While these characteristics provide the correctional organization with an efficient, stable, predictable operation, they also present some serious weaknesses in a rapidly changing society.

Unfortunately today, when technological advances astound the imagination, most correctional organizations are bound by tradition or are in a state of anxious transition toward a behavioralistic approach to organizational structure. To maintain bureaucratic stability, the traditional organization is encumbered by an instinct for self-survival, rigidity, poor communications, lack of creativity, and a general divergence away from its basic objectives.

A bureaucracy is ill-adapted to rapid change and the increasing demands of the public. Such phenomena as increased drug abuse or racial strife can prove to be very disrupting to the tradition-bound justice organization. As corrctional organizations grow, control from centralized bodies becomes more difficult for the administrator. As tasks become more diverse and require more specialized skills, the manager's problems become more complex. The bureaucratic model, having grown out of the industrial revolution, may no longer be applicable in contemporary correctional organizations. The question is, Can the traditional structure remain in an era when not only the public but the professional in the organization is more socially conscious and concerned?

The future of correctional organizations was aptly stated by the Joint Commission on Correctional Manpower and Training:

The general direction which organizational change will take is toward less rigidly structured relationships both within the work unit and between superior and subordinate. It can be predicted that administrative and management practices will move toward a results orientation. This means that corrections will shift from a reliance on task and job descriptions; and bureaus, divisions, sections, and the like to an organizational form more related to the client and his progress toward some sort of goal.[22]

In California a corrections system task force recommended that all correctional organizations follow the general principle of flattening the structure. The task force meant that the bulk of correctional operations should be at the local community level. It was reported that many correctional workers felt they were forced to be people manipulators rather than treatment agents. It was found that there was a general appearance that the organization was run for the convenience of the staff rather than the need of the clients. The task force recommended a flattened organizational structure with increased bilateral communications and decision making at lower levels where accountability to the productiveness of decisions is relevant.[23]

In a noninstitutional correctional organization, the professional caseworker is the keystone of the organization; deputy probation officers and parole officers or agents represent the organization's ability to meet its objectives. All meaningful contact with probationers, parolees, and their families is made by these persons. Furthermore, these caseworkers' day-to-day relationships with outside groups such as courts, police, and other agencies, as well as schools, employers, and therapists, have a vital bearing on the success of the correctional agency.

Since the success of the department depends almost entirely on the ability of these staff members and their supervisors to perform their duties in a competent and professional manner, the organization of the department must take the form that will best support the work of the first-line officer. Line-management positions should be charged with responsibility for planning, supervising, and coordinating services in support of the first-line officers or agents. Any activity which does not further this function, either directly or indirectly, must be seriously questioned. Line managers should fulfill their functions in varying ways, including the provision of training and development; problem solving; case, program, and organizational planning; and evaluation. In larger organizations, staff and special support groups should exist only to support the casework function performed by the deputy probation officer or parole agent. Special support functions might include clerical work; training, research, and development; psychological and fiscal services.[24]

PROBATION ORGANIZATION

In the early years of probation, it was common to find that the appointment and supervision of probation officers and the administration of probation services was a court function. It was not uncommon that in a single city or county there were several probation departments and in other large areas and in many states there was a complete absence of probation services. In later years, there was a trend toward state-administered probation services.[25] The form of probation organizations today varies from state to state but there is a trend toward local services on a city or county basis, especially in larger communities. In some areas the courts administer probation services and in others local governing bodies such as county boards of supervisors control probation departments. In many states, such as California, the provision of adult and juvenile probation services are directed to the county by state law and are often combined into one department under one chief probation officer. The county probation officer serves at the pleasure of the board of supervisors, but also serves as the administrative arm of the juvenile, municipal, and superior courts of the county.

Probation departments that are controlled locally and have combined juvenile and adult services tend to have one of three typical organizational structures. The first applies to very small departments with less than ten officers. In these agencies there is little need for complex organizational structure as each officer must be able to perform a variety of tasks including investigation and supervision of both juveniles and adults. There may be a chief and one assistant who have responsibility for all administrative functions and some casework. A minimal number of support positions are found in the small agency usually consisting of clerical services. Small agencies are sometimes hampered by an inability to offer competitive salaries and benefits to attract the best qualified staff. As might be expected, the highest caliber of probation services are not found in the smaller departments as a rule.

The second model, generally with less than 100 officers, begins to appear more like the traditional bureaucratic structure. Typically there is an administrative executive at the head of the organization, the chief probation officer. Below him we find one or more assistant chiefs and functional division chiefs managing operational units along functional lines. In addition, the medium-sized agency will usually have more support services for administering the organization such as clerical, accounting, and file clerks, etc. There is usually a county juvenile hall which comes under the jurisdiction of the probation department in many areas. The director of the juvenile hall reports directly to the chief probation officer in this sized agency.

In probation departments with over 200 officers, more staff are assigned to specialized functions and to support services. Typically there are four divisions of responsibility: (1) field services, to conduct the initial investigation of referrals, provide various services to the courts, coordinate the placement of minors, and supervise juveniles and adults placed on probation, (2) institutional services, to administer the detention facilities and county-operated places of residential care and treatment, (3) administrative services, to conduct the business operations and coordinate work of centralized support and technical groups, and (4) medical division, to provide medical, dental, and psychiatric services that may be offered by the department.[26] In large organizations like these, there are several special assistants and others who do not fall neatly into an organizational pyramid. They perform such functions as providing employee services including personnel, safety, and employee development. Delinquency prevention officers are becoming more widely used in larger departments. These and several other staff-type functions are sometimes put into a separate division if the agency is large enough to support such a unit.

A typical organizational chart for a medium-to-large probation department is shown in Figure 22.

PROBATION FUNCTIONS

Since probation departments are usually organized along functional lines, a brief description of probation functions is in order at this point. As previously indicated, probation services can be easily divided into adult and juvenile services. Although the age of attaining adult status in the eyes of the law may vary from state to state, most jurisdictions now set the age of majority, for the purpose of justice administration, at 18 years. At the age of 18 or over, persons who commit crimes are dealt with through the municipal and superior courts. If detained, they will be held in city or county jails. Persons under 18 are brought before the juvenile court in which the guiding philosophy is to act in the minor's best interest and with the spirit of correction and not punishment. Persons under 18 years are normally detained in separate facilities called juvenile halls.

Adult Probation Services

Persons who have been arrested, charged, and subsequently found guilty by trial or plea, may be referred to the probation department for investigation prior to sentencing. At this point, proceedings are continued for two to four weeks to allow a probation officer to make a social investigation of the offender and prepare a report and recommendation for the judge. Deputy probation officers act as the information gathering arm of

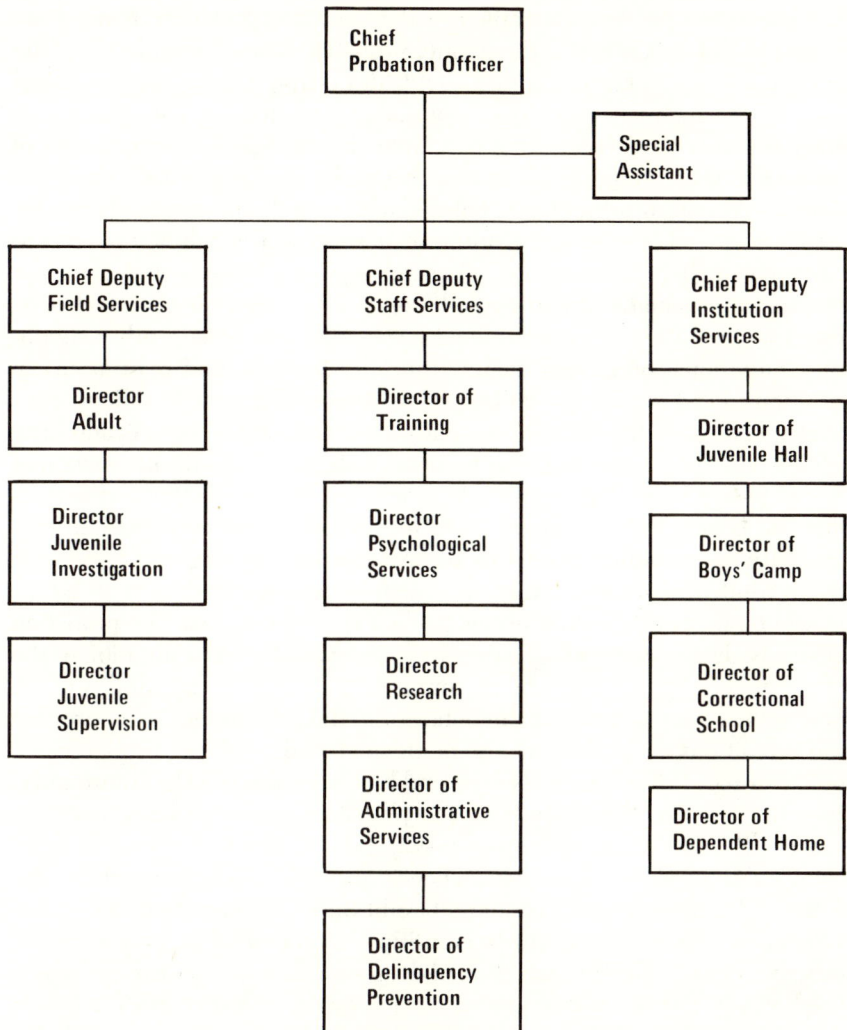

Figure 22.   *Typical Organization: Medium-to-Large Probation Department*

the court, often collecting and presenting the only total background information on the defendant that is available. These officers are not restricted by pre-empting legal advisements and are uninvolved in the role of prosecution or arrest, so they often uncover pertinent factors for presentation to the court that lend unbiased weight to both sides of the scale of justice.

This investigation presents a comprehensive composite of all available information—a description of the offense, the defendant's statements concerning the offense, his plans for the future, statements from references and interested parties, a complete listing and interpretation of any prior record or lack of same, and the deputy probation officer's evaluation of the person and of the facts obtained about him during the investigation and interviews which take place over a period of three weeks. The officer then ends the report with a recommendation for or against the granting of probation. If he recommends that probation be granted, a plan and conditions for probation are set forth, tailored to the needs of the defendant. This plan is designed to achieve the optimum in successful rehabilitation; conditions may include the necessity of abstaining from the use of alcohol, the seeking of psychiatric treatment, the testing of urinalysis to detect drug use, the preclusion of association with specified individuals; other significant conditions sometimes include time in jail, fines, and restitution. In addition to the regular presentence investigation, probation officers conduct special investigations for mentally disordered sex offenders and drug addicts. The adult investigation function makes up a significant portion of the work in a large department. As many as 4,000 to 5,000 investigations may be conducted per year. Each individual probation officer in this specialty may conduct from 4 to 10 investigations per week.

Adult probation services also include the supervision of all adults placed on probation by the municipal and superior courts. The probation officer is always aware of his two-part objective—the rehabilitation of the offender and the protection of the community. It is the responsibility of the probation officer to monitor the behavior of the probationer to assure that the conditions of probation are being met and that the probationer's behavior meets the standards expected by the courts and the community. In order to effect rehabilitation, the probation officer utilizes many resources in addition to his own counseling skills. Referral to employment counseling services, therapists, special problem agencies such as Alcoholics Anonymous and Consumer Credit Bureau (budget counseling) are typical of the resources utilized. Supervising officers may conduct urinalysis testing for the detection of drug and narcotic use; this process is used as a deterrent and an aid in rehabilitation rather than as a simple detection method for the purpose of further prosecution. Probation officers frequently counsel probationers serving time in jail preparatory to their release. The goal is to make the probationer's reintegration into a normal life as smooth as possible.

There are two unique specialties in adult probation supervision. The first is the probation supervision of fathers convicted of failing to provide for their minor children. These men are frequently irresponsible and have severe deficiency in their employability. Criminal proceedings in these cases occur only after all other means of inducement for collection of support monies have failed. Funds collected through enforced probation conditions have a significant impact on the welfare grants for dependent children of these fathers. Probation officers participate in the counseling and job placement of these offenders to help them meet their parental responsibility.

The other specialty, of recent origin, is supervising work furloughs from jail. This probation program is designed to give persons in jail the opportunity to continue working in order to support their families. In addition to its rehabilitative benefits, the program is financially self-supporting. Under work furlough the inmate is released from jail to work at his regular civilian job (or a job secured by the probation officer) at regular wages during the work day. He returns to custody at night or immediately after the completion of his work day. The probation officer's job is to make sure that the probationer does not absent himself from work. In cooperation with jail officials, the prisoner's return to jail is closely monitored. The inmate on work furlough saves the taxpayer a substantial part of the expense of his keep since a charge for his maintenance is made against his earnings. Amounts are also withheld from his paycheck for payment of fines, restitution, and other expressed purposes.[27]

A medium-to-large county probation department will supervise from 5,000 to 10,000 adult probationers at any given time. The average supervision case load per officer may vary a great deal from department to department and within the same department if specialized case loads are developed. Although studies indicate an optimum case load is from 40 to 60, in reality case loads extend to from 100 to 200 and in some agencies as many as 300 cases per officer. Larger case loads reduce effectiveness, minimize personalized service, and increase paper work to an unmanageable proportion of the officer's work time.

Juvenile Investigation Services

This function of probation involves direct service to the juvenile court in its disposition of juvenile offenders and minors whose welfare is endangered. Juvenile court cases usually fall into three distinct categories: (1) dependency proceedings, (2) proceedings that deal with a minor who is in danger of becoming delinquent, and (3) delinquency proceedings. The dependent child is one who is neglected, mistreated, or abandoned. A minor classified as being in danger of becoming a delinquent may be an habitual truant, a runaway, or incorrigible. Delinquent children are those who have violated a local, state, or federal law.

Juvenile intake probation services can be defined as those which intercede between an arrest or discovery of a situation and the formal judicial process. In most larger juvenile courts, probation staff screen all referrals initially, disposing of a majority of them informally without need for adjudication. Referrals to juvenile intake come from various sources such as police, schools, parents, and other agencies. By far the greatest number of referrals emanate from a police investigation and arrest; the police make such referrals either by written communication or by physically transporting the juvenile to the probation detention facility.

Once the referral is made, the probation officer must assess the nature of the offense or situation, the attitude and background of the juvenile and his parents, previous misbehavior and other factors. The officer then can make the decision whether or not to proceed with formal juvenile court action and what initial facts should be presented to the court or whether to release the minor. Most jurisdictions allow the intake officer to counsel and release or place the minor on informal probation if the situation merits such a disposition. The intake officer must also make determinations on the legal residence of the minor and whether the alleged offense or situation is admitted or denied. A jurisdiction of 1.5 million population might generate 25,000 referrals to juvenile intake each year. Of these 10,000 might be passed on for formal juvenile court action.

In recent years there has been a trend toward advisory proceedings in juvenile court with the involvement of attorneys; the testimony of witnesses and the presentation of evidence is very common. This trend and a number of landmark Supreme Court decisions have made the juvenile intake process more significant from a legal perspective. Intake officers now work closely with deputy district attorneys in making decisions on intake disposition. The absence of bail in the juvenile justice system makes necessary a separate proceeding to determine detention. The intake probation officer investigates these matters of detention and makes recommendations to the court.

Juvenile court proceedings are of three types: (1) a detention hearing to determine the need to detain prior to further hearing, (2) a jurisdictional hearing to determine the truth of the allegations, and (3) a dispositional hearing to decide on corrective measures.

Juvenile investigation services refer to social investigatory services subsequent to the decision for formal action and prior to the dispositional hearing. The report prepared by the juvenile investigation probation officer is the main tool for providing background information which the court uses in making its orders. This report is made on the basis of available records of police and probation departments, interviews with the minor, victim, parents, school officials, and others, and special diagnostic services of a psychologist when the need for this type of evaluation is indicated. With this information the probation officer's report reflects an analysis of the offense, the motivations, the minor's identification with delinquent peers, his attitudinal orientation, the parents' strengths and weaknesses, the family's general stability, the minor's physical environment, his school record, and his physical health. The officer relates these factors to alternative plans of treatment and explores the resources available to carry out the suggested treatment.

Probation supervision is recommended for most offenders, but commitments to correctional institutions are also made when appropriate. Occasionally, the officer recommends placement in a foster home or a psychiatrically oriented institution. If probation is recommended, the officer must also recommend the conditions which should be applied. These might include restitution, participation in a work program, special counseling, restriction of associates, or any other restrictions or requirements that will contribute to the minor's rehabilitation. Beyond the court's use of the probation report to impose a disposition, the report becomes the main source of information for making decisions throughout the history of the case. It is forwarded to any institution to which the minor may be committed; it is sent to other jurisdictions should the minor change his residence, and it becomes a permanent part of the probation file.

In addition to processing a minor who appears before the juvenile court, many special investigation services may be assigned to probation. Among these are:

1. Stepparent adoptions—investigation and recommendation for or against adoption of a stepchild.
2. Abandonment—a search for natural parents and investigation of foster parents with recommendation for or against a court declaration of abandonment and subsequent adoption.
3. Civil custody—the investigation of divorced or estranged parents to determine the advisability on which parent should be granted legal custody of the children.
4. Premarriage investigation—the determination of advisability for marriage between underage minors.
5. Inquiries from other jurisdictions about minors residing locally.
6. Financial investigation—the determination of parents' ability to reimburse for the care and keeping of their children who are placed in institutions and foster homes.

Juvenile Supervision Services

The essence of juvenile probation services is usually depicted in the supervision of minors on probation. The purpose of supervision is the successful treatment of juveniles while they are in the community; the result is behavior modification with minimal disruption of the juvenile's normal living environment. To achieve these ends, the supervision officer generally performs the following functions:

1. He visits regularly in the child's home and community to counsel not only with the child but with his parents, relatives, friends, and others involved with the juvenile's life.
2. He locates foster homes and, when appropriate, places minors in foster homes on a temporary basis.
3. He enlists the assistance of law enforcement agencies in locating and/or arresting probation violators.
4. He helps his charges who have physical or emotional problems, find professional assistance.
5. He effects placement of children in one of several department-run rehabilitation programs so that the individual problems of each child may be treated.

The supervising officer's first task is to diagnose the treatment needs of each child in a highly individualized manner. Studies have shown that clients with the most positive attitude about probation are those whose officers exhibit a personal concern for them. A system of classification of cases is needed in order to determine which cases can profit most by individualized attention because, with high case loads, the probation officer cannot provide this service to everyone.

The process of reintegrating the minor into his own community requires that the probation officer make full utilization of all available resources. To do this, he must develop the capability of obtaining services when they are needed. This action makes the officer a services coordinator. It is likely that the time expended in this role will have a greater return in meeting the needs of probationers than any other approach used.

In some probation departments all cases in which the child is placed in a foster home or privately run institution are assigned to officers specializing in these placement-type cases. They must work with the child, the foster parents, or institutional staff, as well as the natural parents. The goal in placement casework is to alleviate the conditions which made it necessary to remove the child from his parents' home.

Support Services

Support services in probation departments serve to make the previously described functions operate efficiently and effectively. As can be seen in Figure 22 these typically include training, psychological services, research, administrative (including fiscal and clerical), and delinquency prevention services.

The training function is of two basic types, entry-level orientation and in-service training. Since rapidly expanding probation departments cannot always recruit enough experienced staff to meet their needs, entry-level positions are frequently filled by qualified but inexperienced men and women. The goal of training these persons is to provide them with the basic knowledge and the skills of interviewing, investigating, and court report writing so that they can be assigned to full case load assignments as soon as possible. Experienced probation officers and managers also need developmental training to sharpen their skills, update their techniques, or prepare them for advancement. The number of staff assigned to the training function depends on the nature of the training program, but it is very important that persons assigned to training have a high level of skill and aptitude as well as an ability to instruct.

Psychological services provide the agency with a readily available in-house resource. Probation officers frequently need to consult with a psychologist in reference to special casework problems. Courts may order psychological evaluations which can be prepared by the staff. Since much of the probation function deals with personality deficiencies, psychologists serve as valuable trainers as well. If there are sufficient staff in this service, they may also provide direct treatment to carefully selected probationers.

Not many probation departments, far too few, have research staff on a full or even part-time basis. So many aspects of probation are subjective and intuitive, it is becoming increasingly vital that techniques, programs, and general methods be tested for validity. As agencies reach the large-department ctegory, statistical procedures and a systems approach become more complex and a research unit using the systems technique can prove most valuable. Practical evaluative research can also assist the administrator in seeking funds for experimental programs.

Administrative services are most vital and ineffective operation of this support service can easily cripple the entire organization. Control and accurate accounting of expenses and income, the preparation of the budget, and theprovision of a wide variety of clerical services are important to the success of all probation programs.

Delinquency prevention or community resource liaison is becoming an integral part of medium and large probation departments. As probation enlists community support, it extends its expertise about the causative factors of delinquency into the community and thus probation agencies are sought for knowledge in this field. Staff are assigned to serve as speakers representing the department, and as consultants to service organizations in their efforts to plan, organize, and coordinate programs for the prevention of crime and delinquency. Staff may also enlist, screen, and train volunteers who work directly with probation officers.

Institution Services

Institutions for juveniles at the local level are frequently under the administration of the chief probation officer. These institutions can be divided into three general types: the detention facility known widely as juvenile hall, the home for dependents, which is separate from the facility for delinquents, and the camps, ranches, and schools for treatment of delinquents. In some counties the juvenile hall facility is used as a short-term commitment facility as well as for detaining juveniles pending court appearance or placement. All treatment institutions have staff who counsel the juveniles and prepare them for release to their own community. Education, vocational training, recreation, and after-care supervision are common to probation-department-operated treatment institutions. These and other institutional programs are discussed fully in the following chapter.

PAROLE ORGANIZATION

Before discussing the organization of parole, remember the client for parole is a man, woman, boy, or girl who has been committed to a state-operated institution for an extended period of time. Most sentences are indeterminate or flexible in some way. Because of this, bodies known as parole boards are formed to make decisions on when to release and when to return a parolee to institutional care. Parole boards should be independent decision-making bodies that act in the interest of the general public. They have some judicial powers and responsibility. For this reason, they should neither be under the control of the correctional agency whose clients they evaluate nor should their policy be dictated by the agency. While parole boards should be independent, they should develop close, cooperative working relationships between the board and agency staff.

A California parole task force described the functions of a parole board.

> The duties of parole boards should be to establish policies and procedures regarding all aspects of the paroling function; to make all decisions regarding the granting, revoking, and terminating of parole (including the setting and modification of conditions of parole)....
>
> Both the number of boards and the number of members on each should be no larger than necessary to adequately perform their functions.
>
> Appointments should be through merit selection, and members should have an educational and experiential background which would enable them to understand the causes of illegal behavior and methods by which such behavior could be modified.[28]

The President's Commission on Law Enforcement and Administration of Justice asserted, "While there should always be a maximum time for confinement, the law should not establish mandatory minimum sentence."

They also noted that parolees should be permitted opportunity to provide for their own defense at revocation hearings.[29]

In adult parole matters, the paroling authority is generally not part of the same administration as the institution or parole organization. Juvenile parole boards tend to involve staff of training schools in making the decision to parole. The basic argument for placing release decisions in the hands of institutional staff is that they are most familiar with the offender and are responsible for developing programs for him, thus they are most sensitive to the optimum time for release. It must be remembered that institutional staff might place undue emphasis on the offender's institutional adjustment.

The president's commission found several methods to promote closer coordination between staffs of institutions and releasing authorities. One extreme is to integrate the releasing authority within a centralized correctional organization with a parole board appointed by that agency. In the youth authority structures of Illinois, Massachusetts, Ohio, Minnesota, and California, the power of release is given to a board that has general control over the entire correctional system, both in institutions and in the community treatment process. This type of structure has not been used in the adult arena. In juvenile parole, the main issue has been whether a central authority should control release or whether this decision should rest with the institutions. Most authorities feel that the final decision should be with a central correctional authority, but that detailed input from institutional staff is needed in this process.

Releasing authorities face one sort of question when they consider parole for an offender who will be supervised by a trained parole officer with a small case load working intensely with the offender and community agencies. The questions are very different when considering release to a parole officer who is so overburdened that he can give no more than token supervision. As in probation, the main themes of parole supervision are control and assistance. Ideally, parole programs are geared to the individual's special needs much the same as probation treatment. Research is needed to develop an effective classification system through which offenders can be described and types of treatment prescribed which would have the most potential for success.[30]

Juvenile Aftercare (Parole)

There are over 42,000 youth from 8 to 21 years in training schools throughout the country at any given time. Programs needed for their aftercare must be of a wide variety to meet the child's individual needs. Parole programs must be flexible and creative to meet these needs. Juveniles leave institutions more sophisticated or more dependent on the institution's structuring. They return to the home environment frequently no better than it was when they left. Aftercare is the last step of the correctional process and to achieve its objective it must be an integral part of the institutional program.

The president's commission made several recommendations relevant to juvenile parole:

1. Responsibility for aftercare should be vested in a state agency which is administratively responsible for institutional and related services for delinquent children.
2. The law under which a juvenile enters a state training school should provide that the agency granted legal custody should have the right to determine when he should leave the institution.
3. The law should provide that a juvenile remain in the school for an indefinite period of not more than three years and no specified minimum before being released on parole.
4. Maintain an adequate statistical recording system with uniform data on parole automatically reported to a central statistical agency.
5. The authority to approve placement should be vested in the parent state agency.
6. The standard caseload for parole officers should not exceed 50 with one pre-release investigation being considered equal to three cases under supervision.
7. Parole officers should be selected on the basis of merit. They should possess a bachelor's degree in one of the behavioral sciences, and salaries should be adequate, commensurate with the qualifications, high trust, and responsibility required. Staff development programs should be provided with staff assigned specifically to the training function.
8. Parole services need to be diversified to meet the varying needs of juveniles released from institutions. Such methods as group counseling, family counseling, job finding, and employment counseling are critical as is the use of foster homes, halfway houses, and group homes. Expanding use of paraprofessionals, new careerists, and indigenous community workers make parole aftercare for juveniles more likely to succeed.[31]

All of these desirable standards may exist only if sufficient funding is available. The states seem most likely to have the needed resources.

A recent effort to improve parole effectiveness is the Increased Parole Effectiveness Program (IPEP) begun in 1971 by the California Youth

Authority with the assistance of funding through the California Council on Criminal Justice. The specific objectives of IPEP were to reduce crimes committed by parolees and thereby free 400 institutional beds by April 1, 1973. To do this, plans were made to increase time for case services on a planned differential based on individual need, to improve treatment plan development, and to find new alternatives for wards in the community. The size of individual case loads varies from 20 to over 100 depending on the planned services for each case.[32]

This California agency also places emphasis on community-based services as in their special community parole center program. The goal of this effort is to increase parole effectiveness by initiating relationships with wards, family members, and relevant community resources on a continuous basis from the time the minor enters the institution until he returns to the community. Emphasis is placed on prerelease planning, limited case loads in economically depressed and socially disorganized urban areas. Thus, the parole centers become an integral part of the community serving not only parolees but their families, peers, and others who reside in the immediate community. Volunteers from the area are solicited to become actively involved in these community improvement projects. Techniques employed through the community centers include individual, group, and family counseling, psychiatric services, special school programs, marital counseling, increased surveillance, and out-of-home placement. These techniques are being studied to determine their effectiveness as are all special programs of the California Youth Authority.[33]

Administrative Structure in Parole Organizations

Unlike probation, parole organizations are not diversified functionally. A common model separates juvenile and adult into separate agencies each having two functional distinctions: institutions and parole services. Both usually have administrative services and provision for training, research, and a number of lesser functions. As previously discussed, the parole board is not found as part of the administration structure of the parole organization. Figures 23 and 24 depict typical organizations.

Communications in the Organization

As can be seen, there are excessively long lines of communication in parole organizations. This is also true in probation departments that are large and decentralized. These long lines of communications with their multiple layers of deputies, directors, region directors, district directors, and unit supervisors are dysfunctional and disruptive for an effective modern correctional organization. The top administrator tends to become encapsulated at the peak of the hierarchical structure. In

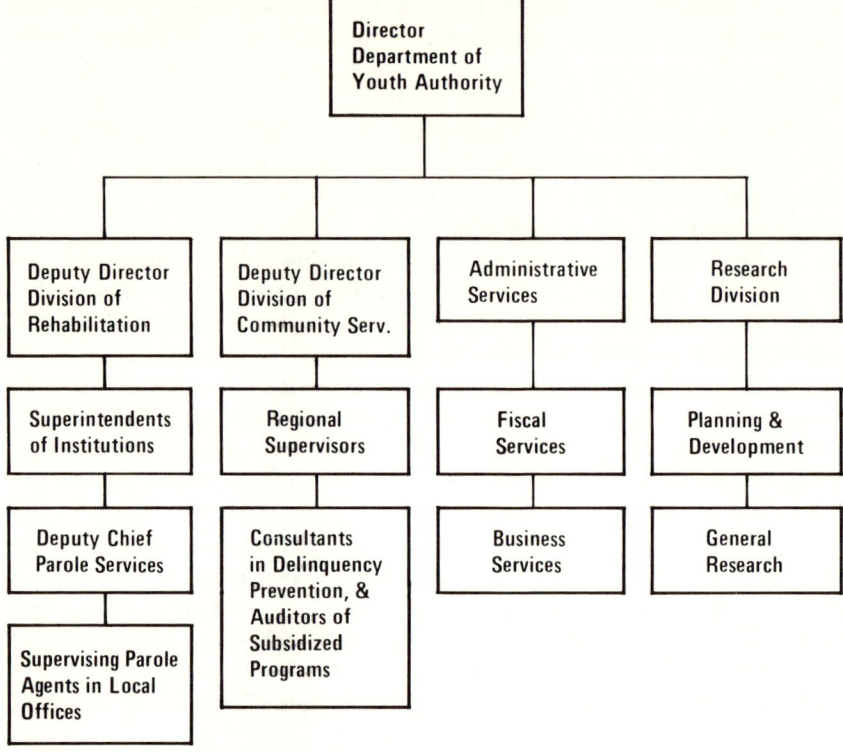

Figure 23.   *Typical Juvenile Parole Organization*

turn, this encapsulation affects his capacity to make decisions based on the best set of information. The fact that information does not flow smoothly and unrestrictedly is an inherent problem with all hierarchically arranged organizations. Therefore, it is important that new models be developed to handle the problem of communicative interference which occurs between levels of the organization. To reduce organizational "noise" between the working and the policy levels, the new structure should reduce the distance and provide for a greater degree of integration between them.[34]

For the past 30 years, there has been a trend toward centralization and integration of correctional services. The concept of a coordinated correctional system possessed of a variety of rehabilitative services and custodial facilities has been the principal cause for the proliferation of large hierarchical structures. As late as 1951, the noted correctional authority Richard McGee stated that the single department with a professional administrator was undoubtedly the most satisfactory administrative form developed at that time. In recent years, a rationale has emerged for

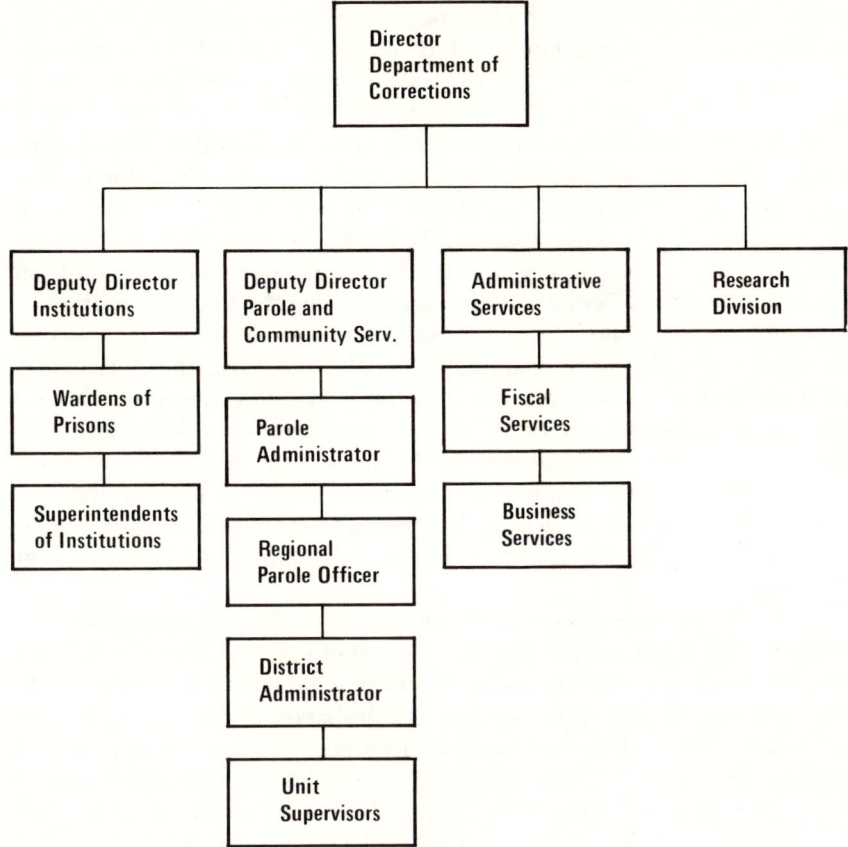

Figure 24. *Typical Adult Parole Organization*

purposeful decentralization of services, a development which will have a significant influence on organizational communications. This flattened structure will stimulate creativity and innovation but may pose new communication problems as the flow of information vertically upward and downward will become less efficient. Nevertheless, contemporary correctional authorities believe that the reintegration of offenders must take place in the community and that it cannot be achieved unless a broad spectrum of community interests is drawn into the task.[35]

In the 1971 study of California's correctional system, all task force reports indicated low worker morale; the staff rated the quality of communications as poor. Staff perceived a significant problem in the general organization of corrections. Many employees saw an inherent conflict in the organization; on the one hand, it is purportedly oriented to the client, his needs and problems; on the other hand, it exhibits an authoritarian administration and style which appear to be more concerned with the problems of the organization's maintenance and survival. These findings are related to the fact that large centralized organizations have poor communication lines among and between different levels of staff; in such organizations, communication tends to be organized so that factual information flows up and decisions and control directives flow down. The consequence is a curious inversion of the original problem for which decision making was necessary. Decisions on what to do about an offender's problem may be made at a level far above and removed from the actual problem. Removal of the decision from the locale of its origin is inevitably accompanied by an attendant loss of ability to review that decision and to be held accountable for the results of the decision. A flattened organizational structure develops lines of communication and encourages interaction among client, worker, and supervisor; as a result decision making takes place nearest to the point of relevance. Furthermore, feedback on the result of the decision is readily communicated with such an organizational structure. It is easier to exercise accountability for the productivity of decisions than to exercise control and authority over decisions.[36]

Faulty communication results in failure, on the part of some staff, to comprehend departmental policies. Line staff may feel they are not getting the word from the top and in return may be unable to communicate this deficiency to the administration. In probation departments, it is not unusual for line staff to be unable to accurately express the department philosophy on key issues. Typically, line staff and supervisors rate communications—downward and upward—lower than do administrators and department heads. Serious breaches of communication in hierarchical organizations can occur if chains of command are bypassed.

A study of communications in California probation departments found, as would be expected, that there was a better flow of information between the chief and his staff in the smaller departments. It was also found that, in some larger agencies, communication was facilitated because those in the lines of communication were able to talk and to listen effectively. It was also noted that the opportunity given some staff to share in decision making assisted the communication process. Unfortunately, the majority of line staff and most supervisors feel they have no voice or little say in the decision-making processes that shape the direction of their organizations.

CONTEMPORARY CORRECTIONS AND MANAGEMENT IN THE FUTURE

There has been very little systematic inquiry into correctional operations; the sparsity of study in correctional management is readily apparent to the student of correctional administration. There have, of course, been many innovative and creative efforts to improve the system and provide management programs geared to produce maximum service and direction to the correctional objective. Studies of probation appear to be centered in California. A number conducted since 1948 have disclosed weaknesses in probation. Ineffectiveness seems to be related to high work loads, inadequate standards of performance, and insufficient support services. In addition to numerous studies, the president's commission recognized the need for a strong and versatile mixture of corrective community services. The challenge of providing these services seems to center around the need for financial support of localized agencies and programs and the need to staff probation and parole services with people who are skilled enough to make rehabilitation of convicted offenders in the community a realistic prospect.

Probation Subsidy

In 1963, the California legislature financed a study of probation services to be made by the Board of Corrections. As a result of this study, the board took the position, in line with that of contemporary correctional theory, that the most effective services should be offered at the local level. The assumptions are: (1) Crime and delinquency are products of the community and, therefore, resolution of the problems must be in the community. (2) Local treatment has the advantage because the offender remains close to his family and social ties which bind him to conformity. (3) Local treatment is less expensive for the taxpayer since it permits the offender to maintain financial self-sufficiency for himself and his family.

As a result of these findings, the board recommended a state subvention system, a cost-sharing program to aid probation services which was subsequently made law and is known as Probation Subsidy. This is a system whereby the state pays participating counties for each juvenile or adult who is retained at the local level instead of being committed to state institutions. The system, operative in 1966, has had unprecedented success in reducing the necessity for commitment to state institutions by upgrading local rehabilitation services. Probation services of a high quality can be provided at one-sixth the expense of institutional treatment at the state level. Since 1966, the state has experienced an estimated savings of $126 million over and above the cost of subsidy for that period ($60 million to local probation departments). Available funds given to local agencies have been used to expand and enrich probation services.

In order for a participating county to receive subsidy funds, a degree of probation supervision substantially above the normal must be employed using new techniques instead of routine supervision. Standards have been set to operationalize the spirit of improved services:

>   1. *Personnel standards*—securing the best available manpower for program.

2. *Workload*—reduction to a case load substantially below a maximum of 50.
3. *Span of control*—no supervisor to manage a unit of more than six deputy probation officers.
4. *Classification*—diagnostic classification of cases and application of differential treatment based on individual need.
5. *Clerical assistance*—adequate clerical staff to free professionals from all nonprofessional responsibilities.
6. *Support services*—provision of improved training, psychological services, volunteer services and research.

Care must be taken in administering a probation subsidy system to preserve community protection and not to jeopardize the public safety for the sake of financial enrichment. The goal should be to improve services, but never at the cost of alienating the community at large. The selection of cases for special probation supervision and the decisions relevant to probation violation are critically important if such a program is to succeed.

It has been said, and I believe, that subsidy represents the most innovative approach to correctional field services ever conceived. Though the number of probationers being served is less than 12 percent of the total, there has been a strong impact upon all of probation. Subsidy has been a stimulus to professional creativity in methods of treating or supervising those who might otherwise be committed to institutions. As a result, all probation has developed an awareness that supervision of probationers can be more meaningful by using special strategies such as reduced case loads, more frequent contacts, more supportive treatment in the probationer's natural environment, and additional training of probation officers in case work methods, group therapy, and family counseling.[37]

Community-based Field Services

One of the directions recommended for corrections in the future by the President's Commission on Law Enforcement and Administration of Justice was that the system attempt to reintegrate offenders into the community. It is expected that the correctional function should be less punitive, less an instrument of revenge and retribution, and more a deterrent to criminal activity. The implications for the manager are significant. The managers of reintegrating programs need to cooperate with the varied centers of influence which control the resources needed by individual offenders.

The relevant influence centers are dispersed throughout the community in schools, neighborhood centers, employment services, and recreational facilities. The manager must understand the purposes and values of all community institutions, services, and agencies that influence his organization's effectiveness. Functioning of community-based corrections is dependent on the integration of probation and parole services into the fabric of local community life. Cooperation with law enforcement, bringing police and probation together at the line level in order to synthesize the justice system objective, is most likely to meet success in a community-based program. Closer working relationships with school officials and sharing of client goals for readjustment is also applicable to the community-based program.

Steps that can be taken to stimulate community-based treatment include: (1) operating decentralized neighborhood or storefront-type offices in a less formal or foreboding manner, (2) using indigenous workers who can contribute significantly in areas not open to the probation or parole officer, who is unfamiliar with lifestyles, local culture, and local concerns, (3) acquiring the support of local service organizations and agencies to enrich programs and stimulate local involvement, and (4) enlisting a wide range of local volunteer services to the community-based correctional program and its clients. In areas where such approaches have been tried, there has been significant success in stimulating local interest, involvement, and a sense of responsibility. Community-based programs fit the modern correctional system as is shown in figure 25.

Differential Treatment

The correctional system of the future will be more precise in gearing its treatment program to the individualized needs of the probationer or parolee. Diagnosis of offenders and prescription of treatment methods and techniques are becoming more refined and diligent research will enable the practitioner to predict treatment outcomes more reliably. Some offenders require rigorous supervision and control while others need little or no direction. Some will benefit from group therapy, while others require individual counseling or mainly assistance in finding work or completing their education. In order to utilize these diagnostic techniques, the manager of the future must be fully aware of his workers' skills, talents, preferences, and training. Assignment of cases will no longer be only on the basis of geography. Further, the manager and the administrator must have enough knowledge of the diagnostic and differential treatment system to apply it effectively. The administrator should enlist his research support services to test the validity of the diagnostic system employed and the effectiveness of the application of differential treatment.

Concern for Fairness

As in all of the justice system, Corrections too must be increasingly sensitive to due process, fairness, and objectivity in handling offenders.

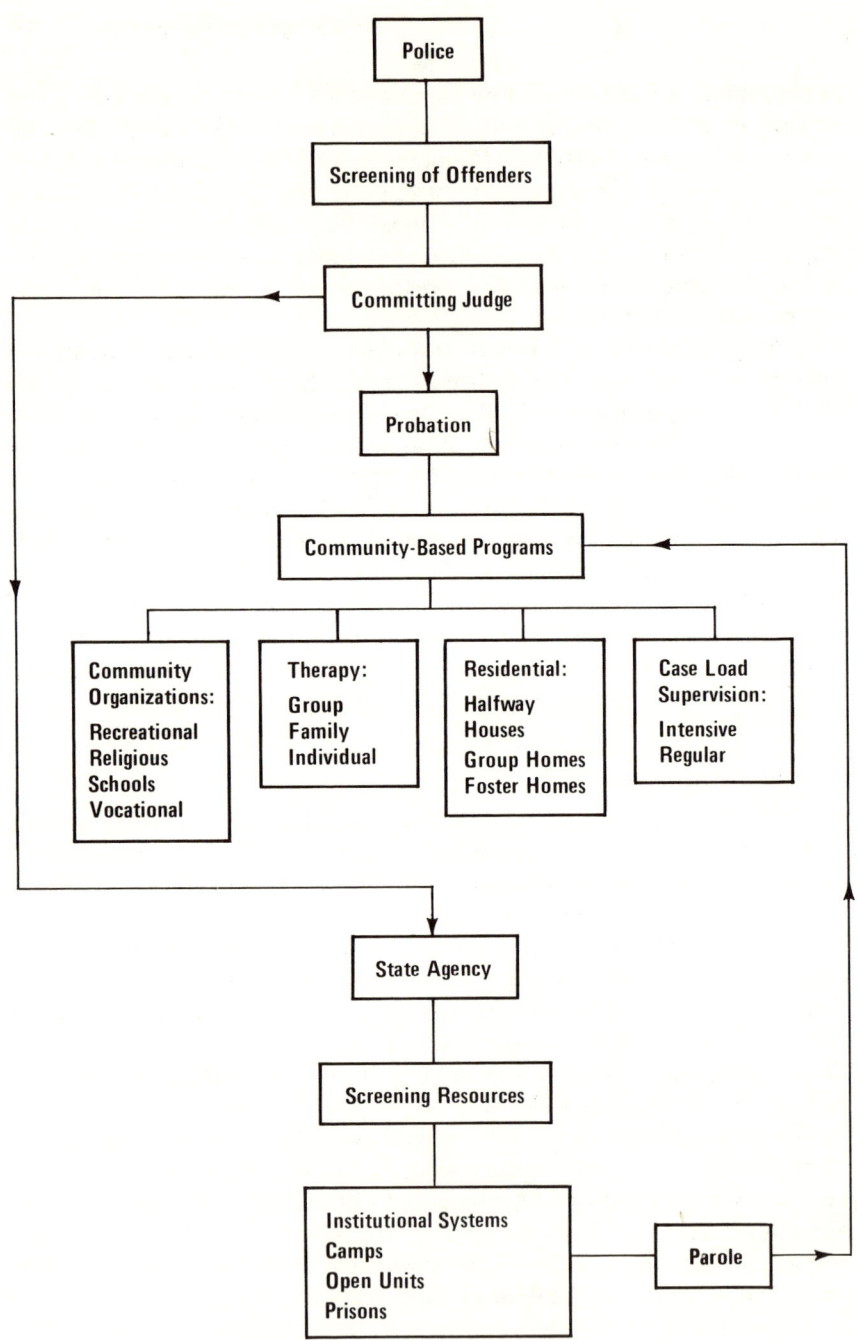

Figure 25.   Justice System Flow to Community-Based Services
Source: Task Force on Corrections, President's Commission on Law Enforcement and Administration of Justice, *Corrections Task Force Report*, p. 91.

The administrative prerogatives in making decisions that affect the offender are increasing; this increase necessitates a concern for fair administration of justice. Such matters as placement in various programs, discretionary options in handling probation and parole violations, and the variety of available resources accentuate the responsibility of the correctional manager. During the presentence phase of the corrections agency role, we see increasing use of legal counsel and a tendency toward more formalized advisory proceedings in the case of juvenile court, all of which is indicative of a trend toward fairness and due process for the accused and the convicted offender. As this trend continues, written records will be required to support key decisions such as parole revocation or change in custody status. There will be an increase in administrative review and offenders will have more access to relevant information and the right to challenge evidence which is antagonistic to his position. Corrections will have to protect its clients from arbitrariness and insensitivity in order to avoid legalistic interference of its processes. The Corrections manager of the future will have to be better informed and more secure about the substantive and procedural ingredients of due process.[38]

Bridging the Gap between Probation and Police

Suffice it to say that to discuss in detail the issue of communications, differing values, historical backgrounds, and organizational management styles between police and probation would go far beyond the scope of this text. Nevertheless, the administrator or manager in a correctional agency is immediately confronted with the issue of how he will work in concert with the police toward the common objective of the justice system. Law enforcement and corrections in the traditional sense are at once at odds with each other and striving toward a common goal. Simplistically, the policeman states that he works diligently, often at great risk, to apprehend offenders endangering the public safety and then the probation officer in conjunction with the courts "undo" the apprehension by releasing the offender back into the community without, in the eyes of the policeman, any apparent change in the offender or his danger to the community. On the other hand, the traditionalist probation officer may accuse the policeman of rousting his client, harassing him to a point of interference with the treatment program.

The question is, How shall these apparently diametrically opposed opinions of each other's role be brought together and be directed toward a common objective? Fortunately there is a trend toward enlightenment in law enforcement and probation. As training, education, and improved communications take place, each discipline is becoming more sophisticated and aware of its function as a part of a greater system. The emphasis on community-centered correctional programs can do much to bring these two disciplines together, at least to a point of understanding. In order to stimulate greater cohesiveness, many agencies now engage in mutual exchange training programs such as "ride alongs" and visits by police to correctional institutions. The decentralization of probation services and the assignment of a deputy probation officer as a liaison officer or directly to a duty station in the police facility are trends which ease differences and facilitate interagency communication. The interrelationship of roles must be clearly understood. Feedback to police on dispositional decisions with full explanation is necessary and joint decision making on specific cases is most desirable. Police participation on an active level in juvenile diversion programs is a particularly effective method of improving police-probation relations.

Meeting the Manpower Needs of Probation and Parole

Administration of the justice system faces innumerable challenges; present trends reflect an ever-increasing need for more and better-trained personnel. To meet these needs, one must consider several areas: (1) the manpower shortage for each position according to specified criteria, (2) the availability of qualified personnel, (3) the feasibility of expanding the pool of qualified personnel, (4) the strategies and costs of expanding educational programs in fields feeding the manpower pool, (5) strategies for improving agency efficiency in recruiting by promoting professionalism and increasing salaries, and (6) strategies to recruit from sources other than the standard manpower pool of behavioral science college graduates.[39]

In 1965, across the nation 21,000 full-time probation and parole officers were employed in 1,647 probation and parole agencies. Two-thirds of these agencies employed fewer than five officers and only 26 had over 100 officers. Of the 21,000 officers, 5,100 were administrators and supervisors and 450 were trainers representing 1 manager for every 4 officers and 1 trainer for every 60 officers on an average. By 1966, there were 28,780 officers employed, but probation and parole executives estimated a need for an additional 6,614 to meet the needs for effective agency operation.[40]

The president's commission noted the following regarding correctional manpower:

> Changing corrections into a system with significantly increased power to reduce recidivism and prevent recruitment into criminal careers will require above all else, a sufficient number of qualified staff to perform the many tasks to be done.[41]

RECRUITMENT. Difficulties in recruiting qualified probation and parole officers have traditionally been deterred by low salaries, long hours, and lack of ongoing contact with colleges and universities. Strides have been made in recent years, especially in California where salaries are now competitive with many other professional or semiprofessional positions in government. Entry level salaries surpass those of police and generally match most professions at the entry level ranging from $10,000 to $12,000 per year in larger departments. Other jurisdictions are not so fortunate. Many small agencies require graduate degrees and pay salaries not much above the poverty level. There is also evidence of growing ties with advanced education institutions, but primarily again in the larger agencies.

Civil service merit systems provide the guidelines for standards of recruiting, screening, and hiring in most jurisdictions. Too often, undue stress is placed on seniority rather than merit; entry requirements may be rigid and unrealistic; and obstacles to removal prevent the elimination of less-than-adequate staff. Although many devices have been developed to screen applicants, the best and most reliable is screening during a probationary period of on-the-job training. Entry requirements in the majority of agencies include the age of at least 21 years, a B.A. degree, sound body and stable personality, and the absence of a serious criminal record. Some agencies around the country do not require a degree and in others a masters of social work is necessary.

Contemporary corrections must look to additional manpower sources. For example, the use of subprofessionals can be increased by redesigning the role of the professional as a coordinator of services. New positions for subprofessionals, such as community workers, can be developed in order to expand the effectiveness of programs in the community. The use of volunteers can also ease manpower shortages. Experiments have also been done in using offenders and ex-offenders to supplement the caseworker's efforts.

Special attention should be given to the administrative and managerial manpower needs of corrections. Traditionally these persons have been recruited from the rank and file staff in both juvenile and adult fields. Very few have had special training or preparation for managerial responsibilities. The needs and trends discussed in this chapter put a premium on managerial skill. Most correctional managers need more training in public administration. They need to know and understand organizational development, the dynamics of administrative decision making, the principles of personnel management, and the use of data and research findings in order to effect organizational change.[42]

TRAINING. Training can be identified as a critical area of manpower needs. The development of individuals within an organization can combat bureaucratic inertia, stimulate creativity, and allow the organization to flex with change. Probation and parole have long been criticized for not having adequate training programs for their staff. A 1965 study found that more than half of all corrections agencies in the nation had no organized training program. In agencies that do have training programs, few have central training units. While full-time trainers are desirable, the primary responsibility for training rests on the immediate supervisor who must stimulate and oversee the process of converting information into skilled practice.

Staff development deficiencies were noted in a 1964 study of probation in California.

> Few departments have effective continuous staff development programs. As a result, working personnel cannot keep abreast of the latest developments in the field, even assuming they had time for staff development, which they do not. As a result, probation staff often have limited knowledge about treatment, their own capability for treatment, or the treatment resources of the community in which they work.
>
> Staff development programs for first line supervisors and middle management personnel are inadequate, and in most departments nonexistent. Most supervisors move into their positions from treatment assignments. They have no preparation for supervision and learn by doing. Often what they learn is wrong, and what they do fails to make the most effective use of available manpower. In turn, supervisors are promoted to middle management positions without training and without preparation. The mistakes that they were able to make as supervisors are now compounded by the new position of authority and responsibility they command."[43]

There is very little evidence to show that the observations of 1964 have changed; the system of not training managers tends to proliferate itself because the decision for or against investment in training programs lies with the very same managers who are victims of the system.

Larger departments are committed to providing staff with in-house, in-service training. This system is desirable because the agency is best able to identify its training needs. Smaller agencies need assistance from the states and from federal grants. All departments should make use of training resources available in the community. Staff should be encouraged to better themselves academically by the provision of tuition reimbursement, time off, and improved promotability.

Universities and colleges can help to plan in-service training programs. Faculty members can serve as trainers or consultants. The need for more collaboration among colleges, universities, and correctional agencies is widespread. Departments need to make use of external trainers for specialized programs, i.e., for training and managerial techniques, complex classification, treatment systems. This can be done by contractual agreement with other agencies that have this capability.

EVALUATION AND RESEARCH

No correctional manager has been able to avoid the simple question, How successful is your program? To answer it, one must first consider the nature of success in a discipline that is normative and ridden with different values. The most effective rehabilitative program may have only immediate results—the client may return to antisocial behavior as soon as he is free from the constraints of the system. To measure success by change that is lasting might be more reasonable, but change in behavior may not be indicative of attitudinal change which will have long-lasting effect in the client's lifestyle, sense of responsibility, and conformity to accepted moral values. For how long can or should the agency follow the probationer or parolee after the expiration of his term of supervision? There is a tendency to see the unsuccessful clients and forget the many successes. Nevertheless, the administrator must have an ability to evaluate the effect and worth of the programs of his agency. If community-based corrections are to be accepted by a doubting public, scientific evidence of effectiveness will be demanded with increasing frequency. Legislatures and the general public have a right to expect these tests of effectiveness for the sake of the public welfare and the large sums of money spent on correctional programs.

Sufficient resources must be allotted for research and evaluation to expand the measurement capabilities now available to most probation and parole agencies. Where necessary outside funding for consultation and direct research should be sought from various grant programs. The aid of universities and colleges for program research should be solicited whenever possible. Assistance from graduate schools is sometimes available at no cost. It is imperative that new approaches for reducing crime on the part of offenders on probation be tried, but new approaches, as well as current programs, need evaluation. This can occur only when managers first determine their objectives in measurable terms and then commit themselves to objective evaluation. There is danger that such efforts become busy work or a novelty, unless there is a serious commitment to follow through on the results of research by modifying or eliminating the ineffective programs.[44]

Today, research has gained a foothold in correctional operations, but it remains a strange and sometimes frightening spector to many administrators. They believe it is worthwhile to support research but many are unfamiliar with the methods and vocabulary of this new area. It is recognized that widespread research could cast doubt and uncertainty on existing rehabilitation practices on which extensive investments have been made at the persuasion of the administrator. Nevertheless, administrators of the future will have to adjust to the tentativeness of available knowledge. They will need to understand basic research methodology, its capabilities, and its limitations. They will need to understand the principles of sampling, control groups, degrees of significance, the hypothesis, and the determination of research activity targets.

In addition to understanding basic research methods, administrators will need a broad knowledge of theory in the social and behavioral sciences. They will need special knowledge about deviant behavior and its treatment and how their agency fits into the larger picture of the Criminal Justice System.[45]

SUMMARY

The origin and very principle of noninstitutional corrections stems from the most local level of citizen concern. As probation and parole agencies were developed, each took on its own structure and design to meet the needs of its community. All exist to accomplish a common objective, to rehabilitate offenders in the community without jeopardizing community safety. Probation and parole are subsystems of the Corrections or output phase of the justice system.

Rehabilitation is the process by which an offender is restored to a productive, law-abiding role in his community. It involves a modification of attitudes and behavior achieved through corrective treatment; it is based on enlightened diagnosis which reflects an understanding of the complex personal and social factors that cause criminal or delinquent behavior. It is vital to the success of these systems that caseworkers accurately assess an offender's amenability to treatment. In many cases, rehabilitative efforts can best be served by placing the offender in the community under the supervision and guidance of a trained probation officer or parole agent. Offenders who present a danger to their community or whose rehabilitation can only be served in a custodial setting should be incarcerated.

Probation is a conditional release of a convicted offender or juvenile who, after promising and indicating an ability to behave acceptably, is placed under the supervision of a probation officer. Probation offers a viable alternative to incarceration; jail is a costly, often less successful method of rehabilitation. Parole also offers a conditional release, but only after the benefits of institutional treatment have been exhausted. It is not expected that everyone placed on probation or parole will succeed. Agencies that employ highly trained staff and utilize the available resources should expect success in two-thirds of the cases placed on probation; at least one-half of the parolees should experience complete success. By success we refer to the absence of need for further incarceration.

Probation and parole deal with multifaceted social problems presented by their clients and a wide range of services are required to ameliorate these problems. These resources are found in the community and in other agencies and organizations, but many large departments are beginning to rely on their own resources more and more. The provision of internal resources such as psychological, diagnostic, prevention, employment-placement, and family-counseling services have made contemporary probation and parole organizations diverse and in some cases so cumbersome that the real objective of the agency becomes obscure. The correctional administrator must face this challenge and maintain a clear direction that can be seen and understood by the staff. Nevertheless, correctional agencies must be prepared to deal with the several causes of criminal and delinquent behavior such as personality deficiencies, breakdown of the family unit, poor housing, lack of education, unemployment, cultural and economic deprivation, and discrimination, to name a few.

The principal skill required for accomplishing these functions of probation and parole is the management of services. The knowledge and techniques employed are drawn from all the behavioral sciences. The one-to-one contact between probation officer and probationer can and should be augmented by the full utilization of resources to add manpower to the system and promote local involvement. To this end, probation departments should enlist the services of volunteers, community workers, paraprofessionals, and in some cases former clients. These manpower needs can best be met by instituting greater emphasis on community-based treatment services. Thus, the probation or parole officer becomes a coordinator of a broad range of services contributing to the corrections objective.

If probation and parole organizations are to function smoothly toward the system's objective, the pitfalls and shortcomings of bureaucratic organization need to be minimized. Careful articulation of objectives and goals, open communications, and meeting manpower needs are all needed to accomplish the purpose. The effective manager will recognize his function as one of goal setting, planning, organizing, staffing, monitoring, and evaluating. In order to make his work effective, he will guide the organization so that all services center on the client and contribute to the way in which the staff actually works with the client. Wise selection of qualified persons, appropriate staff development, and reasonable workloads are minimum requirements for the effective organization in corrections much the same as for any other organization.

A recognized deficiency in corrections has been its inability to accurately and scientifically measure the effect of its efforts. Today the need for evaluation and research is greater than ever before due to diversification, experimentation with new programs and techniques, mounting expenses, and public concern for safety and protection in the communities. Research should evaluate existing programs and identify deficiencies, assist in the development of new programs and measure their effectiveness, develop methods of predicting behavior more accurately, and apply modern technology to the collection of data, its storage, retrieval, and analysis. Coupled with an active research program should be a willingness to abandon any service or program shown to be ineffective and a willingness to try new methods and techniques.

Notes

1. Cresap, McCormick, and Paget, "Los Angeles County Probation Department Management Survey" (unpublished report, prepared by management consultants for the county of Los Angeles, California, April 1965), pp. ii–2.
2. The President's Commission on Law Enforcement and Administration of Justice, *Task Force Report: Corrections* (Washington, D. C.: U. S. Government Printing Office, 1967), p. 60.
3. Board of Corrections, Human Relations Agency, *Coordinated California Corrections: Field Services* (Sacramento, California, 1971), pp. 1–2.
4. Task Force on Probation and Parole, "Report to Attorney General Evelle J. Younger" (Sacramento, California: mimeographed, 1972), pp. 4–5.
5. Michigan Crime and Delinquency Council of the National Council on Crime and Delinquency, "The Saginaw Probation Demonstration Project" (unpublished report, National Council on Crime and Delinquency, New York, 1963).
6. Robert M. Carter, A. W. McEachern, and Herbert R. Sigurdson, "The Uncertain Future of Criminal Justice" (unpublished paper, University of Southern California, School of Public Administration, Los Angeles, California, 1970), p. 9.
7. Board of Corrections, Human Relations Agency, *Coordinated California Corrections: The System* (Sacramento, California, 1971), p. 17.
8. Harold M. F. Rush, *Behavioral Science, Concepts and Management Application* (New York: National Industrial Conference Board, Inc., 1969), pp. 26–30.
9. Carl Terwilliger and Stuart Adams, "Probation Department Management by Objectives," *Crime and Delinquency* 15: 228.
10. Ibid., p. 229.
11. Ibid., pp. 236–37.
12. Ibid., pp. 236–37.
13. Board of Corrections, *Field Services*, p. 7.
14. National Conference on Parole, *A Manual and Report, Parole in Principle and Practice* (New York: National Probation and Parole Association, 1957), pp. 182–83.
15. Board of Corrections, *Field Services*, p. 14.
16. California Welfare and Institutions Code, Article I, Chapter 937, Section 1700.
17. California Department of the Youth Authority, *Parole Manual* (Sacramento, California: revised 1966), Section 502.10.
18. Board of Corrections, *Field Services*, p. vi.
19. Ibid.
20. The President's Commission, *Task Force Report: Corrections*, p. 28.
21. Board of Corrections, *Field Services*, p. vi–vii.
22. Fels Marshall, "Specialized Manpower in a Changing Correctional Climate," *Perspectives in Correctional Manpower and Training*, Staff Report on Joint Commission on Correctional Manpower and Training (Lebanon, Penn.: Sowers Printing Co., 1970), p. 48.
23. Board of Corrections, *Coordinated California Corrections: The System*, pp. 37–38.
24. Cresap, McCormick, and Paget, "Los Angeles County Probation Department Management Survey," pp. vi, 1–2.
25. The American Correctional Association, *Manual of Correctional Standards* (New York: The American Correctional Association, 1959), pp. 511–512.

26. Cresap, McCormick, and Paget, "Los Angeles County Probation Department Management Survey," p. vi–3.
27. T. C. Esselstyn, George Kirkham, and Alvin Rudoff, "Evaluating Work Furlough," *Federal Probation* (March 1971), p. 34.
28. Board of Corrections, *Field Services*, p. 10.
29. The President's Commission, *Task Force Report: Corrections*, pp. 65–66.
30. Ibid., pp. 67–68.
31. Ibid., pp. 150–54.
32. Department of the Youth Authority, *A Guide to Treatment Programs* (Sacramento, California: 1972), p. 1.
33. Ibid., pp. 9–10.
34. Board of Corrections, *The System*, p. 37.
35. Elmer K. Nelson, Jr., and Catherine H. Lovell, *Developing Correctional Administrators, A Research Report of the Joint Commission on Correctional Manpower and Training* (Washington, D. C.: 1969), pp. 7–8.
36. Board of Corrections, *The System*, pp. 37–38.
37. Board of Corrections, *Field Services*, p. 67.
38. Nelson and Lovell, *Developing Correctional Administrators*, p. 14.
39. Herman Piven and Abraham Alcabes, *Probation/Parole: Pilot Study of Correctional Training and Manpower*, U. S. Department of Health, Education, and Welfare (Washington, D. C.: U. S. Printing Office, 1967), pp. 3–4.
40. Ibid., pp. 8–9.
41. The President's Commission, *Task Force Report: Corrections*, p. 93.
42. Ibid., p. 98.
43. Board of Corrections, *Field Service*, p. 90.
44. Ibid., p. 98.
45. Nelson and Lovell, *Developing Correctional Administrators*, p. 16.

Review Questions

1. Describe the role of probation in the criminal justice and juvenile justice systems.
2. What are the principal differences between probation and parole? What do they have in common?
3. Justify rehabilitation of offenders in the community under the supervision of a probation or parole officer.
4. What education, training, and skills are needed to equip the contemporary probation or parole officer to perform his function in the system?
5. Discuss the disadvantages of measuring an organization's success in quantitative terms.
6. Describe the potential difficulties in stating an objective for a probation department.
7. What are the advantages of community-based field supervision programs?
8. Name and describe the major functions of a probation department.
9. What factors contribute to poor communications in a probation or parole agency?
10. Discuss ways in which probation and police can work more cooperatively.
11. Describe the advantages of probation subsidy.
12. What is the significance of research for probation and parole administrators?

13 Administration of Correctional Institutions

> Putting a man behind bars is supposed to pay his debt to society. Once he has paid it, he is given a suit of clothes, maybe a $10 bill, and released. But he often is back—in a week, a month, a year—because he can't make it outside. *Today* there is more hope for rehabilitation. It starts from the moment the door clangs shut behind the convict—sometimes before.
>
> L. Dana Gatlin, "Crime Menace,"
> *The Christian Science Monitor*
> Second Section, May 31, 1966*

Changing times are having an impact upon the entire justice system. Social change is occurring in the community, and among other things, it has affected the composition of the inmate population in both juvenile and adult correctional institutions. It is evident that progressive measures are required to offset the increase in crime and delinquency. This chapter examines the administrative function and organizational structure of juvenile and adult institutional care. Although the spectrum is very broad between juvenile treatment, jails, and the state prison, the material is intended to describe the general scope of the correctional process and to highlight the role of management.

As a subsystem, correctional institutions generally occupy a position between probation and parole in the total Criminal Justice System. If

---

*Quoted with permission from The Christian Science Monitor © 1966 The Christian Science Publishing Society, All rights reserved.

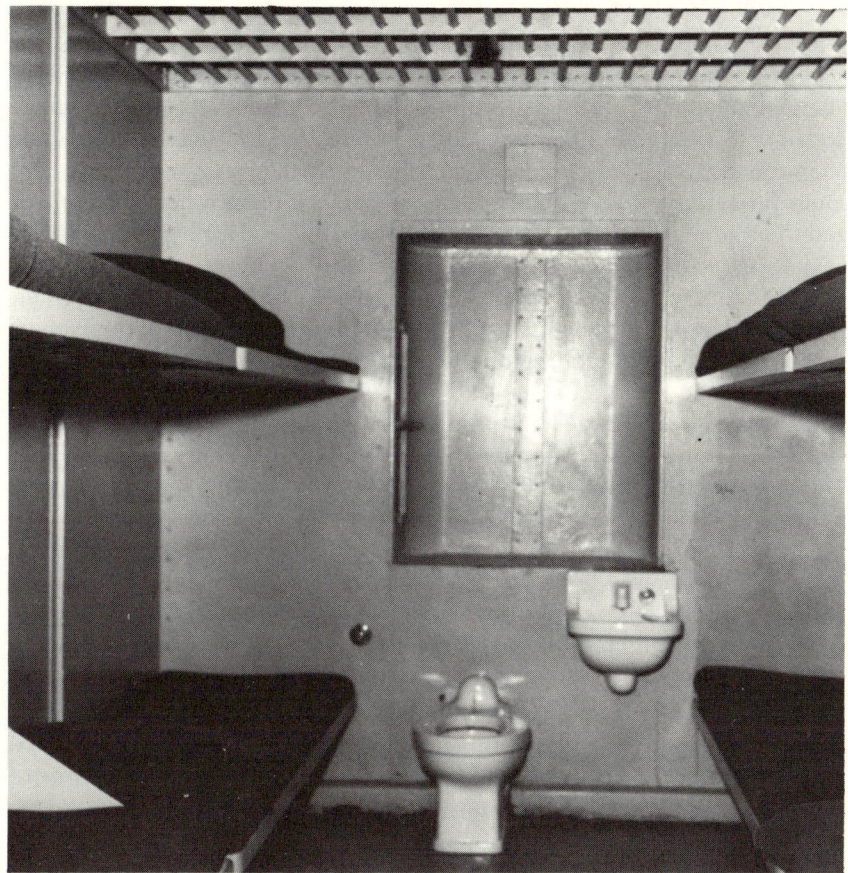

Jail
Courtesy: Sheriff's Department, Riverside County, California

institutional care is required, it should ideally occur in a continuous, coordinated, and integrated process with the other segments of the system.

The 33 principles of The American Correctional Association were revised and reaffirmed in 1960 at the association's nineteeth annual congress. Principle XI is hereby presented as a preface to the text:

> The organization and administration of correctional institutions and agencies is one of the more complex areas of public administration and deals with one of the most involved of social problems. It is essential that the administration of the correctional agencies meet the highest standards of public administration and that all employees be selected in accordance with the best available criteria and serve on the basis of merit and tenure system.[1]

EARLY DEVELOPMENT

The American correctional system is an extremely diverse amalgam of facilities, theories, techniques, and programs. It handles nearly 1.3 million offenders on an average day; its annual operating budget is over a billion dollars.[2] Correctional operations are administered for juvenile and adult offenders by federal, state, county, and municipal governments. Further, some jurisdictions have developed meaningful programs for the control and treatment of offenders while others have displayed little progress in the advancement of correctional reform.

Modern corrections display evidence of evolution in thought and practice, each attempting to cope with the difficult problems of punishing, deterring, and rehabilitating offenders.

Until the middle of the eighteenth century, European corrections was motivated principally by punishment and retribution. Most crimes were dealt with by corporal punishment, and a great many by execution. The death penalty was freely prescribed by statute as deterrence; transportation and banishment to other lands were also used for the purpose of isolating the offenders from society so that they could not commit other crimes, sometimes referred to as incapacitation. Notions of punishment still underlie much of corrections today.

In the late eighteenth and early nineteenth centuries, criminals were viewed as persons, not possessed by evil, but who had deliberately chosen to violate the law because it gave them pleasure or profit. Jeremy Bentham notably proposed that the rational response to crime was to penalize lawbreakers in the measure deemed necessary to offset the pleasures of illicit gain and to effect deterrence. Consequently, imprisonment was developed as the major correctional tool. It was intended to serve as a place for reflection in solitude, leading to repentance and redemption. During this era, confinement of long-term prisoners was not only a substitute for corporal and capital punishment, but it also served to overcome the evil conditions existing in the jails, where men, women, and children slept indiscriminately on the floors of filthy compartments, liquor was sold at the jail bar, and neglect and brutality were accepted as standard practice.

Penologists report that a Quaker organization under the leadership of Dr. Benjamin Rush established the first penitentiary (derived from the word *penitence*) in the world in 1790 at the Walnut Street Jail in Philadelphia. A block of cells was constructed in the jail to provide solitary confinement for hardened criminals in order to eliminate moral contamination from the other prisoners and to force them to meditate on the evil of their ways. A small exercise yard was attached to each cell. And although the penitentiary was merely a reconverted and enlarged jail, it did serve the entire Commonwealth of Pennsylvania and received prisoners from all over the state.[3] The facility attracted wide attention because the discipline was good, strict silence rules were enforced, the sexes were separated, liquor was not sold, and the treatment was humane. An excellent history of the beginnings and early years of American prisons, originally published in 1922 by the Prison Association of New York, was reprinted in 1967.[4]

In 1815, New York established a state prison at Auburn that imposed the silent system, with individual confinement at night and congregate work during the day. Harsh discipline with regimentation and strong security measures were introduced at the prison. The Walnut Street Jail and Auburn systems rivaled each other for many years. European penologists came to America to examine both institutions. The Europeans generally adopted the Pennsylvania system as being more humane and treatment-oriented. On the other hand, most American states adopted the Auburn plan as being more economical and feasible to administer. Vestiges of the Auburn plan are seen in many of the large penitentiaries and prisons in the United States today.[5]

Eventually, the Pennsylvania system, with its cellular isolation, was abandoned in the United States because it was so inconvenient to manage. On the other hand, the Auburn plan was less expensive to construct and permitted the development of congregate labor in the workshops and factories, which further reduced costs of prisoner maintenance. Prison labor was exploited beyond reason.

A punitive philosophy predominated the prison field during the mid-nineteenth century, marked by rigid repression, mass regimentation, silence rules, severe punishment, poor and insufficient food, confinement in small, unsanitary, poorly lighted cells, and lack of anything but the most rudimentary efforts at rehabilitation.[6]

Following the establishment of the prison system, reformers and administrators advocated measures to reduce the length of stay in prison. These measures included reduction of a sentence for good behavior, the indeterminate sentence, and parole. Probation, as a suspended sentence, was also established at about the same time, but principally in the lower courts.

The reformatory concept emerged about the time of the Civil War in an effort to separate young offenders from confirmed criminals. The reformatory at Elmira, New York, became a prototype for this new approach: it emphasized training and a merit system whereby inmates could earn a reduction in sentence through achievement. These principles have remained basic to correctional institutions to this day.

More recently, the idea of individualized treatment has become prevalent. This concept, which recognizes multiple causation of criminal as well as personal characteristics, has led correctional administrators to focus on rehabilitation and modify the institutional milieu. Parole, pre-release plans, and the utilization of community resources have each become part of contemporary treatment.

PURPOSE OF CORRECTIONAL INSTITUTIONS

When students in the field of corrections inquire about the purpose of our prisons and what we expect them to accomplish, they should recall that 95 percent or more of all inmates are released to society.

All components of criminal justice, including corrections, have one ultimate objective, to reduce crime and delinquency. The primary goal of juvenile and adult institutions is the protection of society. Their secondary goals include incapacitation, deterrence, rehabilitation, and reintegration. Simply stated, the basic goal of the correctional system is to provide public protection by aiding in the prevention of crime. The primary methods employed to achieve this objective include control of offenders, correction of offenders, coordination of programming with other public and private resources, research, evaluation, and community involvement.

Generally, the most promising method of reducing the incidence of crime is rehabilitation of the offender. Differential treatment with varying degrees and periods of incarceration must be recognized as the most appropriate way to handle offenders. Excessively harsh penalties may simply backfire by fostering hostility and despair.

It must be noted that correctional institutions have often been built without much prior consideration of the programs they were to house. Authorities have developed the following series of purposes for correctional institutions:

1. To seek to limit confinement to persons actually requiring it, for only as long as they require it, and under conditions that are lawful and humane.
2. To afford both the community and the offender temporary and partial respite from each other in order to facilitate resolution of the crisis which led to commitment.
3. To make the confinement experience constructive and relevant to the ultimate goal of reintegrating the offender into the community and of preventing recidivism.
4. To educate the community and its agencies about the problems of reintegrating offenders in order to elicit their collaboration in carrying out specific rehabilitative efforts and in improving conditions which militate against such efforts.
5. To seek continual improvement in the system's capacity to achieve these ends.[7]

Juvenile Detention and Treatment Institutions

Unlike statutes pertaining to adults, juvenile court law permits a child to be taken into custody for his protection from situations that endanger his health and welfare. This purpose can be served by two distinct types of temporary care:

1. *Detention*—Temporary care of a child who has committed a delinquent act and requires secure custody in a physically restricting facility pending court disposition or the child's return to another jurisdictional agency.
2. *Shelter*—Temporary care in a physically unrestricting facility pending the child's return to his own home or placement for longer-term care. Shelter care is generally used for dependent and neglected children.

Juvenile detention, properly used, serves the juvenile court exclusively. Shelter care is a broader child-welfare service not only for the court but also for child and family agencies, both public and private.

The growth of correctional services, particularly in California, resulted in the development of various types of correctional institutions. Most of the changes have occurred in institutional programs for juveniles which are generally oriented toward providing care, custody, and control of minors under 18 years of age. The strategies of juvenile correction should include special emphasis on environmental modification and changes, peer group influence, family and community involvement, and individual casework.

Influenced by the high volume of juveniles entering the juvenile justice process and the complexity of their needs, various institutional programs have been devised. In California, youths requiring detention are placed in juvenile hall to await disposition of their cases in juvenile court. Dependent and neglected children are given protective services in a segregated unit or facility. County juvenile institutions such as camps, ranches, and schools provide treatment and serve as a backup to the efforts of juvenile court and probation. A juvenile institution is actually a residential facility, often called a training school, for treatment of delinquent youth. A series of state institutions such as the California Youth Authority serves as further backup for those youths whose needs cannot be met at the county level.

A California correctional system study reported:

> The primary goal of juvenile institutions, as well as that of all corrections, should be the *protection of society*, i.e. minimizing the probability of recidivism. Ultimately all correctional programs must be evaluated in terms of their effectiveness in reducing the recidivism of offenders. Their secondary goals, and strategies for attaining goals, should be generally the same as for the rest of corrections, but with specific emphasis based on the nature of institutions and the specific populations juvenile institutions serve. The

secondary goals include *incapacitation, deterrence,* and, particularly, *rehabilitation* and *reintegration.* It is the position of the Juvenile Institution Task Force that rehabilitation and reintegration normally are compatible with the protection of society. That is, society is normally best protected by the effective rehabilitation and reintegration of a youth in society.[8]

The American Correctional Association has outlined the following suggested standards for the operation of an effective institution program for youth offenders.

1. Program for the youthful offender should be flexible.
2. Community rather than institution-based programs should be emphasized.
3. Effective liaison must be maintained with agencies providing related services.
4. Program concepts and requirements must be established.
5. The type, size, and number of institutions must be planned carefully.
6. The institution program should be varied and dynamic.
7. Qualified personnel in adequate number must be provided.
8. An effective system of communications must be established within the institution.
9. A program of records, research, and statistics should be conducted.
10. Effective relationships with the community must be maintained.[9]

Correctional practitioners believe that juvenile training schools should provide reeducative treatment geared to the development of a healthy, happy personality and a successful adjustment to society.

The general public expects the training school to control the child for the period of commitment without a recurrence of delinquent conduct. The school is expected to provide some type of training that will enable the youth to become a contributing member of society.

The value of the institution to the delinquent is that it offers a setting which combines controls, protection, and a totality of treatment which he has not experienced in the community.

A few administrators see the training school primarily as a custodial agency with treatment as a secondary function. A few regard its basic function as educational and see correction as an educative process. But leading practitioners in the field believe that the main purpose of institutional placement is treatment and that training schools must be essentially treatment institutions with an integrated professional service, i.e., education casework, psychology, medicine, and vocational rehabilitation and religion.

The most widely accepted goal of institutions for delinquents is to train, re-educate and rehabilitate the children under care and that the modern method of accomplishing this is the individualized application of an integrated treatment program.

Jails—Community Detention

The jail is the oldest of all institutions for the detention of law violators. Its original function was for pretrial detention of persons charged with crime. Later, it came into use for the service of short sentences. Today, most jails serve a dual role as places of confinement for persons awaiting court action and for convicted offenders serving short sentences.

The American jail system falls into three general classes:

1. *The lockup.* This is a security facility, usually operated by the police department, for temporary detention of persons held for investigation or awaiting a preliminary hearing. Usually the period of detention does not exceed 48 hours; persons who must be held longer are transferred to the city or county jail.
2. *The jail.* In most instances this institution houses both offenders awaiting court action and those serving short sentences, usually up to one year.
3. *The workhouse, jail farm, or camp.* These institutions house minimum custody offenders serving short sentences, usually not more than one year but in a few jurisdictions extending up to several years. Like the jail, they may be operated by the county sheriff or by a governing board of the city or county.[10]

The county jail has become a point of concern among jail administrators, students, and those interested in the problems of criminal justice and corrections. Until recently, the number of jails in the United States was unknown. However, in January 1971, the Law Enforcement Assistance Administration published the results of the first national jail census: there were 4,037 jails in the United States.[11] The survey also found that 52 percent of all persons in jail had not been convicted of any crime, and of this group, four out of five were eligible for bail, but could not raise the funds.

County jails in California are best thought of as being two facilities:

1. A detention unit which houses prisoners who are somewhere in the process of adjudication from arrest to the finding of guilt or innocence.

2. A correctional facility which houses only those who have been found guilty and sentenced to a term in jail.[12]

When viewed in terms of operational efficiency, county jails process hundreds of thousands of persons each year with relative speed and efficiency.

The county jail is presently in a period of transition from the relatively simple task of keeping people to the more complex task of changing people. The jail philosophy is also undergoing a period of transition.

A stated goal and philosophy provide a framework for action and create a common direction. By law, the sheriff is mandated to operate a jail facility and receive prisoners. Section 4015 of the California Penal Code states:

> The sheriff must receive all persons committed to jail by competent authority. The board of supervisors shall provide the sheriff with necessary food, clothing, and bedding, for such prisoners, which shall be of a quality and quantity at least equal to the minimum standards and requirements prescribed by the Board of Corrections for the feeding, clothing, and care of prisoners in all county, city, and other local jails and detention facilities.

Aerial view of Wayside Honor Rancho
Los Angeles County Sheriff's Department official photograph

There are other laws directing the sheriff to maintain humane conditions in the jail and to assure prisoner safety. In addition, there are permissive statutes which give the counties latitude to operate correctional-type programs of their choosing, such as work and educational furlough (1208 P.C.) and vocational and academic instruction (4018.5 P.C.). In short, the sheriff is *not required* to do any more than house inmates. But, if he has the support of the board of supervisors, he *may* provide correctional programs. In fact, without that support there is very little that he can do beyond "warehousing" the persons serving jail sentences.[13]

It may be assumed that some good is provided for the community by housing inmates in the county jail or that some good is provided for the inmates by permitting them to work or to attend school. However, while these functions are required or permitted in the law, nowhere does the law clearly delineate correctional objectives for jails.

Prison—Correctional Institution

The last recourse of any correctional system, other than the death penalty, is imprisonment.

> Institutions for felony offenders are residential facilities. They are generally called reformatories, prisons, penitentiaries, or correctional institutions. They exist for the confinement and treatment of adult offenders under felony sentences.[14]

While the word *prison* designates institutions for convicted offenders above the level of the county jail, it is no longer an accurate term. State institutions for persons convicted of felonies and serving sentences, generally of more than a year, are of various types today: prisons (called penitentiaries in some states), reformatories for men and women, road and forestry camps, farms, and special institutions for insane and mentally defective criminals. The word "correctional" rather than penal institution has become more acceptable; however, the term "prison" is still used for convenience.

The primary mission of corrections, which it shares with law enforcement, is to reduce crime. The specific goals of prisons are incapacitation, deterrence, and rehabilitation. Prisons contribute to crime reduction if the confinement they impose incapacitates persons who otherwise would commit serious crime and if rehabilitation occurs during confinement. Deterrence is achieved more by certainty of punishment by confinement than by severity of penalties beyond a minimum severity already exceeded in most prison cases through concern with incapacitation. Therefore, reduction of crime by deterrence depends more on the efficiency of the police and the courts than on prisons. Incapacitation is more readily achieved than rehabilitation, and the necessity for incapacitation is determined by the extent of failure in rehabilitation. Thus, the primary problem confronting prison management is increasing rehabilitation.[15]

INSTITUTIONAL ORGANIZATION AND MANAGEMENT

The central administration of correctional systems in the United States reflects a wide diversity of organizational patterns from state to state. This diversity of form may be partially explained by difference in size.

The two most popular forms of state administration of correctional systems are for corrections to be (1) a division of a larger department, and (2) a separate department. Both concepts seem to give corrections enough separate identity to allow centralization of budgetary matters and other administrative tasks and simultaneously provide a sufficient framework for professional career service and staff development.

Divisions of corrections may be within larger departments of justice, institutions, or welfare. Corrections is a division of the Department of Justice in Pennsylvania and in the U. S. Bureau of Prisons. It is a division of a Department of Institutions in Vermont, Tennessee, and Washington. It is a division of the Department of Public Welfare or Social Welfare in Virginia, Kentucky, Rhode Island, and Wisconsin. Ohio has its Division of Corrections in the Department of Corrections and Mental Hygiene. Florida has its Division of Corrections in the Department of Health and Rehabilitative Services.

There are separate departments of corrections in Alabama, Georgia, Arkansas, California, Massachusetts, Indiana, Iowa, District of Columbia, and Texas.[16]

Many of the other forms of organization use various kinds of boards of lay persons. There are (1) boards of trustees, (2) ex-officio boards, (3) centralized prison boards, and (4) boards of control. They all have the weaknesses of board administration. Decisions are delayed because of infrequent board meetings, and when decisions are reached, they are often the result of compromise.

Correctional Institutions

The separate department of corrections is considered to be the best administrative setup by most in the field. The advantages of centralization are that it provides better administration in terms of purchasing, accounting, personnel policies, classification, statistical research and identification facilities, and training facilities. Interdepartmental contracts are easier to negotiate and implement in a separate department.[17]

The *Manual of Correctional Standards* lists the following elements of a good state system for the administration of correctional functions:

1. *The Separate Department.* The correctional system should be administered by a separate state department.
2. *The Name.* It should have a dignified and appropriate title, such as "Department of Corrections."
3. *The Single Administrator.* The department should have a single administrative head.
4. *The Parole Board.* Any quasi-judicial functions such as the granting of paroles and the fixing of terms in jurisdictions having an indeterminate law should be vested in a board of not less than three persons.
5. *Laws, Rules, and Regulations.* Orderly and consistent administration should be insured by a body of written laws, rules, regulations, statements of policy, and manuals of procedure.
6. *Administrative Planning and Research.* Orderly growth and dynamic development of the organization should be provided for by means of a staff unit concerned with long-term planning and research.
7. *Financial Support.* The correctional functions must receive an adequate share of the state's revenues.
8. *Legislative Relationships.* The department must maintain a close and effective relationship with the legislature.
9. *Political Interference.* Precautions should be taken to guard against improper political interference.
10. *Personnel Policy.* The personnel policy must have as its objective the development of a professionalized career service.
11. *The Internal Organization.* The internal organization of the department should be developed on a basis of the generally understood principles of "line and staff" organization. The central office staff should be adequate to provide competent supervision over all functions.
12. *Community Resources.* The state department and each of its local offices and institutions should make a continuous effort to make use of all possible community resources in the improvement and enrichment of the correctional program.
13. *Relations to Local Units of Government.* The state department should be given regulatory or administrative responsibility over local correctional services to as great an extent as proves practicable in view of our traditional emphasis on local autonomy.

14. *Leadership Responsibilities.* The director of corrections and other policy-making officials of the department should assume a position of statewide professional leadership in correctional matters and not limit themselves merely to carrying out the necessary administrative functions provided by law.[18]

Juvenile Institutions

Juvenile institutions with their historic emphasis on the protection and treatment of children have tended to be less autonomous than adult penal institutions. The link between them and welfare services, based on protection of the child, has tended to draw juvenile institutions into centralized administrative services.

In 46 states, juvenile institutions are administered by a central agency. In 21 of these states, the central agency is a correctional institution. The next most common pattern, used in 14 states, places juvenile institutions under the welfare department.

Nineteen of the 58 counties in California operate their own juvenile treatment facilities under the supervision of the county probation officer. As of February 1971, there were 68 county juvenile facilities in the state. All of these were being subsidized by the state under legislation passed in 1965. These institutions included 47 facilities for boys (mainly camps and ranches), 18 for girls (primarily short-term treatment units and day centers), and three coeducational facilities.[19]

Jails

The organization and management of jails is almost exclusively a local concern. A national survey estimated the number and distribution of jail facilities by level of government, as shown in Table 1.

Table 1. – *Estimated Distribution of Jails and Other Local Correctional Institutions by Level of Government, 1965*

	NUMBER	%
City Institutions	762	22.0
County Institutions	2,547	73.3
City-County Institutions	149	4.3
Other	15	.4
TOTAL	3,473	100.0

Source: National Survey of Corrections from The President's Commission on Law Enforcement and the Administration of Justice, *Task Force Report: Corrections* (Washington, D. C.: U. S. Government Printing Office) 1967, p. 79.

Although the distribution shows that jails are overwhelmingly a county or city-county function, there are some exceptions. In Alaska, jails are administered by the Youth and Adult Authority; in Connecticut, by the State Jail Administration; and in Rhode Island, by the Department of Social Welfare.

Most jails continue to be operated by law enforcement officials. The basic police mission of apprehending offenders usually leaves little time, commitment, or expertise for the development of rehabilitative programs, although notable exceptions demonstrate that jails can indeed be settings for correctional treatment. Many law enforcement officials, particularly those administering large and professionalized forces, have advocated transfer of jails to correctional control.

The most compelling reason for making this change is the opportunity it offers to integrate the jails with the total corrections network, to upgrade them, and to use them in close coordination with both institutional and community-based correctional services. As long as jails are operated by law enforcement officials, no matter how enlightened, it will be more difficult to transform them into correctional centers. As a major step toward reform, jails should be placed under the control of correctional authorities who are able to develop the needed program services. The trend should be away from the isolated jail and toward an integrated but diversified system of correctional facilities.[20]

There are basically two types of administrative organizations for county jail and detention facilities in the state of California. In the first type, correctional facilities such as jails and camps fall directly under the supervision and control of the sheriff. This is by far the most common pattern, followed by 52 counties throughout the state. In the second pattern, which is found in the remaining six counties, minimum security facilities for prisoners are administered by agencies other than the sheriff's office. However, in all 58 counties, maximum security facilities fall under the direct authority of the sheriff's office. While there are historical reasons for the sheriff administering the county jails and camps, in recent years there has been growing concern about the wisdom of placing correctional services uder the direct authority of an agency whose aim is law enforcement.

In 1969, there were 203 city-operated jails and two city-operated camps in California.[21] In addition, the counties of the state operated 58 main county jails, 46 adult county camps and farms, and 62 other facilities including branch jails, work furlough facilities, medical detention wards, and substation jails.[22] All of these facilities are operated by city and county law enforcement officials.

ADMINISTRATIVE ORGANIZATIONAL STRUCTURE

The larger the institution, the greater the need for an organizational structure which sets forth a definite chain of command, division of responsibility, and channels of communication.

In general terms, it may be said that the best organizational structure for an institution is one which best serves to carry out all of its objectives. Before an effective organizational structure can be developed, the objectives of the institutions must be established: then and only then can a workable plan be designed. This structure then will serve to define lines of authority, establish lines of communication, and solve the problems of relationships among the personnel covered by its organization chart.

The following goals should be considered in building the organizational structure:

1. The maximum program efficiency and effectiveness possible with the personnel available.
2. The recruitment of qualified personnel and to provide for their development and improvement.
3. An institutional climate characterized by professional competence, objectiveness, industriousness, good order, high morale, and with a minimum of emotional tensions.
4. An organizational structure capable of meeting emergency situations with the least possible difficulty and damage to the constructive phases of the program.
5. A system to facilitate the lines of communication for orders and information, not only vertically but horizontally to all levels and units of the organization. The importance of maintaining communications within the organization extends to the inmates as well as to personnel. The procedures within the organizational structure should provide for a means of keeping open all channels of communication from the management through the personnel to the inmates and vice versa.
6. Create and maintain a continuous program impact upon the inmates designed to redirect their energies, ambitions, and attitudes toward acceptable standards of social living, and at the same time insure a safe degree of institutional security and public protection.
7. Develop an organization that works harmoniously with all disciplines bringing a balanced impact on the inmate.[23]

I. Correctional Institution

A good organizational structure for an institution for adult prisoners will include the following features:

A. THE SINGLE ADMINISTRATOR. Separate departments with single administrators are on the increase. The superintendent or warden should be appointed by the head of the state correctional department. Consistent with the laws and departmental policies and procedures, the institution head should have full authority and responsibility for the management of personnel, inmate, and programs of the institution.

The tone and atmosphere of an institution are a reflection of the personality and leadership of its chief executive officer. Institutions have tended to grow larger and to become more complex as to goals and programs. Accordingly the warden's role must differ from his traditional role in managing a small prison emphasizing custodial control with a minimum of treatment. The changes are illustrated in terms of five important responsibilities involving subordinate personnel and human relations in general.

1. *Decision making.* The warden limits his role to considering policy matters and major problems; he delegates with confidence, to well-trained subordinate executives, sufficient authority for management of daily operations in line with established policy.
2. *Control of prison operations and activities.* The warden depends on sound organizational planning, written manuals of policies and procedures, trained personnel, and an effective communications system.
3. *Public relations.* He provides leadership to involve all personnel in a program aimed at gaining public understanding, good will, and community acceptance.
4. *Personnel program.* He provides leadership and assigns responsibility for recruitment, selection and training, and supervision of personnel.
5. *Executive leadership.* Must be constantly demonstrated by the administrative head. "He must regularly evaluate his total program, insuring its (1) united endeavor for reaching objectives set by him and/or department policy, (2) he also should be ready to set new goals or objectives when it is apparent that additional programs will more effectively deal with the total problem.[24]"

B. ORGANIZATIONAL FRAMEWORK. Factors to be taken into account in planning the organizational structure of an institution include objectives, programs, quantity and caliber of personnel, location and layout of the physical plant, and the number and kinds of inmates.

The institution should be managed by organizing like functions under major administrative subdivisions. However, the grouping of the functions and the number of administrative units may vary, depending on the number and kinds of inmates and the nature of the institutional program.

Plan No. 1, shown in Figure 26, is an organizational chart for a large institution for male adults, with a population up to 2,000.

1. Custodial and treatment functions are organized under separate divisions and management.
2. Because of program size, industrial and business services are managed separately.
3. Staff specialists should be provided to render assistance to management in the following areas: public relations, management analysis, personnel management and training, civil defense, general inspections, and special investigations.

C. ORGANIZATIONAL SUBDIVISIONS. Organizational subdivisions should be specified to provide appropriate levels of authority and responsibility through the chain of command. A plan and description of the institutional organization should include a chart of organization.[25]

D. PLAN AND DESCRIPTION OF ORGANIZATION. Clear policy statements for treatment and other procedures are important. A manual of policy and procedures can be developed as a vehicle to communicate the policies and procedures to everyone in the organization. The manual could be coded, with the first digit designating the area of concern and a hyphen separating it from a second set of digits, designating the consecutive order or importance of the directive. For example, a manual of policies and procedures in an institution might be coded as follows:[26]

1. Administration
2. Personnel
3. Custody
4. Classification
5. Treatment Program
6. Records
7. Business and Accounting
8. Medical
9. Maintenance
10. Industries
11. Farms
12. Research

E. PERSONNEL CONTROLS AND DEVELOPMENT. A program of personnel development must be maintained. It should include the analysis, description

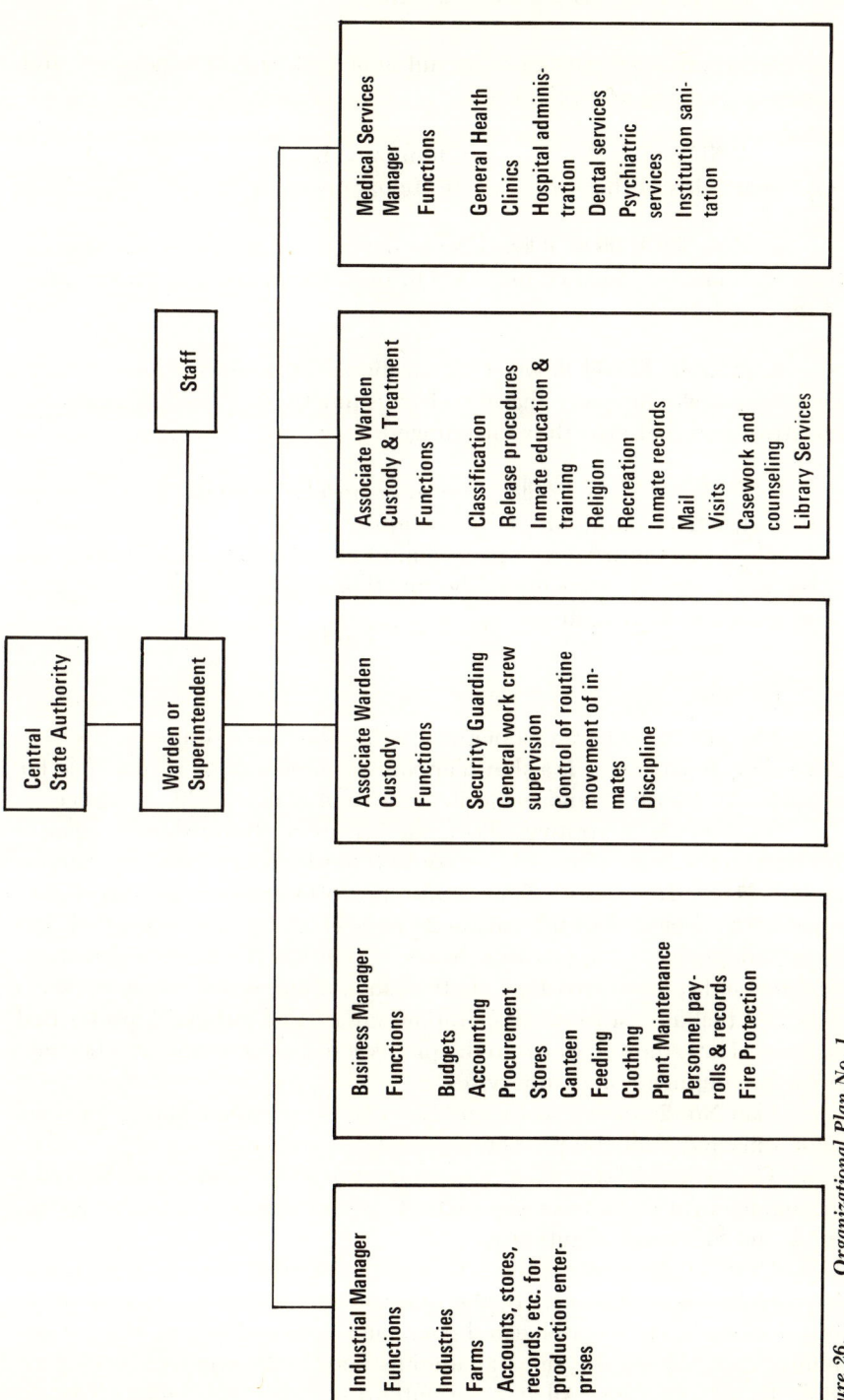

Figure 26. *Organizational Plan No. 1*

Source: American Correctional Association, *Manual of Correctional Standards*, 3rd Ed., 1966 Plan B, p. 319.

and classification of positions; recruitment and selection policies, and in-service training and promotion.

F. MAINTAINING TEAMWORK. A system must be developed for coordinating the activitis of the various institutional divisions.

G. COMMUNICATION WITH INMATES. A constructive system of communications with inmates must be provided through the organizational structure of the institution.

H. REGULAR REEVALUATION. Organizational structures should be reviewed annually to assure that the chart is functioning, that programs are effective, and that growth is encouraged.

I. COMMUNITY RELATIONSHIPS. A system must be maintained for developing constructive community relationships.[27]

The trend toward developing community programs for inmates in the correctional system is changing the function of the institutions, bringing new goals and high visibility.

II. Jails

The jail administrator operates within the policy framework of the governing department. If a sheriff appoints a deputy to be responsible for the jail, the sheriff should prescribe a general policy for his guidance.

As chief administrative officer, the jail administrator should organize his staff on the basis of areas of responsibilities such as security, program, and business management. Time requirements for the various tours of duty must be so arranged as to provide 24-hour coverage where needed. He should deputize by appointing heads of units and delegating responsibilities and authority to them. He then should supervise their activities to ascertain that all institutional operations are carried out in the prescribed manner. Thus, the key words to the professional jail administrator become organize, deputize, and supervise.

Plan No. 2, shown in Figure 27, is an organizational chart for a jail with a maximum of 100 prisoners.

The pyramidal structure, sometimes called the *scalar principle*, is the arrangement of units from the highest (jail administrator) to the lowest (rank and file) level of authority.

Unity of command is the principle that requires only one person to be responsible for the jail. In the diagram, the sheriff is responsible to his electorate. He has delegated command responsibility to the jail administrator. Within the jail, the administrator is the one person responsible for all activities. All lines of authority and reponsibility converge on him.

Administration of Correctional Institutions   365

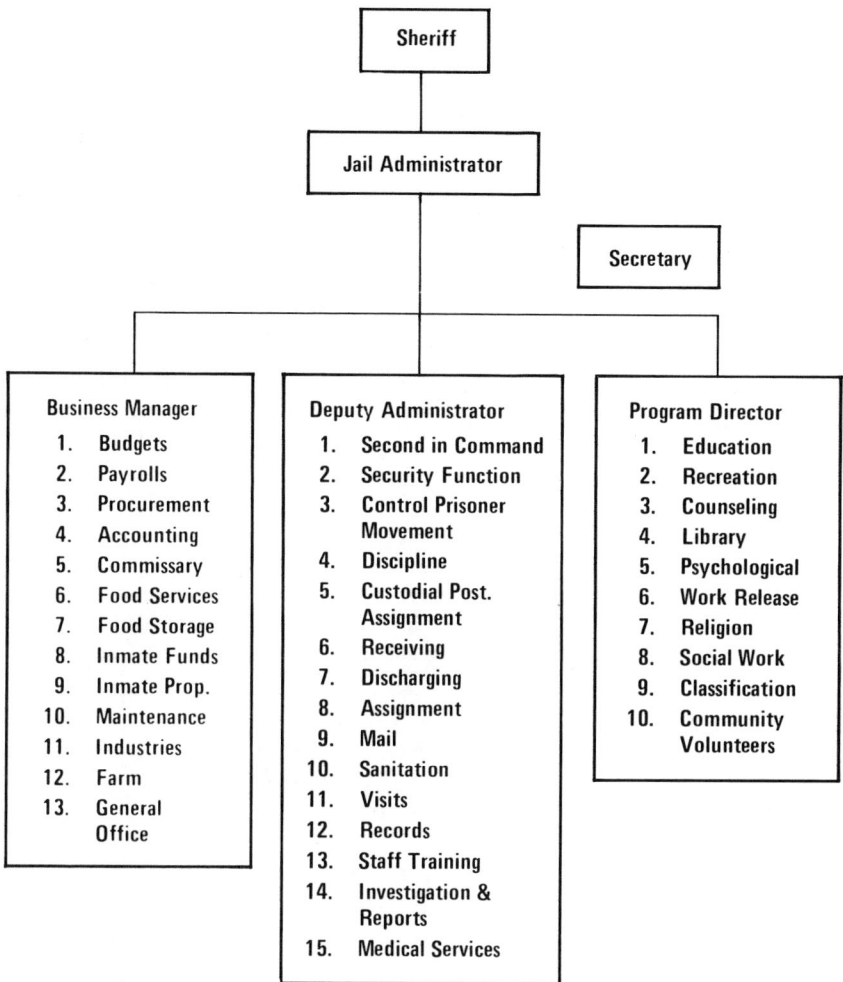

Figure 27.   Organizational Plan No. 2
Source: Manual on Jail Administration, (Washington, D.C.: National Sheriff's Association, 1970), p. 4.

   Chain of command is the linkage between the jail administrator and the rank and file. In the illustration, the administrator would issue instructions to the program director on matters relating to academic education. The program director would pass such orders down to the employee responsible for that function. In like manner, requests from that employee would go to the administrator through the program director.
   Channels of communication generally follow the same procedure except when there is lateral communication between persons on the same

level of authority; i.e., when the librarian coordinates an activity with the director of vocational training.

The span of control describes the operations immediately under the direction of the administrator. In Figure 27, the business manager, deputy administrator, and the program director are within the span of control of the jail administrator. The employees responsible for vocational training, academic education, and the library are in the program director's span of control and not that of the jail administrator.[28]

Furthermore, the United States Bureau of Prisons suggests that a jail can be administered most effectively if the operation is divided into manageable functional units. The functional units of the jail include fiscal management, personnel administration, operations, fiscal planning, program planning, and community relations. Within each of these units, the functions of setting objectives, planning, decision making, and control can be exercised.

> *Objectives.* The development of objectives is the first step in rational management, for they serve as a method of measuring effort, progress, change, and results. They serve as the basis for planning, in every area of management, for without them planning could not be done. Objectives also serve to make the activities of the organization rational.
>
> *Planning.* Planning is an organized method of problem solving in which the problem is identified and studied, alternative solutions are examined, and a course of action selected. Without planning, the jail administrator runs the risk of administration by crisis—solving each problem as it arises without taking into account the long-range implications of the solution.
>
> *Decision Making.* Everyone in the jail from the jail officer to the administrator makes decisions. The jail officer is guided in his decisions by policies, procedures, and schedules called standing plans. During escapes and riots, decisions are made on the basis of emergency plans. Standing plans and emergency plans are methods of making decisions in advance.
>
> *Exercising Control.* The objectives of control are: (1) to monitor the operation of the jail to ensure that objectives are being met, (2) to evaluate the effectiveness of policies, procedures, and programs, and (3) to identify or predict problems before they reach a critical stage.
>
> An administrator has a number of tools at his disposal that he can use to exercise control of the jail. These include reports, records, and deadlines. The achievement of objectives can be accomplished by the use of these methods. Objectives can be measured by records and reports. Program development and planning can be controlled by the establishment of schedules or deadlines. Where plans require specific stages, deadlines can be set for each stage, thus monitoring and controlling the development of the plan.[29]

III. Juvenile Institutions

The administrative structure of the training school is a vehicle for carrying on treatment in the institution and should be so ordered as to make possible the efficient conduct, coordination, and integration of all parts of the program. No set pattern of administrative organization would adequately fit all training schools because of differences in size, age group served, types of services provided, personnel, budget resources, and community attitudes. However, an administrative organization should: (1) limit closely related functions to departments, sections, and units, (2) delineate working relationships and facilitate the coordination of staff efforts, and (3) clearly define lines of responsibility, authority, and delegation of authority.

In every training school there are at least two related but different kinds of functions; programs, such as group life, religion, clinical services, education, and recreation, and business management, such as budget, accounting, and housekeeping. Some schools break down the first group of functions for administrative purposes into program resources and clinical services.

A superintendent with superior administrative ability, a liking for children, a belief in treatment, and a familiarity with the procedures and techniques of treatment is indispensable to efficient operation of a training school.

Further, a superintendent is the administrative head of the institution, responsible for coordinating its various activities, for establishing and maintaining acceptable standards throughout the school, and for the school's community relationships. He should appoint all personnel and be responsible for preparing and expending the budget and for interpreting the finances of the school to the budget-approving authorities and to the general public.[30]

PERSONNEL MANAGEMENT

The administrative personnel who manage the correctional system merit special comment. This group may well be the key to introducing much-needed changes. Estimates indicate that there are more than 17,000 middle managers and supervisors at work in corrections.[31] Traditionally, these persons, like the top administrators, have been recruited from rank-and-file staff in both juvenile and adult fields. Very few have had special training or preparation for managerial responsibilities.

The trend toward change in correctional agencies puts a premium on managerial skill. The lowering of barriers between institutions and the outside community as well as efforts to eliminate the schism between custody and treatment, demands flexible and sophisticated performance of management functions.

Correctional managers need more training in public administration. To effect organizational change, they need to know more about the nature of formal organizations, the dynamics of administrative decision making, the principles of personnel management, and the use of strategic information and research findings. The correctional manager needs the same opportunities for personal development that have been urged for other staff: educational leaves, extension courses, institutes, and workshops. Beyond this, universities need to develop curricula leading to careers in correctional administration.

Jail Administration

The first essential for the operation of a jail is adequate personnel. The most securely constructed jails and prisons have not prevented escapes by way of the front door and over a 30-foot guarded wall when the guard force was deficient in numbers and in quality.

The climate of the jail can be depressive, detrimental to constructive resocialization programs, and contributory to recidivism. It can also be conducive to good morale, good discipline, and a desire for self-improvement. Either condition is the result of the attitude and efficiency of the jail in terms of acceptable standards.

Ranks and Titles. Appropriate designations should be made in accordance with the organizational structure.

Job Satisfaction. Working conditions and compensation should lead to retention of employees due to good morale.

Recruitment. Every potential manpower pool should be approached for qualified applicants.

Basis for Selection. Qualifying and competitive testing should be the means of obtaining employees.

Employee Probation. A period of time for the purposes of training, observation, and evaluation should be established.

Training. A program designed to prepare employees to perform their duties efficiently and to advance within the profession should be provided.

Personnel Officer. A qualified staff member should be given the responsibilities of personnel administration.

Discipline. A system for dealing with employee disciplinary matters should be prescribed.

Assignments. Posts and responsibilities should be assigned on an objective basis.

Duty Schedules. A means of advising employees, well in advance, of their duty and pass days should be devised and posted.[32]

PHYSICAL PLANT—FACILITY FUNCTIONS

When viewed nationally, correctional institutions are seen as large, antiquated, ill-equipped and poorly staffed, and deprived of interaction with the community. What interaction exists is more likely to hinder the inmate than help.[33] The institutions exist in an information vacuum and are handicapped by a lack of public support. The horizon is dotted by large, multipurpose custodial facilities which are wasteful of both offenders and staff.

Although California's correctional facilities have had a national reputation for providing superior services to inmates, it is still true that many of its institutions are large, fortress-like, concrete structures, generally isolated from the community and frequently operated within an information vacuum. California's correctional institutions receive sporadic public support. At times, the public is willing to support institutions that are antiquated, as demonstrated by its tolerance of a jail that is a century old.[34]

It is exceedingly difficult to generalize about correctional institutions because they present such diversity of characteristics. Some have changed very little over many years. Others, however, have become progressive and have adopted advanced practices and procedures. Institutions in America are both varied and in various stages of development.

Institutions have become increasingly specialized, with separate facilities for males and females, felons and misdemeanants, adult and youthful offenders, and those requiring maximum, medium, and minimum security.

1. A maximum-security facility is a walled institution where the inmates are kept in cells and guarded to prevent their escape.
2. A medium-security institution is enclosed by an industrial type of wire fence. Many of the inmates sleep in dormitories and are permitted to work in a less restricted environment.
3. A minimum-security institution is an open facility, usually an honor farm or camp. The prisoners live in unlocked and unfenced buildings and generally work outdoors. While at work, the inmates are under supervision of overseers rather than under the surveillance of guards. In this type of institution, there is a minimum emphasis on preventing escapes.

Experience has shown that among comparable groups of inmates, escape attempts are less frequent in minimum-security facilities.

Juvenile Detention

A new type of architecture has been tested during the past ten years. Well over 100 specially designed detention facilities have been built in this period, most of them embodying the National Council on Crime and Delinquency's basic principles of detention home design and each replacing a county jail or makeshift facility. Group units are of the same sex and rarely exceed 15 youngsters, except in two eastern cities and larger western juvenile halls, where 20 is the usual size of the group.[35] Most of the modern detention homes have individual rooms, visual and auditory control, attractive but foolproof furnishings, and equipment designed to facilitate constructive supervision.

COEDUCATIONAL FACILITIES. Coeducational activities play an important role in a varied state program. In this connection, most administrators of training schools serving both boys and girls on one campus are strongly in favor of joint facilities and an integrated program.

Proponents of the coeducational system point out that it helps to create a more normal and natural atmosphere in an otherwise abnormal setting and is similar to the condition the child will face upon return to his own community. They also believe that isolation or separation of adolescents tends to create problems and that the opportunity for healthy association with both sexes is desirable.

Admittedly, problems of supervision are intensified under a coeducational system. However, its proponents point out that these problems can be successfully dealt with through a good selection process, adequate staff-to-student ratios, comparatively small populations, and appropriate physical layout of the plants.

Coeducational schools integrate their children in a variety of ways which range from attending an occasional social event or entertainment to joint classroom attendance, sharing the same dining facilities, and daily social activities such as dances, skating parties, mixed choirs, plays, and athletic events. Such a program recognizes that the youngsters are going back into a coeducational community and attempts to prepare them accordingly.

Experience has also shown that wholesome contacts with the opposite sex while in the training school cause boys and girls to have more pride in their personal appearance, that the children are better able to adjust after they are released, and that the frequent contacts tend to relieve the tension and excitement that comes when adolescents see each other less frequently.[36]

Redefined objectives and new staff requirements call for more than care and custody. The better detention homes now adhere to standards of social work and provide casework and clinical services, a full and varied school and activities program, and a professional diagnostic report on the child in detention. Use of professional personnel has increased markedly.[37]

CALIFORNIA JUVENILE INSTITUTIONS. A California correctional system study identified the following state facility standards:

> *Type.* Local correctional agencies should have a range of institutional programs and services available, including "diagnostic study centers, small residential treatment centers for seriously disturbed children, facilities for various age and coeducational groupings, foster homes, forestry camps, and other community-based facilities."
>
> *Size.* The capacity of any juvenile facility, including state institutions, should not exceed 100 (which is the present California law for county facilities).[38]
>
> "Living groups in a training school should consist of not more than 20 children. Forestry camp population should total no more than 40 to 50." More specifically, "standards generally call for the living unit to have a maximum capacity of 20 where groupings are homogeneous; the size for a heterogeneous group, or a group of severely disturbed children, should be from 12 to 16. Girls should have private rooms."
>
> *Planning.* No new institution or major additions to existing facilities should be authorized without first planning them around the specific type of program to be carried out in the institution. No new institutions or any major additions to existing facilities should be authorized unless the facilities are in locations conducive to the task of reintegrating their clientele into the community.[39]

CORRECTIONAL COSTS AND LOCATION OF JUVENILE AND ADULT OFFENDERS

On any one day in the United States, about 1¼ million persons — more than the population of 16 states—are under the jurisdiction of state and local correctional agencies and institutions. In addition, many thousands more are serving from a few days to a few weeks in a variety of local lockups.

Of the total volume of offenders, 28 percent are juveniles and 72 percent are adults. The number of adults under probation and parole supervision and in correctional institutions (876,412) is more than the number of enlisted personnel (846,684) in the United States Army for 1965.

More than 400,000, or one-third, of all juvenile and adult, offenders are found in institutions; over 800,000 (two-thirds) were in communities under probation or parole supervision, about 20 percent of them on parole or aftercare status after having served time in an institution.

The estimated cost of operating state and local correctional services in 1965 was almost $1 billion ($940,467,494), about 80 percent of this allocated for institutions. Of that allocation, more than half was used to support state adult correctional institutions. Local institutions and jails accounted for about 16 percent of all expenditures; juvenile detention accounted for about 6 percent of the total. Only 14.4 percent of correctional costs were allocated for probation services, including supervision of offenders and preparation of social studies to aid courts in making dispositions.

Of the total cost, one-third ($314,569,795) was for juvenile detention, institutions, and aftercare.

Costs for local services for misdemeanants accounted for 18.7 percent of the total, with only 3 percent going for probation services and 15.7 percent for confinement of misdemeanants.[40]

DIAGNOSIS AND CLASSIFICATION

Article IV, Section 14 of the Standard Act for State Correctional Services proposes:

> Persons committed to the institutional care of the department shall be dealt with humanely, with efforts directed to their rehabilitation, to effect their return to the community as promptly as practicable. For these purposes, the director shall establish programs of classification and diagnosis, education, casework, counseling and psychotherapy, vocational training and guidance, work and library and religious services; he may establish other rehabilitation programs; and he shall institute procedures for the study and classification of inmates.
>
> Women committed to the department shall be housed in institutions separate from institutions for men.[41]

The diagnosis and classification of prisoners is a relatively recent development in the correctional field. Varying forms of diagnostic facilities have come into existence as the emphasis has turned toward individualized treatment of the offender. The type of diagnostic unit varies, depending primarily upon the type, nature, and qualifications of correctional personnel. Classification is defined as:

> The organized procedures by which diagnosis, treatment-planning, and the carrying out of the component parts of the general treatment program are coordinated and focused on the individual in prison and on parole. . . . It is the process through which the resources of the correctional institution can be applied effectively to the individual case.[42]

The primary objective of classification is the development and administration of an integrated and realistic program of treatment for the individual with procedures for changing the program as needed. This objective is attained in the following manner. First, the individual's problems are analyzed by use of every available diagnostic technique, including social investigation, medical, psychological, and psychiatric examinations, and educational, vocational, religious, and recreational studies. A treatment and training program is then developed in staff conference during or after a personal interview with the inmate and a frank discussion of its purposes with him. The program must be carried out and revised as needed, for this dynamic process cannot be effective unless modifications are made in accordance with the changing needs of the individual inmate. What is done for the inmate in the institution then needs to be correlated with his program on parole.

Classification is therefore neither specific training nor general treatment, but rather the process through which the resources of the correctional institution can be applied effectively to the individual case.[43]

In addition, the American Correctional Association has reported the following:

> Classification . . . contributes to a smoothly, efficiently operated correctional program by the pooling of all relevant information concerning the offender, by devising a program for the individual based upon that information, and by keeping that program realistically in line with the individual's requirements. It furnishes an orderly method to the institution administrator by which the varied needs and requirements of each inmate may be followed through from commitment to discharge. Through its diagnostic and coordinating functions, classification not only contributes to the objective of rehabilitation, but also to custody, discipline, work assignments, officer and inmate morale and the effective use of training opportunities. Through the data it develops, it assists in long-range planning and development, both in the correctional system as a whole and in the individual institution.[44]

Classification programs have been administered under three general systems of organization: the classification clinic, the institutional classification committee, and the reception center. The earliest type, the clinic, was a separate administrative unit. Because of its isolation, its recommendations were seldom considered. The second type, the classification committee, consists of personnel representing all institutional departments having contact with individual inmates. They meet together as a whole or in subgroups to consider and to direct the care and treatment program of each individual inmate. The latest step in the development of the classification system is the reception center.

The Reception Center

The reception period, immediately following admission to prison, is possibly the most important phase of the inmate's total period of incarceration. Many inmates enter the correctional system with guilt, anxiety, resentment, self-pity, depression, remorse, and hostility. Very few bring with them any reality-based understanding of the correctional program and its mission.

The reception center is a central unit where each new prisoner is sent for a comprehensive study and diagnosis and the formulation of a treatment program in his behalf. He is then assigned to an institution which best meets the needs of his planned program of treatment.

Further, an essential feature of the classification process is the admission-orientation program. A period ranging from 30 to 60 days is generally allocated to the admission and orientation of new inmates. This permits the offender to be segregated from the general inmate population. Orientation may include a review of the rules and regulations of the institution, the philosophy of corrections, the facilities, and programs available at the institution.

1. CALIFORNIA YOUTH AUTHORITY RECEPTION CENTERS. Treatment is considered the most important aspect of the correctional process. Consequently, an effective classification system is essential to enable each offender to be assigned to a program that is best suited to his needs.

A 1971 juvenile institution task force revealed that the Youth Authority has special reception centers which perform classification functions for all committed wards. It operates three separate reception centers or units: the northern reception center receives both boys and girls, the southern reception center is for boys only, and there is a reception center for girls at the Ventura School. In addition, some of the wards committed by the criminal courts are referred to the reception center at the Deuel Vocational Institution operated by the department of corrections. The three Youth Authority reception centers evaluate each ward for an average of four weeks.[45] The evaluation process is somewhat longer at the Deuel Vocational Institution. Reception centers make recommendations as to the type of program in which the youth should be placed.[46]

2. RECEPTION AND CLASSIFICATION. A 1971 California Prison Task Force presented the following recommendations regarding reception and classification procedures:

> 1. The reception process should be shortened from the current period of six to eight weeks to a period of approximately 30 days.

2. The reception and diagnostic process should be shortened and revamped to include a systematic "follow-up," which would determine whether or not the recommendations of the reception process are carried out. Also, in the revamping of the reception process, there should be more definite separation of young offenders from old, and the less criminally oriented from the more sophisticated.
3. Efforts should be made throughout the system for a more differential allocation of institutional population based on program need. A careful typological analysis of the prison population and a thorough review of classification practices and policies should be undertaken in an effort to effect better institutional placement.
4. Efforts should be taken to coordinate more closely institutional programs with parole planning.[47]

RECORD AND STATISTICAL CONTROLS

Every correctional organization should have well-organized, accurate, up-to-date records.

One of the weakest areas of correctional statistics is in providing current and useful reports, not only for the administrator, but for public use. Most states require that all departments issue annual or biennial reports.

The following are some of the uses for records and reports:

1. Evaluation of past performance. Reports that give figures on amounts, kinds, frequency, and costs are useful in evaluating past performance.
2. Information for future planning. Records of planning for new construction, program planning, budgeting, and personnel increases must be carefully prepared.
3. Documentation of administrative actions. Records must be kept on any administrative actions and decisions that may be subject to review by higher authority or by the Courts—for example, approval of disciplinary actions, forfeiture and restoration of good time, personnel actions, and purchase authorizations.
4. Descriptions of events and incidents. Records should be kept of all special events and unusual incidents, including tours, holiday observances (such as a religious program given by a church group), accidents, escapes, and disturbances.[48]

The type of records that an institution keeps is determined by the needs and the statutory requirements of the jurisdiction in which it is located. Most institutions keep records of population movement, admissions and discharges; food and supplies; disciplinary action; maintenance; medical data; and special programs. In addition, reports on drug use are required by law.

Institution records are important and should always be available for administrative purposes. The records should include data on the daily population, identification of inmates (including vital statistics, photographs, and fingerprints), social background, prior criminal history, and other case record information. In addition, the records should contain a locator card which enables the control center to determine inmate's cell or dormitory, and a visitor's and correspondence card. Case records should be considered confidential, but should be available to the appropriate staff through proper channels.

Further, regular monthly, quarterly, and semiannual reports are of inestimable value to administrators. These reports generally contain data, which should be readily accessible, on such items as movement of population, per capita expenditures, personnel information, summaries of special studies, and analysis of current trends. In essence, this information is required for effective management.

A California prison task force in 1971 recommended:

> The Department's existing "unit records"-type system should be replaced with the computerized information system which emphasizes program-type data for management purposes. Such a system should be designed to include follow-up data along with current data on programs and offenders, so that separate programs may be evaluated as to their relative effectiveness for different types of offenders in the long run. Cost-effectiveness estimates of the long-run economic consequences of specific programs for different types of offenders should also be undertaken.[49]

Adequate records also need to be kept for research. Statistics on persons coming into the institution, on diagnoses from the evaluations of the offenders, and on the outcome are all necessary for adequate research programs. With the aid of computer technology, these records are within reach of most correctional institutions and agencies.

COMMUNITY-BASED CORRECTIONS

In recent years, community-based corrections has received considerable attention as a progressive approach to reintegrating correctional clients into the community. Community-based corrections encompasses community service centers, halfway houses, and prerelease programs, work release and study release programs, neighborhood centers and projects, and all other community resources that can be used with correctional clients.[50]

There are some inherent problems in developing these services as alternatives to institutionalization. Correctional administrators and legislators must be supportive of the programs and create conditions favorable for their development. Demonstration projects or models of successful programs should be implemented in various areas. Effective leadership and personnel skilled in special community programs are essential. In view of the limited experience of the prototype models, it is difficult to clearly define the administrative structure of the new community programs. The planning of community programs also requires the involvement of social service agencies such as welfare, mental health, state employment, and vocational training.

The President's Task Force Report on corrections revealed:

> One of the most critical problems in developing new community programs is to secure the involvement and participation of the community itself. Too often, promising programs such as halfway houses have failed simply because the community was not prepared to tolerate them. Thus, it is essential that the public be brought into planning early and that correctional managers make intense efforts to insure citizen understanding and support.[51]

1. **PHILOSOPHY AND OBJECTIVES.** An institution, especially the jail or training facility, should be considered as part of the community. The primary objective of the facility is to protect the community by preparing each inmate for a responsible role when he returns to the community. Therefore, the institution should utilize community resources and establish appropriate programs for those offenders who do not pose a threat to the public safety. Experience has shown that the public is more receptive to community treatment programs for misdemeanants than for felons.

Community release programs strive to prepare and gradually reintegrate the offenders back into the mainstream of society under the restraints of constructive supervision by the jail administration. After all, most inmates are sentenced for relatively short terms, a few months to one year, and they will then be released in the community. Progressive jail administrators can provide inmates with a meaningful opportunity to reestablish themselves in society as opposed to remaining bitter and isolated in confinement.

2. **WORK RELEASE.** There is no more practical, acceptable, economical, and potentially rehabilitative community release program than work

release. Basically, this program releases the inmate from the institution during certain hours for the purpose of maintaining private employment, seeking gainful employment, or participating in a trade-educational training program. The program is used primarily with short-term inmates at the county jail level or with prison inmates who are preparing for release on parole.

Any work release program should include at least the following:

   a. The selection of suitable prisoners.
   b. The careful investigation of each job by a jail staff to make certain it is lawful and that inmates will not be exploited or that regularly employed persons will not be displaced.
   c. That arrangements will be made for the transporting of prisoners to and from such employment, and that they will have the necessary work clothes and tools.
   d. That all wages earned in such employment are properly recorded and disbursed.[52]

Properly administered work release is an ideal procedure for helping the inmate make the transition back to society—it benefits the inmate, his family, and society. His day-to-day participation in community life will provide a firm basis for gaining self-respect and reestablishing himself when he is released. While away from the jail, he is required to make decisions regarding his behavior the same as a free citizen.

The law and the administration of work release vary from state to state. Work release may be referred to as work furlough (California), day parole (Wisconsin), outmate (Pennsylvania), or semi-liberté (France). It is difficult to make a generalization regarding the work release program; however, the concept of providing rehabilitation and offering a solution to the age-old problem of a defendant losing his job because of a jail sentence is universal.

The success of any community-based correctional endeavor depends upon the acceptance, involvement, and support of the community. The primary objective is to organize a broad range of community resources and support. The professions, labor, law enforcement, business, and the general public should be represented on an advisory planning committee.

Management of the work release program will entail a selection of participants, development of employment opportunities, supervision, collection and administration of funds, housing work release prisoners, and solving special problems. The problems vary with the structure and organization of the program and the type of inmate involved in the program. The most frequent problems include irregular work schedules, inmate use of intoxicants, AWOL, transportation, and possession of contraband.

Work release opportunities have been limited in some regions because the correctional institution is located in rural areas where jobs are not plentiful and community conditions are different from those of the metropolitan areas to which most inmates return. Since the early 1960's, the U. S. Bureau of Prisons, and more recently some state correctional departments, have attempted to overcome this problem by establishing community residential centers.

During the coming decade, it is anticipated that work release programs and other facets of community-based corrections will be expanded to new dimensions. It may very well be that community-based correctional services holds the future of corrections.

RESEARCH AND EVALUATION

To secure maximum efficiency in the administration of justice and attain the objectives of new trends in the field of corrections, much research is undoubtedly needed. Very little has been done to determine correction's batting average by evaluating the effectiveness of what is done to, for, and with the arrested law violator. If a business knew as little about the performance of its product and the explanation for its performance after it reached the market as corrections knows about the performance of its graduates and the reasons for their performance, the business would surely fail. Products that had to be taken in for repairs as often as correctional graduates are returned for more rehabilitation would soon be off the market.

The most conspicuous problems in corrections today are lack of knowledge and unsystematic approaches to the development of programs and techniques. Changes in correctional treatment have been guided primarily by what Wright calls "intuitive opportunism,"[53] a kind of goal-oriented guessing.

In the past, research studies in the field of corrections have consistently been evaluated as more effective when they are conducted by persons identified with a research project than by outside evaluators. Further, social and behavioral sciences are being used increasingly to develop more effective and efficient programs to modify criminal and delinquent behavior. They will be used even more so in the future. Heretofore, correctional programs have operated on faith, hope, and charity, without adequate assessment and evaluation. If "experimental programs" scare correctional administrators, the present "trial-and-error" programs should scare them more.[54]

In 1967, the President's Task Force on corrections reported:

> The first requirement for an efficient use of research in correctional program development is an organizational arrangement that calls for

integration of the functions of administration, treatment, and evaluation. Prior to the introduction of research, there was only one communicational channel within the system: the channel between administration and treatment. With the advent of research, the channels of communication increase to three.

There is a need to overcome such barriers through the development of a common commitment subscribed to by administrators, program operators, and researchers. The gap between administrator and treater could be substantially lessened if management committed itself to specific treatment strategies which would be given adequate tests and if it shared program decisions with treatment personnel. The gap between administrator and researcher could be narrowed through adoption of a common frame of reference as to the role of evaluation in the total management process. The gap between treaters and researchers could be lessened through mutual commitment to the goal of improving treatment by evaluation. Treaters would be called upon to enter actively into the evaluation process and would be seen as indispensable collaborators in research. Research would be seen as an aid rather than a threat to the treatment of the offender.[55]

A basic principle of good correctional practice is that research and evaluation must be an integral part of every program. Programs must be held accountable for producing reasonably acceptable results. Thus, the field of corrections needs to evaluate continually what it has done, how it is doing, and what new strategies are needed to improve overall performance.

Basically, there are two types of research that are particularly relevant to corrections. The first is essentially a compilation of descriptive data such matters as thulation movement and client characteristics. This kind of information is necessary for budgetary considerations, population projections, and general planning. The second type of research, sometimes called action research, pertains to involvement in program planning and evaluation. The researcher should not be an isolate in an ivory tower but should be part of a team, along with administrators and line staff, in deciding program goals, helping to develop specific strategies and criteria for measuring success or failure, observing the program as it is carried out, evaluating and interpreting the results, and disseminating the finds or conclusions to other correctional practitioners.

At the county level in California, some effort has been made in recent years to gather descriptive population data. As yet, however, these efforts have not resulted in a well-developed record-keeping system. Whatever available data exist are received and published by the Bureau of Criminal Statistics. The second type of research, however, is still a novelty. Many administrators of county facilities believed that sophisticated research was too complicated or extensive for their departments, and that its findings were of questionable value. They also felt that action research is more properly the responsibility of the state. In short, there is not much local understanding of or commitment to action-research.[56]

A California Correctional Task Force in 1971 recommended:

1. Every institutional program should be evaluated continuously in order to determine whether or not each is achieving its stated objectives. Failure to accomplish these objectives, provided reasonably adequate resources are available, should result in modification or elimination of the program.
2. County agencies, as well as the state, should substantially increase their commitment to evaluation and research both philosophically and by allocating significantly greater resources for this function.
3. Research activities should be team efforts (involving administrators, line workers, and research staff) and should concentrate on determining and disseminating information about what does and does not assist in accomplishing the goals of corrections.
4. The state and counties should enter into a collaborative effort of program research and evaluation. The state should play the primary role in planning, carrying out, and disseminating the results of correctional research, with active participation and cooperation from the counties. Research assistance and information should be provided for the counties without charge, but counties should be able to contract with the state or outside sources for extensive individual projects.[57]

In the future, research and evaluation will increasingly become built-in components of correctional programs. A significant beginning was made in 1971 in a self-accreditation project of the American Correctional Association to evaluate all correctional programs. This effort was funded by The Ford Foundation and participation was on a voluntary basis.

Today, automated data systems are a high priority for research. Computers are already being used in some of the larger, more progressive correctional systems for administrative purposes in classification, reduction of custody, accounting and printing checks for inmates as well as staff, and assessing the inmate's progress on probation, parole, as well as in institutions. Research with technological assistance will have a major impact upon the future of Corrections.

SUMMARY

Correctional institutions, including jails and juvenile training facilities, are in a period of transition. Although institutional operations may have appeared static to some observers, this is certainly no longer the case. The nature of the inmate population has changed. Further, juvenile and adult corrections are beginning to feel the effects of public enlightenment.

The basic objective of correctional institutions has remained essentially the same: to protect the public. However, in most jurisdictions, the philosophy and approach have been modified. Growing emphasis has been given to differential treatment based upon individual needs. In addition, the diagnosis and classification of inmates entering the correctional system have become more important in planning treatment.

This material is intended to sketch the development of corrections and then to draw attention to the administrative organization and structure of juvenile institutions, jails, and correctional institutions and their various components. Today's correctional administrator is confronted with new challenges. Further, he must be familiar with modern organization methods and techniques. A correctional institution of any type cannot be operated successfully over a long period unless careful attention is given to the development of a sound organizational structure based upon recognized principles of administration and the goals of the parent agency.

In addition to examining correctional administration and its objectives, this chapter highlights numerous components of the system — personnel management, the physical plant, reception center, community-based corrections, records and statistical controls, and research and evaluation. The general theme that is woven into the contemporary correctional process is the reintegration of the offender into the mainstream of community life.

Recent trends in the field of corrections have focused upon the development and utilization of alternatives to incarceration. The underlying factors have involved overcrowded conditions in jails and correctional facilities, a belief that every offender does not require incarceration; and a realistic movement toward community treatment.

Richard McGee states "The correctional field is on the threshold of revolutionary changes which will take place gradually as they are tested by scientific methods."[58] As a prerequisite to change, political leaders, judges, public interest groups, and public-information media must be educated in the potential of community-based corrections. The projection of future operational methods should also consider technological advancement and the need to utilize research methodology, analysis, and computers to classify an offender for a rehabilitation program.

The task of corrections includes building or rebuilding solid ties between the offender and community to integrate or reintegrate the offender into community life—restoring family ties, obtaining employment, education, and securing a place for the offender in society. The use of probation has already been expanded, and construction of new correctional institutions has already declined. The reorganization of institution programs, especially the county jail, is envisioned with increased use of the halfway house, work furlough, work-study release programs, and community service centers. Correctional administrators are challenged to mobilize public and private community resources and utilize volunteers as a means of enhancing correctional services and bridging the gap between the institution and the community. Every effort should be made to bring the community into the institution and the institution into the community.

Notes

1. The American Correctional Association, *Manual of Correctional Standards*, 3rd ed., 1966, p. xx.
2. National Survey of Corrections, Federal Bureau of Prisons and the Administrative Office of the U. S. Courts, 1965.
3. Harry Elmer Barnes and Negley K. Teeters, *New Horizons in Criminology*, 2nd ed. (Englewood Cliffs, N. J., Prentice-Hall, 1951), p. 394.
4. Orlando F. Lewis, *The Development of American Prisons and Prison Customs, 1776–1835* (Montclair, N. J.: Patterson Smith, 1967), p. 350.
5. Vernon Fox, *Introductions to Corrections* (Englewood Cliffs, N. J.: Prentice-Hall, 1972), p. 12.
6. The American Correctional Association, *Manual of Correctional Standards*, p. 11.
7. Joint Commission on Correctional Manpower and Training, *Manpower and Training in Correctional Institutions: 1969* (Washington, D. C.: U. S. Government Printing Office, 1969), p. 36. (Should be ordered from the American Correctional Association.)
8. *Correctional System Study*, California Board of Corrections, July 1971, p. 18.
9. The American Correctional Association, *Manual of Correctional Standards*, pp. 579–80.
10. Ibid., p. 43–44.
11. TIME Magazine, January 18, 1971, p. 48.
12. California Correctional System Study, Jail Task Force Report, July 1971, p. 9.
13. Ibid., p. 8.
14. The President's Commission on Law Enforcement and Administration of Justice, *Task Force Report: Corrections* (Washington D. C.: U. S. Government Printing Office, 1967), p. 209.
15. California Correctional System Study, Prison Task Force, July 1971, p. 70.
16. Fox, *Introduction to Corrections*, pp. 140–41.
17. Ibid., p. 141.
18. The American Correctional Association, *Manual of Correctional Standards*, pp. 151–52.
19. Department of the Youth Authority, "Average Length of Stay, Costs, and Bed Capacity of County Operated Juvenile Homes, Ranches, and Camps," State of California (Sacramento, March 1971).
20. The President's Commission, *Task Force Report: Corrections*, 1967, p. 79.
21. Board of Corrections, *A Study of California County Jails*, State of California (Sacramento: April 1970), p. 11.
22. Ibid., p. 11.
23. The American Correctional Association, *Manual of Correctional Standards*, pp. 313–14.

24. Ibid., p. 316.
25. Ibid., p. 314.
26. Fox, *Introduction to Corrections*, pp. 361–62.
27. The American Correctional Association, *Manual of Correctional Standards*, p. 314–15.
28. The National Sheriff's Association, *Manual of Jail Administration*, (Washington D. C.: 1970), pp. 4–5.
29. "The Jail: Its Operation and Management," U. S. Bureau of Prisons, 1970, pp. 104–106.
30. "Institutions Serving Delinquent Children," U. S. Department of Health, Education, and Welfare, 1962, pp. 18–19.
31. The estimate is based on a ratio of one supervisor for every six employees, derived from the data of the National Survey of Corrections. (President's Commission on Law Enforcement and Administration of Justice, *Task Force Report: Corrections*, 1967, p. 98.)
32. The National Sheriff's Association, *Manual of Jail Administration*, pp. 8–9.
33. Joint Commission on Correctional Manpower and Training, *Manpower and Training in Correctional Institutions: 1969* (Washington, 1969).
34. California Correctional System Study, Institutions, July 1971, p. vi.
35. California's "Standards for Juvenile Halls" calls for two adults with each group of 20 during the day and evening shifts after school hours and on weekends. NCCD standards set 15 as the maximum.
36. "Institutions Serving Delinquent Children," U. S. Department of Health, Education, and Welfare, 1962, pp. 9–10.
37. The President's Commission, *Task Force Report: Corrections*, p. 121.
38. California Welfare and Institutions Code, Section 886.
39. California Correctional System Study, Juvenile Institutions Task Force Report, July 1971, pp. 21–22.
40. The President's Commission, *Task Force Report: Corrections*, pp. 192–93.
41. National Council on Crime and Delinquency, Standard Act for State Correctional Services, Volume 3, No. 3, July 1967, p. 414.
42. The American Correctional Association, *Manual of Correctional Standards*, pp. 352–53.
43. Ibid., p. 353.
44. Handbook on Classification in Correctional Institutions, American Correctional Association, New York, 1947, p. 10.
45. Department of the Youth Authority, Annual Statistical Report: 1969, State of California (Sacramento, 1970), p. 5.
46. California Correctional System Study, Juvenile Institutions Task Force Report, July 1971, p. 31.
47. California Correctional System Study, Prison Task Force Report, July 1971, p. vi.
48. "The Jail: Its Operation and Management," U. S. Bureau of Prisons, p. 147.
49. California Correctional System Study, Prison Task Force Report, July 1971, p. xi.
50. Fox, *Introduction to Corrections*, p. 215.
51. The President's Commission, *Task Force Report: Corrections*, p. 44.
52. "Community Work—An Alternative to Imprisonment," Correctional Research Associates, Washington D. C., December 1967.
53. John C. Wright, "Curiosity and Opportunism", *Trans-Action* 2: 38–40.
54. Gordon P. Waldo, "The Dilemma of Correctional Research," *American Journal of Corrections* 31: 6–10.
55. The President's Commission, *Task Force Report: Corrections*, p. 14.
56. California Correctional System Study, Juvenile Institutions Task Force, July 1971, p. 65.
57. Ibid., pp. 91–92.
58. Richard A. McGee, "What is Past is Prologue," *The Annals*, January 1969, p. 1.

Review Questions

1. Trace the early development of corrections in the United States.
2. Describe the subsystem of correctional institutions as it relates to probation and parole.
3. What are the objectives of correctional institutions?
4. Evaluate the punishment vs. the treatment approach in corrections.
5. Discuss the function of the jail.
6. Define "correctional institution."
7. Why is a separate department of corrections considered the best administrative forum?
8. What are the advantages of the single administrator?
9. What factors are taken into account in planning the organizational structure of an institution?
10. Discuss and compare the difference between minimum, medium, and maximum-security facilities.
11. Describe the proponents of coeducational juvenile treatment institutions.
12. Discuss the function of the reception center.
13. What is the objective of the classification process?
14. Why are records and statistical controls important to administration?
15. What is community-based corrections?
16. Evaluate work release.
17. Why is research important to the future of corrections?

14 Public Relations

"Those were the days" is a familiar line. Another one is "the good old days" or "way back when." Whatever or whenever those days were, they are no longer here. To hang tenaciously onto an elusive shadow based on memories of only the good parts of yesterday is to engage in idle daydreaming. Today and tomorrow are the only days that the criminal justice administrator can do anything about. It is most important that every possible effort be made to do some critical self-analysis and to initiate some positive public relations activities that will enhance the department's probability of achieving its objectives.

There are many facets to a public relations program for a criminal justice agency. Because there are different types of agencies, we make no attempt to develop a standard program in this chapter. Our approach is to discuss concepts of public relations as they apply universally to the Criminal Justice System, leaving to the reader the task of developing a specific and comprehensive program that will most adequately serve the needs of the agency he is planning to enter. In this chapter, we cover the topic on the premise that there are essentially three components to a typical public relations program: (1) community relations, (2) public relations, and (3) press relations.

First, let us consider community relations. This term implies human interaction, a face-to-face personal relationship between individuals in the community at large and the individual members of the department, who also represent the community. Once these human relationships are thoughtfully and effectively initiated into a program, they would be

Los Angeles County Sheriff's Department official photograph

self-generating: each person would participate spontaneously in the interfacing activities on a no-host basis to achieve a maximum in mutual understanding between the community and the department.

The second component, public relations, is a managed and carefully organized effort to present to the public an accurate and total picture of the organization's philosophies and its activities. Public relations involves salesmanship and press-agentry. It is a matter of presenting to many segments of the community that information about the department which affects them. Although the product is a service instead of milk or oven cleaner, the general advertising theme is similar. There is less spontaneity involved in a public relations program than in the community relations approach because an effective program must be carefully designed, programmed, and rehearsed. As with the community relations concept, the public relations approach may help to develop a better public

Los Angeles County Sheriff's Department official photograph

understanding of the role the department plays in the community. But the purpose is to "sell" the department and its product: service, justice, protection, rehabilitation, crime reduction, or whatever the administrator chooses to emphasize. The objective is achieved if public relations produces a strong tendency to "buy" the department and to endorse its programs. The "public relations" concept involves a one-way presentation which may or may not involve any change in attitudes on the part of the criminal justice agency in question.

The third component, press relations, requires a mutual understanding between representatives of the press and the department and a feeling for each other's role, in a continual one-to-one relationship, on a cooperative basis. The everyday cooperative relationship with the press should be open, honest, and frank.

However, cooperation obviously does not extend to supplying information that would be detrimental to a prosecution or to the public safety or convenience. Sometimes, the press will have access to information that is detrimental to the department in question. The rule still applies: be honest and frank with the press. An explanation for a certain course of action, even though it turned out to be the wrong course, will produce fewer problems than an attempt to gloss over an item or evade it when questions are asked. There are certain items of information that are best withheld in the judgment of the criminal justice administrator. Conflicts are inevitable as certain press representatives will insist upon more information to satisfy their "need to know." But the administrator whose policies on news dissemination are consistent and well known will have much less grief than his counterpart who changes policy with the wind.

The second aspect of press relations involves the public relations approach. It is extremely important that the department's ongoing sales campaign include the press at every opportunity. News items of human interest, or unusual occurrences that might be of interest to a reading and a viewing public should be called to the attention of the person preparing news releases for the department. Items the administrator believes to be of interest which have already occurred rather than those in progress or about to occur may be the subject of a brief but interestingly written news release. Crime statistics and trends, new probation methods, or a new concept in work furlough are all items of general interest which should be prepared with the administrator's interpretation or explanation.

COMMUNITY RELATIONS

Community involvement, participation, and influence are all important to the criminal justice agency if its objectives and goals are to be met. The dynamics of human behavior and its effect upon the success or failure of a single program or an entire department must be taken into account by the administrator when he tries to gain the willing cooperation of the many "communities" that he serves. Actually, he serves the community of young potential violators, the community of nonviolators, the community of liberals and of conservatives, homeowners, landlords, taxpayers, welfare recipients, victims, suspects, the persons in various socioeconomic strata, parents, labor, management, the managers, and the managed. Each community has some common denominator for the same individuals may belong to many communities. Nevertheless, all of these community interests must be served by the Criminal Justice System.

Community relations involves an interaction among the administrators, manager, supervisors, and other personnel in the department with the total community and all of its parts. Whether the interaction be in the course of occupational and professional pursuits or in informal away-from-work activities, the criminal justice practitioner can never divest himself of his professional role. As many others have said on many occasions, every contact and every impression should be a positive one because it may be the only one.

Following are a few community relations techniques for consideration.

1. SELF-EVALUATION. If certain advertising agencies would have their way, anyone who wonders about his popularity must first make a quick inventory to ascertain that he is using all the best products to gain social acceptance. So it is with the criminal justice agency. The image the agency presents should be one that others would want to associate with. Personal

conduct and appearance should be pleasant and inoffensive; and most people do reasonably well in that. But what about the building that greets the first-time visitor? Is it pleasant and does the visitor feel welcome? It seems that a dull depressing gray is about the only color used for public buildings, and this has an adverse effect on the visitor. There should be pleasant surroundings, the facilities should be clean, and the decorations should be businesslike and appropriate. The courtroom design and appointments should be in keeping with traditions and procedures and should hold the people present in awe of the proceeding and physical arrangements so that they will conduct themselves in a subdued and respectful manner.

Personal dress, grooming, and conduct must be professional and appropriate to the role each person plays. An individual should not only be suited to the position that he fills but he should also be believable in his role.

Cultural understanding is achieved in many ways.
Courtesy: Police Department, Pasadena, California

2. **CULTURAL UNDERSTANDING.** Every culture has distinctive characteristics that tend to distinguish one individual from another. An understanding of an individual's heritage, customs, and cultural differences—no matter how subtle these differences may appear—will lead to a more favorable relationship between two persons. Reference to another individual in derogatory terms or by inadvertent use of "trigger words"[1] should not be tolerated even when they are allegedly used in jest. Use of the terms and phrases may become a habit and actually become a regular part of an individual's vocabulary. An understanding of the various cultures of people living in an area leads to a deeper understanding of the individuals of different heritage than one's own.

3. **PROFESSIONAL CONDUCT.** There is a quiet dignity to the professional man or woman. He has an objective, impartial attitude which may be reflected in both words and actions and in a professional detachment from personal display of emotional involvement. Gratuities and special favors may be offered, but once accepted, the person offering the favors tends to expect some sort of preferential treatment at some future time. The criminal justice practitioner should be approachable and a good listener, but not to the point where he assumes the posture or the reputation of an overly familiar busybody. The professional attitude should be extended to one's telephone speech and etiquette as well as to face-to-face contacts.

4. **ADVISORY COMMITTEES.** If we are to effectively serve a community on the basis of real needs, it is necessary to "sound out" representative members of that community. Some community leaders identify themselves through popular elections, but most are indigenous leaders and serve no official roles. They should be ferreted out and invited to participate as advisors on ad hoc or standing committees to provide valid feedback to current or proposed policies and procedures which affect the public. Care should be taken to select only individuals who are recognized as representatives of the community where they live. People who are chosen by the agency and designated as "representatives" when in fact they are not, may actually worsen any strained relationships the department may have with the community.

5. **VOLUNTEERS AS AIDES OR PARA/PROFESSIONALS.** Many student and adult volunteers may never see employment in criminal justice occupation, but their brief exposure to the field may more than compensate for any lost time or motion that their inexpertise may cause. Osmosis is sometimes a more valuable learning tool than some form of "hard-sell" indoctrination.

6. **PLAY POLITICS.** Partisan political participation is hazardous to any criminal justice practitioner, and should be discouraged in every way

possible. Campaigning on behalf of a candidate is a kind of political activity that should be considered improper conduct. The administration of justice is supposed to be nonpartisan, and any aggressive leadership role that a deputy probation officer, for example, would take in any type of partisan politics may raise serious doubts as to his ability to think and act impartially in his official capacity.

7. PARTICIPATE IN COMMUNITY AFFAIRS. As a private individual, the police officer, or court clerk, or parole officer, or any other person involved in criminal justice has a private life to lead as neighbor, parent, and spouse. He should worship if and how he chooses, hold memberships in whatever organizations he wants, and actively participate in various community affairs. Because of the social nature of his position, he can be encouraged to continue to direct his attention toward getting deeply involved in community affairs.

Ask a cop!
Courtesy: Police Department, Costa Mesa, California

8. TALK TO THE COMMUNITY. Take every opportunity to explain the criminal justice role and to directly address criticism. Program committee chairmen are always looking for another guest speaker to fill that luncheon spot, and they should be reminded that good speakers are available.

9. COMMUNICATORS WANTED. The police officer and the lawyer must both have the ability to communicate by oral and written methods, as well as by nuances and other subtle indicators of attitudes. Convictions are won, riots are prevented, and most work is done effectively by the well-qualified and carefully trained communicator. Human interaction is essentially little more than another form of communication, and the criminal justice practitioner must be an expert in this art.

PUBLIC RELATIONS

As the term is used in this chapter, *public relations* is the process of presenting the entire Criminal Justice System, but especially our own department, in the best possible light in order to gain public understanding, support, and cooperation. The process involves press-agentry, salesmanship, image-building, and the other techniques that most businesses and industries employ to present their products or services in the best possible light. Presidents are elected, milk gains favor, books are sold, colleges become internationally famous, celebrities reach stardom, and criminal justice agencies gain acceptance when they employ public relations methods. The greatest judge in the world gains that stature for three reasons: first, the world knows of his existence; second, he continually does something worthy of greatness; and third, he has sufficient publicity to focus the world's attention on his deeds. Without a good press, the judge and his few colleagues might be the only ones to know of his greatness.

Partisan political activity by the professional in criminal justice is often a form of masochism. Such activity draws the ire of many quarters in the community. A nonpartisan public posture seems to lend itself best to one's effectiveness as an objective, and judicious image as a police officer, parole agent, deputy probation officer, prosecutor, or judge. Party membership usually creates no problem; but when an individual participates in aggressive party leadership, which necessarily calls for vocal and relentless criticism of an opposing view, then whatever action he takes may be interpreted as motivated by whatever bias he has so vehemently articulated as a political advocate.

Conversely, public relations is a form of political activity in which the professional attempts to gain stature and acceptance as well as cooperation from all segments of the community in a way that is irrelevant to political differences. Each actor must play his role in a convincing manner. The result will be a believable performance that the public will accept as a true characterization of the role the actor is playing.

Following are a few suggested methods for creating and maintaining an appropriate image through public relations efforts.

1. PUBLIC UNDERSTANDING OF PHILOSOPHY. The policies and philosophies of the department should be clearly articulated and well publicized. For example, if a court chooses to take a hard stand on certain types of traffic violations, that information should be made public. If the police department policy is to arrest all vice operators, the police chief should inform all concerned his officers will enforce that policy. A court-approved philosophy that calls for probation officers to seek alternatives to confinement of juveniles and to attempt redirection efforts in the community environment should be made known to the public and to the police officers. Public awareness of what is happening is a lion's share of the battle, particularly when the problem involves individuals who have been convicted of serious crimes and have been sent to the institution for what the public perceives as punishment.

Press releases, annual reports, and printed brochures may be utilized to disseminate information about department attitudes and procedures. Television and radio interviews and the public speaking circuit should also be considered as avenues of communication. Some cities have merchant associations that support a welcome wagon to make newcomers feel welcome in the community and to introduce them to the local merchants. Another letter of greeting from the local chief of police, or the state's department of fish and game, or harbor police might serve as an excellent vehicle for passing on critical information about curfew laws, leash laws, hunting and fishing rules, and directions on how to contact the agency for more detailed information or assistance.

2. PUBLIC SPEAKING. Program committee chairmen are often hard-pressed for speakers on many occasions. A series of well-prepared half-hour talks with interesting visual aids, brochures, and other supplements to a prepared speech can do a great deal of good for the department when given by a carefully trained department representative. The nature of the business that we are in—jails and institutions, law enforcement, the courts, and field casework—limits or forbids public access to the facilities. Motion pictures, videotapes, and slide programs can be used to take the audience on a vicarious tour through the labyrinths of the prison on the outskirts of town. Such a presentation may prove quite valuable in dispelling misunderstandings or unwarranted misgivings about allowing the institution to be there in the first place.

The speaker's platform is an excellent medium for addressing unfounded rumors and distorted criticism based on half-truths or founded in someone's imagination. Although ethics often prohibit an administrator from discussing a matter pending in court, there are many questions on policy and procedure which can be answered. The speaker may explain why certain security measures are taken, or why an officer must use force, or perhaps why the bartered plea is an absolute necessity in the average municipal court. Whatever the leading questions or criticism may be about the particular component of criminal justice represented by the speaker, he will have the floor and will be able to respond to the questions or criticism.

3. POSITIVE ACTION PROGRAMS. An ethnic minority may be aggrieved about alleged or real discrimination. While carefully avoiding any "showcase" attempt to display a fair and unbiased attitude on the part of the department, it may be possible to employ members of that unrepresented minority or to direct a series of programs specifically to overcome the particular barrier or difficulty. Sometimes, a shift in the arrangement of public relations priorities may solve a problem that may have been inadvertently caused by placing too much emphasis on what may have seemed to be a higher-priority need.

Open house, tours, dedication, or memorial ceremonies—There are many occasions when the department may become legitimately involved in some holiday or special-interest day by sponsoring some type of ceremony. Interesting displays, presentations, and planned activities may draw a substantial crowd and pay valuable dividends in goodwill.

4. YOUTH ACTIVITIES. Boy Scout Explorer posts, athletic leagues, olympics, and various contests can be easily sponsored by many criminal justice agencies, whose purpose is to prevent criminal conduct and to guide young people into the appropriate channels where they may avoid development of a social or criminal behavior pattern. Sponsorship of bicycle safety contests and a variety of different activities on the school grounds may lead to lasting relationships under conditions conducive to good fellowship.

5. ENLIST SPOKESMEN. Within the community, one can usually find certain individuals who feel quite positive about the efforts of police, or the courts, or probation programs. Sometimes, such an individual is found on field trips or at special visits of volunteers. There are times when such a spokesman may say the same thing as an institutional administrator, but the effect is different. Whenever someone is identified as one who may help communicate to at least some small percentage of the community what it is that the police administrator, for example, wishes to communicate, the wiser avenue to take might be to provide information to such a spokesman and leave the rest to him.

6. RUMOR CONTROL. Rumors run rampant when emotions are high, such as during a rally or demonstration. By suggestion, sometimes by

deliberate implantation, unfounded rumors may be created and perpetuated beyond imagination and they will spread like brushfires. Dramatic methods may have to be employed to curb some untruthful rumor, but usually the more effective way to stop a rumor during the preliminary stages is to make sure that certain indigenous community leaders are instantly provided with truthful information so that they can seek out the source of the rumor and squelch it before it is blown all out of proportion. In some of the more concentrated urban centers, it may be wise to identify the community leaders and to establish a liaison so that a rumor control center or similar mechanism may be put into operation when the need arises.

7. OVERCOME COMMUNITY INDIFFERENCE. Dealing with the special interest groups whose desires are well known through their publicity may be a lesser problem than dealing with the much larger percentage of the public whose desires are unknown. If the Criminal Justice System is to meet the needs of the communities it serves, deliberate efforts should be made to ascertain what it is that the communities need and expect. One approach to this problem has been attempted in surveys to determine community standards, which may document certain moods of the people to enforce closure of certain bars and similar business houses that allow certain types of entertainment, such as nude-lewd shows. What is lewd may be defined according to the community standards rather than by a single judge who visits the place of so-called entertainment and makes a decision on whether the show is too risqué for the clientele it serves.

8. A BUSINESSLIKE OPERATION. Establish a businesslike operation and present an image to the public that the taxes that pay for the operation are well spent. Telephone courtesy and personal contacts in reception areas should be maintained as if every visitor were a paying customer. A voice of authority and that of an officious martinet have different sounds and different meanings. People should be treated with courtesy, respect, and quiet dignity. Although a suspect may have been jailed for some atrocious crime, there is no reason why his visiting relatives should be treated as though they were suspects in the same crime. A deliberate effort must be made to avoid development of pompous conduct on the part of the employees who must deal with the public.

PRESS MEDIA RELATIONS

Every department must have a comprehensive press policy and every representative of the press must know what it is. While the larger agency may have a public information officer, the smaller agency must rely on spontaneous assignment of the individual in charge of the office or the activity to double as the press agent. An ideal arrangement would be to train everyone to speak well and to present a good image for the television cameras and the millions of people comprising the viewing public. An alternative is to designate certain individuals who have such qualities to release all information. Then, whenever a newsworthy event occurred, the appropriate individual would be notified immediately so that the "press relations office" would be open for business. Although everyone should have a "nose for news," it is imperative that certain individuals should not be allowed to capture the media representatives and monopolize the news at the expense of the other members of the department. "Exclusives" must be avoided: all reporters and television and radio newscasters should have equal access to news items and all other general-interest items generated by the department.

What is the *Press*? When asked, one might immediately respond by listing the local newspapers and the radio and television stations that serve the immediate area. Actually, the press has a much larger constituency. It includes thousands of newspapers representing the entire political and social spectrum of viewpoints, television and radio stations (am and fm), hundreds of news services, magazines of all types, and many free-lance journalists who chase the news for the fees they can earn depending on the salable quality of their manuscripts. In a happening of major interest, it will be necessary to accommodate literally thousands of press representatives. And it would be wise to consider all segments of the press when developing the department's news policy, because there can be no discrimination toward a certain journalist whose paper represents a particular point of view.

A very worthwhile investment in future news coverage is to provide background for the press by allowing media representatives to accompany the practitioner while he is performing his duties, to be present during normal and routine working activities. In this manner, the reporter gets a feeling for the many roles on which he will report, and develops insight into the reasons why the prosecutor or the police officer takes certain action.

The news media involves a public service: providing the public with information that it needs to know and is entitled to have. A general policy of total cooperation should underlie any other set of rules that might guide release of information to the press. Cooperation, of course, is a two-way process, and it involves an understanding and an acceptance on the part of the press that the public interest also requires that certain information be withheld.

Items of information, such as statistics, progress reports, personal accomplishments, internal activities of general public interest, and human interest stories would be provided to the press on a continuing basis. Sometimes, when the information is about something that has already happened, a well-written news release should be prepared. If the story is used, it may be changed into the writer's own style, but often this kind of information will be used whenever the newspaper or other publication is looking for material to fill partially unused columns, and the information is particularly valuable to them if the timing is not critical.

GENERAL GUIDELINES ABOUT ARRESTED PERSONS. Trial by press might be a valid reason why an accused person will be given a change of venue[2] in the interest of his receiving a fair trial. An arrested person may be photographed by the press, but in no circumstances should the accused be posed or deliberately paraded before cameras to satisfy demands by the photographers. The accused is innocent until proven guilty in court.

Information about a person who has been arrested and accused of a crime should be limited to the basics: (1) name, (2) address, (3) vital statistics such as description and date of birth, (4) a brief description of the offense—but not the details—for which the arrest is made, (5) basic information about the victim, (6) a statement of the charges, and (7) only that information on the crime which will not interfere with the fair trial of the accused.

Most information about the individuals who are the victims, witnesses, or accused in criminal proceedings is private information held by a public agency, and it is not public information.

PRESS RELEASES. An individual should be designated to provide information to the press, and he will have the authority to limit the amount of information to be released. A press policy for routine release of information and for unusual occurrences should be published and followed by all members of the department, including the chief executive and his staff. The ideal site to notify the press would be at a central repository for such information, such as a newsroom, or through a conference telephone at a central location to ensure that the same information is being provided all of the press at the same time and in the same manner.

A press board may be provided in the newsroom for copies of all reports that are available to the press, and for other newsworthy items. It may be possible to provide a continuous tape with basic information about the day's occurrences to any authorized news representative. Armed with this basic information, the reporter can then seek out the information officer and fill in what details he needs for those items which he will use. Press conferences and other methods of news release, such as closed-circuit television presentations and coverage of certain investigations, may be utilized to assure comprehensive news coverage.

SUMMARY

In this chapter, we have discussed the challenge of public relations in three basic categories: press media relations, public relations, and community relations. Because the typical criminal justice agency communicates with the public through the press, a good relationship with the press is imperative, and every effort should be made to strive toward a mutual cooperative relationship. In the category of public relations, the agency would do well to develop a comprehensive public relations program that reaches every segment of the community and addresses many different portions of the community by way of the most effective form of communication. In the category of community relations, the overriding requisite for success of the agency is that the image it presents should be representative of its true strength and integrity.

Courtesy: Police Department, Pasadena, California

Notes

1. Trigger words are words that may have no derogatory significance attached to them when used in one context, yet when used carelessly in the presence of someone who is sensitive to them may offend him.
2. A case is transferred to another judicial jurisdiction when it is believed that the defendant can receive a fair trial in another area because the potential jurors have no information about the case or no prejudged attitudes.

Review Questions

1. What are the three components to a typical public relations program?
2. Which of the three components has as its objective the development of mutual understanding between the community and the department?
3. Are salesmanship and press-agentry characteristic to community relations or public relations, according to the author?
4. What should be the attitude of the criminal justice agency toward the press?
5. Is it wise to withhold certain information from the press? If so, how do you handle criticism by the press for not divulging the information?
6. What is a "trigger word?" Give at least five examples in the area in which you live.
7. What about gratuities—are there times when it is okay to accept them rather than cause a "scene?"
8. Is it wise practice to utilize unpaid and nonprofessional volunteers? Why? Why not?
9. What do you believe the professional's attitude should be toward "playing politics?"
10. List five of the eight suggested methods discussed in this chapter for creating and maintaining an appropriate public image.
11. Add at least two of your own to the list you just completed.
12. When we speak of "press" people, who are we talking about in the area where you live?
13. What information may be released to the press about an arrested person?

Bibliography

Adams, Thomas F. *Police Patrol Tactics and Techniques.* Englewood Cliffs: Prentice-Hall, 1971.
Allen, L. *Management and Organizations.* New York: McGraw-Hill, 1958.
American Correctional Association. *Handbook on Classification in Correctional Institutions.* New York: American Correctional Association, 1947.
──────. *Manual of Correctional Standards.* 3rd ed. New York: American Correctional Association, 1966.
National Survey of Corrections. Federal Bureau of Prisons and the Administrative Office of the U. S. Courts. Washington, D. C.: U. S. Government Printing Office, 1965.
Athos, Anthony G., and Coffey, Robert E. *Behavior in Organizations: A Multi-Dimensional View.* Englewood Cliffs: Prentice-Hall, 1968.
Barnard, C. *The Function of the Executive.* Cambridge, Mass.: Harvard Press, 1938.
Barnes, Harry Elmer and Teeters, Negley K. *New Horizons in Criminology.* 2nd ed. Englewood Cliffs: Prentice-Hall, 1951.
Board of Corrections, Human Relations Agency. *Coordinated California Corrections: Field Services.* Sacramento, California, 1971.
Bristow, Allen P. *Effective Police Manpower Utilization.* Springfield: Charles C Thomas, 1969.
California Correctional System Study, *Prison Task Force.* Sacramento: California State Printing Office, July 1971.
Carter, Robert M., McEachern, A. W., and Sigurdson, Herbert R. "The Uncertain Future of Criminal Justice." Unpublished paper, University of Southern California, School of Public Administration, Los Angeles, California, 1970
Cresap, McCormick, and Paget. "Los Angeles County Probation Department Management Survey." Unpublished report prepared by management consultants for the county of Los Angeles, California, April 1965.
Crockett, Thompson S. and Stinchcomb, James D. *Guidelines for Law Enforcement Educaton Programs in Community and Junior Colleges.* Washington, D. C.: American Association of Junior Colleges, 1968.
Department of Defense. *PERT Guide for Management.* Washington, D. C., 1963.
Downs, Anthony. *Inside Bureaucracy.* Boston: Little, Brown, 1967.
Drucker, Peter F. *The Effective Executive.* New York: Harper & Row, 1967.
──────. *General and Industrial Administration.* New York: Harper & Row, 1954.
Esselstyn, T. C., Kirkham, George, and Rudoff, Alvin. *Evaluating Work Furlough.* Federal Probation, March 1971.

Fayol, Henry (a French industrialist). *General and Industrial Administration.* London: Sir Isaac Pitman and Sons, 1949.

Fox, Vernon. *Introduction to Corrections.* Englewood Cliffs: Prentice-Hall, 1972.

A. C. Germann, Frank D. Day, and Robert R. J. Gallati. *Introduction to Law Enforcement and Criminal Justice.* Springfield: Charles C Thomas, 1971.

Gourley, G. Douglas. *Effective Municipal Police Organization.* Beverly Hills, Calif.: Glencoe Press, MacMillan Co., 1970.

_____, and Bristow, Allen P. *Patrol Administration.* Springfield: Charles C Thomas, 1970.

Gulick, L. "*Papers and Science of Administration*", *Notes on the Theory of Organization.* New York: Institute of Public Administration, 1937.

Hanna, Donald G., and Gentel, William D. *A Guide to Primary Police Management Concepts.* Springfield: Charles C Thomas, 1971.

_____, and Kleberg, John R. *A Police Records System for the Small Department.* Springfield: Charles C Thomas, 1969.

Holcomb, Richard L. *Police Patrol.* Springfield: Charles C Thomas, 1971.

Iannone, N. F. *Supervision of Police Personnel.* Englewood Cliffs: Prentice-Hall, 1970.

ICMA. *Municipal Finance Administration.* 5th ed. Chicago: 1955.

_____. *Municipal Police Administration.* 5th ed. Chicago: 1961.

_____. Report #206 Management Information Service, *Preparation of a Police Manual.* Chicago: 1961.

Jacobs Company, The. *Report on Police and Fire Classification and Day Studies.* Chicago: Jacobs Company, 1970.

Joint Commission on Correctional Manpower and Training. *Manpower and Training in Correctional Institutions.* Washington, D. C.: U. S. Government Printing Office, 1969.

Kassoff, Norman C. *The Police Management System.* Washington, D. C.: International Association of Chiefs of Police, 1967.

_____. *Organization Concepts.* Washington, D. C.: International Association of Chiefs of Police, 1967.

Katz, Daniel, and Kahn, Robert L. *The Social Psychology of Organizations.* New York: John Wiley and Sons, 1966. Quoted in Whisenand.

Kenney, John P. *Police Administration.* Springfield: Charles C Thomas, 1972

Koontz, Harold, and O'Donnell, Cyril. *Principles of Management: An Analysis of Managerial Functions.* 4th ed. New York: McGraw Hill, 1968.

Leavitt, Harold J. *Managerial Psychology.* Chicago: University of Chicago Press, 1958.

Leonard, V. A. *The Police Communications System.* Springfield: Charles C Thomas, 1970.

_____. *The Police Detective Function.* Springfield: Charles C Thomas, 1970.

_____. *The Police Enterprise: Its Organization and Management.* Springfield: Charles C Thomas, 1969.

_____, and More, Harry W. *Police Organization and Management.* 3rd ed. Mineola, New York: The Foundation Press, 1971.

_____. *Police Traffic Control.* Springfield: Charles C Thomas, 1971.

Lewis, Orlando F. *The Development of American Prisons and Prison Customs, 1776–1835.* Montclair, New Jersey: Patterson Smith, 1967.

Likert, Rensis. *New Patterns of Management*. New York: McGraw-Hill, 1961.
Mager, Robert F., and Beach, Jr., Kenneth M. *Developing Vocational Instruction*. Palo Alto, Calif.: Fearon Publisher, 1967.
Malcolm, Donald G., and Rowe, Alan J., eds. *Management Control Systems*. New York: John Wiley and Sons, 1960. The Proceedings of a symposium held at System Development Corporation, Santa Monica, Calif. July 29–31, 1959.
Marshalls, Fels. "Specialized Manpower in a Changing Correctional Climate", *Perspectives in Correctional Manpower and Training*. Staff Report on Joint Commission on Correctional Manpower and Training. Lebanon, Pa.: Sowers Printing Co., 1970.
McGee, Richard A. "What is Past is Prologue." *The Annals*, Jan. 1969.
McGregor, Douglas. *The Human Side of Enterprise*. New York: McGraw-Hill, 1960.
McMahon, Arthur W., and Millet, John D. *Federal Administration*. New York: Columbia University Press, 1939.
Michigan Crime and Delinquency Council of the National Council on Crime and Delinquency. "The Saginaw Probation Demonstration Project." Unpublished report, National Council on Crime and Delinquency, New York, 1963.
Montilla, Robert. *Correctional Planning and Resources Guide*. Washington, D. C.: Office of Law Enforcement Assistance, 1969.
Mooney, J. D. *The Principles of Organization*. New York: Harper & Brothers, 1947.
National Conference on Parole, A Manual and Report, *Parole in Principle and Practice*. Washington, D. C.: National Probation and Parole Association, 1956.
National Sheriff's Association. *Manual of Jail Administration*. Washington, D. C.: National Sheriff's Association, 1970.
Nelson, Elmer K., Jr., and Lovell, Catherine H. *Developing Correctional Administrators, A Research Report of the Joint Commission on Manpower and Training*. Washington, D. C.: U. S. Government Printing Office, 1969.
Newman, William H. *Administrative Action: The Techniques of Organization and Management*. 2nd ed. Englewood Cliffs: Prentice-Hall, 1963.
_____, and Summer, Jr., C. E. *The Process of Management*. Englewood Cliffs: Prentice-Hall, 1961.
Pfiffner, John M., and Sherwood, Frank P. *Administrative Organization*. Englewood Cliffs: Prentice-Hall, 1965.
Phillips, Jewell Cass, Abraham, Henry J., and Ewing, Cortez A. M. *Essentials of National Government*. 3rd ed. New York: Van Nostrand Reinhold Company, 1971.
Piven, Harold, and Alcabes, Abraham. *Probation/Parole: Pilot Study of Correctional Training and Manpower*. U. S. Department of Health, Education, and Welfare. Washington, D. C.: U. S. Government Printing Office, 1967.
The President's Commission on Law Enforcement and Administration of Justice, *Task Force Report: Corrections*. Washington, D. C.: U. S. Government Printing Office, 1967.
Redfield, Charles E. *Communication in Management*. Chicago: University of Chicago Press, 1954.

Reed, Thomas H. *Municipal Government in the United States.* New York: The Century Company, 1926.
Rush, Harold M. F. *Behavioral Science Concepts and Management Application.* New York: National Industrial Conference Board, Inc., 1969.
Sayles, Leonard R., and Strauss, George. *Human Behavior in Organizations.* Englewood Cliffs: Prentice-Hall, 1966.
Schein, Edgar H. *Organizational Psychology.* Englewood Cliffs: Prentice-Hall, 1965.
Schultze, Charles L., with Hamilton, Edward K., and Schick, Allen. *Setting National Priorities: The 1971 Budget.* Washington, D. C.: The Brookings Institution, 1970.
Sigler, Jay A., and Getz, Robert S. *Contemporary American Government: Problems and Prospects.* New York: Van Nostrand Reinhold Company, 1972.
Simon, H. A., and March, J. G. *Organizations.* New York: John Wiley and Sons, 1958.
Smith, Bruce. *Police Systems in the United States.* Rev. ed. New York: Harper & Brothers, 1960.
Smith, Henry Clay. *Psychology of Industrial Behavior.* 2nd ed. New York: McGraw-Hill, 1964.
Smith, R. D. *Inspection and Control.* Washington, D. C.: International Association of Chiefs of Police, 1964.
Task Force on Probation and Parole, "Report to Attorney General Evelle J. Younger." Mimeographed, Sacramento, Calif., 1972.
Terwilliger, Carl, and Adams, Stuart. "Probation Department Management by Objectives." *Crime and Delinquency* 15 (April 1969).
Waldo, Gordon P. "The Dilemma of Correctional Research." *American Journal of Corrections* 31 (November-December 1969).
Weber, Max. *The Theory of Social and Economic Organization.* Edited by Talcott Parsons. Translated by A. M. Henderson and Talcott Parsons. New York: Oxford University Press, 1947.
Welfare and Institutions Code. California Legislature, 1971.
Whisenand, Paul M. *Police Supervision Theory and Practice.* Englewood Cliffs: Prentice-Hall, 1971.
Wiener, Norbert. *Cybernetics: Control and Communication in the Animal and the Machine.* New York: John Wiley and Sons, 1948.
Wilson, O. W., and McLaren, Roy Clinton. *Police Administration.* 3rd ed. New York: McGraw-Hill, 1972.
―――. *Police Planning.* Springfield: Charles C. Thomas, 1952.
Worthy, J. C. *Big Business and Free Men.* New York: Harper & Brothers, 1959.
Wright, John C. "Curiosity and Opportunism." *Trans-Action* 21 (January-February 1965).
Youth Authority, California Department of, *A Guide to Treatment Programs.* Sacramento: State Printing Office, 1972.
Youth Authority, California Department of, *Annual Statistical Report: 1969, State of California.* Sacramento: State Printing Office, 1970.
―――. *Parole Manual.* Sacramento: State Printing Office, rev. 1966.

INDEX

Aberdeen patrol plan, 250-51
"Accidents," 256, 260
Accountability, 24
    minimizing dual, 24-27
Administration, Whisenand's definition of, 15
Administrative Action (Newman), 16
Alcohol, Tobacco, and Firearms. (ATF), Division of, 10
American Correctional Association, 347
Appeal channels, 67, 83-84
Appeal system, 120
Application form, employment, 96-97
Athos, Anthony G., 22, 34, 60
    on leadership, 126
    on line-staff relationships, 43, 44
Augustus, John, 300
Authority, 21-24, 135-36
    delegation of, 22, 53
    as key to management job, 22
    line, 43, 56, 136
    line of, 23
    relationships, 53-54
    staff, 43, 56, 136
Authority-responsibility relationship, 17, 21-24, 68-70
Auxiliary, 43

Background investigation, 100-101
Barnard, Chester I., 135,136
Beach, Kenneth M., 149
Benevolent associations, 117-19
Blair, Carol Ann,
    on educational and training needs of corrections personnel, 152-153, 190

Blanchard, Bob, 155
Booking desk, 3
Brainstorming, 88, 225
Brewer, Donald D.,
    on educational and training needs of corrections personnel, 152-153, 190
Bristow, Allen P., 248
    on Aberdeen patrol plan, 250-251
    degrees of specialization and, 52
    on deployment of patrol officers, 253-254
    on Salford patrol plan, 251
"Buck-passing," 23
Budget
    cycle, 233-35
    defined, 223
    function, 226, 227-28
    line-item, 226, 229-30
    performance, 226, 228-29
    as planning tool, 223-24
    process, 232-37
    types of, 226-30
Bureau of Narcotics and Dangerous Drugs, 2, 10
Burkhead, Jesse, 226, 228, 229

Chain of command, 23
    Pfiffner and Sherwood on, 24
Challenge of Crime in a Free Society, The, 291
Charisma, 135
Citations, traffic, 290
Civil Service Commission, 11
Civil service examinations, 99
Classification (of prisoners), 372-73, 374-75

Cliques, 58
"Closed shop" concept, 92
Coffey, Robert E., 22, 34, 60
   on leadership, 126
   on line-staff relationships, 43, 44
Command, chain of, 23, 24
Committees, 77-78
Communication
   administrative, 67-85
   barriers to, 70-72
   inspections and, 81-83
   manuals as medium of, 75-77
   mass, 74-75
   meetings as medium of, 78-80
   overcoming barriers to, 72-74
   in parole organizations, 329-332
   staff, 80-81
Community relations, 386-87, 389-93
Compensation plan, standard, 116
Competition, excessive, 131-32
Complaint, 278, 289-90
Control, 56-57
   Kassoff's guidelines for, 134-35
   methods of, 36-38
   peer, 251
   rumor, 395-96
   span of, 27-29
Coordination, 35, 56-57, 136-38, 216
   Hanna and Gentel on, 137
   Kassoff on, 137
   Kenney on, 137
   Sayles and Strauss on, 137
Correctional institutions
   administration of, 346-83
   early development, 348-49
   organization and management, 356-67
   personnel management, 367-69
   physical plant, 369-71
   purpose of, 350-59
   records of, 375-76
Corrections, 2, 5, 7-9, 12-13
   community-based, 376-79
   educational and training needs of employees in, 152-153
   education for, 144-45, 187-88

Corrections (cont)
   future development of, 332-40
   noninstitutional, 302-304
   organizational structure of, 314-17
   President's Task Force on, 379-80
   research and evaluation, 379-81
   training for, 190-93
Courses. *See also* Curriculum; Education; *and* Training
   advanced officer, 203-204
   appraisal of, 151
   development of, 150-51
   executive development, 200-202
   middle management, 202
   specialized short, 204
   supervisory, 202-203
Court component of Criminal Justice System, 1-2, 4-5, 11-12
   administration of, 286-98
   Crime Commission report and, 291-97
   model timetable for, 294-95
   professional preparation for, 145
   records and reports of, 289-91
   reorganization of, 297-98
Court of Claims, 12
Court of Military Appeals, 12
Court of Systems and Patent Appeals, 12
Courts martial, 12
Credit unions, 117
Crime, organized, 271, 272
Crime index, 282
Criminal Justice System, 1-13, *See also* Corrections; Court component of; *and* Police component of
   components of, 1
   goals for, 16
   individual processed through, 2-5
   professionalization within, 69
   systems approach to, 5-9
Crockett, Thompson S.
   on associate degree program in law enforcement, 154

Crockett, Thompson S. (cont)
   on need for education beyond high school level, 145-146
Curriculum
   development, 147-51
      laundry list approach to, 147-48
      systems approach to, 148-49
      task force (California), 155-82
      three phases of, 149-51
   law enforcement
      Rutgers University, 185-86
      University of Long Beach, 183-85
      University of Maryland, 183
Custodial officers, 191
Customs Court, 12
Cybernetics, 37

Defense attorney, 4
Departmentation, 46-48, 49
   Newman's six key considerations in, 21, 58
Department of Justice, 10, 274
"Depolicing", 94
Detention, juvenile, 350-53, 358, 370-71. *See also* Correctional institutions; Corrections; Jail; *and* Prison
Developing Vocational Instruction (Mager and Beach), 149
Direction, 135-36. *See also* Control
Discipline, 119-20
   negative, 138-39
   positive, 138
Division of Alcohol, Tobacco, and Firearms (ATF), 10
Drucker, Peter F., 54, 69, 79, 80, 88, 123, 125-26, 132

Education, criminal justice, 119, 142-204
   college and university role in, 154-88
   for corrections, 144-45

Education, criminal justice (cont)
   for court, 145
   versus training, 145-47, 152-53
Educational programs, law enforcement, 183-188
Effective Executive, The (Drucker), 69, 88
Emergency mobilization and operations of police agency, plan for, 214-16
Employees. *See also* Personnel
   education and training of, 119
   motivation of, 129-33
   three basic needs of, 129-31
   unionization of, 118
Enforcement, selective, 258-59
Essay evaluation method, 108
Evaluation
   of parole, 341-42
   of performance, 133
   of personnel, 102-13
   of probation, 341-42

Fairness
   in corrections, 335-36
   in courts, 293
Fayol, Henri, 23
Federal Aviation Authority of the Department of Transportation, 11
Federal Bureau of Immigration and Naturalization, 2
Federal Bureau of Investigation (FBI), 10, 281
Federal Bureau of Prisons, 13
Federal Communications Commission, 11
Federal government
   law enforcement and investigative agencies of, 10-11
   police power of, 10
Federal Road Aid Act of 1916
Federal Trade Commission, 11
Files (police). *See also* Records
   bicycle license, 278
   crime location, 277
   identification, 277-78

Files (police) (cont)
    intelligence, 278
    pawned object, 277
    report or complaint, 278
    serial number, 276-77
    stolen object, 277
Follett, Mary Parker, 35

Gentel, William D., 70
    on coordination, 137
    on leadership skill, 125
    on PPBS, 230
Gourley, G. Douglas, 11, 26, 28, 55
    on Aberdeen patrol plan, 251
    on investigation, 264
    on purposes of police planning, 218-19
    on Salford patrol plan, 251
Government Budgeting (Burkhead), 226
Grapevine, 80

Halo effect, 105
Hanna, Donald G., 70
    on coordination, 137
    on investigation, 264
    on leadership skill, 125
    on PPBS, 230
Health and accident insurance, 117
Hearsay, 270
Holcomb, Richard L., 246
Human Side of Enterprise, The (McGregor), 127

Iannone, N.F., 61
Immigration and Naturalization Service, 10
Increased Parole Effectiveness Program (IPEP), 328
Individual, development of, 134
Inspections, 81-83
    authoritative, 82
    intelligence, 82
    purposes for, 83
    staff, 82

Internal Revenue Service, 10
Interstate Commerce Commission, 11
Interview, employment, 97-101
"Intuitive opportunism", 379
Inventory control, 238-39
Investigation, 262-65
    Bristow on preliminary criminal, 248
    collision, 260
    of employee background, 100-101
    Gourley on continuing, 264
    Hanna and Gentel on, 264
    records, 280-81
    vice, 266-67

Jail
    administration, 368-69
    community detention, 353-55, 358-59
    function of police agency, 267-68
Job descriptions, 91-94
Journal of Criminal Law, Criminology and Police Science, 99
Judge, 4-5
Juvenile detention, 350-53, 358, 370-71
Juvenile function of police department, 265-66

Kahn, Robert L., 7
Kassoff, Norman C.
    on challenging individual, 128
    on characteristics supervisors must have, 125
    on control, 134-135
    on coordination, 137
    on need for planning, 208
    on supervisory role, 123
Katz, Daniel, 7
Kenney, John, 70
    on coordination, 137
    on planning, 216
    on PPBS, 230-31, 232
    on specialization, 49

Kennedy, John (cont)
    "team concept" of, 50
    on team policing, 251
    on training of supervisors, 200
Koontz, Harold, 21, 22, 24, 26, 34, 35, 36
    on concept of staff, 56
    on functions of manager, 54
    on planning, 218

"Lateral entry" concept, 93
Law Enforcement Assistance Administration, 155
Leadership, 124-128. *See also* Manager; Personnel management; *and* Supervision
    challenging individual and (Kassoff), 128
    economic considerations and (Schein), 127-128
    three basic types of (Athos and Coffey), 126
    through fear, 131
Lejins, Peter P., 155
Leonard, V.A., 28, 43
    on development of individual, 134
Liberty, Richard R., 286n, 297
Likert, Rensis, 35
    on leadership style, 126-27
    on line-staff relationships, 44-45
    on material to be communicated through medium of meetings, 80
Line, 43, 246
Line authority, 43, 56
Line functions of police department. *See* Police department, line functions of
Line-staff concept, 43
Local conditions, 58
Lockheed, 133

McGee, Richard, 330
McGregor, Douglas
    on types of managers, 127

McLaren, Roy C.
    on planning, 208
McNamara, Robert, 230
Mager, Robert F., 149
Management
    "divine right" authoritarianism in, 135-36
    fiscal, 221-40
    of personnel, 87-121, 367-69
    planning as tool of, 218-19
    principal function of, 34
    principles of police, 242-46
    Whisenand's definition of, 5
Manager
    functions of, 54
    types of (McGregor), 127
Managerial qualities
    Drucker on, 125-26
    Kassoff on, 125
    Koontz and O'Donnell on, 124
Manuals of rules and regulations, 119
    constitutionality and validity of, 76-77
    as medium of communication, 75-77
Mark, Jack A., 185
Montilla, Robert, 187-88
Motivation, 129-33, 218
"Mugging" process, 3
Municipal Finance Officers Association, 229

Narcotics, dangerous drugs, 2, 10, 267
National Association of Trial Court Administrators, 289
National Crime Information Center, 274
National Firearms Act, 10
National Institute for Law Enforcement and Criminal Justice, 195
National Safety Council, 256, 281
Newman, William, 16, 18, 24, 55
    on departmentation, 21, 58
    on dual subordination, 25
    on usefulness of committees, 77
New Patterns of Management (Likert), 35

Nowiki, Stephen, 99

Objectives, 16-17, 35
   police department, 244-46
   statement of, 210-12
O'Donnell, Cyril, 21, 22, 24, 26, 34, 35, 36
   on concept of staff, 56
   on functions of manager, 54
   on planning, 218
Offenses
   Part I, 282
   Part II, 282-83
"Open system," Katz and Kahn on, 7-9
Organization, 38
   informal, 84
   table of, 17, 42
   Whisenand's definition of, 15
Organizational chart, 17, 46, 59
   impact of, 60-63
   of line authority relationships, *45*
   of staff-line relationship, *45*, 62, 63
Organizational design, 59-63
Organizational management, traditional view of, 30
Organizational plan, 17-18, 42-64
Organizational pyramid, 62
Organizing, process of, 18-21

Parkinson, Northcote, 49
Parkinson's Law, 49
Parole, 5, 8, 299-344
   community-based program of, 311-14
   definition of, 300
   evaluation, 341-42
   goals, 304-306
   historical development of, 300-301
   juvenile, 327-29
      objectives of, 311-12
   meeting manpower needs of, 338-40
   objectives, 309-12
   organization, 326-32

Parole boards, functions of, 326
Parole officer, 192-94
Paternalism, 131
Patrol, 246-56
   Aberdeen plan for, 250-51
   beat, 250
   deployment, 252-56
   fluid, 254
   Holcomb on, 246-47
   Salford plan for, 251
   statistical controls useful in, 279-80
Penitentiaries, 13
People-movers, 84
Performance measurement, 133
Personnel, *See also* Employees
   development of, 133-34
   evaluation
      methods, 106-110
      qualities considered in, 103-105
      suggestions for, 110-13
      uses for, 102-103
   interviews, 97-98
   management, 87-121, 367-69
      guidelines for, 116-120
   promotion of, 114-116
   psychological screening of, 99
   rank-ordering of, 59-61
   recruitment and selection, 94-97
   testing, 98-100
Pfiffner, John M., 43, 69, 84, 135-36
   on chain of command, 24
   on concept of staff, 56
   on span of control, 28, 29
Planning, 207-220
   defined, 208
   Kenney on, 216
   need for, 208-209
   process, 209-18
   value of, 218-19
Planning Program Budget System, (PPBS), 223, 230-32, 239
   step-by-step procedures, 231-32
Police academies, *143*, 188-89, 195
   basic, 197-98
   length of, 196
Police Administration (Kenney), 50
Police Chief, 256

Police component of Criminal Justice
   System, 1, 10-11
Police department
   line functions of, 246-68
      civil division, 268
      investigation, 262-65
      jail, 267-268
      juvenile, 265-66
      patrol, 246-56
      traffic, 256-62
      vice investigation and
         enforcement, 266-67
   organizing, 246-74
   staff functions of, 268-74
      business office, 268-69
      communications, 269
      community relations, 274
      inspections and internal
         affairs, 272
      intelligence, 271-72
      personnel, 273-74
      property and evidence
         control, 270-71
      records, 269-70
      research and development,
         272-73
      technical services, 271
      training, 274
Police officer
   discretionary powers of, 249
   psychological screening of, 99
   training of, 195-99
Police organization, 242-83
   Whisenand on, 6-7
Police Organization and Management
   (Leonard and More), 28
Police Patrol: Tactics and Techniques
   (Adams), 250
Police power
   of federal government, 10
   of state governments, 11
Police Science Degree Programs
   (Mark), 185
Policies, 75
President's Crime Commission
   (1967), 155
Press media relations, 388-89,
   396-99
Press releases, 398

Prison, 355-56. *See also* Jail *and*
   Penitentiaries
Prisoners
   classification of, 371-75
   reception of, 374-75
Probation, 5, 299-344
   community-based program of,
      311-14, 334-35
   definition of, 299-300
   evaluation, 341-42
   functions, 318-26
   goals, 304-306
   historical development of,
      300-301
   meeting manpower needs of,
      338-40
   objectives, 306-309
   organization, 317-18
Probationary period of employment,
   101
Probation officer, 5, 192-94
Probation reports, 291
Probation services
   adult, 318-20
   California study of, 333-34
   juvenile
      investigation, 321-23
      supervision, 323-24
Professionalism
   trade union membership and,
      118
Promotional procedure, 114-16
Prosecutor, 4
Public relations, 387-88, 393-96
Purchasing, 237-38

Rand Corporation, 230
Ranking evaluation method, 106-108
Rank structure, relative, 59-61
Rating scale evaluation method, 108
Ream, Norman J., 133
Reception (of prisoners), 374-75
Records, *See also* Files
   correctional, 375-76
   court, 289-91
   police department, 269-70,
      274-78
Recruitment, 94-97

Regional Criminal Justice Training Center (R.C.J.T.C.), 143, 144
Regulations, manuals of, 75-77
Residence requirements (for police agency employment), 94-95
Responsibility, 21-24
Rules, manuals of, 75-77
Rumor control, 395-96

Safe Streets Act of 1968, 48, 189-90, 219
Salford patrol plan, 251
Sayles, Leonard R., 30, 34, 50, 59, 67, 68, 83
   on coordination, 137
   on department-imposed work standards, 281
   on paternalism, 131
Schein, Edgar H., 127-28
Secret Service, 10
Sherwood, Frank P., 43, 69, 84, 135-36
   on chain of command, 24
   on concept of staff, 56
   on span of control, 28, 29
Silva, J. Winston, 155
Slott, Irving, 195
Smith, Henry Clay, 96, 97
   on utilization of sociometry, 130-31
Sociometry, 130
Specialization, 48-53
   advantages of, 52
   degrees of, 52-53
   disadvantages of, 50-52
   pseudo-, 49
Staff, 43, 246
Staff assistants, 55
Staff authority, 43, 56
Staff functions of police department. *See* Police department, staff functions of
Staffing, 36
Statistical controls (police department), 279-83
Stinchcomb, James D.
   on associate degree program in law enforcement, 154

Stinchcomb, James D. (cont)
   on need for education beyond high school level, 145-46
Strauss, George, 30, 34, 50, 59, 67, 68, 83
   on coordination, 137
   on department-imposed work standards, 281
   on paternalism, 131
Strike, 118
Supervision, 123-40. *See also* Personnel management
   functional, 136
   limiting scope of, 27-34
   staff, 136
Supervisor
   accessibility of, 33
   Kenney on training of, 200
   work requirements for, 32
Systems analysis
   Criminal Justice System and, 5-9
   police organization and, 6-7

Task analysis, 87-94
   by Los Angeles Police and Fire Departments, 93
"Team Concept," Kenney's, 50
Team policing. *See also* Aberdeen patrol plan *and* Salford patrol plan
   Kenney on, 251
   Whisenand on, 252
Tennessee Valley Authority (TVA), 229
Tenney, Charles W., Jr.
   on models for law enforcement curricula, 183
   on training, 146
Tenure, 101
Terminal performance objectives, 148
Tests. *See also* Civil service examinations
   ability and aptitude, 99-100
   psychological, 98
   situational, 99
Traffic functions, 256-62
   collision investigation, 260
   direction of traffic, 259-60
   drivers' education, 260-61

Traffic functions (cont)
    enforcement of laws, 257
    statistic controls useful to, 279-80
    traffic engineering 261
Training, criminal justice, 119, 142-204
    college and university participation in, 189-90
    for corrections personnel, 190-93
    field, 196, 198-99
    in-service, 190, 195
    on-the-job, 142
    roll call, 199
    specialized, 188-90
    Tenney's definition of, 146
    versus education, 145-47, 152-53
Training officer, 196
Treasury Department
    law enforcement agencies of, 10

U.S. Supreme Court, 12

Unity of command, principle of, 24, 26
    contradiction to, 27
    exceptions to, 27

Vice investigation and enforcement, 266-67
Vocabulary as leadership qualification, 125
Vollmer, August, 50

Warrant, 290
Whisenand, Paul, 6, 7, 15
    on team policing, 252
Wiener, Norbert, 37
Wilson, Orlando W.
    on planning, 208
Wilson, Woodrow, 256
Work, division of, 42-48
Working conditions, 119
Work release program, 377-79
Wright, John C., 379